W9-CLJ-269

THE NON-EXISTENCE OF GOD

Is it possible to prove or disprove God's existence?

Arguments for the existence of God have taken many different forms over the centuries: the ontological, cosmological and teleological arguments; arguments which invoke miracles, religious experience and morality; and prudential arguments such as Pascal's Wager. On the other hand are the arguments against theistic belief: the traditional problem of evil; the logical tensions between divine attributes such as omnipotence, omniscience and eternity; and arguments from the scale of the universe.

In *The Non-existence of God*, Nicholas Everitt introduces and critically assesses these arguments and examines the role that reason and knowledge play in the debate over God's existence. He draws on recent scientific disputes over neo-Darwinism, the implications of 'big bang' cosmology, and the temporal and spatial size of the universe; and discusses some of the most recent work on the subject, such as the writings of Reformed Epistemologists, and Plantinga's 'anti-naturalism' argument in favour of theism. Everitt's controversial conclusion is that there is a sense in which God's existence is disprovable, and that even in other senses a belief in God would be irrational.

Contents: 1. Reasoning about God 2. Reformed Epistemology 3. Ontological arguments 4. Cosmological arguments 5. Teleological arguments 6. Arguments to and from miracles 7. God and morality 8. Religious experience 9. Naturalism, evolution and rationality 10. Prudential arguments 11. Arguments from scale 12. Problems about evil 13. Omnipotence 14. Eternity and omnipresence 15. Omniscience 16. Conclusion.

Nicholas Everitt is Senior Lecturer in Philosophy at the University of East Anglia, UK. He is the co-author of *Modern Epistemology* (1995).

THE NON-EXISTENCE OF GOD

Nicholas Everitt

Routledge
Taylor & Francis Group

LONDON AND NEW YORK

First published 2004
by Routledge
2 Park Square, Milton Park, Abingdon, Oxon, OX14 4RN

Simultaneously published in the USA and Canada
by Routledge
270 Madison Avenue, New York, NY 10016

Reprinted 2005

Routledge is an imprint of the Taylor & Francis Group

Typeset in Sabon by The Running Head Limited, Cambridge
Printed and bound in Great Britain by MPG Books Ltd, Bodmin

British Library Cataloguing in Publication Data
A catalogue record for this book is available from the British Library

Library of Congress Cataloging in Publication Data
The non-existence of God / Nicholas Everitt.—1st ed.
p. cm.
Includes bibliographical references and index.
1. Atheism. 2. God—Proof. 3. Faith and reason. I. Title.
BL2747.3.E94 2003
212'.1—dc21   2003011943

ISBN 0–415–30106–8 (hb)
ISBN 0–415–30107–6 (pb)

Heaven

Fish (fly-replete in depth of June,
Dawdling away their wat'ry noon)
Ponder deep wisdom, dark or clear,
Each secret fishy hope or fear.
Fish say, they have their Stream and Pond;
But is there anything Beyond?
This life cannot be All, they swear,
For how unpleasant if it were!
One may not doubt that, somehow, Good
Shall come of Water and of Mud;
And, sure, the reverent eye must see
A Purpose in Liquidity.
We darkly know, by faith we cry,
The future is not Wholly Dry.
Mud unto mud! – Death eddies near –
Not here the appointed End, not here!
But somewhere beyond Space and Time,
Is wetter water, slimier slime!
And there (they trust) there swimmeth One
Who swam ere rivers were begun,
Immense of fishy form and mind,
Squamous, omnipotent, and kind;
And under that Almighty Fin,
The littlest fish may enter in.
Oh! Never fly conceals a hook,
Fish say, in the Eternal Brook,
But more than mundane weeds are there,
And mud, celestially fair;
Fat caterpillars drift around,
And Paradisal grubs are found;
Unfading moths, immortal flies,
And the worm that never dies.
And in that Heaven of all their wish,
There shall be no more land, say fish.

Rupert Brooke

Contents

——•◉•——

vii

CONTENTS

CONTENTS

Preface

———◦◯◦———

When I was a philosophy student, I once told my tutor that I would like to write an essay on the existence of God. 'My interest in my maker ceased when I read Hume's *Dialogues*', he loftily replied, leaving me in no doubt that my interest should be similarly short-lived. I never wrote the essay, but nor, in spite of reading Hume's *Dialogues*, did I lose the interest. Since those distant days, the philosophy of religion has enjoyed a remarkable renaissance. In those bad old days, with a few honourable exceptions, it was dominated by the woolly pieties and cross objections of third-rate thinkers. Since then, the field has been taken over by imaginative, creative thinkers who are themselves cutting-edge contributors in other areas of philosophy. These philosophers have brought with them an array of the sharpest weapons in the armoury of analytic philosophy. This combination of able thinkers and sophisticated techniques has transformed the field in the last few decades.

The Non-existence of God is intended as a modest contribution to this new way of tackling the philosophy of religion. The book began life as a rather bland introduction to the field. It aimed to be accessible to those who had not studied philosophy before, it was determinedly non-partisan, and it covered not just questions about God, but related issues in the philosophy of religion such as life after death and the meaning of life. In working on the book, I have come to abandon all of those early aims. First, writing at an elementary level was too restrictive. Points had either to be more simplified than I was comfortable with, or else to become intolerably prolix. This problem was solved by changing the intended audience, which is now at third-year undergraduate and postgraduate level. This has allowed the material to become more sophisticated and more original while still remaining, I hope, clear and accessible.

Second, the book has become avowedly more partisan. I still try to make the strongest case I can for positions which ultimately I think are mistaken (there is after all not much point in showing that the weakest defence of a position is open to attack, if other defences are invulnerable). But my own views on the various issues are much more transparent, and in many places I am arguing a case rather than simply expounding a set of arguments and objections. This change of commitment is reflected in the title.

Third, the focus of the book has narrowed to an exclusive concern with God. This is partly for reasons of space, and partly because of all the topics in the philosophy of religion, the issue of God seems to me to raise by far the most interesting set of philosophical problems. The topic of God is a huge philosophical river junction, a confluence into which flow streams from metaphysics, the philosophy of mind, epistemology, the philosophy of science, moral philosophy, and the philosophy of logic, and of course from the history of philosophy.

In writing the book, I have benefited from discussions with a number of colleagues, but I would like to pay especial thanks to Alan Hobbs, Jerry Goodenough and Alec Fisher, who have been invaluable in helping me to clarify ideas, to detect dud arguments, and in general to act as a sounding board for a wide range of speculations. For the errors which remain in the text, I of course am responsible.

Finally I should like to thank the editor and publisher of *Philosophical Papers* for permission to use material from the article 'Why Only Perfection Is Good Enough', *Philosophical Papers* 2000, 29: 155–8.

Nicholas Everitt
University of East Anglia
Norwich

1

—·◦◯◦·—

Reasoning about God

I find every sect, as far as reason will help them, makes use of
it gladly; and where it fails them, they cry out, 'It is a matter of
faith and above reason'.

(Locke 1964 vol. 2: 281)

The central role of the existence of God

Our principal concern will be with the question of whether God exists. The
reason for making this the primary focus is not that the existence of God is
the only interesting philosophical issue raised by religion. All religions which
accept the existence of God consist of much more than a bare assertion of
his existence. They consist as well of a set of doctrines about what kind of
being he is and what significance his existence has for human life. Some religions, such as Judaism, Christianity and Islam, defend historical claims
about the life histories of various individuals, such as Moses, Jesus or
Mohammed; some put forward metaphysical claims (such as the doctrine of
reincarnation or of life after death, or the possibility of intercessionary
prayer, or Christianity's doctrine of the Incarnation). Beyond the area of
doctrine, most religions also involve an ethical and a ritual system. They aim
to provide a set of rules or recipes by reference to which individuals can lead
the good life, and sometimes by reference to which forms of social organisation can be judged. It is in this area that claims are sometimes made that
religion can supply a meaning or purpose for human existence – or, more
strongly, that *only* religion can do this. So most religions commit themselves
to a good deal more than the bare assertion of God's existence.

But there is nonetheless good reason for making the primary focus of a
text such as this the existence of God. For a belief in God is not only essential to most religions (arguably to all, depending on the definition of
'religion' one favours); it is also what gives the point to the other parts of a
religion. There would be no point in debating detailed issues about the ritual
appropriate to a religion, unless one accepted the existence of the God on

whom the religion was supposedly based. There would be no point in following a set of edicts because they had a supposedly divine origin, unless one accepted the existence of the God from whom they were supposed to originate.

Furthermore, it is to discussions of God's existence that a number of able thinkers have devoted themselves, in a tradition running from early Christian thinkers such as Anselm; through Aquinas and other medieval scholastics; on through Descartes, Locke and Leibniz in the seventeenth century, Hume and Kant in the eighteenth, Mill in the nineteenth, Russell and Mackie in the twentieth, Swinburne, Plantinga and others in the twenty-first. The last few decades in particular have seen a philosophical resurgence of interest in the claims of theism. Contemporary thinkers about God have been able to draw on a wide variety of new ideas, from logic, from the philosophy of science, from probability theory, from epistemology, and from the philosophy of mind. What adds to the philosophical interest of this tradition of debate is that the participants in it have made wildly contradictory claims. At one extreme, Descartes claims that the existence of God can be known with greater assurance than I can know any claim about the physical world (such as for example that I have two hands), and also with greater assurance than any mathematical truth (such as for example that 2 + 2 = 4). At the other extreme is the conclusion which Hume reaches at the end of his *Natural History of Religion*: 'The whole is a riddle, an aenigma, an inexplicable mystery. Doubt, uncertainty, suspence of judgement appear the only result of our most accurate scrutiny, concerning this subject' (Hume 1976: 95).

The need to appeal to reason

Our central topic, then, is the existence of God. Since it is neither obviously true that he exists, nor obviously true that he does not, we need to examine what *reasons* there are to think that he exists, what *reasons* there are to think that he does not, to weigh them against each other, and thereby come to *the most reasonable view* we can.

So much seems obvious. But already, according to some thinkers, we have gone wrong. Some thinkers believe that this appeal to reasons for and against a belief in God is entirely inappropriate. We can distinguish between three different ways in which the appeal to reason has been thought inappropriate. One group of thinkers has claimed that it is somehow impious or even blasphemous or at least superfluous to reason about God's existence. A second group, while not holding that it is impious, maintains that it is pointless because there are no reasons to be given. A third group allows that there are reasons to be given, but claims that all such reasons are inconclusive, and hence incapable of settling the issue anyway. Let us look in more detail at these three kinds of reservation about a search for reasons.

The claim that it is wrong to appeal to reason

According to thinkers in the first group, even if it is sensible to look for supporting evidence for some (perhaps most) of the beliefs we form, we stray from the path of righteousness in using this approach to the question of God's existence. Human reason, they claim, is a feeble tool, whose use should be confined to mundane matters and not extended to holy mysteries. An early statement of the feebleness of human reason can be found in the famous (or should one say infamous?) remarks by Tertullian (c. 160 to c. 220 AD) in connection with the Incarnation that 'just *because* it is absurd, it is to be believed . . . it is certain *because* it is impossible' (quoted by B. Williams in Flew and MacIntyre 1963: 187).[1] Later medieval writers who reiterated this mistrust of reason included St Peter Damian (1007–72), Manegold of Lautenbach (d. 1103), and Walter of St Victor (d. 1180). Commenting on Peter Damian, for example, Copleston notes that he believed that:

> God in his omnipotence could undo the past. Thus though it happens to be true today that Julius Caesar crossed the Rubicon, God could in principle make the statement false tomorrow, by cancelling out the past. If this idea was at variance with the demands of reason, so much the worse for reason.
>
> (Copleston 1972: 67)

This medieval hostility to reason persisted in some Catholic writings of the sixteenth century. St Ignatius Loyola, the founder of the Jesuits, wrote:

> That we may be altogether of the same mind and in conformity with the Church herself, if she shall have defined anything to be black which to our eyes appears to be white, we ought in the like manner to pronounce it to be black.
>
> (quoted in Hollis 1973: 12 fn.)

A rather more vigorous expression of the misleadingness of reason is found in Luther's remark that 'We know that reason is the Devil's harlot, and can do nothing but slander and harm all that God says and does . . . Therefore keep to revelation and do not try to understand' (quoted in ibid.).

Could it be a virtue to believe something not on the basis of supporting reasons, but on faith? That will depend on how we interpret the term 'faith'. Some people draw a distinction between having faith *in* something, and having faith *that* something is the case, and claim that the relevant sense in a religious context is the former. But it seems quite clear that you cannot have faith in something unless you think that it exists. In this respect, having 'faith in' is like trusting, or revering or loving or admiring. I can sincerely urge you to put your trust in the Citizens Savings Bank – but not if I think that no such bank exists, nor if I have no idea whether there is any such bank. You can admire (say) the architect of the Parthenon – but not if you think that there was no architect. Again, you can revere (say) David Hume – but not if you think that there never was such a man. So even if having faith in God is a central religious ideal, it *presupposes* having a belief that God exists, having a faith *that* God exists.

So what is it to believe something 'on faith'? Some people use the term 'faith' in such a way that to believe something on faith is to believe it without any supporting reasons, or even (bizarrely) when the evidence one has goes against one's belief – see, for example, Tertullian quoted above. What should we make of the claim that we may, or even should, form our beliefs 'by faith' in this sense of the word? Let us note first of all that in this sense of the word 'faith', the common phrase 'to believe something *on the basis of faith*' is a logical solecism. It suggests that there are two possible bases for a belief: either you can believe something on the basis of reasons, or you can believe it on the basis of faith. But 'faith' in this sense denotes the *absence* of a basis – and the absence of a basis is not an alternative kind of basis. To believe something 'on the basis of faith' would be more clearly expressed as believing something when you have no reason to think that your belief is true, when you have no justification for your belief, when you have no supporting evidence. It is not to have supporting evidence of a special (perhaps supernatural) kind. If there is any supernatural evidence, and it does indeed support a certain conclusion, then it is rational to use it in forming your beliefs and irrational to ignore it. So someone who believes that there is such evidence is wrong to denigrate the claims of reason – such a person wants to use reason themselves. The claim that a belief that God exists (or does not exist) needs supporting evidence does not imply that such evidence must be of any particular kind (such as 'scientific' or 'naturalistic'). If (and it is a big 'if') there are kinds of evidence which are non-scientific and non-naturalistic, which are supernatural, and they are genuinely *evidence* (i.e. they really do make it more likely that the belief is true) then it would be irrational to ignore such non-standard evidence.

Further, it is unclear that even those like Luther who regard reason as 'the Devil's harlot' can entirely dispense with it. Luther urges us to 'keep to revelation'. But which revelation? Presumably people can be mistaken in thinking that God has revealed himself to them. Moses claimed that God had spoken to him – but so too did the Yorkshire Ripper, Peter Sutcliffe. Sutcliffe claimed to have received instructions from God, and there is no reason to doubt that his claim was sincere. On the basis of those instructions, he murdered nine young women (Cross 1995: 242). His grisly case raises sharply for us the question of how true revelations can be sorted out from false ones. Anyone who appeals to revelation as an alternative to reason, as Luther does, will surely nevertheless want to follow 'the Devil's harlot' and claim that there are *good reasons* for thinking that Sutcliffe's 'revelation' was a false one; and further (perhaps) that there are *good reasons* for thinking that Moses' was a true one. The only alternative seems to be that there are no grounds at all for thinking that God did reveal himself to Moses and not to Peter Sutcliffe – and that looks like a very unattractive option.

In fairness to theism, it should be noted that many theists, when they speak of faith, do not have in mind the irrational belief apparently endorsed by Luther. What they have in mind is a form of belief which is rational, in the sense that it is supported by the available evidence, but which isn't accompanied by a deep understanding of what it is that is believed. An example will make this clear. If a mathematician tells me that Gödel's Theorem (which says that it is impossible to formulate an axiomatisation of arithmetic which is both complete and consistent) is true, I may well believe her, because she is an expert and in a position to know, and she has no reason to deceive me. I have a belief, and it is a rational belief for me to hold, since I have good supporting evidence. But the grounds of my belief are so very different from and inferior to the grounds that the mathematician herself has, that it would be natural to give them different labels, to say that I believe Gödel's Theorem as a matter of faith, whereas the expert sees exactly how and why the theorem *must* be true. In a similar way, a theist might well argue that a person who grows up in a religious community where all the recognised experts accept the existence of God, has good grounds for himself accepting the existence of God. But when he reaches intellectual maturity, he might well then seek to understand for himself what the evidence is for the existence of God, evidence that is to say which does not simply consist in the fact that many able people believe in his existence. Such a person would display, to use Anselm's phrase, 'faith seeking understanding'.

We could represent diagrammatically the difference between these two meanings for the term 'faith'. The first conception is portrayed in Figure 1.1 and the second in Figure 1.2 (overleaf).

In the second sense of faith, it is of course rational to accept things as a matter of faith. But in this second sense, when someone tells us that she accepts something on faith, we can at once ask what reason she has for what she accepts. Accepting something on faith commits her to having a reason

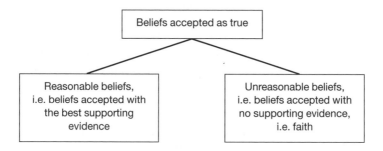

Figure 1.1

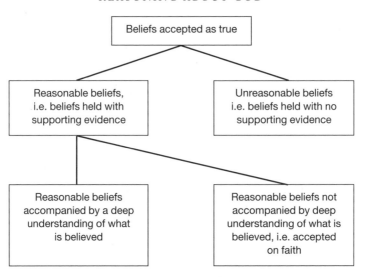

Figure 1.2

for what she believes; and we can then raise the question whether the reason is indeed a good one. It is this sense of faith that Locke was evidently using when he said: '*faith* is nothing but a firm assent of the mind: which, *if it be regulated, as is our duty,* cannot be afforded to anything but upon good reason' (Locke 1964 vol. 2: 281, second italics added).

A different sort of consideration has persuaded some modern philosophers (who are sometimes called Reformed Epistemologists) that there is no need to provide substantive reasons for God's existence. Plantinga, for example, has argued that the demand for reasons is a product of a certain conception of (what he calls) warranted belief, and that that conception has been shown to be false. According to Reformed Epistemology, a believer can be fully warranted in believing a number of claims about God even if she cannot produce any argument in favour of such a belief, and even if she has no evidence or reason which can support the belief, or show it to be true or even probably true.

This sounds like a thorough-going rejection of the role of reason in the justification of beliefs about God, of the kind expressed by Luther. And certainly Plantinga himself wants to connect his views about religious belief with those of Reformation theologians like Calvin (hence the label *Reformed* Epistemology). We will look at Plantinga's position more closely in the next chapter, but here we can note that in fact it is a good deal less hostile to reason than it sounds. In the first place, Plantinga distinguishes between reasons and warrant, and although he says that a warranted believer does not need reasons for her central beliefs about God, she does need warrant –

although she does not need to know what her warrant consists in. Second, although the believer does not need reasons for her own belief to be justified, Plantinga never denies that there are reasons, both for and against beliefs about God. The warranted believer may be called upon to put forward and defend the pro-belief reasons, and to criticise the anti-belief reasons – in other words, to engage in reasoning about the existence and nature of God, in just the way that I am now urging both the believer and the sceptic to do.

It is an interesting philosophical question whether any of our beliefs have to be held without any supporting reasons. That is to ask whether we can give reasons for our reasons, and reasons for our reasons for our reasons, and so on indefinitely, or whether there are some things which we are justified in accepting without supporting reasons or grounds. But if there are any such things, a belief in God is prima facie not one of them. If reasons for and against a belief are available (and we shall shortly assert that they are available in the case of God's existence), then we should use them to the best of our ability, not resolutely shut our eyes to them. A juror in a criminal case who pronounces on the guilt of the accused while making sure that her judgement is based on no supporting reasons would rightly be thought outrageously irresponsible; and the same condemnation should attach to those who think that such an approach is appropriate when deciding about the existence of God.

The claim that there are no relevant reasons

We ought, then, so far as we can, to base our beliefs about the existence of God on whatever reasons are available. But *are* there any relevant reasons which will enable us to decide the question? The very existence of such reasons is what is called into question by the second group whom we described above as sceptics. Such anti-rationalists, whether they are for or against a belief in God, think of religious belief as essentially a non-rational option, a 'leap of faith' (or 'a leap for scepticism') because they think that whether a belief or disbelief in God *should* be supported, it *cannot* be supported; and it cannot be supported because there are no reasons available either way. Kierkegaard, for example, tells us that even if God exists, it would be 'folly' to try to prove that he does: either we would have presupposed in our argument the very thing which we were trying to establish; or else, at the end of the argument we would still need to make a non-rational 'leap' beyond the conclusion of the argument. Either way, it is futile to engage in reasoning about the existence of God (S. Kierkegaard, *Philosophical Fragments*, quoted in Hick 1964: 211). A twentieth-century stance which is in the same tradition can be found in the writings of Wittgenstein. These remarks are notoriously difficult to interpret; but, speaking of controversies about religious doctrines, he remarks: 'These controversies look quite different from any normal controversies. Reasons look entirely different from normal reasons. They are, in a way, quite inconclusive. *The point is that if there were evidence, this would in fact destroy the whole business*' (Wittgenstein 1978: 56, italics added).[2]

The crucial thought here is not just that there are no reasons, but more strongly that it is essential to religious belief being the sort of thing that it is that there should not be any reasons. If one's beliefs were reasonable, *ipso facto* they would no longer be religious.

It is easy to refute this second sort of anti-rationalism. All that is necessary is to point out that if one actually consults the relevant literature, it is *full* of arguments for and against the existence of God, advanced by both believers and non-believers. There are, to mention only a few examples of such arguments, Aquinas's 'Five Ways'; the traditional triumvirate of the ontological, cosmological and teleological arguments (all of which come in several versions); the argument from miracles; the argument from religious experience; and so on. The whole domain is dense with arguments. One suspects that many of those who proclaim, as if it were an obvious truth, that 'you cannot prove or disprove the existence of God' are simply unacquainted with the huge literature of arguments which attempt to do precisely that.

The claim that reasons are inconclusive

Of course, establishing that there are arguments is not by itself to say that any of the arguments is any good, or is sufficient to prove (or disprove) God's existence. And it is this fact which is seized upon by the third kind of sceptic whom we distinguished above. They are willing to allow that we are entitled to reason about God's existence, and they are not so rash as to allege that there are no arguments to be considered. Rather, they assert that at the end of the exercise, we still will be unable to discover good grounds either for asserting or for denying that God exists. Freud for example tells us that

> all of them [i.e. religious doctrines] are . . . insusceptible of proof. No one can be compelled to think them true, to believe in them . . . just as they cannot be proved, so they cannot be refuted. We still know too little to make a critical approach to them.[3]
>
> (op. cit. p. 31)

But against this third sort of sceptic, we need to make three points. First, it would be impossible to establish whether any of the traditional arguments for and against the existence of God is any good without looking at each of them in detail. So the third sort of scepticism, far from making rational scrutiny of the arguments unnecessary, actually requires it.

Second, although it is certainly a possibility that *none* of the arguments in this area has *any* force at all, that would on the face of it be a rather surprising conclusion. The arguments, after all, have been produced by some of the most powerful intellects of (predominantly Western) civilisation; and although this does not of course prove that they are good ones, it does create a prima facie assumption that *some* of them will have at least *some* force. As we will notice shortly, even though the arguments taken singly may well fall short of being conclusive, they may nonetheless have sufficient weight, especially if taken collectively, to make it rational to come down on one side or the other.

Third, we must admit that it is also a possibility that the arguments for God's existence have some weight, and the arguments against his existence have some weight; and that the two weights *exactly* balance. If this were so, then it would be true that reason did not favour one side rather than the other. But aside from the fact that such an exact balance of argumentative force is very unlikely, the force of this concession is undermined by the fact that such an equality between the conflicting arguments could be established only by a detailed study of the arguments themselves. So again, contrary to the claim of the third set of irrationalists, we must allow ourselves to be seduced by 'the Devil's harlot' reason.

I suggested above that non-believers as well as believers can be guilty of ignoring the need to defend their position by an appeal to reasons. Equally, we need to notice that many believers in God, as well as non-believers, have fully recognised the importance of adducing reasons in support of their position. The long tradition of debate mentioned above about the existence and nature of God contains mostly believers in God insisting that his existence and at least some of his attributes can be known by reason. In his *Summa Contra Gentiles*, Aquinas draws a distinction between some truths about God which (he thinks) surpass 'all the ability of human reason', and 'truths which the natural reason is . . . able to reach'. As an example of the first, he mentions the doctrine of the Trinity. As examples of the second, he mentions the truths 'that God exists, that He is one, and the like', and he continues: 'In fact, such truths about God have been proved demonstratively by the philosophers, guided by the light of the natural reason' (Aquinas 1975, Book 1: 63).

When Descartes asserts that it is absolutely certain that God exists, this is not because he feels a burning conviction within his breast, even less because he has made a 'leap of faith'. It is because he believes that he has found an absolutely watertight argument which *proves* that God exists. The same would have been true of Leibniz, of Cudworth and of Samuel Clarke in the seventeenth and eighteenth centuries. Locke, Berkeley, Butler and the careful natural theologians of the eighteenth century such as Ray, Derham and Paley, in producing their arguments, perhaps would not have called them 'watertight', but would certainly have thought that they made it highly reasonable to believe in God. In our own day, the writings of Richard Swinburne provide an excellent statement of the general assumptions underlying such a position. He writes that

> The present book [i.e. *The Existence of God*] assumes that the claim that there is a God is not demonstrably incoherent (i.e. self-contradictory), and hence that it is proper to look around us for evidence of its truth or falsity . . . The book is written in deep conviction of the possibility of reaching fairly well justified conclusions by rational argument on this issue . . . It is a conviction which was explicitly acknowledged by the vast majority of Christian (and non-Christian) philosophers from the thirteenth to the eighteenth centuries; and, I believe, shared, although acknowledged less explicitly, by many Christian and non-Christian philosophers from the first to the twelfth century.
>
> (Swinburne 1979: 1–2)

There is, then, a long and distinguished tradition of rational enquiry into the existence and nature of God, a tradition to which both believers and non-believers have contributed their opposing arguments. This text aligns itself firmly with this tradition, and against the various forms of irrationalism noted above.

Whether someone has good reasons v. whether there are good reasons

One other point about the role of reasons in our investigation requires comment. We need to distinguish between a *biographical* or *sociological* enquiry into why some people have believed or disbelieved in God; and an *epistemological* enquiry into whether there are any good reasons for either belief or disbelief. It may well be that when we look at the intellectual biographies of certain believers and disbelievers, we find that they held their beliefs for poor or inadequate reasons or perhaps for no reasons at all. Perhaps Ms Theist believed in God merely because she had an unconscious need to believe in a father figure; while Mr Sceptic believed that God did not exist merely because he was brought up in an atheistic household. These facts would be of interest to the biographers of Ms Theist and Mr Sceptic respectively; but they are of no interest at all to us. We are interested in the question of what *good reasons* there are for or against God's existence, and no light is thrown on that question by discovering people who hold their beliefs without having good reasons for them. Even if it turns out that all believers (or all non-believers) are irrational, in that they have no good grounds for what they maintain (or deny), that leaves entirely open whether there are any good reasons for what they maintain (or deny). Of course it is *sensible* to look in the first place to believers for arguments in support of beliefs in God's existence and nature, and to disbelievers for arguments against such beliefs. But this is a purely pragmatic policy: there may well be cogent arguments which believers and disbelievers alike have overlooked.

This is why non-rational explanations of the existence of religious belief, of the kind offered by e.g. Marx and Freud, are largely irrelevant to our enquiry. Suppose for example that 'religion is the opium of the people' as Marx famously claimed in his 'Critique of Hegel's *Philosophy of Right*' (see Marx 1971: 116). Suppose that Marx is right in thinking that religion is part of a set of beliefs and attitudes whose effect is to reconcile the exploited members of society to their lot, and to convince them that revolution would inevitably be futile or even impious. Suppose furthermore that it is *because* religion has this effect that it is promulgated by 'the ruling class'. Suppose even that widespread religious belief is impossible in a fully just society, as Marx seems to have thought. None of this is sufficient to show that the doctrines of religion are false. It does not even show that there are any good reasons for thinking that those doctrines are false, or that there are no good reasons for thinking that they are true.

In a similar way, we can suppose with Freud that 'Psychoanalysis has made us familiar with the intimate connection between the father-complex and belief in God; it has shown us that a personal God is, psychologically, nothing other than an exalted father' (Freud 1973 vol. xi: 'Leonardo da Vinci': 34).

But this has no direct bearing on the question we are going to consider. Even if many people's (or even everyone's) belief in God was a kind of wishful thinking, that would do nothing to show that the belief was not true, nor that there are no reasons for thinking that it is true.

It is worth emphasising this point, because some commentators have claimed the opposite. Gaskin, for example, claims that

> the sort of thing Freud has to say is very damaging to the truth claims of religion . . . It is clearly a very powerful way of shedding doubt upon the rational integrity of a belief if I can both explain the causes of the belief and show how these involve wanting or needing to believe what is in fact believed.
>
> (Gaskin 1984: 34)

Gaskin is a little misleading here. First, he says that Freud's remarks threaten the *truth* of religion. But you cannot threaten the truth of a claim merely by showing that those who accept the claim have engaged in wishful thinking. It is perfectly possible for beliefs arrived at by wishful thinking to be true; and as the familiar joke reminds us, the fact that someone is paranoid does not show that she is not in fact persecuted. Second, if someone does arrive at their beliefs by wishful thinking, they have by definition not arrived at those beliefs by good reasoning. But that does not show that there is no process of good reasoning which could have been used to support the belief. Perhaps beliefs which have in fact been arrived at by wishful thinking could have been arrived at (and subsequently defended) by cogent reasoning. Since we are concerned not with the biographical question of whether this or that particular person used good reasons in arriving at their beliefs, but with the impersonal question of whether there are any good reasons for or against their beliefs, it is a mistake to think that critiques like Freud's (or Marx's) have much relevance. Third, however, it *is* true that *some* of Freud's claims do threaten both the truth and the rationality of religious belief. I quoted earlier the passage where he says that some religious beliefs are 'incompatible with everything we have laboriously discovered about the reality of the world'. But the point here is that this is a claim which cannot possibly be established by Freud's investigations into the nature of the human mind. Investigating the human mind will not tell you for example whether the universe was created by an omnipotent and caring being. That kind of claim can be established only by a (rational) comparison of the religious beliefs in question with what we have discovered about the universe, and trying to decide (rationally) if there really are any incompatibilities.

It is of course possible for a theorist to go further than saying that religious views have a socially repressive role to play, or are motivated by deep-seated psychological needs. It would be possible to claim that religion and its doctrines are 'nothing but' a means of achieving class subordination; or that a belief in God is 'nothing but' a hankering after a father figure. It is not entirely clear what a phrase like 'nothing but' means in such contexts; but if it is meant to imply that the beliefs are false, then such a claim would indeed be centrally relevant to our concerns. But again we need to be clear that claims like this cannot be established by Marxist social, political and economic analysis; nor by Freudian psychological investigations. They can be established only by a painstaking analysis of all the traditional arguments for and against the truth of the beliefs in question – in other words, by engaging in the philosophy of religion.

I said above that these socio-economic and psychoanalytic explanations for the prevalence of religious belief do not have 'much' relevance. For there is one situation in which reference to them might be useful. Suppose that we decide that there are no good grounds for believing in the existence of God. The question might then be raised 'Why in that case are so many people believers?'. Marxist, Freudian and other similar theories could then explain why the belief was held in the absence of good reasons, by invoking various social or psychological mechanisms which maintained the belief in the absence of supporting reasons. The implication of this is that an appeal to these social or psychological mechanisms can have a role to play only after the relevant philosophical work has been done. It cannot be a substitute for that work.

The variety of reasons

So far, we have argued that it is proper and necessary to look for good reasons to support the beliefs we form about God's existence and nature. But we should not approach this search for reasons with unrealistically high expectations. We need to recognise that reasons can vary in strength. At one extreme, there will be those which provide absolutely conclusive support for (or against) a position. At the other extreme, will be reasons which raise (or lower) by only a minute amount the probability that our conclusion is true. In between, there will be reasons which can be ranged along a spectrum of strength. In ordinary life, we recognise the existence of this spectrum by deploying such locutions as:

> A proves B beyond all doubt
> A is overwhelming evidence for B
> A is very strong evidence for B
> A is strong evidence for B
> A makes B more likely than not
> A is good evidence for B
> A is fairly good evidence for B
> A makes B a real possibility
> A suggests that B
> A is some evidence for B
> A is weak evidence for B
> A marginally increases the likelihood that B.

The reason for emphasising this spectrum is in order to remind ourselves that in the philosophy of religion, as elsewhere in daily life, being guided by reason does not mean demanding 'proof' before we accept anything as true. The term 'proof' can of course be interpreted in many ways, but we rightly (i.e. reasonably or rationally) believe many things which we cannot prove. For example, I believe that my car will start when I next turn on the ignition and starter switch. This is a rationally defensible belief (the car has been very reliable in the past, it is regularly serviced, it is kept in a locked garage so is very unlikely to be interfered with, etc.). But the evidence that I have, good though it is, cannot be said to *prove* that the car will start next time. Nor would I be being rational or reasonable if I said 'I cannot prove the matter either way, therefore I cannot form any defensible view of the matter'.

In a similar way, being guided by reason in debates about God does not consist in refusing to accept anything until it can be proved. It is adjusting one's beliefs in the light of the evidence which is available. If this evidence is conclusive, well and good. But we should be prepared for it to fall in a murky area where it seems to have some force but not very much. Two factors make the situation even more difficult. First, since there are many arguments for the existence of God, one is required to *combine* a number of arguments which individually may be weak but which collectively may be much stronger, and it is often very unclear how to arrive at such a judgement of collective strength. Second, since there are also a number of arguments *against* the existence of God, the same combining exercise has to be carried out for them, and then the force of those two conflicting sets of considerations balanced against one another.

Theism (and its more specific varieties), atheism, agnosticism

I have said that the primary focus is on the existence and nature of God. This means that our topic will be narrower than Christianity in one way and wider in another. It will be narrower in that many doctrines central to Christianity, or to certain streams within it, such as the Incarnation, or the Trinity, or life after death, will be ignored altogether. But it is wider in that it will be addressing a belief held by all those who believe in God, by whatever name. It will thus probably cover most forms of Judaism and most forms of Islam. It will also cover those, perhaps numerous, individuals who do not identify with any organised or named religion, but nevertheless declare a belief in God. But it will not cover religions (such as Hinduism, or Buddhism, or Jainism) which are not monotheistic. As a convenient name for such a belief in God, I shall use the term 'theism', and call those who accept theism 'theists'. Following my remarks above about proof not being the relevant concept here, I shall not require that a theist believes that the existence of God can be proved, but only that she thinks at least that the existence of God is more likely than not. In a similar way, I shall use the term 'atheist' to mean not someone who thinks that God's existence can be disproved, or who is absolutely certain that God does not exist, but someone who thinks it at least more likely than not that God does not exist. And I shall use the term 'agnostic' to mean someone who thinks that God's existence and his non-existence are equally probable.

In what follows, the examples used and the authors quoted will be drawn almost wholly from the context of debates about Christianity. The reason is that this is the only context with which I have any familiarity. But we need to remember that the real topic is theism, not Christianity. We must not therefore credit (or burden) the theist with doctrines peculiar to Christianity, to which her theism does not commit her.

How the term 'God' is to be understood

Our next task is to consider how we are to understand the term 'God'. (Following normal philosophical convention, when I am referring to the

14

word, I enclose it in quotes, thus: 'God'; when I wish to talk about what the word supposedly refers to, I use no quotes, thus: God. So 'God' refers (supposedly) to God.) The first question we need to decide is whether we should interpret the term 'God' as a proper name, like 'George Washington' or 'Shakespeare' or 'Julius Caesar'; or as a description like 'the President of the USA', 'the author of such plays as *Hamlet* and *King Lear*' or 'the Roman general who defeated Pompey and was assassinated by Brutus'. This might seem a curious and unimportant point to raise, and indeed according to some accounts there is no significant difference between proper names and descriptions (see e.g. Quine 1961: 7). But there are some good reasons for thinking that the logical behaviour of names and of descriptions is different (see e.g. Kripke 1980, Lecture 1) and if that is so, the cogency of some objections to at least one classical argument for God's existence (the ontological argument) will depend on how we interpret the term 'God'.

Certainly, the word 'God' appears to casual inspection to be a proper name. It takes a capital letter, as names do; it is not normally preceded by either the definite article 'the' or the indefinite article 'a'; it does not naturally take a plural form. (It is true that we speak of 'gods' with a small 'g' – but we do not speak of Gods, or Allahs or Yahwehs in the plural.) In all these respects, 'God' appears to be a proper name. But if 'God' is a proper name, then it seems that we cannot meaningfully ask what 'God' means, or ask for a definition of 'God'. If I tell you that Brutus assassinated Caesar, you might ask me what 'assassinated' means, or how I would define it; but you could not ask me what 'Brutus' or 'Caesar' means. These are words that certainly refer to people, but they do so without themselves having a definition.

Nonetheless, it is also common in debates about God to ask for and to give various definitions of 'God', and this suggests that perhaps 'God' is more like a description, perhaps equivalent to something like 'the supreme Being'. And the phrase 'the Lord' or 'the Lord God' is not linguistically odd, again suggesting that the term 'God' is more like a description than a name. At all events, I shall take it that 'God' is a description, or (more accurately) shorthand for one. But then for which description in particular is it a shorthand? Will 'the supreme being' do? It is, I think, certainly on the right lines in capturing what many theists have had in mind. But even for a provisional definition, we need more detail. I propose then provisionally to adopt the following understanding of the term 'God': he is the creator and preserver of everything, a being who is omnipotent, omniscient, and perfect. He is in some sense a conscious or minded being, in that he is the subject of various psychological predicates (he knows everything, he cares for humankind, he has plans, he has wishes (e.g. about how we should behave), etc.). He is eternal, and omnipresent; and he is without bodily parts. Finally, he is an appropriate object of worship.

Some of these characteristics are perhaps implied by others. Perhaps God's omniscience and his moral perfection imply that he is the subject of psychological predicates; perhaps his moral perfection implies that he cares for humankind; perhaps his moral perfection and his concern for humankind imply that he is a fit object of worship. These are questions which we do not need to settle here. All we need is a working definition which can allow the debate to begin. In due course, we can return to parts of this definition/description and examine more carefully the problems which they throw up.

Why should anyone accept this definition, and what should be said to objectors who say 'That's just your definition of God. Who is to say that yours is the right one? I have my own different definition'. The short answer to these questions is that the definition is not 'just my' definition: it is a definition which can claim historical and linguistic accuracy. A huge tradition of people over the last two millennia who have declared a belief in God have understood 'God' in substantially the sense defined – or, if they have not been sufficiently intellectually reflective to put it in these terms, they have belonged to churches and other institutions whose official theorists articulated the beliefs of the church in these terms. A review of writings by theists, from the third century AD to the twenty-first century, from orthodox Catholics to committed Calvinists, reveals a very wide consensus about the properties which God has, and which are taken to be essential to his nature. It is true that the agreement is not universal, and it is true that two people who agree, for example, that God is eternal may attach different senses to eternity. But there is sufficient overlap to justify the assumption that they are all talking about the same topic. To say this is not to say that any individual cannot define the term 'God' differently. Anyone is free to be a linguistic deviant. But they should not then assume that they are participating in the debate about the existence of God to which the great thinkers of the past have contributed.

Further reading

Flew (1966, Chapters 1, 2 and 9) is an eloquent insistence on the need for a rational approach to the philosophy of religion, as is Gaskin (1984, Chapter 2). Stephen Davis (1997, Chapter 1) has an excellent discussion of the nature and point of proofs about theism. McLellan (1987) provides a useful discussion of the attitude of Marx and Engels, and of later Marxists, to religion, and contains a helpful bibliography. Freud's view of religion can be found scattered in his writings, but important texts are 'The Future of an Illusion', 'Leonardo Da Vinci', 'Totem and Taboo' and 'Moses and Monotheism'. Plantinga's position is succinctly stated in his contribution 'Reformed Epistemology' in Quinn and Taliaferro (1997), and a more extended version can be found in Plantinga and Wolterstorff (1983: 16–93), or in Plantinga (2000). Jonathan Barnes (1972: 66–70) has a sensitive discussion of whether 'God' is a proper name or a description, an issue that is interestingly followed up by Gellman (1997: 20–36).

2

---◦◯◦---

Reformed Epistemology

I believe that there are a large number (at least a couple of dozen) good arguments for the existence of God.

(Plantinga 2000: 170)

it is entirely right, rational, reasonable, and proper to believe in God without any evidence or argument at all.

(Plantinga 1983: 17)

Introduction

According to the picture which we have presented in Chapter 1, the right way for the open-minded enquirer to approach the question of God's existence is to look for grounds or reasons or evidence for thinking that God does exist, then to do the same for thinking that he does not exist, and finally to perform a metaphorical subtraction of one from the other. This will then yield the net grounds, or the grounds all-things-considered, for believing that God does or does not exist.

We were considering thinkers who rejected this approach either on the grounds that reason was a corrupting or inappropriate faculty, or because there are no relevant reasons, or because the reasons are all inconclusive. In this chapter, I will consider the claims of so-called Reformed Epistemology (RE for short), which offers a more cautious and more qualified rejection of some of the claims about the role of reason that were advanced in the first chapter.

The term 'Reformed Epistemology' and the related expression of 'the Reformed objection to natural theology' spring from the fact that thinkers in this tradition see themselves as heirs to the Protestant Reformation of the sixteenth century, and to the work of Calvin in particular. The movement has come to particular prominence in the epistemology of religious belief in the last few decades with the work of Plantinga, Wolterstorff, Alston and others; but it will be convenient to take Plantinga as the main exponent of this line of thought.

Plantinga's opposition to the position recommended in Chapter 1 is clear and stark. In the words which form the motto for this chapter: 'it is entirely right, rational, reasonable, and proper to believe in God without any evidence or argument at all' (Plantinga 1983: 17).

But how can such a position be defended? Plantinga approaches this question indirectly by first trying to show how those who reject his position are relying on a particular epistemology, classical foundationalism. He claims that it is classical foundationalism which supplies the rationale for an acceptance of what he calls evidentialism, the thesis that a belief in God can be justified, right, rational, etc. only if it is supported by evidence or reasons. He seeks therefore to show that classical foundationalism is deeply flawed, and hence that there is no good reason to accept evidentialism. This then clears the ground for his positive account of how theistic belief can be 'proper' even if it is not based on any evidence or argument. We need first, then, to see what classical foundationalism is, and how it is supposed to support evidentialism.

Classical foundationalism

Many of the things which we believe, and rightly believe, we accept on the basis of other things that we believe. I believe that Mary is a better swimmer than Fred because I also believe that when they have competed against each other Mary has been able to swim further and faster than Fred, and I have inferred the first belief from the second. I may believe that good weather is likely tomorrow because I believe that there is a red sky this evening, and again I have used the second belief to support the first. In such cases, if the first belief is to be justified it must not just be caused by the second, it must be genuinely supported by the second, although how this relation of support is to be understood is something that has divided foundationalists.

Sometimes, there are more than just two beliefs connected by these justificatory links. I might hold one belief A on the basis of another belief B; hold B on the basis of belief C; and so on. For example, if I am working my way through a geometrical proof, I may accept the conclusion because I can see that it is supported by the penultimate step; and I accept the penultimate step because I can see that it is supported by the prepenultimate step; and so on.

Given this still very sketchy picture of what the structure of our set of justified beliefs looks like, it is natural to think that it needs supplementing in one respect in particular. I may be able to justify A by appealing to B, and justify B by appealing to C, and justify C by appealing to D. But how far back does this regress of justification go? Does it go back infinitely? Does it eventually go around in a big circle, so that I end up appealing to my starting point, belief A, in order to justify my belief Z? Or does it eventually stop at some basic beliefs that do not need to be supported by any further beliefs? Given the finitude of human beings, the first option has generally been thought to be untenable. A number of philosophers (so-called coherentists) have argued in favour of the second option, but they have faced the obvious objection that arguing in a circle cannot provide real justification. If your justification for belief A is belief B, it must not also be the case that your justification for B is A; and on the face of it, the same would be true if we had a larger circle with n beliefs (for any value of n) rather than a very small circle with just two beliefs. Accordingly, most philosophers have opted for the third alternative and accepted that there must be some basic beliefs which do not need to be supported by any further beliefs. In other words, they have accepted a version of foundationalism.

Foundationalism thus complicates the simple picture of justification sketched above by distinguishing between two classes of beliefs. The first kind have been called basic, or foundational, beliefs, and the second kind have been called derived or inferred beliefs. The picture now is that if I am to be a rational or a reasonable person, then I must be entitled to all my basic beliefs, and all my non-basic or derived beliefs must be supported by my basic beliefs, or by beliefs which in turn are supported by my basic beliefs.

That leaves the foundationalist with the question 'What entitles you to accept any beliefs as basic? What entitles you to accept them even though they are not supported by any of your other beliefs? In other words, what makes a basic belief *properly* basic, where a properly basic belief is defined as a belief which I am justified in accepting, even though my justification does not lie in the fact that I have derived it from any of my other beliefs?' To answer this question, different foundationalists have given different answers. But classical foundationalists have wanted to include at least and at most two kinds of belief within the category 'basic belief'. First, they have claimed that some propositions are self-evidently true. The implication of calling a proposition *self*-evidently true is that in order to see that it is true, you do not have to look beyond the proposition itself: you can 'see' (in a non-visual sense) that it is true, just by considering it. For example, 1 + 1 = 2 does not need any proof: we can just see straight off that it is true. If someone really doubted whether it was true, we could make sense of her doubt only by assuming that she did not really understand what addition was – or perhaps what meaning attaches to '1' or '2' or '='. Other examples of self-evident propositions would plausibly include the following: if A is identical to B, and B is identical to C, then A is identical to C; if a proposition p is true, and p entails q, then q is true; and whatever entails a falsehood is itself false. No doubt there are also many others of the same kind.

The second kind of belief that classical foundationalists have been willing to admit as properly basic is those that (to put it loosely) describe one's current conscious state. Thus if I believe 'I am now thinking of my dinner', then foundationalists maintain both that I am justified in holding this belief, and also that my justification does not lie in the fact that I hold some other belief which supports this belief. My belief 'I am now thinking of my dinner' is properly basic. One's knowledge of one's own sensations has in a similar way generally been thought to be properly basic. If I believe that I am in pain, then my belief is justified, but not by virtue of being supported by any of my other beliefs. Beliefs about the input of one's senses has usually been treated in the same way. Thus beliefs such as 'I have the impression of a red patch in my visual field' have been treated as properly basic. Some foundationalists have allowed that beliefs about the physical world, if they simply report what one can see, hear, taste, etc., could also count as basic (because although they are justified, they are not supported by other beliefs). But most foundationalists have restricted properly basic beliefs about sensory input to beliefs about sense impressions, sense data, etc. Further, most foundationalists have thought that basic beliefs were not merely ones which it was epistemically right or proper or permissible for you to hold, but further that they were true, and had some kind of especial security – they were indubitable, or incorrigible, or even infallible, or absolutely certain.

Where does a belief in God fit into this picture of the structure of our justified beliefs? Very few theists have wanted to say that 'God exists' is self-evident, in the way in which beliefs in mathematics and logic can be. But equally 'God exists' does not simply report one's current conscious state, either one's thoughts or one's sensory awareness. It follows that if classical foundationalism is true, 'God exists' cannot be a basic belief. If it is to be justifiably believed at all, it must be a derived belief: the only way in which it can be justified is by showing that it can be supported by some other beliefs that one has, perhaps in some complicated chain of reasoning. Theists have risen to this challenge, and tried to produce arguments (e.g. the ontological and cosmological argument, the argument to design, the argument from miracles, etc.) to show that a belief in God is indeed a rational derived belief.

This, then, is the underlying epistemology of classical foundationalism which, Plantinga maintains, supplies the rationale for the claim that if a belief in God is to be reasonable or rational or proper, it must be defended by and supported by reasons or evidence. Plantinga now undertakes to show that classical foundationalism is untenable, and that we therefore have no good reason to require theism to be based on evidence. Ultimately he intends to show that theism can be a properly basic belief.

Plantinga's attack on classical foundationalism

The attack begins by pointing out that classical foundationalism commits us to widespread scepticism. Many of the beliefs which, according to common sense, we rightly hold do not fit within the category of basic beliefs, nor can they be derived from our basic beliefs. Accordingly, they cannot be justified at all. As an example, take my belief that I remember having toast for breakfast this morning. This is not self-evident. One cannot see that it is true simply by inspecting the proposition itself as one can with $1 + 1 = 2$. But nor does it simply report my current conscious state: even if we think that my remembering something requires that I should be in a certain conscious state, it clearly requires more than this. It also requires that something should have happened in the past, namely that I ate toast for breakfast. It therefore cannot be considered a basic belief. But nor can I derive it from any of my basic beliefs. I somehow know 'straight off' that I remember having toast for breakfast, without having any grounds or evidence for that belief. Even if when challenged I can produce evidence for other people that my claim is true, I can know without needing to produce any such evidence, and even if there is no evidence. Yet people are sometimes justified in believing that they remember having toast for breakfast, so it follows that classical foundationalism must be false.

But, Plantinga urges, worse is to follow for classical foundationalism. Not only would it commit us to widespread scepticism, it also suffers the crippling defect of being (in a large sense of the term) self-refuting. To see why this is so, let us spell out explicitly what the classical foundationalist is saying about justified beliefs. She is claiming:

> (A) A belief that p is justified only if p is properly basic (i.e. self-evident or a report of one's current conscious state) or is derivable from properly basic beliefs.

But what is the status of (A) according to classical foundationalism? Would a classical foundationalist be justified in believing (A) to be true? According to (A), she would be justified in believing (A) only if (A) is properly basic, or is derivable from beliefs which are properly basic. In fact, Plantinga points out, classical foundationalists have not produced any argument to show that (A) can be derived from other beliefs which are properly basic. So they must believe that (A) is properly basic. But since (A) is not self-evident, nor is it a report of one's current conscious state, it cannot be properly basic. So either (A) is false, or if it is true, no rational person could believe it. Either way, no rational person could accept (A). So classical foundationalism is 'bankrupt', and with its failure disappears any rationale for thinking that theism needs to meet the evidentialist requirement. By implication, the way is open to classify 'God exists' as a properly basic belief, and hence as a belief which can be justifiably held in the absence of any supporting reasons or evidence – contra the claims of Chapter 1.

The alternative view proposed by Reformed Epistemology

If classical foundationalism turns out to be a bankrupt epistemology, what alternative does RE offer? Perhaps surprisingly, the replacement has some close parallels to what it replaces: it offers what we might call Reformed foundationalism. It accepts that our justified beliefs can all be divided into the two great classes, basic and derived; that our derived beliefs are justified only if they are supported by our properly basic beliefs, directly or indirectly; and that all the beliefs described by classical foundationalism as properly basic are indeed properly basic. Its central difference from classical foundationalism is that it insists that the class of properly basic beliefs, those which we are entitled to hold without having any reasons or evidence to back them up, is very much wider than classical foundationalism allows. For as we have just seen, Reformed foundationalism classifies both memory beliefs and a belief in God as properly basic. From this basic difference flow a number of other differences. First, RE does not require that our properly basic beliefs should be indubitable or incorrigible or infallible – it does not even require that they should be true. It says only that it must be permissible to hold such beliefs even when you have no supporting reasons or evidence. Second, it allows that there can be good arguments against any given person's properly basic belief; and that when a person comes to know of these objections to what she believes, she is entitled to continue with this belief only if she can show where the objection goes wrong. For example, suppose I remember (as it seems to me) that last week there was a forest fire in the local woods. RE allows that memory beliefs can be properly basic, so I am fully entitled to believe that I remember there was a forest fire, even though I do not have any reasons for this belief. Suppose someone then produces good evidence that my belief is false – perhaps eyewitness reports of people who were in the local woods but who deny that there was a fire. I am then no longer entitled to hold on to my memory belief. If I retain it as a basic belief, it will not be *properly* basic for me. But then suppose that I investigate the matter further, and discover that all the eyewitness reports relate to the day before the day on which I remember the fire occurring. I then have evidence to undermine the initial reports which seem to disprove my initial memory belief, and I can revert to my original memory belief as a properly basic belief. In a terminology which has been increasingly common, the eyewitness reports are a *defeater* for my original memory belief; and my discovery of the discrepancy in dates is a defeater of that defeater. So, although there is a defeater to my original memory belief, I have a defeater for that defeater, and for this reason I can retain the original belief not merely as basic, but as properly basic.

However this still leaves some loose ends. The most obvious of these is the justification for putting a belief in God in the category of properly basic beliefs. Can *any* arbitrarily chosen belief count as properly basic, according to Reformed Epistemology? If not, what are the criteria for being properly basic, and what grounds are there for saying that theism meets these criteria?

In addressing these questions, Plantinga denies that just any belief, no matter how crazy, could count as properly basic. He gives the example of someone believing that the Great Pumpkin returns every Hallowe'en. Such a crazy belief might be held as basic by a given person, that is to say they do not *in fact* support that belief by inferring it from any other beliefs that they hold. But they would be open to epistemic criticism for holding the belief – it would not be a *properly* basic belief. What, then, distinguishes a belief in God and a belief in the Great Pumpkin? Why is one but not the other properly basic? Plantinga admits that he cannot produce a set of necessary and sufficient conditions for proper basicality; and while admitting that this is a gap in his overall position, he denies that it is a serious objection. He makes the point that we can often know that something is *not* a such-and-such even though we cannot produce criteria for something being a such-and-such. In particular, the fact that we cannot produce such criteria does not commit us to saying that just anything counts as a such-and-such. Confronted by a mouse-like creature, I might know that it was not an elephant, without being able to supply a set of necessary and sufficient conditions for being an elephant.

Given that the lack of such criteria is indeed a gap in the account provided by RE, how then can we proceed to fill the gap? Plantinga's suggestion is that we must proceed inductively. We must gather a wide variety of examples of beliefs which on serious reflection we take to be properly basic, and a similar sample of those which we take not to be properly basic. We must then try to extract from such examples a provisional set of necessary and sufficient conditions for proper basicality, a set which we can then test against further examples. There is of course no reason to suppose that everyone will agree initially on what beliefs are properly basic. Some theists will think that a belief in God is not properly basic because they think that it needs to be supported by evidence; most atheists will think that a belief in God is not properly basic, nor properly derived, because they will think that it is not a defensible belief at all. Other theists will think that a belief in God is properly basic, and they will take the claim that a belief in theism has that status as a datum which any putative set of criteria for proper basicality must accommodate.

The dispute between RE and its opponents thus reaches an impasse: they cannot agree on a starting point. However, Plantinga does add a few more details to try to make RE more acceptable. First, he implies that the impasse does not reveal a defect in RE. It is not that there is a small set of beliefs which can be correctly identified as properly basic, and the REist is being irrational and obstinate in insisting on enlarging it to include theism. To think that *that* is the position would already be to prejudge the case against

RE. For from the RE perspective, precisely the same is true of the opponent of RE. From the point of view of RE, it would be just as true to say that the REist has identified a correct set of properly basic beliefs, including theism, and her opponent irrationally refuses to acknowledge them. The fact is that there is no neutral starting point. There can be no bipartisan agreement on what the data are which our epistemological theories need to accommodate. The consequence is that the sceptic will think that the REist has put forward a question-begging defence of theism, and the REist will think that the sceptic has mounted a question-begging attack. But, Plantinga in effect is saying, although the REist may feel sad that the sceptic cannot see the weakness of her (the sceptic's) attack, she (the REist) should not think that she has no adequate reply to the attack. She has what is (by her own lights) a good reply, and that is all that she needs.

Second, Plantinga points out that although properly basic beliefs are not based on *reasons*, they can have *grounds*. The crucial distinction is that reasons for a belief B have to take the form of further *beliefs* from which one reasons to B as a conclusion. By contrast, the grounds of a belief are never further beliefs from which one reasons but simply *experiences*; and one does not *reason* from the experience to the belief, it is the mere occurrence of the experience which supplies at least prima facie justification for the belief. For example: if, being in pain, I come to believe that I am in pain, I do not have to reason my way to this belief from other beliefs. It is the mere occurrence of the pain itself which grounds and hence justifies my belief that I am in pain. Similarly, if I believe that I see a pink wall in front of me, then although normally I will not have reasoned my way to this belief, it will be grounded in the occurrence of a certain kind of visual experience.

In an analogous way, Plantinga claims, beliefs about God can be grounded, even though they are properly basic. He provides the following examples: reading the Bible, I come to believe that God is speaking to me; having done something wrong, I feel guilty, and spontaneously believe 'God disapproves of what I have done'; finding life 'sweet and satisfying', I have a spontaneous belief that God is to be praised and thanked; being in danger, I have a spontaneous belief 'God will help me if I ask'. Strictly, of course none of these beliefs is theism itself, i.e. the belief that God exists, so they do not show that theism per se is a properly basic belief. But the main aims of RE would clearly be secured if beliefs about God, of the kind just described, were all properly basic. For the sake of convenience I will continue to follow the RE tradition of speaking as if what is in question is the proper basicality of the belief 'God exists' rather than of these more specific beliefs.

Before we go on to assess this position, let us note further four points of clarification. First, RE is not saying that *every* person's belief in the existence of God is properly basic, or that one person's belief in the existence of God will be properly basic at *every* time in their lives. There are two main ways in which a belief in God might fail to be properly basic:

(a) It might not be basic at all. A particular believer might reason their way to the existence of God, in which case their belief would be derived, not basic, and hence not properly basic.

(b) It might be basic but not properly basic. I might begin by holding a belief in God as a properly basic belief, then I come across some strong atheist arguments to which I have no answer. But I still hold to my belief in God. Here my belief is still basic (I do not derive it by reasoning from any of my other beliefs), but it is no longer properly basic. I am not entitled to hold a belief to which I think that there are telling objections. If at a later time I find that I can answer those atheist objections, then my basic belief in God can become properly basic again.

Second, RE is not saying that a belief in God is indubitable, or incorrigible or unrevisable or not open to criticism or objection. It will allow that theism is as open to criticism as the great majority of our beliefs, and if the theist wishes to continue to hold on to her belief as properly basic, RE will say that it is incumbent on her to meet these criticisms when she comes across them. She does need to show that the reasons for thinking that theism is irrational or false or in some other way deficient all fail. What she does not need to do is to find positive reasons for thinking that it is true.

Third, RE is not saying that there are no positive reasons for thinking that theism is true, no arguments by which it *can* be supported. In fact, Plantinga has produced a number of such reasons. The claim is only that the theist does not *need* to appeal to any such arguments in order to defend her belief in God: the belief in God can be fully justified even if the believer knows nothing of any supporting arguments, and even if it should turn out that none of the pro-theist arguments succeeds.

Finally, RE is not defending a *general* hostility to reason in relation to theism, of the kind that a number of authors from Chapter 1 displayed. It maintains that critics of theism need to produce reasons for thinking that theism is either false or irrational, and that theists need to produce reasons to argue against these atheist objections. The absence of good argument from either of these domains would be a proper object of epistemic criticism. So it is allowing that there can be good arguments in favour of theism; there can be non-foolish objections to these arguments; there can be (in principle at least) good arguments against theism; and there can be non-foolish objections to these arguments. The only limitation which RE imposes on reason is that it maintains that a belief in theism *can* be fully justified (not that it always is), in the absence of any good supporting arguments.

Assessment

I will argue that Plantinga is wrong to think that theism can be a properly basic belief, but that even if he is right, the consequences for the role of reason in religion will be relatively small.

To see why it is implausible to think of theism as properly basic, we need to look again at what Plantinga says about the 'grounding' of other properly basic beliefs. In each case, he invokes some kind of experience as being what grounds the belief in question. Thus, the belief that I am in pain is grounded in my feeling of pain; the belief that I am perceiving a tree is grounded in my sensory awareness of a tree; my belief that someone else is in pain is grounded in my perception of her pain behaviour; my memory belief about having breakfast this morning is grounded in my having 'a certain past-tinged experience that is familiar to all but hard to describe' (Plantinga in Sennett 1998: 153). In each case, Plantinga says that the belief is properly basic and that the 'experience is what justifies me in holding it; [the experience] is the ground of my justification, and by extension, the ground of the belief itself' (ibid. p. 152).

Whether or not we accept this general picture of the relationship between belief and experience, we can see a certain plausibility in it. There is, we could say, a certain correspondence between the content of the experience and the content of the belief. It is not that the experience triggers in me a belief about something completely unrelated. It is my feeling of pain that grounds the belief that I am in pain, not, for example, the belief that there is no highest prime number or that $E = mc^2$, or that all life on Earth descends from a single source.

But now let us see what grounding Plantinga says there is for theistic beliefs. He claims that Mary's belief that God is speaking to her is grounded in her experience of reading the Bible; her belief that God disapproves of what she has done is grounded in a feeling of guilt; her belief that God can help is grounded in a feeling of danger; her belief that God is to be thanked and praised is grounded in a feeling that life is sweet and satisfying.

It is clear from these examples that the relationship between properly basic non-theistic beliefs and their grounds is very different from the relationship between properly basic theistic beliefs and their grounds. The relationship is very much closer in the former case than in the latter, and makes it intelligible why Plantinga should claim that grounding is a form of justification. But in the theistic case, there is simply a huge gap between the belief and what is supposed to ground it. Take the case where I feel guilty about something. How can a feeling of this kind, ground and hence justify a belief in the existence of, for example, a being who created the universe from nothing? Or of a being who is eternal? Or of a being who is non-physical? Of course some theists have argued that there is some indirect and unobvious connection between the existence of morality and the existence

26

of God. They have thought that a good argument could be constructed to show that anyone who recognised moral constraints as genuinely binding was logically committed to the existence of God; and we will be looking at their position in Chapter 7. But that is not what Plantinga is saying. For he is claiming that the theistic belief is properly basic, and hence although it is justified, it does not need any supporting argument. Intuitions will vary on such a case, but it looks as if someone in whom feelings of guilt trigger the belief 'God disapproves of what I have done' is suffering from a cognitive malfunction. Whether or not there any good arguments for the existence of God, or for thinking that he disapproves of what I have done, feelings of guilt are simply the wrong sort of thing to supply a justification.

Consider again the experience of reading the Bible. What belief ought this to ground as a properly basic belief? Given that the experience of pain grounds the belief 'I am in pain' as properly basic, and the experience of seeing a red patch grounds the belief 'I am seeing a red patch' as properly basic, one might have thought that if the experience of reading the Bible grounds any belief as properly basic, it would be the belief 'I am reading the Bible'. But the belief which Plantinga says is grounded by this experience (the belief that God is speaking to me) is at a huge epistemic distance from the experience. The belief involves a hypothesis about the source of the text I am reading, a cosmological speculation about the dependency of all reality on some single principle, an assumption that that principle has some very specific qualities, and so on. Even if all of these hypotheses are true, and even if it is possible to justify a belief that they are true, the mere experience of reading the Bible is simply the wrong sort of thing to provide such justification.

We will return in Chapter 8 to the issue of religious experience, but for the moment we can simply say that given the kind of hypothesis that theism is (i.e. a large-scale cosmological hypothesis, postulating the existence of an entity with a variety of unique, unobservable properties), it would be very surprising if the occurrence of an experience could by itself (i.e. without any surrounding reasoning) justify a theistic belief. It therefore seems unlikely that theism could be a properly basic belief.

However, let us suppose for the sake of argument that this line of criticism is wrong, and that theism can be properly basic. From what has already been said, we can see that this does not mean that everyone, everywhere, at every time is right, rational etc. to believe in God without evidence or argument, but only that it is *possible* in specific contexts for a particular believer's belief to be right, etc. in the absence of argument. But now we need to notice an ambiguity, or at least a duality, in some of the concepts of epistemic approval ('justified', 'entitled') which Plantinga uses. Following (as he believes) the classical foundationalists themselves, he gives these terms a deontological or quasi-ethical twist. He connects them with the concepts of epistemic praise and blame; rights, duties, and negligence. Let us call this the 'duty' sense. Given this construal of the terms, when the believer asks herself 'Is my belief in God epistemically permissible?' she is asking herself 'Am I entitled to hold this belief? Do I violate any of my epistemic duties in holding this belief? Have I been careless or negligent in forming it? Am I open to epistemic reproach? Have I been, for example, gullible, overhasty, or biased?'. RE maintains that some believers can honestly answer these questions in a way that shows that belief to be beyond epistemic reproach, and hence to be justified, legitimate, etc., even though it has not been arrived at by reasoning or argument.

But there is a second and quite different sense which we could give to this cluster of terms, which I will call the 'truth-indicator' sense. In this sense, the question 'Is my belief justified?' is not asking about me and my epistemic procedures, it is asking whether there are any pointers to the truth of what I believe. Whereas the duty sense is focused on *my believing* what I believe, the truth-indicator sense is focused on *what I believe*. There can of course be a connection between them. If my epistemic procedures have all been properly followed, then that fact could be a good indicator that the belief that I end up with is true. But in principle, these are two different kinds of assessment, directed at two different objects, the believing and the proposition believed. We are familiar with the idea that two people who hold the same belief might not be equally rational in holding it: in arriving at the belief, one has fulfilled her epistemic duties, and the other has not. But this is quite separate from asking impersonally whether there is any reason to think that what they both believe is true.

We can now see that even if Plantinga is right in thinking that a believer can be 'entirely right, rational, reasonable, and proper to believe in God without any evidence or argument at all' (op. cit. p. 103), this is beside the point. That conclusion can indeed be a comfort to the believer, in assuring her that she is free from reproach in holding on to her theism even though she cannot offer any supporting argument or evidence. But it is beside the point, because many believers will quite properly want to ask themselves the further question 'Given that I do not violate any epistemic duties in holding this belief, what reasons are there for thinking that the belief is true?'. In other words, they want to focus not on the degree of conscientiousness of this or that believer, but on the truth of the matter about God's existence.

This is connected with a further point. Plantinga approaches the matter from the point of a believer. This is of course entirely reasonable since he is a theist. But it means that his starting point is that of someone who already holds a belief in God who asks herself the question 'Am I rational or reasonable or entitled to hold what I believe?'. But there is an alternative starting point, which is perhaps in current Western society at least as common. It is the starting point of someone who does not antecedently think that theism is true, nor that it is false, but who is enquiring in an open-minded way what reasons there are for accepting either theism or atheism. It seems that in relation to such a person, RE can only say 'Well, if you accept theism, you could be justified (in the duty sense), because your belief might be a properly basic one'. But that is not the question which the enquirer wants answered. She is asking what reasons there are for thinking that theism is true, not about the epistemic propriety of those who accept it.

There is one final query to raise. Suppose we grant that the category of properly basic beliefs is not intrinsically problematic. We grant that some beliefs are straightforwardly properly basic. Perhaps we think of beliefs such as '1 + 1 = 2', and 'I am in pain' as uncontroversially in this category, and perhaps some memory beliefs too. But what in the domain of religion is a Reformed Epistemologist asking us to include as properly basic? As we noted above, strictly speaking it is not theism itself (i.e. the thesis that God exists) which Plantinga says is properly basic but a series of beliefs from which theism follows obviously and uncontroversially. They were claims like 'God disapproves of what I have done', 'God will help me if I ask' and so on. But now the Great Pumpkin objection must return. How many beliefs about God can be counted as properly basic? How many kinds of beliefs can the theist claim that she is justified in holding even though she has no evidence to think that they are true? As we will see in Chapter 9, it may be that proper basicality is meant to cover some very specific beliefs about God's intentions, for example, the belief that God has created humans with a set of cognitive faculties which will yield mainly true beliefs when those faculties are properly used in the environment for which they were intended. So what other beliefs can count as properly basic? Can I have properly basic beliefs about Vishnu or Zoroaster or Zeus? If I am a Protagorean, can 'Man is the measure of all things' be properly basic for me? Plantinga's concession that he cannot produce a set of necessary and sufficient conditions begins to look more damaging for theism. Equally, the way forward which he recommends (gathering a wide range of examples of what we agree to be basic and non-basic beliefs) does not look promising, because there is no reason to think that Reformed Epistemologists and their opponents will be able to agree about the status of theistic beliefs.

The consequence is that although it seems at first as if RE is a major challenge to the need for argument and reason defended in Chapter 1, closer examination shows that this is not the case. First, there are good reasons for rejecting the claim that theism is properly basic. Second, even if theism is properly basic, the challenge RE presents is of restricted scope. It is restricted because RE allows full scope for reason in the presentation of anti-theist arguments, and in attempts by the theist to undermine these objections. It also allows that there are some cogent pro-theist arguments, and some serious objections to those arguments. Third, the challenge of RE is anyway not one which the non-theist needs to meet, because it is one which the theist cannot raise without begging the question.

Further reading

The locus classicus for Reformed Epistemology is the collection of papers edited by Plantinga and Wolterstorff (1983) – see in particular the papers by Plantinga 'Reason and Belief in God', reprinted in Sennett (1998), and by Wolterstorff. For later developments of these ideas see the two papers by Plantinga and Wolterstorff respectively in Quinn and Taliaferro (1997), and Plantinga (2000). Criticisms of RE from within theism can be found in Quinn (1985 and 1993). Plantinga replies to the first of these papers in Plantinga (1986). An overview of the debate can be found in Hasker (1998). *Philosophical Books* (vol. 43, April 2002) published a symposium on Plantinga (2000), with articles by Sudduth, Wykstra, and Zagzebski, and a reply by Plantinga. Alston's version of RE can be found in Alston (1991), with a critique in Sudduth (1995).

3

—·◦◯◦·—

Ontological arguments

> When considered generally and impartially, this famous onto-
> logical proof is really a most delightful farce.
> (Schopenhauer 1974: 14–15)

Introduction

We can begin our consideration of arguments for God's existence with the
first of three large groups of arguments (the ontological, the cosmological
and the teleological) which have gained a sort of classic status as arguments
for God's existence. Just as Aquinas's Five Ways were once thought of as
one significant cluster of arguments, so are these three. But there is only a
historical reason for this. They are not as a group obviously any stronger
than other arguments and there is no reason for separating them out for special treatment. The only reason that they are treated as a triumvirate is that
Kant declared in his discussion of God's existence that they constituted the
only three possible proofs for the existence of God (he did not include his
own attempted proof from morality).

Of the three classic proofs, the ontological is in several ways the most
peculiar. It would probably be true to say that of the purported proofs that
we will consider, all but this one have functioned for at least some theists as
the factor that initially convinced them of the intellectual defensibility of
theism. No doubt many people accept one or more of the arguments *after*
they have already come to accept the existence of God. The arguments then
function for them as a post hoc justification for what they already believe –
and they are none the worse for that. But nevertheless for *some* people, the
arguments probably function as what initially persuades them of the truth
of theism. But it seems unlikely that the same could be said of the ontological argument: it is difficult to believe that anyone has been converted to
theism simply by studying the ontological argument.

An ontological argument is typically one which starts from the mere idea
or concept or notion of God, and, simply by examining the content of this

31

idea, seeks to infer the existence of God. It thus proceeds wholly a priori, not using as a premise any assumptions about the existence or nature of the contingent universe or of its contents. And typically, the conclusion of the argument is not merely that God exists, but that he exists *necessarily* – that is to say, he not only does exist, he could not have failed to exist.

Overall, the argument has had a rather bad press philosophically. It was first propounded by St Anselm, an eleventh-century Archbishop of Canterbury. In the thirteenth century, it was rejected by St Thomas Aquinas. A different version of it was revived in the seventeenth century by Descartes, and different versions again were endorsed by Spinoza and by Leibniz. It was heavily and some would say conclusively criticised in the eighteenth century by Hume and Kant, attacks which were strengthened by the writings of Frege in the nineteenth century (although he did not discuss the ontological argument as such). In the twentieth century, it has had some able supporters, such as Norman Malcolm, Alvin Plantinga and Charles Hartshorne. But the balance of modern philosophical opinion would be heavily weighted against the argument, and the main dispute centres not on *whether* the argument fails, but on *where and how* it fails.

Anselm's version

Anselm starts off with what he treats as a definition of God. He says that God is a being than which none greater can be thought. He does not tell us explicitly what he means by greatness, but we can take it that he is drawing on a Christian tradition which sees God as being the greatest in terms of knowledge, greatest in terms of power, greatest in terms of goodness, and so on. It is in this sense that God is a being than which a greater cannot be thought. Anselm now identifies his opponent with the fool mentioned in Psalms 14: 1 ('The fool has said in his heart "There is no God"'), and he continues as follows:

> when this same Fool hears what I am speaking about, namely 'something-than-which-nothing-greater-can-be-thought', he understands what he hears, and what he understands is in his mind, even if he does not understand that it actually exists . . . Even the Fool, then, is forced to agree that something-than-which-nothing-greater-can-be-thought exists in the mind, since he understands this when he hears it, and whatever is understood is in the mind. And surely that-than-which-a-greater-cannot-be-thought cannot exist in the mind alone. For if it exists solely in the mind, it can be thought to exist in reality also, which is greater. If then that-than-which-nothing-greater-can-be-thought exists in the mind alone, this same that-than-which-a-greater-*cannot*-be-thought is that-than-which-a-

greater-*can*-be-thought. But this is obviously impossible. Therefore there is absolutely no doubt that something-than-which-a-greater-cannot-be-thought exists both in the mind and in reality.

(Anselm 1998: 87–8)

The argument thus suggests that prima facie we might think that we can distinguish between the idea of God on the one hand, and God's reality on the other. After all, in general, we can distinguish between our ideas of things and the things themselves, and we know that in some cases there are no real things corresponding to our ideas. We can, for example, have the idea of unicorns and dragons, faster-than-light rockets and perpetual motion machines, although no such things exist. Why can't the atheist in a similar way agree that he has the idea of God but deny that there is a really existing God who corresponds to this idea?

Anselm's claim is that in the case of God, the idea and the reality *must* go hand in hand: the very content of the idea entails that God really exists. For, if we try to imagine a situation in which the idea exists but God does not, it would turn out that it was not the idea *of God* which we were thinking of. Given, then, that both the atheistical fool and the theist are contemplating the same idea (as they must be if the fool is to deny what the theist asserts), it follows that willy-nilly the fool *is* committed to the existence of God.

We can summarise the argument more formally as follows:

(1) When the fool hears 'A being-than-which . . . etc.', he understands it (premise, which must be granted by a fool who tries to deny that there is such a being).
(2) Whatever is understood is in the mind (premise – true by definition). So:
(3) When the fool hears 'A being-than-which etc.', such a being exists at least in his mind (from (1) and (2)).
(4) If a being-than-which . . . etc. existed only in the fool's mind, it could also be thought of as existing in reality as well, and this is greater (premise). So:
(5) If a being-than-which, etc. existed only in the fool's mind, it would not after all be a being-than-which . . . etc. (from (4)). So:
(6) A being-than-which . . etc. cannot exist only in the mind (from (5)). So:
(7) A being-than-which exists both in the mind and in reality (from (6)).

Anselm's argument was famously criticised by one of his contemporaries, the monk Gaunilo, who produced what is usually called the 'lost island' objection. Gaunilo said that if Anselm's argument succeeded in proving the existence of God, a parallel argument would prove the existence of a perfect island, full of every conceivable delight. For we understand what is meant by speaking of such an island, so the island exists at least in our understanding. But if the island existed only in our understanding, we could think of such an island as existing in reality, and that would be better still. So this most marvellous island cannot exist only in our understanding but must exist in reality as well. Now, says Gaunilo, we can see that this 'lost island' argument does not really prove the existence of a perfect island, and since it has exactly the same structure as Anselm's argument for God, it follows that Anselm's argument is a failure too. (For a text of Gaunilo's objection, see Anselm 1998: 105–10; Davies 1993: 60; or Plantinga 1974: 89.)

One of the twentieth-century defenders of the ontological argument, Plantinga, has argued that Gaunilo's objection fails – and by implication that all similar attempts at reductio ad absurdum refutations of Anselm will like-wise fail. Plantinga argues that the concept of a most perfect island is impossible. The very concept is self-contradictory, and hence no argument could succeed in proving the existence of such an island. The reason that the concept is self-contradictory is this: whatever features contribute to the per-fection of an island (Plantinga suggests Nubian maidens, dancing girls, palm trees and coconuts), it is always possible to imagine an island with twice as many, and *that* island would be more perfect than the one we originally thought of (Plantinga 1977: 91). By contrast, there *is* an intrinsic maximum to the qualities in terms of which God is normally defined (knowledge, power, goodness). For once we have imagined a being who knows every-thing, can do *anything*, etc., we cannot imagine another being who has those powers to a higher degree.

But this objection to Gaunilo seems less than compelling. Given an island with a certain degree of F, where F is some desirable feature, there is no reason to accept that an island with twice as much would be any better. You *can* have too much of a good thing – and Plantinga's own examples neatly illustrate this. Even if we grant that an abundance of coconuts contributes to the perfection of an island, we cannot assume that doubling and redoubling repeatedly the number of coconuts would keep improving the island. Clearly there would come a point where the superabundance of coconuts became a positive nuisance. The same point surely goes for palm trees – and presum-ably at *some* point even for Nubian maidens and dancing girls.

So this rebuttal of Gaunilo's 'lost island' objection fails, and Anselm's argument seems to be exposed to the objection. But Anselm himself also offers a different line of reply to Gaunilo (Anselm 1965: 119–21; Hick 1964: 27). Like Plantinga, he tries to show that the concept of God and of a perfect island are different in a way which would undermine the parallel which Gaunilo has set up. He says that a being than which none greater can be conceived cannot be thought of as non-existent, since if it could be thought of as non-existent, it could be thought of as having a beginning and an end, which is impossible. Anselm does not say why it is impossible but his reasoning may have been that if something had a beginning, its coming into existence would be dependent on the creative action of something else; and if it could cease to exist, then its continued existence would be depen-dent on the refraining from action (action of an annihilating kind) of some other being; and each of these kinds of dependence would be incompatible with the nature of a being than whom none greater can be thought. The implicit contrast with the island seems to be this: an island is by its very nature the sort of thing which can be thought of as having a beginning and an end in time. It can therefore be thought of as non-existent. But if it can be thought of as non-existent, its existence cannot follow from the mere thought or idea of it. So, Anselm can say, there *is* a difference between Gaunilo's 'lost island' argument, and Anselm's original argument.

But this line of defence for Anselm in fact fails, for a reason which is best brought out by considering some remarks by Hume. Hume tells us that

> The idea of existence . . . is the very same with what we conceive to be existent. To reflect on anything simply, and to reflect on it as existent, are nothing different from each other. That idea [i.e. of existence], when conjoined with the idea of any object, makes no addition to it.
>
> (Hume 1960: 66–7)

Hume was not explicitly commenting on Anselm or the ontological argument when he made those remarks. But they clearly have a direct bearing on what Anselm is claiming. There are two ways in which we could interpret what Hume is saying, and both of them are fatal to Anselm. The first way would be to say that the idea of existence is conjoined to the idea of *every* thing, not just to the idea of God. To think of God is certainly to think of God as existing, but equally to think of a table or a cloud or a unicorn is to think of the table, the cloud and the unicorn as existing. This is not to say that when we think of an x, or of an existent x, we must *believe* that x exists. We can certainly think of things which we know not to exist. The point is that when we think of them, we think of them *as* existing. It is rather that if told to think of a tiger, and then to think of it as existing, the second command adds nothing to the first. To comply with the first is necessarily to comply with the second.

But in that case, the contrast on which Anselm is relying must collapse. For he is assuming that in every case except when we are thinking of God, we *can* think of entities without thinking of them as existing. He assumes that it is only in the case of the maximally great being that when we think of it, we *have to* think of it as existing – from which Anselm wrongly infers that we must accept that it really does exist. But Hume's point shows that when we think of something, even if we have to think of it as existing (because thinking of anything is thinking of it as existing), it does not follow that we have to accept that it really exists. Thinking of God and thinking of unicorns are precisely on a par here, and if Anselm's argument proved the existence of God, it would also prove the existence of unicorns.

But there is a second way in which Hume might intend his remarks. Perhaps his point is not that the idea of existence is conjoined to every other idea, but that it is conjoined to *no* other idea. He does say, after all, 'that idea [i.e. of existence], when conjoined with the idea of any object, *makes no addition to it*' (my emphasis), and we might well think that an idea which 'makes no addition' to anything to which it is added is not a real idea at all. Interpreted this way, Anselm's contrast between thinking of a maximally great being, and thinking of it as existing would again collapse. If the 'as existing' makes no addition to the thought of the maximally great being, then clearly the thought of it as existing will be the same as the bare thought of it. Anselm wanted to use the 'as existing' as a bridge from the mere thought to the real existence of the maximally great being. What Hume's sharp little comment shows is that taken one way, it is a bridge which not just God but everything we can think of would have to cross; taken another way, it is a bridge that nothing, not even God, could cross. Either way, the underlying assumption which Anselm makes that an ontological argument will work for the concept of God and for that concept alone, is untenable.

But even if we were not persuaded by Hume's comments, Anselm's argument faces a further conclusive objection. It suffers from a crippling confusion about what is involved in existing in the understanding. Briefly, what Anselm is assuming is: (1) that there are two ways in which a thing might exist: either in the mind, or in reality, and (2) that existing in the mind is an inferior way of existing. Both of these assumptions are false.

Consider the first assumption. Something that exists *only* in the mind does not exist *at all*, just as a non-existent tiger is not one kind of tiger. I understand the phrase 'tenth planet of the Sun', so that to use Anselm's terminology, we could say that the tenth planet of the Sun 'exists in my mind'. But that is compatible with saying that the tenth planet of the sun does not exist *at all* – or more idiomatically, that there is no tenth planet. The situation is not, as it were, that astronomers have located the tenth planet in my mind, and then have the further task of locating it in the solar system. What is 'in my mind' is better described as a bit of linguistic competence, not a shadowy planet.

A parallel point applies to thinking of a being than whom none greater can be thought. That I understand the phrase does not show that such a being has at least one kind of existence, namely in my mind, and might possibly have another kind of existence, namely in reality. All it shows is that I have some linguistic competence.

So Anselm's first assumption about two kinds of existence is mistaken. And since there are not the two kinds of existence which he supposes, it follows that he is mistaken too in thinking that one kind of existence is superior to the other.

It might be thought that this is to attribute to Anselm a blunder of which he is not guilty. After all, his argument contrasts: (a) existing in the mind alone, and (b) being thought of as existing in reality. But the contrast which we have just attributed to him is that between (a) above and (c) existing in reality as well as in the mind. Even if the contrast between (a) and (c) is untenable, it might well be thought that the contrast between (a) and (b) is defensible, and hence that Anselm's argument can escape this attack.

However, this is a too kind reading of Anselm, for two reasons. First, it is clear that the conclusion which he thinks he can defend is that God exists, not just that he must be *thought of* as existing. The end of Chapter 1 of *Proslogion* says 'Without doubt, therefore, there exists, both in the understanding and in reality, something than which a greater cannot be thought'. Second, if Anselm were seeking to defend only the more modest claim that God must be thought of as existing, the Humean criticism which we mentioned earlier would bite. The fool will reply to Anselm, 'If you think of God, you think of him as existing, just as if you think of anything, you think of it as existing. But that does not show either that he does exist, or that if we think of him, we must believe that he exists.'

Descartes and the ontological argument

Writing some 600 years after Anselm, Descartes produced a different version of the ontological argument. (We might note in passing that he seems not to have regarded it as the main argument for God's existence. In the *Meditations*, his main argument is a causal argument, which comes in Meditation 3; the ontological argument is produced almost in passing in Meditation 5. But on the other hand, in the *Principles*, written some three years after the *Meditations*, the order is reversed, so perhaps not very much should be made of the relative importance which Descartes attached to the two arguments.)

As with Anselm's proof, Descartes's is so brief that it can be quoted in full:

> Certainly, the idea of God, or of a supremely perfect being, is one which I find within me just as surely as the idea of any shape or number. And my understanding that it belongs to his nature that he always exists is no less clear and distinct than is the case when I prove of any shape or number that some property belongs to its nature. Hence . . . I ought . . . to regard the existence of God as having at least the same level of certainty as I have hitherto attributed to the truths of mathematics.
>
> (Descartes 1984 vol. 2: 45)

The argument looks so brief as to be almost ludicrous. It amounts to:

Existence belongs to the nature of God (premise).

So:

God exists (conclusion).

A paragraph later, Descartes expands the argument to the following:

(1) God is by definition a being with all perfections.
(2) Existence is a perfection. So:
(3) God has the perfection of existence (from (1) and (2)). So:
(4) God exists (from (3)).

We might well feel that this cannot be a proof of the existence of God because if it were, we could establish the existence of anything simply by making existence part of the nature or essence or definition of anything. A unicorn, for example, is a hoofed quadruped with a horn in its forehead; let us define a new term 'shunicorn' which by definition is a hoofed quadruped with a horn in its forehead that also (by definition) possesses the perfection of existence. I can then argue thus:

(5) A shunicorn is by definition a being with the perfection of existence. So:
(6) Shunicorns exist.

This *must* be a bad argument, whatever we think is wrong with it; and if Descartes's ontological argument is on a par with this, it is worthless.

Descartes does try to distinguish his ontological argument from ludicrous arguments like the shunicorn one. He claims that whereas ideas like that of a shunicorn are somehow bogus and artificial, the idea of God is not. Speaking of the idea of God, he says that the idea is 'not something fictitious which is dependent on my thought, but is an image of a true and immutable nature' (op. cit. p. 47). And we find the same thought reiterated in the *Principles* where he says that

> the idea of a supremely perfect being is not an idea which was invented by the mind, or which represents some chimera, but . . . it represents a true and immutable nature which cannot but exist, since necessary existence is contained within it.
>
> (op. cit. vol. 1: 15)

Because of this, he says, the ontological argument is not a case of thought trying to impose itself on reality (as he might complain in the shunicorn case), but instead is a case of reality forcing us to think in a certain way. But how acceptable this line of thought is will depend on whether he can tell us what a true and immutable nature is, why God is a true and immutable nature, and why shunicorns are not true and immutable natures.

He gives three reasons for thinking that God is a true and immutable nature: (1) he (Descartes) cannot conceive anything but God himself to whose essence existence necessarily pertains; (2) it is not possible for him to conceive two or more Gods in this same way; and, given that one God exists, it is necessary that he exists from and to eternity; (3) he perceives many other attributes of God, none of which he can remove or alter (op. cit. vol. 1: 44).

But each of these reasons is strikingly weak. To take the first, we can say to Descartes 'But a shunicorn is something to whose essence existence necessarily belongs, for we have just defined it as such'. If he replies 'No, because the idea of a shunicorn is fictitious: you have just arbitrarily made it up', he needs to explain how one can tell whether an idea has been made up. Certainly the *word* 'shunicorn' was made up; but the same is true of the word 'God' (or 'Dieu', 'Gott', 'Deus', etc.). But Descartes must think that that does not show that the associated idea or concept is in any way made up. So if a made-up word like 'God' can refer to something with a true and immutable nature, why cannot the same be true of a made-up word like 'shunicorn'?

What about the second reason? Why should the fact (if it is a fact) that we cannot conceive of more than one God show that God is a true and immutable nature? If uniqueness is an essential feature of such a nature, we can easily add a uniqueness condition to our definition of a unicorn (we can define a 'uni-shunicorn' as a shunicorn such that there is only one of them). As before, Descartes can say that this is playing around with words. But as before, he supplies no grounds for distinguishing between saying that we cannot conceive of more than one God, and saying that we cannot conceive of more than one uni-shunicorn.

As for Descartes's third reason, that we cannot diminish or change in our imagination the other properties of God, this is simply false. We can, for example, imagine a being who is omniscient but not perfectly good, or who is perfectly good but not omnipotent, etc. Of course Descartes can then say that it is not *God* whom we are talking about, since God by definition must have all these qualities. But in *that* sense, we cannot change or diminish the properties in our definition of a shunicorn or a uni-shunicorn, for if we did, we would no longer be speaking of shunicorns or uni-shunicorns.

It seems, then, that Descartes's ontological argument is badly exposed. If his argument established the existence of God, it would also establish the existence of shunicorns; and since the shunicorn argument is absurd, so must the God argument be too. Nor, of course, is it just shunicorns whose existence we would be able to prove. There would be shlions, shtigers, shrhinos, etc., where a shlion is by definition anything that is a lion and exists – and similarly for shtigers, shrhinos, etc. Equally we would be able to establish the *non*-existence of all sorts of things. Let a blion be defined as a lion with the further property of non-existence. It would then follow that the world contains no blions – although of course it does contain things (namely lions) which are absolutely indistinguishable in every way from what blions would be like if they existed. Of more significance theologically perhaps, we would be able to prove that the Devil did not exist:

(7) The Devil by definition lacks every perfection.
(2) Existence is a perfection. So:

(8) The Devil lacks existence (from (7) and (2)). So:

(9) The Devil does not exist (from (8)).

What generates this logical quagmire is the assumption that existence is a property that things have or lack, indeed that it is a perfect property. So how does Descartes defend the idea that existence is a perfection? Surprisingly, he says nothing at all in defence of the claim in the *Meditations*, but simply refers to the fact as if it were obvious; and his subsequent references to it are equally cavalier (op. cit. vol. 2: 46, 47). One of Descartes's contemporaries, Gassendi, spotted this undefended and implausible assumption of Descartes's and commented thus:

> existence is not a perfection either in God or in anything else; it is that without which no perfections can be present.
>
> For surely that which does not exist has no perfections or imperfections, and what does exist and has several perfections does not have existence as one of its individual perfections; rather, its existence is that in virtue of which both the thing itself and its perfections are existent . . . if a thing lacks existence, we do not say it is imperfect, or deprived of a perfection, but say instead that it is nothing at all.
>
> (op. cit. vol. 2: 224–5)

These points are well made. What Gassendi is saying is that assertions (and denials) of existence should not be thought of as ascribing (or denying) a property to something. We can elaborate on Gassendi's insight in the following way.

Descartes's background assumption is that when we say, for example, 'Mary is kind', 'Mary is pretty', 'Mary is wise', etc., the sentence functions by first of all using the subject term 'Mary' to pick out in thought, or identify, or refer to, the being about whom we are going to say something; and then using the predicate expressions 'is kind', 'is pretty' etc. to ascribe to the being whom we have picked out the properties of being kind, pretty, wise, etc. Descartes implicitly tries to interpret assertions of existence in the same way: he assumes that when one says 'Mary exists', the subject term 'Mary' is used to pick out the being to whom we are going to ascribe a property, and then the predicate 'exists' is used to ascribe the property of existence to the being so-picked-out.

The mistake that is involved in this Cartesian interpretation of assertions of existence can be brought out by reflecting that if I have already succeeded in picking out the being to whom I am referring, then I have *already* presupposed that Mary exists. So to add the word 'exists' to the term 'Mary' seems redundant. 'Mary exists' becomes a quasi-tautology – which surely it ought not to be. And worse is to follow when we consider negative existential sentences. Consider, for example, 'Father Christmas does not exist'. If we accept the assimilation of existential sentences to subject/property assertions, this sentence must work in the following way: the subject term 'Father Christmas' serves to pick out the being to whom we are referring; and the predicate expression 'does not exist' then serves to say of this being whom we have just picked out that he does not exist. Here, the problem is that if we have succeeded in picking out Father Christmas, in order to say anything at all about him, it surely follows that he must exist. So if what we then say of him is that he does not exist, we seem to be involved in a self-contradiction.

The moral that Gassendi is implicitly pointing to is that we must not interpret existential sentences as subject/predicate sentences with the same structure as, for example, 'Mary is wise'. Descartes makes exactly this mistake, and indeed goes one further by saying that 'God exists' is a subject/*defining* predicate sentence.

Plantinga and the ontological argument

In our own day, Plantinga has offered an argument which at first glance is strikingly unlike that of either Anselm or Descartes. But it warrants the label 'ontological argument' since like theirs, it seeks to prove the existence of God entirely a priori, proceeding from the mere concept of God. Plantinga casts the argument in the language of 'possible worlds' and it will be convenient for us to follow him in this respect. So let us first get clear how 'possible worlds' talk is to be understood.

We commonly think that the world could have been different in various ways from the way in which in fact it is. Some differences would have been very small (for example, a moment ago you might have blinked although in fact you did not); some differences would have been very large (for example, it could have been the case that life never developed on earth); and other differences would have been all-embracing (for example, if the laws of physics had been completely different from what they are). Possible worlds talk is a way of expressing these various possibilities. Thus to say 'There is a possible world in which you blinked a moment ago' is to say '(In this actual world), it could have been the case that you blinked a moment ago'. To say 'In *every* possible world, 2 + 2 = '4' is to say '(In this actual world), 2 + 2 necessarily equals 4'. More idiomatically, 2 + 2 not only *does* equal 4, it *has to* equal 4. To say 'There is no possible world in which bachelors are married' is to say '(In this actual world), bachelors *cannot* be married'. So the point of using possible worlds talk is to have a convenient way of expressing claims about what *must* be so, what *cannot* be so, what *could have been* different, etc.

Three points of clarification need to be remembered:

(a) Although it is customary to speak of possible *worlds*, and of ways in which the actual *world* could have been different, the phrase 'the world' should not be given its customary reference of the Earth. Rather, it is a reference to the universe as a whole. It is the whole universe which could have been different from the way in which it is, not just the Earth.

(b) The phrase 'could have been different' can be interpreted in a variety of ways. Sometimes when we say that something could have been different, we mean only that *as far as we know* it could have been different. We do not know of anything which necessitated things being as they actually were. This epistemological reading of 'could have been different' is not what is intended by possible worlds talk. To say that something could have been the case is rather to say that the supposition that it was the case is not self-contradictory, in a fairly broad sense of that term. Thus it could have been the case that the laws of physics were different from what they are because the supposition that, for example, $E = mc$ instead of $E = mc^2$ (in Einstein's famous formula) is not self-contradictory. By contrast, it could not have been the case that bachelors were married, since the supposition that they are married *is* self-contradictory. In a parallel way, to say that something must be true, and hence that it is true in all possible worlds, is to say that the supposition that it is not true is self-contradictory. And to say that something cannot be true, and hence that there is no possible world in which it is true, is to say that it is self-contradictory.

(c) I have spoken so far as if talk about possible worlds applies only if we are envisaging things as being different from how they in fact are. But in fact the actual world is one possible world. For the way things actually are is a possible way for them to be, i.e. the supposition that they are like that is not self-contradictory.

Armed with this vocabulary, we can now approach Plantinga's proof. He begins by introducing the idea of excellence, understood in a special sense. A being is excellent (in this technical sense) to the extent to which he is knowledgeable, powerful, and morally good. By implication, a being is maximally excellent if and only if he is maximally knowledgeable, maximally powerful, and maximally good, a set of properties which Plantinga equates with being omniscient, omnipotent and morally perfect.

Now it seems possible that a being might be maximally excellent in our world, but not in some other possible world. His excellence might be, as it were fragile in this sense: given the contingencies of this world, he is indeed morally excellent, but had these contingencies been different (i.e. had he existed in another possible world), he would not have been maximally excellent.

Now consider two possible beings, A and B. A is maximally excellent in this world, B is maximally excellent in some other possible world. But whereas in yet other possible worlds, A is less than maximally excellent, B is maximally excellent in all other possible worlds. It then seems that we ought to say (Plantinga implies) that although A and B are (in this world) of equal excellence, B is *greater than* A. He is greater than A because his maximal excellence is more robust than A's. It is more robust, in the sense that no matter how different things might have been, he would still be maximally excellent. We might indeed say that B is *maximally great*, in the sense that he displays maximal excellence with maximal robustness: his excellence is so robust that it survives in every possible world.

So, we can help ourselves to this claim:

(1) A being has maximal greatness if and only if it has maximal excellence in every possible world.

If we now ask ourselves whether it is *possible* that there is a maximally great being, it seems (Plantinga implies) that we should say 'yes'. After all, agreeing that something is at least possible in this sense apparently says no more than that it is not absolutely impossible; and if we were to say that such a being was absolutely impossible, Plantinga would rightly challenge us to prove its impossibility. So:

(2) It is possible that some thing is maximally great.

But this is simply to say

(3) There is a possible world in which some thing is maximally great.

But something can have maximal greatness only if it exists in every possible world since maximal greatness is defined as being maximally excellent in every possible world (see (1) above), and if it exists in every possible world, clearly it exists in this world. So we can say

(4) (In this world) there is something which is maximally great.

But from this and (1), it at once follows that:

(5) (In this world) there exists a being of maximal excellence.

This in turn implies:

(6) (In this world) there exists a being who is omnipotent, omniscient and morally perfect.

And this implies:

(7) God exists.

The argument contains no *obvious* blunders – the premises seem to be plausible, and each of the steps seems to follow logically. And yet starting with some definitions and mere possibilities, we seem to have conjured God into existence. What should the sceptic say about this argument? Clearly the crucial premise is (2). This is saying that it is possible for there to be a being who exists in every possible world (and who, moreover, is maximally excellent in every possible world). But this already begins to sound very controversial. It is saying that it is possible for there to exist a necessary being (since a being is necessary if and only if it exists in every possible world). And since premise (2) is already saying that that necessarily existing being has the divine attributes (or a core of them at least), premise (2) is already saying that God exists in every possible world, including of course this one. So, the sceptic may well say, with a premise as controversial as that, it is hardly surprising that you can derive a conclusion like (7). In effect, the argument comes down to saying

(A) God exists in every possible world.

So:

(B) God exists in this world.

No doubt the argument is valid – but the premise looks much too strong to be acceptable to anyone except those who are antecedently convinced that God exists – and indeed exists as a matter of necessity. So someone who is sceptical about the conclusion will be sceptical about the premise to the same degree.

Could Plantinga defend the premise? Perhaps he could. It is not implausible to accept some such principle as the following:

(C) If a being X exists, although he might not have existed (or: there are some possible worlds in which he does not exist), then he could not be God.

In effect, this is just another way of saying that anything which is to count as God must exist necessarily. But the right response for the sceptic to make at this point is to say that if the only options are that God exists of necessity, or that God's existence is impossible (because God cannot exist in some possible worlds and yet not in others), the correct conclusion to draw is that God's existence is absolutely impossible.

But how could this claim be defended? The sceptic might challenge premise (2) above in the following way. Premise (2) says that it is possible for there to be a being such that it has necessary existence, and also that it possesses a range of moral and intellectual properties, the ones which Plantinga describes as excellences. But how could one entity display both kinds of quality? The most plausible candidates for meeting the first condition are abstract entities like numbers, or concepts, or propositions; the only candidates known to meet the second condition are human beings. How could there be one entity which met both conditions? It is like assuming that since some things (namely, people) are cheerful, and other things (namely, even numbers) are divisible by two, we can understand the concept of something which is both cheerful and divisible by two.

So Plantinga's version of the ontological argument suffers from a question-begging premise of doubtful intelligibility. Once we have unpacked what premise (2) is saying, we see that no one who is either sceptical or open-minded about the existence of God will accept it as a starting point; and that even if such a person were tempted by the premise, there is some difficulty in understanding how it could be true.

The Malcolm/Anselm version

Malcolm claims that there are two versions of Anselm's argument. According to Malcolm, Anselm's first version relies on the assumption that to exist in reality is greater than to exist in the understanding alone. But this, he says, is equivalent to treating existence as a perfection, i.e. as a property which the greatest conceivable being would have. And, he continues, Kant has shown that existence is not a property. Consequently, this version of the argument fails.

However, Malcolm says that Anselm has a second argument, which perhaps he did not distinguish from the first. This second argument comes in a later chapter (Chapter 3) of *Proslogion* (and is also hinted at in Anselm's reply to Gaunilo, outlined above (pp. 34–5). According to Malcolm, whereas Anselm's first argument turns on the claim that existence is a perfection, the second turns on the different principle that existence-*as-matter-of-necessity* is a perfection. We can elucidate what this means using the language of possible worlds which we have outlined above. Some entities exist in some possible worlds, but not in others; whereas it is at least possible for an entity to exist in every possible world. Beings who exist in some possible worlds but not in others have only *contingent* existence, whereas beings who exist in every possible world have existence-as-a-matter-of necessity, or necessary existence.

Why should it be thought that necessary existence is greater than contingent existence? Malcolm suggests a rationale for such a view as follows: a being which exists only contingently might have not existed (this is part of the force of calling it contingent: there are some possible worlds in which it does not exist). Consequently, if it does exist, it must either owe its existence to something else, or else it just *happens* to exist, without being caused to exist by anything. But each of these two possibilities is incompatible with maximal greatness. The first would mean that the being was a dependent and hence not omnipotent being; the second would mean that the being was in a certain way arbitrary. Since both of these two possibilities can apply only to a less than maximally great being, it follows that a maximally great being can have only necessary existence. If it exists at all, it exists in every possible world. What this means, says Malcolm, is that if it is possible that such a being exists, then it does exist, and furthermore exists necessarily. So the only way in which a maximally great being could fail to exist is if its existence is impossible. So, *is* a maximally great being possible? Malcolm takes it for granted that it is, thence infers that a maximally great being exists necessarily, and draws the conclusion that, so understood, Anselm's argument is a sound proof of the existence of God.

But there are at least two compelling reasons for thinking that Malcolm's version of the argument fails. The first arises from the argument's assumption that necessary existence is a perfection; the second from a failure to show that God has necessary existence. Let us take them in turn.

In defence of the idea that necessary existence is a perfection, Malcolm takes up some remarks which Anselm made in his reply to Gaunilo, to the effect that a being who did not exist necessarily would have only a dependent existence. Since its *non*-existence is possible (i.e. there are possible worlds in which it does not exist), its continued existence is dependent on the non-occurrence of any events which would destroy it. But we can grant Malcolm this and still think that necessary existence need not be a merit. Why should the fact that something could be destroyed be a demerit in it? This clearly cannot be a universal truth: for some types of entity, the fact that they are biodegradable is a definite merit, and for most artefacts, it would surely be *disastrous* if, once created, they were indestructible! So, there is no warrant for thinking that the impossibility of the non-existence of an entity is any sort of merit in that entity.

Malcolm invokes the idea that God is often thought of as being by definition unlimited; and since dependence would be a kind of limitation, it follows that God cannot be a dependent being, and hence that he must exist necessarily. This may be true, but it still gives us no reason for thinking that necessary existence is a merit. The mere fact that something is true of God does not make that something admirable. If God exists, it might be that God is admirable, but that fact could hardly make *existence as such* admirable. Equally, if God *exists necessarily*, he might be admirable, but it would not follow that *necessary existence* is admirable. So Malcolm is unsuccessful in showing why we should accept that necessary existence is a perfection or a great-making property.

But there is a second problem with Malcolm's defence of the ontological argument. His defence turns essentially on the claim that necessary existence is a different concept from existence per se, and in the version he defends, the conclusion of the argument is that God exists necessarily. He interprets this to mean that God exists in all possible worlds, in other words, 'God does not exist' is not merely false, it is self-contradictory, in the wide sense of that term. But if we examine his line of reasoning closely, we will see that it does not justify such a conclusion. Malcolm says that God is by definition an unlimited being, and hence one who cannot have a dependent existence. Given this, it will follow that God (if he exists) is a being who cannot be either created or destroyed (since that would reveal a dependence on the action of his creator, or the inaction of his potential destroyer). But it does not follow from that that God (if he exists) exists in every possible world. All that follows is

> Necessarily, if God does not exist at time t, he will not exist at t + 1 (since he cannot be created); and necessarily, if he does exist at t, then he will exist at t + 1 (since he cannot be destroyed).

For all that Malcolm has said, the following scenario is possible: in some possible worlds, God always has existed and always will exist (and hence can have a non-dependent existence); but in other possible worlds, God never has existed and never will (and hence he does not have necessary existence). Malcolm's error is in confusing the absolute independence which he claims (quite plausibly) must characterise God (if he exists), with necessary existence.

For both of these reasons, Malcolm's version of the argument fails.

Hartshorne's version

Hartshorne agrees with Malcolm that there are two versions of the ontological argument to be found in Anselm; he agrees that of these two versions, the first is unsound and the second is sound; but he disagrees with Malcolm about the form which the second version takes. Hartshorne provides a concise statement of what he takes this second version to be, and it can be quoted in full:

> 'q' for '(Ex)Px' There is a perfect being, or perfection exists
> 'N' for 'it is necessary (logically true) that'
> '~' for 'it is not true that'
> '∨' for 'or'
> 'p → q' for 'p strictly implies q' or 'N ~(p & ~ q)'
>
> 1. $q \to Nq$ (Anselm's Principle: perfection could not exist contingently)
> 2. $Nq \lor \sim Nq$ (excluded middle)
> 3. $\sim Nq \to N \sim Nq$ (form of Becker's Postulate: moral status is always necessary)
> 4. $Nq \lor N \sim Nq$ (inference from (2, 3))
> 5. $N \sim Nq \to N \sim q$ (inference from (1): the necessary falsity of the consequent implies that of the antecedent (modal form of modus tollens))
> 6. $Nq \lor N \sim q$ (inference from (4, 5))
> 7. $\sim N \sim q$ (intuitive postulate (or conclusion from other theistic arguments): perfection is not impossible)
> 8. Nq (inference from (6, 7))
> 9. $Nq \to q$ (modal axiom)
> 10. q (inference from (8, 9))
>
> (Hartshorne 1973: 50–1, punctuation changed)

This quotation from Hartshorne gives us the logical skeleton of his argument. Let us spell it out more fully in English. We then find that it amounts to the following:

(1a)   If there is a perfect being, this is necessarily true (assumption).

(2a)   Either it is necessarily true that there is a perfect being, or it is not necessarily true that such a being exists (law of excluded middle).

(3a)   If it is not necessarily true that a perfect being exists, then it is necessary that it is not necessarily true that such a being exists (modal status is necessary). So:

(4a)   Either it is necessarily true that a perfect being exists, or it is necessary that it is not necessarily true that such a being exists (from 2a and 3a). So:

(5a)   If it is necessary that it is not necessarily true that a perfect being exists, then it is necessary that such a being does not exist (from 1a). So:

(6a)   Either it is necessarily true that a perfect being exists or it is necessarily true that such a being does not exist (from 4a and 5a).

(7a)   It is not necessarily true that there is no perfect being (assumption). So:

(8a)   It is necessarily true that there is a perfect being (from 6a and 7a).

(9a)   If it is necessarily true that there is a perfect being, then there is a perfect being (assumption). So:

(10a) There is a perfect being (from 8a and 9a).

The argument is certainly valid, in the formal sense that the conclusion follows from the initial assumptions. So the only point at which it is open to criticism is in its premises. Some of these are quite uncontroversial, for example (2) and (9). Others, such as (3) and (5), could be challenged on technical grounds. But the assumptions which are unobvious are (1) and (7). Assumption (1) tells us that if God exists at all, his existence is a necessary truth. In terms of the 'possible worlds' vocabulary which we introduced earlier, if God exists at all, he exists in every possible world. He cannot, in other words, exist in some possible worlds and not in others. So if he exists in *any* possible worlds, he exists in them all. So what (1) implies is that if it is *possible* for God to exist, then it follows that he does exist. Assumption (7) then tells us that it is indeed possible for God to exist; which in conjunction with what (1) implies, leads to the conclusion that he does exist. So a simplified version of Hartshorne's argument would be:

(a)   If it is possible that God exists, then he exists.
(b)   It *is* possible that God exists. So:
(c)   God exists.

Why, then, should we accept (1)? This assumption is very close to the assumption which, as we saw above, both Plantinga and Malcolm make, namely that a maximally great being must have necessary existence (Plantinga), and that God cannot have merely contingent existence (Malcolm). How, then, can Hartshorne defend his version of the assumption, which tells us that if God exists at all, he exists necessarily? He does so by claiming that non-existence is a defect, and that the defect which characterises contingent non-existence also characterises contingent existence. Since God is by definition a perfect being, he cannot have a defective kind of existence, and hence cannot have a merely contingent existence. 'Non-existence is indeed a defect . . . [Furthermore] there is a deficiency in the ordinary manner of failing to exist which carries over into the ordinary manner of existing; and neither, therefore makes sense in combination with perfection' (op. cit. p. 60).

This is a very strange metaphysics. If non-existence is a defect, what is it a defect in? Surely not in the thing which does not exist? If there is to be a defect, there must be something (something real) which has the defect. Is it then a defect in the other things which do exist? It can be true that the non-existence of one thing is a defect in another. It would be a defect in a car if it had no windscreen. But this is because a car needs a windscreen if it is to function normally. It would not be a defect in a car if it had no propeller, because cars do not need propellers to function normally. So examples like this do not help to give a sense to the idea that non-existence per se is a defect. On the contrary, they bring out the fact that non-existence can be a merit just as well as a defect. If I am at all concerned about petrol consumption, I could well regard it as a merit in my car that it does not have a supercharger that would increase the fuel consumption. Could Hartshorne mean that non-existences are a defect in *the universe at large*, rather than in this or that particular thing? This idea is scarcely intelligible, and surely not one which could appeal to a theist. For it would have the consequence that the universe is a *massively* defective place. There are so many *kinds* of thing that do not exist (red unicorns, yellow unicorns, striped unicorns, etc.); and for each kind of thing that does not exist, there are so many individual things of that kind that could have existed but do not. Whether we interpret the thesis that 'non-existence is indeed a defect' as locating the defect in the non-existent things, in particular existent things, or in the world at large, the claim turns out either to be senseless, or to be irrelevant to Hartshorne's argument.

What deepens the puzzle is that whatever kind of defect we manage to detect in non-existence has also got to be present in contingent *existence* (see the previous quotation from Hartshorne). We have, or more accurately Hartshorne has, here surely transgressed the limits of sense.

But although Hartshorne emphasises the claim that non-existence is a defect, perhaps he does not really need it. What he really needs is not the claim that *non*-existence is a defect but the claim that *contingent* existence is defective, for from that he could infer that God cannot have contingent existence, and hence that if he exists at all he must exist necessarily. As we saw above, Malcolm tried to argue that God could not have a merely contingent existence; and as we also saw, he produced an invalid argument which turned on a misunderstanding of the implications of saying that God cannot be a dependent being. Hartshorne's defence of the non-contingency of God moves in suspiciously similar territory. He tells us that 'To exist contingently is to exist precariously, or by chance . . . But to exist precariously or by chance is an imperfection, appropriate only to imperfect individuals' (op. cit. p. 61).

But Hartshorne here is just plain wrong. Contingent existence is *nothing to do* with 'precarious' existence or existence 'by chance'. If A exists contingently, then A exists in at least one possible world (the actual world) but not in all possible worlds. It could well be the case that in all the possible worlds in which A existed, its existence is absolutely secure and non-precarious, and further that it is indefinitely extended in time. Indeed, this is exactly the sense which some theists attach to God's existence. Swinburne, for example, says that the proposition 'God exists' is contingent, that God nonetheless exists in a range of possible worlds (including the real one), and that within the real world he enjoys eternal existence.

It seems, then, that however we interpret him, Hartshorne cannot find a convincing defence for the claim that contingent existence is defective; and without such a defence, he has no grounds for the claim that God's existence must be necessary. And without *that* claim, his ontological argument (1)–(10) above collapses.

But even if the above attack on premise (1) is waived, the Hartshorne argument is still open to attack over premise (7). Premise (7) claims that it is possible that God exists. Remember that this must be taken in the logical, not the epistemological sense of 'possible'. The claim is not that, so far as we can tell, there is no impossibility in there being a God. The claim is that there is at least one possible world in which God exists. That will be true only if God's defining properties are individually intelligible, and collectively self-consistent. There have been many attempts to show that this twofold requirement is not met, and we shall be considering them in due course. For now, we can simply observe that Hartshorne makes no attempt to meet any of these standard critiques of the concept of God, and to that extent he is not entitled to help himself to premise (7) as if it were uncontroversial.

Where ontological arguments go wrong

So far, we have looked at five versions of the ontological argument, and found serious fault with all of them. But now we might wonder whether there is some pervasive error which must infect all ontological arguments, or whether it might be possible to devise a sound version. The conventional wisdom is that there *are* some general faults which all ontological arguments display. They can be summed up in three slogans:

(i) Existence is not a property.

(ii) Existential statements are second order statements.

(iii) No existential statements can be logically necessary.

Let us take these in turn, and see if they can give us any reason to think that no future version of the ontological argument can be any more successful than those we have looked at.

(i) Existence is not a property

We have already come across the idea that existence is not a property in looking at Gassendi's criticism of Descartes, and in particular in his remark 'what does not exist has no perfections or imperfections, and what does exist and has several perfections does not have existence as one of its individual perfections' (ibid.).

But it is usually Kant who is credited with developing the idea that existence is not a property (or that 'exists' is not a real predicate) and applying it with devastating force to the ontological argument. So how does Kant achieve this?

He first draws a distinction between what he calls 'merely logical' predicates and what he calls 'real or determining predicates'. Although he speaks as if it is a division between predicates per se, what he later says makes it clear that it is really a distinction between *uses* of predicates that he is concerned with. He says that any grammatically appropriate expression can be used as a predicate, and can hence qualify for the term 'logical' predicate. But to be counted as a real predicate, an expression has to go beyond what is implicit in the subject concept. Thus if I say 'Circles are round', 'are round' is being used as a merely logical predicate: it does not go beyond the subject concept 'circles'. But if I say 'Plates are round', 'are round' is being used as a real or determining predicate, since merely by examining the subject concept *plate* in as much detail as you please, you would never be able to determine whether or not plates are round.

Kant then asserts that 'exists' can only ever be used as a merely logical predicate, and hence that statements of the form 'God exists' cannot be really subject–predicate in form. The implication is that if 'exists' cannot be a predicate, then *a fortiori* it cannot be a defining predicate. Since Kant takes a defender of the ontological argument to be committed to the thesis that 'exists' is a defining predicate of God, Kant claims to have found a conclusive refutation of the ontological argument.

Unfortunately Kant's attack is very confused, and anything but conclusive. In the first place, it is not at all clear that the ontological argument *must* regard 'exists' as part of the definition of God. The version which comes closest to this is perhaps Descartes's (see the passage quoted on p. 37). But it is a criticism which does not apply very obviously to the Anselmian version, even less to the versions which have developed since Kant's day, such as those by Plantinga and Hartshorne. Although all defenders of the ontological argument are committed to saying that 'God exists' is a necessary truth, they are not committed to saying that it is true *by definition*.

Second, Kant has no good ground for his central claim that 'exists' is not a real predicate. Of real predicates, he tells us that they enlarge the concept of the subject, and are not already contained in the concept of the subject. The problem with his critique is that 'exists' passes one and perhaps both of these tests. Suppose that I say 'Tigers exist'. To determine whether tigers exist, I have to investigate the world empirically, not simply analyse the concept. So the predicate 'exists' is not contained in the concept of a tiger. So 'exists' passes Kant's second test for being a real predicate. Does it also pass the first test? It is difficult to be sure since he does not tell us how to discover whether a predicate 'enlarges' a subject or not. But there are some grounds for thinking that Kant is committed to saying 'exists' *does* enlarge the subject. For he insists that all existential judgements are synthetic, and that in a synthetic judgement, the predicate always adds something to the concept of the subject. This appears to commit him to saying that 'exists' does enlarge the subject concept, and hence that 'exists' passes both tests for being a real predicate.

Kant's problem is that he needs to reconcile three claims which on the face of it are mutually incompatible:

(1) 'Exists' can be used only as a logical predicate, and hence can neither add to nor enlarge the subject concept.
(2) 'Exists' occurs only in synthetic judgements.
(3) In synthetic judgements, the predicate always adds to the subject concept.

Although, therefore, Kant's name is particularly associated with the assertion that 'exists' is not a real predicate, we will look in vain to him for a cogent defence of that thesis. Indeed, it seems that Kant's own words commit him to denying the thesis as well as to asserting it.

(ii) Existential statements are second order statements

Let us start by defining an existential statement as one which either asserts or denies the existence of something. A positive existential statement will be one which asserts existence, and a negative existential statement will be one which denies existence. So, 'There are striped tigers', 'God is real', and 'Numbers exist' are all positive existential statements; 'There are no striped tigers', 'God is a fantasy', and 'Numbers do not really exist' are all negative existential statements.

The slogan that existential statements are second order is one which is particularly associated with the work of Frege. Frege was not concerned with the ontological argument as such, but he was very much concerned with the logic of existential statements. He developed a theory which is widely accepted today and which has been applied to the ontological argument in an attempt to expose its basic weakness. We can summarise it as follows:

(a) Statements of number are statements about concepts not about objects.
(b) Existential statements are statements of number. So:
(c) Existential statements are statements about concepts not about objects.

Let us see what these claims mean.

(a) Statements of number are statements about concepts not about objects

Frege starts with the familiar thought that when we apply numbers to collections of objects, it is usually not the case that the number applies to each member of the collection taken separately. If we say 'The army has battle-hardened divisions' the term 'battle-hardened' applies to each individual division, and attributes the property of being battle-hardened to each of them. But if we say 'The army has ten divisions' the term 'ten' does not apply to each division. It does not attribute a property to any division, and in fact applies to none of them. What then does the term 'ten' apply to? What entity or entities is it true of? One natural answer might be 'If not to each of the divisions then to the collection as a whole'. But Frege rejects this answer. He points out that the army can be regarded as ten divisions, or one hundred regiments, or two thousand platoons, or ten thousand men. It is the same collection of men in each case, although a different number applies as we shift our focus. So the number cannot be a property of the whole collection, any more than of the component divisions. What then does it belong to? Frege reasoned that since the number changes as we change the concept under which we bring the army (division, regiment, platoon, etc.), we must really be saying something about the concept, rather than about what the concept applies to. He thus arrives at the conclusion that to say 'There are ten divisions' is to say 'The concept *division* has ten instances'. We are really talking about the concept *division*, not about the military unit, the division. Similarly to say 'There are ten thousand men' is (Frege maintains) to be understood as saying 'The concept *men* (in the sense of soldiers) has ten thousand instances'. This account of the logic of numerical statements can very naturally be extended to cover those cases in which we want to use the number 0 in describing the number of something: we want to say that there are *no* so-and-sos. Perhaps the army contains no VCs. On Frege's account, this should be understood as saying 'The concept *army member who is the holder of a* VC has no instances'.

53

(b) Existential statements are statements of number

Can existential statements be accommodated within this account of how numerical statements work? Frege's simple solution is that a negative existential statement is the same as a numerical statement using zero, and a positive existential statement is a denial of a numerical statement using zero. So, to say 'Striped polar bears do not exist' is to say 'There are no striped polar bears', which in turn is to say 'The concept *striped polar bear* has no instances'; and to say 'There are giraffes in Africa' is to say 'The concept *giraffes in Africa* has some (indeterminate number of) instances'. Existence (and non-existence) are thus not attributed to objects at all – even less are they necessary or defining attributes of objects.

(c) Existential statements are statements about concepts

We can thus see how existential statements both positive and negative are statements about concepts, not about objects. To say 'God exists' is not to make a statement about God, but about the concept *God*. It is to say 'The concept *God* has at least one instance'. To say that existential statements are second order is to say that they attribute properties to concepts, not to objects – they attribute the property of having instances. To say 'The woman in the corner is wise' is a first order statement, since it attributes a property (wisdom) to an object (the woman in the corner). But to say 'There is a woman in the corner' is a second order statement since it is not about an object (a woman) but about a concept. It says 'The concept *woman in the corner* has at least one instance'.

This makes clear how Frege's analysis of existential statements complements Kant's. Kant was able to tell us that existence is not a property, that 'exists' is not a real predicate, and hence that existential statements cannot be subject–predicate statements. But he was confused about *why* 'exists' is not a real predicate, and was quite unable to give us a positive account of how existential statements work. Frege supplies this lack. He shows us that in a statement like 'God exists', although *grammatically* 'God' is the subject term and 'exists' is the predicate, from a deeper logical point of view 'God' is not the subject and 'exists' is not the predicate. The real subject is 'the concept *God*', and the real predicate is not 'exists', but 'has instances' or 'applies to something'. Frege thus completes the argument for saying that existence is not a (first order) property (or 'exists' is not a predicate), and hence that it cannot be a defining (first order) property of anything, not even of God.

(iii) No existential statements can be logically necessary

The third slogan that is sometimes invoked to explain the necessary failure of all possible versions of the ontological argument is that no existential statements can be logically necessary. This is a slogan that is well-embedded in traditional empiricism. (Malcolm 1964: 153–4 provides a useful list of twentieth-century philosophers who have endorsed this slogan.) But why should we think that this slogan says anything true?

One line of thought is that the only way in which a statement of the form 'xs are F' can be necessarily true is if 'are F' is part of the meaning of the word 'x'. Thus 'Vixens are female' is necessarily true, it is said, because being female is part of the definition of the word 'vixen'. By contrast, 'Vixens are shy' is not necessarily true, because being shy is not part of the definition of 'vixen'. So, if 'God exists' were necessarily true, 'exists' would have to be part of the definition of 'God'. But (so the argument continues), after Kant and Frege, we have very powerful grounds for saying that 'exists' is not a real predicate and *a fortiori* not a defining predicate. Ergo 'God exists' cannot be necessarily true.

Construed thus, we can see that slogan (iii) presupposes the correctness of slogans (i) and (ii). But even if we accept slogans (i) and (ii), there are grounds for resisting (iii). As will become clear in the next section, there are many plausible candidates for necessary existential statements, and none of them presuppose that 'exists' or 'does not exist' are predicates, or are part of the definition of the relevant subject terms.

Can the ontological argument survive?

From what we have said so far, we can infer that no future version of the ontological argument can be valid if it treats 'exists' as a defining predicate of God – at least, if we find the analysis of existential statements provided by Frege convincing. But we did not find any good grounds for accepting the current slogan that no existential statements can be logically necessary. So that leaves open the possibility that there might be a sound argument to a necessarily true existential conclusion of the form 'God exists' provided that the argument did not rely on the assumption that 'exists' was a real predicate ascribable to individual things. Let us consider a range of concepts and some associated existential statements (see Table 3.1 overleaf).

In the case of 1, it would be universally agreed that you cannot derive any existential statements from an exhaustive examination of the mere concept. Determining whether there are mammoths requires you to look beyond the concept to the empirical world. With 2, by contrast, it seems that we *can* derive an existential statement. We can derive the negative existential claim 'There are no such beings' – and we know that there are no such beings

Table 3.1

Concepts	Existential statements
1 Woolly mammoth	There are woolly mammoths.
2 Married bachelor	There are no married bachelors.
3 Prime number between 5 and 7	There is no prime number between 5 and 7.
4 Highest natural number	There is no highest natural number.
5 Prime number between 10 and 15	There are two prime numbers between 10 and 15.
6 God	God exists.

because the concept is self-contradictory. In a parallel way, we can derive existential statements from concepts 3 and 4. We can derive the claims 'There are no prime numbers between 5 and 7' and 'There is no highest natural number'. On the face of it, these are straightforward existential claims, denying the existence of certain numbers, just as 'There is no snow-covered mountain in East Anglia' is a straightforward negative existential claim. Of course, numbers are very different kinds of entity from mountains, so there are differences between these types of statement. But the claims about numbers nonetheless seem to be genuinely existential.

Now, if it is possible to derive negative existential claims from mere concepts, surely it ought also to be possible to derive positive existential statements. What would be an example of such a derivation? Presumably it would be something like statement 5. Merely by considering the concept of a prime number between 10 and 15, we can see that there must be such a number – in fact, we can see that there are two such numbers, 11 and 13. Notice that in arriving at all these existential claims, both negative and positive, we do not have to include 'exists' or 'does not exist' explicitly in the concepts we start with. Our concepts are not '*non-existent* prime number between 5 and 7' or '*existent* prime number between 10 and 15'. Of course the existential claim is implicit in the concept – that is simply to say that it can be derived from the concept. But its being implicit does not require us to include it as part of the definition of the concept.

If this line of thinking is correct, it seems that we do not have any proof that *no* version of the ontological could work. For we can agree that 'exists' is not a predicate, that it cannot be a defining predicate, that existential statements are second order statements à la Frege, and still not be able to rule out the possibility of there being statements that are both logically necessary and existential, or rule out the possibility that starting with a mere concept, we could deduce an existential statement.

But how much comfort can the theist draw from this concession? After all, it might be said, even if we are willing to allow that numbers do really exist, existential statements about numbers are a poor model in terms of which to understand an existential statement about God.

Whether the parallel is really poor is a question to which we will have to return. But perhaps surprisingly, a number of God's qualities would make good sense if God was conceived of on the model of numbers. Numbers do not exist in space and time – and the same could be true of God. Numbers are immaterial entities – and so is God. Because they are immaterial, numbers cannot be divided into parts – nor is God divisible. Numbers do not change – and God is often described as immutable. The existence of numbers might be said to be self-explanatory – and God is sometimes described as a self-explanatory being. Of course there are some disanalogies as well, principally arising from God's personal qualities, and his capacity to cause changes in the material world.

Our final judgement therefore should be that no current version of the ontological argument is sound, and that consequently theism cannot be shown to be rational by appealing to any current version. But for the atheist to allege that it is in principle impossible to derive existential conclusions from mere concepts would be to go too far. Not until we are clear about the existential status of abstract entities like numbers, and the extent to which the existence of God could satisfactorily be modelled on that of such abstract entities, will we be in a position to endorse the aphorism from Schopenhauer with which this chapter began.

Further reading

Anselm's ontological argument and Gaunilo's objection can be found in Anselm (1965). Extracts are reprinted in Hick (1964), Plantinga (1968) and Barnes (1972). Hick and Plantinga, and also B. Davies (1993) have the text of Gaunilo's objection. Anselm's argument is assessed and partly defended in Malcolm (1964) and Plantinga (1974). It gets a more hostile review in Gale (1991), and in Martin (1990) who also reviews the Malcolm and Plantinga versions. Descartes's version can be found in Descartes (1984), vol. II, which also includes Gassendi's objection. Wilson gives a good discussion of Descartes. Plantinga's version is defended in Plantinga (1974, 1977), and Gale (1991) supplies a critical assessment. A good introduction to contemporary 'possible worlds' talk is in Kim and Sosa (1995) under the entry 'Modality and possible worlds'. Malcolm's version is in Malcolm (1964) (but first published in *The Philosophical Review* vol. 69 no. 1, 1960) and is criticised by Bennett (1974), Martin (1990) and Gale (1991). Hartshorne's version is in Hartshorne (1973), with a critique in Martin (1990). Kant's analysis of the ontological argument is in Kant (1963) (see especially A 592– A 603), the whole of which is reprinted in Hick (1964). Everitt (1995) is a recent attempt to make sense of it. Frege's analysis of existential statements is in Frege (1974) (see especially sections 46ff). Van Inwagen (1995) defends the claim that there are serious difficulties in knowing whether ontological arguments are either sound or unsound, on the grounds of a general modal scepticism. The most comprehensive recent treatment of the ontological argument, with a very extensive bibliography, is Oppy (1995).

4

Cosmological arguments

> I think that some versions of . . . the Design Argument and the
> Cosmological Argument are as good as any philosophical
> argument that has ever been presented for any conclusion.
> (Van Inwagen in Morris 1994: 47)

Introduction

In contrast to ontological arguments, all versions of the cosmological arguments rely on at least one empirical premise. It is characteristic of most versions of the arguments that this premise is (or these premises are) extremely
general. It might be, for example, simply the fact that the universe exists, or
that it contains some things which depend on other things, or that it contains change, or that it displays orderliness. Other arguments which we will
be looking at later invoke much more specific empirical premises, for example, concerned with the existence of religious experience or of morality. But
cosmological arguments are arguments from the universe (or cosmos) in
general.

It is an argument with a longer history than the ontological argument. Its
origins go back to the Ancient Greeks, and it resurfaces in Western philosophy with the writings of Aquinas in the thirteenth century. Aquinas
offered five ways of proving the existence of God, of which the first three are
usually regarded as versions of the cosmological argument. Descartes in the
seventeenth century produced an argument which is often called a cosmological argument. But in fact Descartes's version does not really fit the
definition given above, since its main premise is not some very general fact
about the universe but on the contrary a very specific one: that Descartes
has an idea of God. Leibniz supported one version of the argument, and
other versions continued to receive endorsement through the eighteenth century from writers like Clarke and Wollaston. At the hands of Hume and
Kant it received severe criticism, but it has continued into the twentieth century with powerful supporters. In his debate with Bertrand Russell,

Copleston relies on a cosmological argument, and the official position of the Catholic church is that an argument of this form is sufficient to convince any rational and open-minded person that God exists.

The First Cause argument

One popular version of the cosmological argument can be expressed as follows: the state of the universe as we see it now was caused by the state of the universe as it was a moment ago; and how it was a moment ago was caused by how it was two moments ago. And how it was two moments ago was caused by how it was three moments ago; and so on. But (so the argument goes) this regress cannot go on infinitely. Therefore there must have been a first cause, and this first cause was (as the originator of everything) God.

Aquinas endorsed a version of this argument in the second of his so-called Five Ways, but it has also received endorsement from contemporary writers such as Davies and Craig.

In one version, the argument turns essentially on the impossibility of an infinite series of past times, or past events, whether these events are thought of as causes or not. We will look at this contention in the next two sections. In other versions, the argument concedes that an infinity of past times is possible, but denies that an infinity of past *causes* is possible, or at least claims that if there were such an infinity, nothing would be (ultimately) explicable. We will turn to this version in the third of the following sections.

Clarifying the concept of infinity

The concept of infinity was philosophically puzzling for centuries. It was easy enough to say that if something was infinite, then it had no limits or boundaries. But this claim provided no real clarification, since no one had any clear idea of how to define 'limit' or 'boundary'. (The surface of a sphere seems to have nothing that would naturally be called a limit or a boundary, and yet the surface is clearly not infinite.) In the nineteenth century this confusion was removed by the work of mathematicians, in particular by Cantor. To understand how his work was able to bring clarity and precision to a previously obscure and woolly concept, we need to grasp three concepts: what it is for two sets to be *equivalent* to each other; what it is for one set to be a *subset* of another; and what it is for one set to be a *proper subset* of a second. These concepts can be defined as follows:

> Set A is equivalent to set B = the members of A can be paired in a one-to-one correspondence with the members of B, i.e. so that each member of one set is paired with just one member of the other set and vice versa.

Set A is a subset of set B = every member of A is a member of B.

Set A is a proper subset of set B = every member of A is a member of B but not vice versa.

Let us take these in turn. From the first definition, we see that, for example, the set of Beethoven symphonies and the set of planets of the sun are equivalent, in this technical sense of 'equivalent'. For each symphony can be paired with a planet, a different symphony for each planet, and a different planet for each symphony. The set of suits in a pack of playing cards is equivalent to the set of the Apostles, since each suit can be paired with just one Apostle, and vice versa. A simpler but less accurate way of understanding set equivalence is thus to say that two sets are equivalent if they have the same number of members. Given this more intuitive understanding of the idea of set equivalence, we can see that the set of current American Presidents is equivalent to the set of current British Prime Ministers. The first set has one member, and the second set has one member, so we see that trivially they can be paired with each other.

The second definition tells us that given sets A and B, A is a subset of B if and only if every member of A is also a member of B. Thus the set of current British Prime Ministers is a subset of the set of British Ministers, since every member of the first set (which in fact has only one member) is also a member of the second set. The set of human beings is a subset of the set of mammals, since every member of the first set, i.e. every human being, is also a member of the second set, i.e. is also a mammal. Notice that by this definition, every set counts as a subset of itself. This is so because if A and B are the same set, then clearly every member of A is a member of B, and thus set A meets the condition for being a subset of set B, and equally B is a subset of A.

The third definition tells us that given sets A and B, A is a proper subset of B if and only if every member of A is a member of B but it is not the case that every member of B is also a member of A. So, to use our previous examples, the set of current British Prime Ministers is not only a subset of the set of British Prime Ministers, it is also a proper subset. For whereas every member of A is a member of B, it is not the case that every member of B is also a member of A: there are members of the set of British Prime Ministers who are not members of the set of current British Prime Ministers. Again, the set of human beings is not only a subset of the set of mammals, it is also a proper subset of the set of mammals, for every human being is a mammal, but not vice versa.

Given these three definitions, it is now possible to produce a precise definition of infinity:

A set has infinitely many members = the set is equivalent to a proper subset of itself.

As a simple test of this definition, let us see how it applies in some cases where we might feel that our pre-reflective understanding of the concept of infinity is firmest. Take the sequence of natural numbers 0, 1, 2, 3, 4, 5, 6, and so on. We normally (and rightly) regard this set as infinite: for any number in the sequence there is a higher one. Now consider the sequence of even numbers 0, 2, 4, 6, 8, 10, and so on. We normally and rightly regard this sequence as being infinite: for any number in the sequence, you can obtain the next number by adding two. There is no highest even number, just as there is no highest natural number. Yet clearly the set of even numbers is a proper subset of the set of natural numbers, since every even number is a natural number, but not every natural number is an even number. But equally clearly the two sets are equivalent, since every member of one set can be paired with a member of the second set, each member of one set getting a different member of the other and vice versa. The simple way to represent this is obviously:

0, 1, 2, 3, 4, 5, 6 . . .

0, 2, 4, 6, 8, 10, 12 . . .

Hence the set of natural numbers is an infinite set by our definition. By contrast, the set of (say) human beings who have ever lived will not be infinite, since although it doubtless contains billions of members, it has no proper subsets which are equivalent to itself. (We are not here trying to *prove* that there are infinitely many natural numbers or finitely many human beings, but only seeking to show how the definition of infinity which Cantor provided picks out sets which we would antecedently think of as infinite and excludes sets which we would antecedently think of as finite.)

Given this clear account of what infinity is, universally accepted by mathematicians, it is possible to go on to prove a number of interesting theorems about infinite sets. For our point of view, there are several important points to notice about this clarified concept of infinity. First, the definition has been achieved without invoking any fuzzy ideas of boundaries or limits or edges. Second, the concept as defined applies primarily to *sets*, and to sets which have discriminable elements or members. Talk of, for example, infinite love or infinite wisdom will make no sense unless wisdom can be thought of as a set with discriminable members (for example, units of wisdom perhaps?). Third, given the match between the definition of infinity and the set of natural numbers, we can use as a rough and ready test for whether a set is infinite the question 'Is there a one-to-one correspondence between the members of the set in question and the natural numbers?'. If there is, the set is infinite; if there is not, then the set is finite.[1] Fourth, although this definition treats infinity as a *number*, it does not treat infinity as a number which occurs somewhere in the sequence of natural numbers. It is not that infinity is a very big natural number, which we could reach if we went far enough along the sequence of natural numbers: infinity is not a member of the sequence of natural numbers at all. Finally, notice how this definition of infinity renders redundant questions like 'But how can a finite mind grasp something infinite? Surely what is infinite must always transcend finite understandings?'. The short answer is that finite minds can grasp the idea of infinite by putting together the two sub-ideas of *set equivalence* and *being a proper subset of*, precisely in the manner indicated.

Suppose, then, that someone advanced the hypothesis that past time is infinite. This would mean that the members of the set of past times were in one-to-one correspondence with the set of natural numbers. What are 'the members of the set of past times'? An obvious way to interpret this would be to identify the members with some arbitrary unit of time, such as a second, a minute, a year, a century, etc. To say that past time was infinite would then be to say that the members of the set of past seconds (or minutes, or years, etc.) could be paired in a one-to-one correspondence with the natural numbers, and the obvious way to do that would be to pair the present second (minute, year, etc.) with 0, the one before that with 1, the one before that with 2, the one before that with 3, and so on. And just as there is no highest number in the sequence, so if past time is infinite, there will be no earliest time. For every number in the sequence of natural numbers, there will be a higher one, and for every time in the sequence, there will be an earlier one.

Similar thoughts apply to the infinity of space. To say that space is infinite is to say that the set of units of space (inches, miles, light years, parsecs, etc.) can be put in a one-to-one correspondence with the set of natural numbers. Starting from where the observer is, the first inch (mile, light year, etc.) can be paired with 0, the next with 1, the next with 2, and so on. And just as there is no highest number in the sequence, so there is no furthermost inch (mile, etc.).

None of this gives us any reason at all to say that time and/or space *is* infinite. All it does is clarify what is meant by saying (or by denying) that time and/or space is infinite. It shows us that there is nothing paradoxical or self-refuting or self-contradictory about the idea that time and/or space is infinite in extent. But whether either of these claims is *true* is a further question.

Can there be an infinity of past events?

We can now return to the First Cause argument. It will be clear that this suffers from a major weakness. It says that the current state of the universe was caused by an earlier one, and that one by an earlier one, and so on – *but this regress cannot go on indefinitely*. The problem with this version of the argument is that we are given no reason at all for thinking that the italicised phrase is true. An infinite regress is not necessarily a vicious regress. So at the very least the argument needs to be supplemented with a supporting argument to show why the causal regress might not stretch back infinitely in time.

It is true that a number of writers have tried to show that there is something vicious in the idea of an infinite regress, focusing more on a regress of past times rather than a regress of past causes. But typically their remarks wrongly assume that innocuous consequences of the concept are somehow logically vicious.

As an example consider the 'proof' by Moreland that an infinite set of past times is impossible. '[This] series cannot even get started. This is because it has no first member!' (Moreland 1987: 29). The implication is that a series which cannot 'get started' and which has 'no first member' is not one which can terminate in the present. But this is impotent to show that an infinite regress is vicious. Of course an infinite series that terminates in the present does not have 'a first member' (assuming that 'first' means 'earliest in time'). If it did, it would clearly be only a finite series of times. Some of the *elementary* implications of saying that the past series of times is infinite are that the series did not *begin*, that it did not have *an earliest member*, that for every member there is an *earlier* member, and so on. Moreland does not show that there is anything vicious about the idea of an infinite regress merely by pointing to such implications – what he needs to do is to show why any of them is supposed to be objectionable.

A second example is found in Helm. Writing of the possibility that God might have existed for an infinite past time, he says:

> such a prospect requires that an infinite number of events must have elapsed before the present moment could arrive. And since it is impossible for an infinite number of events to have elapsed, and yet the present moment has arrived, the series of events cannot be infinite. Therefore either there was a time when God began to exist, which is impossible, or God exists timelessly.
>
> (Helm 1997: 38)

Here the crucial assumption is that 'it is impossible for an infinite number of events to have elapsed and yet the present moment has arrived'. Helm gives no explicit reason to believe this, but perhaps he is moved by something like Moreland's assumption that if a sequence of events is to terminate in the present, it *must* have begun in the past. But this assumption is simply false for those sequences which are infinite: an infinite past series that terminates in the present did not *begin* at all – it has *always* been going on, and therefore has no earliest member. (In a similar way, an infinite future series that begins in the present will never end – it always will be going on, and will have no last member.)

As a final example, we can turn to Craig's section of Craig and Smith (1995). Craig seeks to prove that although there may be nothing wrong with the mathematical concept of infinity *per se*, it is something that cannot apply to the actual world. There can be, as he puts it, potential infinities but not actual infinities. By this he means that although there can be collections with members where, no matter how many members we count, we could always count more, there cannot be any collections that are actually infinite. To illustrate the contradictions implicit in the concept of an actual infinity, he asks us to imagine a library with an infinite collection of books where every book was coloured either black or red. He then continues:

> We would probably not balk if we were told that the number of black books and the number of red books is the same. But would we believe someone who told us that the number of red books in the library is the same as the number of red books *plus* the number of black books? For in that latter collection there are all the red books – just as many as in the former collection, since they are identical – plus an infinite number of black books as well.
>
> (op. cit. p. 12)

We are meant to agree here that the assumption that there are infinitely many books leads to absurdity, and hence that the assumption must be absurd itself. But Craig has unfairly loaded the dice. Of course, we know antecedently that no library contains infinitely many *books* because we know that books take a finite time to write, and there have only been finitely many people in the history of the universe who have written a book. So of course there have only ever been finitely many books in the universe. But this is a fact about books, and the conditions of their production. It tells us nothing at all about infinity. If it were telling us an important truth about infinity, then the following argument ought to have equal force against the infinity of the set of natural numbers:

> We would not balk at being told that the number of even numbers and the number of odd numbers is the same. But would we believe someone who told us that the number of even numbers is the same as the number of even numbers *plus* the number of odd numbers? For in that latter collection there are all the even numbers – just as many as in the former collection, since they are identical – plus an infinite number of odd numbers as well.

In fact, this argument and Craig's do have equal force, i.e. none at all, as an objection to the very idea of infinite collections. While recognising that Craig's library, and other homely examples which he produces, have an intuitive appeal, from a logical point of view they have no force.

We conclude then that the First Cause argument cannot be defended by supposing that it is logically impossible for there to have been an infinity of past times. But what about the idea of an infinity of past *causes*? Can that idea be shown to be paradoxical? Many writers have thought so, and in the next section we turn to consider them.

Can there be an infinity of past causes?

What is the problem with the idea of an infinite series of causes? Aquinas argues in the second of his Five Ways that there cannot be an infinite regress of causes, because if the regress were infinite, then there would be no first cause, and if there is no first cause, there can be no subsequent or later events. So there must, he says, be a First Cause 'to which everyone gives the name of God'.

But this line of argument is worthless. The claim that if there is no first cause, there can be no later events is simply false. The whole point about an infinite sequence is that it does not have to *start* (i.e. to have an earliest or first member) in order to *continue*. If we assume that nothing happens without a cause (as Aquinas here does), then all that is required for the occurrence of later events is the occurrence of *earlier* causes, not of a *first* cause. If the regress of causes is infinite, then for *every* event we pick, it will be preceded by an earlier cause – which in turn will be preceded by an earlier cause, and so on.

A different line of attack comes from the thought that although it might be logically possible for there to be an infinite regress of causes, it would leave something radically inexplicable. For some theists, what would be left inexplicable would be some particular event; for others, what would be left inexplicable would be the existence of the whole infinitely long chain of causes and effects, i.e. the existence of the universe itself.

As a charming example of both of these concerns, consider these analogies from the eighteenth century:

> Suppose a chain hung down out of the heavens from an unknown height, and every link of it gravitated towards the earth, and what it hung upon was not visible, yet it did not descend but kept its situation; and upon this, a question should arise 'What supported or kept up this chain?' Would it be a sufficient answer to say that the first (or lowest) link hung upon the second (or that next above it), the second (or rather the first and second together) upon the third, and so on ad infinitum? For what holds up the whole? A chain of ten links would fall down, unless something able to bear it hindered; one of twenty, if not stayed by something of yet greater strength, in proportion to the increase of weight; and therefore one of infinite links certainly, if not sustained by something infinitely strong, and capable to bear up an infinite weight. And thus it is in a chain of causes and effects tending or as it were gravitating towards some end. The last or lowest depends, or (as one may say) is suspended upon the cause above it; this again, if it be not the first cause, is suspended as an effect upon something above it; and so on. And if they should be infinite, unless (agreeably to what has been said) there is some cause on which all hang or depend, they would

be but an infinite effect without an efficient cause; and so to assert there is any such thing would be as great an absurdity as to say, that a finite or little weight wants something to sustain it, but an infinite one or the greatest does not . . .

Suppose a row of blind men, of which the last laid his hand upon the shoulder of the man next before him, he on the shoulder of the next before him, till the foremost grew to be quite out of sight; and somebody asking, what guide this string of blind men had at the head of them, it should be answered, that they had no guide nor any head, but one held by another, and so went on, ad infinitum, would any rational creature accept this for a just answer? Is it not to say that infinite blindness (or blindness if it be infinite) supplies the place of sight, or of a guide?

(Wollaston 1726: 67, 67 fn.)

Wollaston's point here is not that there could not *be* an infinitely long chain, but that even if there were, the fact that it was infinitely long would leave something *unexplained*. He seems to be saying that you cannot explain what holds up the lowest link by invoking the second link, since it is just as puzzling what holds up the second link. By parity of reasoning you cannot explain the second by appeal to the third, the third by appeal to the fourth, and so on, all the way along the infinitely long chain. The implication is that wherever you stop in your regress of explanation, your stopping point will be just as puzzling as the original question about the first link.

But he also says that in his imagined scenario there would be a puzzle about what supports the whole chain itself. 'What holds up the whole?', he plaintively asks. The short answer to Wollaston's puzzles here is that the fact that the lowest link holds its position is explained by the fact that it is supported by the second, the position of the second is explained by the fact that it is supported by the position of the third, and so on all along the infinite chain. As for what holds up the whole chain, we will have to return to the question shortly of what could be meant by asking for an explanation of the universe as a whole. But we can note here that, like Craig's library of books, Wollaston's chain is a misleading analogy. In all our experience, chains are *always* of finite length, and if they are suspended vertically, they are *always* supported by something that is not itself a chain or another link in a chain. A chain might be hanging from a nail in the wall, it might be held aloft by a person, and so on. By contrast, in all our experience of series of events, we have never experienced an event which did not depend on a predecessor, and if we try to think of what an event might depend on other than a predecessor, no answer comes to mind. Our background expectations about the nature of physical chains of links are therefore very different from our background assumptions about causes in general, and we cannot assume that what seems obvious with the former will also apply to the latter.

Does the Big Bang theory help the First Cause argument?

We have so far been arguing that there is no good ground to accept a priori that the regress of times and causes *must* be finite. In the terminology introduced in Chapter 3, it is logically possible that there is an infinite series of past causes which has brought about the present state of the universe. Equivalently, there is a possible world (which may be this one) in which an infinite series of past causes brings about the current state of the world. There is therefore no good a priori ground for saying that the universe began to exist, hence no ground for saying that it must have been caused to begin to exist by any creator. But having said that it is *possible* that the universe has existed for an infinite time and those who have argued otherwise are mistaken, we now need to agree that as a matter of empirical fact, current cosmological theory seems to provide scientific support to the claim that the universe has existed for only a finite past time (roughly 15 billion years).

Since the theory of the Big Bang and of the expansion of the universe forms a backdrop to some discussion of the cosmological argument, it may be helpful to give a *very* simplified layman's account of what lies behind such talk. In 1929, the American astronomer Hubble discovered that the distant stars seemed to be moving away from us, and the further they were from us, the faster it seemed that they were receding. Naively, this might suggest that the earth was stationary at the centre of the universe. It might suggest that the earth was at the centre of a sphere whose surface was expanding outwards. However, Hubble also showed that from any other point in the universe, the appearance would be the same: from whatever star or other vantage point, X, one made one's observations, all other celestial bodies would seem to be receding from X, at a speed proportional to their distance from X. If we assume that what seems to be the case really is the case, then we live in a universe where every body is moving away from every other body. Instead of the earth being at the centre of a gigantic sphere, it is more helpful to think of the earth and all other celestial bodies as like points on the surface of a huge balloon which is being inflated. As the balloon is inflated, every point on the balloon's surface becomes more distant from every other point, and the further away from each other the points are initially, the faster the rate at which they recede from one another as the balloon is inflated.

This gives us some idea of what is meant by the mysterious-sounding idea that the whole universe is expanding. (We say *some* idea only, because like most of the homely analogies used to explain modern physical and cosmological theories to a lay audience, the analogy has some severe limitations. Our ordinary grasp of physical expansion requires that there should be a space into which the expanding thing expands. But the expanding universe hypothesis does not suppose that there is an infinitely large space into which the celestial bodies move. Rather, space itself is expanding – but not of course expanding *into* anything. The expansion of the universe (including space as part of the universe) is more like the expansion of the economy: the economy can grow bigger without there being some*where* into which it grows.)

If the universe is expanding, then at times before the present it must have been smaller than it was. The further back in time we go, the closer together, and hence the more dense, all the matter in the universe must have been. We come eventually to a point roughly some 15 billion years ago when space and matter were infinitely compressed into a single point of infinite density (see Hawking 1994: 80). Because relativity theory ties the nature of space and the nature of time very closely to the nature of matter, space and time themselves were not then as we know them now. Modern cosmological theory tells us that the universe began with a gigantic explosion of the infinitely dense matter. That is the point at which space began to exist and the first time occurred. Some contemporary cosmologists describe this theory for us in the following way:

> the universe began from a state of infinite density [in the Big Bang].
> Space and time were created in that event and so was all the matter
> in the universe. It is not meaningful to ask what happened before
> the big bang; it is somewhat like asking what is north of the North
> Pole. Similarly, it is not sensible to ask where the Big Bang took
> place. The point-universe was not an object isolated in space; it was
> the entire universe, and so the only answer can be that the Big Bang
> happened everywhere.
>
> (Sandage and Tammann, quoted in Craig and Smith 1995: 43)

Let us take for granted that this cosmological theory is correct and that the universe did have a beginning about 15 billion years ago. Notice that this is not to say that the Big Bang caused the universe to exist, for the phrase 'the Big Bang' refers to a part of the universe itself. It refers to the very first temporal moment in the universe's history. It is not that first the Big Bang occurred and then as a consequence the universe began to exist. Rather the occurrence of the Big Bang was (so we are supposing) the start of the universe. Can the theist get from this point to the conclusion that God exists?

According to Craig, there *is* a plausible argument from the temporal finiteness of the universe to the existence of God. It goes via the thesis that 'everything that begins to exist has a cause of its existence' (op. cit. p. 57). He declares that any defence of this assumption is unnecessary because the assumption 'is so intuitively obvious'; and he then adds (very surprisingly, one may think) 'especially when applied to the universe'! So, the intuitively obvious principle allows us to infer that there is a 'cause of the universe'. What, then, will this 'cause of the universe' be like? Craig continues that 'we may plausibly argue that the cause of the universe is a 'personal being' (by which he means at least a being capable of free choice) (ibid. p. 64). For we need an explanation of why the universe began to exist when it did, rather than earlier or later. The 'plausible argument' which he in fact invokes for saying that the cause must be a personal one is 'an Islamic principle of determination', according to which 'when two different states of affairs are equally possible and one results, this realisation of one rather than the other must be the result of a personal agent who freely chooses one rather than the other' (ibid. p. 66).

So the picture that he presents us with is that some personal being (let us label it X) existed from eternity, and from eternity had chosen or willed to create the universe some 15 billion years ago. Since there was a personal creator of the universe, and since being both personal and creator of everything are two central characteristics of the God of traditional theism, we have a plausible ground for saying that the causal version of the cosmological argument makes it reasonable to believe in the existence of God.

We will argue that every step in this remarkable argument is mistaken: it is not 'intuitively obvious' that everything that begins to exist has a cause of its existence; when applied to the universe as a whole, the claim is not even true, let alone obvious; and even if the universe could have a cause, there is no ground for saying that it must be 'personal'. Let us take these points in turn.

It is of course true that for many of the things which begin to exist, we do discover that they have causes. A table comes into existence because it was shaped by a craftsman; a crater comes into existence because the earth was struck by a meteorite; and so on. From such simple cases, we may well extrapolate and come to expect that *every* beginning of existence will have a cause. But that this need not be so is shown by the development of quantum mechanics which precisely rejects this assumption, and yet is regarded as one of the best-established theories of twentieth- and twenty-first-century science.[2]

What about the universe as a whole – could that have a cause? There is a straightforward reason for saying that the universe as a whole *could not* have a cause. Recall that the phrase 'the universe' is here being used to include space and time as well as matter. This means that there *could not have been* an event preceding the universe and bringing it about, for the simple reason that there was no time before the start of the universe in which that event could have occurred. The first moment of time was the first moment of the universe. If *per impossibile* there had been any event before the supposed start of the universe, that would simply show that the universe had in fact begun earlier than we had assumed.

But suppose there could have been some event which brought about the universe. Why should we accept that this event must have been a free choice? The 'Islamic principle of determination' invoked by Craig is highly implausible – and anyway seems in conflict with the rest of his argument. For suppose that the imagined free agent had not chosen either of the two possible options. If the options are mutually exhaustive (like the existence or non-existence of a universe) then clearly one of them will occur even if the free agent chooses neither (remember that the two options are supposed to be 'equally possible'). That must mean either that the universe could have occurred without any cause at all (contrary to Craig's initial assumption that every beginning of existence requires a cause); or that something else was the cause of the universe (contrary to Craig's assumption that the non-existence of the universe was 'equally possible').

But suppose that we ignore this conclusive objection to the argument, and try to suppose that the universe (and hence time) could have been preceded by a 'personal being' who existed from eternity and who brought the universe into being by willing it to exist. On the assumption that this being exists in time,[3] he clearly cannot be the *cause* of the universe since he is *part* of the universe. He could not be the cause of the temporal framework of the universe if he himself exists within that framework. And we can also make the ad hominem point that it would be inconsistent to argue that the universe could not have existed for an infinite past time, but then to allow that the creator could.

There is a further criticism to be made of the causal version of the cosmological argument. Suppose the objections we have raised so far can all be met. Suppose we can accept that the universe as whole must have a cause, and the cause can be a personal creator whose free choice can explain why the world began to exist when it did. The question must then arise, 'But what explains the existence of the personal creator?'. If we are indeed accepting that everything has to have a cause, that requirement must apply equally to the creator. And clearly the challenge would not have been satisfactorily met if the theist were to postulate some super-creator who created the creator, for then precisely the same question would arise for the super-creator. The only way in which the resort to a creator will block an infinite regress of super-creator, super-super-creator, and so on, is if the creator can have a different *kind* of existence from the universe.

We can distinguish three main ways in which the creator has been thought to have a special kind of existence. One way is to appeal to the idea of self-creation. The theist could then argue that God created the universe and himself. The requirement that everything has a cause would be met by allowing that God was the cause of himself.

The problem with this idea stems from the Humean claim that a cause must precede its effect. If the high wind is to cause the cradle to fall, the cradle must fall after, not before, the wind blows. If the meteorite is the cause of the crater, the crater must not appear until after the meteorite has hit the earth. On this conception of causation, it is clearly impossible for anything to cause itself. For to cause itself, it would have to precede itself;

and obviously nothing precedes itself: nothing occurs earlier than the time at which it occurs.

Kant criticised this Humean requirement that the cause must precede its effect, arguing that a cause and its effect can be simultaneous. He gave the example of a heavy ball resting on a cushion and making an indentation. The pressure of the ball and the indentation which it causes are simultaneous. But although this objection by Kant may be technically correct against Hume, it can afford no comfort to the theist. For Kant agrees with Hume that a cause and its effect must be two distinct things: even when a cause and its effect are simultaneous, there are two distinct events (e.g., in Kant's example, the downward pressure of the ball, and the resultant hollow in the cushion). Applying this to God tells us only that the cause of God need not precede God but would have to be something distinct from him. And then just as a cause that is simultaneous with its effect can itself have an earlier cause, so we could ask for the cause of whatever it was which had God as its simultaneous effect, and we would be embarked on just the sort of regress which the invocation of God was supposed to prevent.

The second and third kinds of special existence with which theists have credited God is to say that whereas the universe exists only contingently, God exists necessarily; and that whereas the universe exists in time, God is in some way 'outside' time. The supposition that God has either of these kinds of existence leads us on naturally to the second main type of cosmological argument, the Argument from Contingency, which we will consider in the next section. But before we embark on the Argument from Contingency, let us draw together the criticisms which we have been making of the causal version of the cosmological argument:

(1) There is nothing logically vicious or paradoxical in the idea that the universe is infinitely old. There could be an infinite series of past events or past causes. However, the best currently available cosmological theory implies that the universe is finitely old and it began about 15 billion years ago.

(2) We have no good grounds for saying that everything which begins to exist has a cause. Familiar middle-sized entities like tables and craters may all have causes, but that is a poor guide to whether absolutely everything that begins to exist has a cause.

(3) There are compelling grounds for denying that the universe could have a cause. If the phrase 'the universe' includes space and time as well as matter, there can be no time before the start of the universe at which a cause of the universe could occur.

(4) Even if all the above objections are waived, the theist would still have to face the challenge 'If everything, including the universe itself, is caused by something or other, what caused the creator?'

The Argument from Contingency

If the cosmological argument is to escape the criticisms which we have so far levelled against it, it clearly needs to take a very different form. The standard way in which theists try to avoid the criticisms is by retreating from the First Cause argument to the Argument from Contingency. The general structure of the Argument from Contingency claims:

(1) The universe (and all its contents) exist only contingently.
(2) If anything exists contingently, something exists necessarily. So:
(3) Something exists necessarily.

And this necessarily existing something is then identified with God. The third of Aquinas's Five Ways presents us with one version of this argument. But since Aquinas's discussion is flawed by some logical blunders,[4] let us consider the version presented by Leibniz. In a paper entitled 'On the Ultimate Origination of Things' he writes:

> neither in any one single thing, nor in the whole aggregate and series of things can there be found the sufficient reason of existence. Let us suppose the book of the elements of geometry to have been eternal, one copy always having been written down from an earlier one; it is evident that, even though a reason can be given for the present book out of a past one, nevertheless out of any number of books taken in order going backwards we shall never come upon a full reason . . . What is true of the books is true also of the different states of the world; for what follows is in some way copied from what precedes . . . And so, however far you go back to earlier states, you will never find in those states a full reason why there should be any world, rather than none . . . Indeed, even if you suppose the world eternal, as you will still be supposing nothing but a succession of states, and will not find in any of them a sufficient reason . . . it is evident that the reason must be sought elsewhere.
> (Leibniz 1968: 32–3)

So far, this seems to be a statement of the First Cause argument. Leibniz is conceding that there is nothing paradoxical in the idea of an infinite regress as such, whether a regress of books or of states of the world. And he allows that if there is such a regress, it is still possible to find a 'reason' for one element in the series, by appealing to a previous element in the series. But he is also claiming that nothing in the series can supply what he calls a 'full' or 'sufficient' reason for the existence either of any element in the series, or apparently for the series as a whole. So far, Leibniz's regress of books is merely a variant on Wollaston's chain of links hanging from heaven. But Leibniz then goes on:

The reasons of the world, then, lie in something extramundane, different from the chain of states or series of things whose aggregate constitutes the world. And so we must pass from physical or hypothetical necessity, which determines the subsequent things of the world by the earlier, to something which is of absolute or metaphysical necessity . . . Since then the ultimate root must be in something which is of metaphysical necessity, and since there is no reason of any existent thing except in an existent thing, it follows that there must exist some one Being of metaphysical necessity, that is, from whose essence existence springs.

(op. cit. p. 33)

Leibniz here clearly sees that if there is to be something which supplies a 'full' reason for the existence of other things without itself requiring a reason in terms of something else, it cannot be simply another member in the series. So what supplies the full reason must have a different kind of existence from that of the members of the series. It must be a being whose existence does not require a reason in terms of something else; and Leibniz follows tradition in thinking that only a being which exists 'of metaphysical necessity' can fill this role; and this being he equates with God.

Assessment of the Argument from Contingency

We can thus see how an argument of this sort can by-pass most of the objections which we raised to the First Cause argument. In the first place, if the argument is sound, it will apply whether the series of contingent things is finite or infinite. As Leibniz says 'even if you suppose the world eternal', you will be unable to get a full reason for anything unless you presuppose the existence of a necessary being.

Second, the necessary being can represent a terminus of explanation. For if we ask 'What is the explanation of the necessary being?', the answer is meant to be internal to the necessary being: you see *why* the being exists when you understand *what* it is. This is what is meant by Leibniz's remark that the being is one 'from whose essence existence springs', and by his comment later that a metaphysical necessity is one whose 'contrary would imply a contradiction or logical absurdity' (op. cit. p. 35). It does not owe its existence to any other being, but only to its own nature. So, to use the terminology we developed in Chapter 2, Leibniz is saying that 'God exists' is logically necessary but the existence of other things in the world is contingent.[5]

We can note in passing the parallels between the ontological argument and this version of the cosmological argument. They are alike in that they have the same conclusion, namely that God not only exists, but exists necessarily, or exists in all possible worlds. But they differ in the route which they take to this conclusion. The ontological argument proceeds purely from the content of the concept of God, without relying on the fact that there also exist contingent things. This version of the cosmological argument relies essentially on an appeal to the existence of contingent things, and not to the content of the concept of God.

But in spite of these seeming improvements on the First Cause argument, we shall argue that the Argument from Contingency is still fundamentally flawed. We can note in the first place how very unGodlike Leibniz's necessary being is. Although Leibniz refers to this being as 'God' (see end of first quotation above), there is no ground in this argument for thinking that the being possesses such traditional attributes as omnipotence, omniscience or moral perfection. There is no ground for saying even that the being is a *person*, rather than, for instance, like some impersonal cosmic force such as gravity. Nor is there any ground for saying that there could be only one such being. If contingent beings presuppose the existence of something necessary, then maybe there is just one necessary being – but maybe there is a large plurality of them. In this case, presumably none of them would count as God. Unless, therefore, we have some good reason to think that there would not be more than one necessary being, we should not adopt theism, even if we are impressed by the Argument from Contingency.

Second, we need to ask for more detail about *how* this necessary being explains the existence of the material universe. What we need is something like an account of the *mechanism by which* the necessary being can produce a universe, or something like a natural law which links states of the necessary being with the production of a universe. I say 'something like' these things, because presumably the linkage between the necessary being and the universe will not be either mechanical or lawlike. But the point of insisting on the need for some analogue to these more familiar forms of nexus is that the theist has not done enough simply to say that there are contingent things on the one hand, and a necessary thing on the other, and that the latter *explains* the former. We are owed some account of what the connection is, or why it is said to be explanatory.

A conventional theist reply here is to invoke the concept of choice, of a person choosing one thing rather than another. So let us assume that we can find some reason outside the Argument from Contingency for cloaking the necessary being of the Argument with personal qualities. The conventional thought then is that God could have chosen to create a universe different from this one, or to create no universe at all, but that for his own good reason he chose to create this one. So we are invited to think of the mechanism referred to on the model of an agent choosing to make something, then consequently acting to make it. We find precisely this view expressed by, for example, Ward, who says explicitly that God 'is a being which exists of necessity but which creates this universe by a free act of will' (Ward 1996: 37).

But then, third, we need to ask what the relationship is between this necessarily existing being and time. Does the being have a temporal existence or not? If it is to be the kind of being who can choose things and consequently bring them about, then surely it has to be a temporal being. And if it is a temporal being, then for reasons given earlier it cannot be the cause of time. But more usually, necessary beings are thought of as being in some way 'outside' time. But although this picks up on the traditional idea that God is timeless, it threatens to render unintelligible the conception of the God/universe link in terms of choice. For choosing is something that takes place at a time, and if X's choices are to explain X's actions, then the choices must precede the action: X must be a temporal being.

But why, it might be asked, could there not be a kind of non-temporal choosing? Perhaps beings like us who exist in time, have to choose and will in time; but couldn't beings who exist non-temporally, choose non-temporally too? The answer is 'no'. Suppose we grant for the sake of argument that the creator could have a thought of the form 'I will a universe of such-and-such a kind to exist'. Since the creator is outside time, this willing does not occur before (nor of course after) the start of the universe which it is supposed to cause. It occurs, but occurs at no time at all. Already it sounds a very suspicious sort of cause. But worse is to follow. The hypothesis of the creator is supposed to explain why the universe began to exist *when* it did, rather than earlier or later. This requires that the creator should be able to have thoughts of the form 'I will the universe to start existing *now* (or in a million units of time from now, etc.)'. But a being who is outside time can attach no sense to terms like 'now' (or 'a million units of time from now' etc.). They can be used and understood only by beings who exist at a time and who persist through time.[6] So even if we leave aside the question of how a mere thought or choice by an immaterial being could bring into existence a material world of space and time, the central problem is that the being would be unable to have thoughts or willings with the requisite *content* to explain the timing of the start of the universe.

Swinburne's argument

A version of the cosmological argument different from those which we have so far considered is defended by Swinburne. He rejects the assumption made by the First Cause version that the universe *must* have a cause: he allows there is no contradiction in the thought that the universe exists uncaused, and hence agrees that if it exists, it exists only contingently. But, Swinburne argues, it is nonetheless *probable* that God exists, given the existence of the universe. He seeks to show this by utilising the parts of probability theory and confirmation theory which scientists standardly use in arriving at their judgements about which scientific theory is best supported by the evidence. Although he does not put it in this way, Swinburne's approach can thus be seen as a challenge to any atheism which is based on science (such as we find in, for example, Dawkins or Atkins): 'In consistency, you must either use probability theory in judging whether God exists, or you must stop using it when you adjudicate between other scientific theories. If you take the first option, you will be committed to theism; if you take the second option, you will be doomed to scientific scepticism.'

Swinburne argues that the probability that God exists, given that there is a universe, is greater than the probability that God existed if there were no universe. So the existence of the universe increases the probability that God exists. In order to defend a judgement of this kind, he needs some way of calculating how high the probability of a hypothesis is, given any piece of evidence. This will clearly depend on a number of factors, such as how high the probability of the hypothesis is anyway, independently of the specific evidence; how far, if the hypothesis were true, it would explain the evidence which one has; and so on. These considerations are given precise form in a theorem of probability theory called Bayes's Theorem. One of the implications of Bayes's Theorem is what is sometimes called the Principle of Relevance, namely:

(A) The probability of a hypothesis (like theism) is raised by a given piece of evidence (such as the existence of our universe)

if and only if

(B) The probability of the evidence (our universe), given the hypothesis (theism), is greater than the probability of the evidence (our universe) alone.

Swinburne therefore tries to establish (B), from which he will then be able to infer (A).

In establishing (B), Swinburne states that if we did not know whether there was anything at all (neither God, nor our existing universe, nor any other universe – not even ourselves), then our existing universe would be *very* improbable, because it is such a very complex entity and would be the sort of entity that would be very unlikely to exist. And given our supposed ignorance of the existence of anything at all, the existence of God, though not very probable, would be more probable than the existence of the universe. But if we did not know of the existence of anything, and then we learnt just that God existed, that would raise the probability that our universe existed. It would raise it because (says Swinburne) it would be so improbable that our universe would have existed if it had not been created by God. So, the probability that our universe exists, given just the existence of God, is greater than the probability that our universe exists, given that we do not know anything else either way. In other words (B) above is true, and since (B) is true if and only if (A) is true, it follows that (A) is true. So, the existence of the universe increases the probability of theism.

Swinburne's argument is a good deal more cautious than those which we have looked at previously. Swinburne does not claim to prove that it is certain that God exists. He does not claim to prove that it is more probable than not that God exists. All he claims is that the existence of the universe *increases the probability* that God exists. His overall strategy is to show that even if none of the traditional arguments for theism by themselves make the existence of God more probable than not, it can still be the case that taken collectively they have this effect, provided that each taken singly raises significantly the probability of theism.

Is Swinburne's form of the argument any improvement on more traditional versions? We can take as unproblematic the elements of probability theory which Swinburne uses. What is contentious is his application of probability theory to the existence of the universe and of God. He tells us that if we start from a position of complete ignorance, the existence of a complex physical entity like the universe is very improbable. But how does he know? The assignment of probability to a claim always requires us to have some relevant background knowledge about two factors in particular. First, I have to know how many possibilities there are, other than the one I am considering; and second, I have to know what the relative probabilities of these possibilities are. So, given that I am choosing a card from a standard, properly shuffled pack, I can say that the probability of my choosing a red card is 26/52, a Queen 4/52, a black Ace 2/52 and so on. And I can say that, because I am assuming that there are 52 possible outcomes, and that all of them are equiprobable. But in trying to judge the probability of a universe like ours existing, how many possibilities are there, and what are the relative probabilities of each of them? Are the possibilities simply that our universe exists or it doesn't, so there are only two possibilities? Or do I need to take account of the fact that there are lots of different possible universes, so there are many more than two possibilities? And what grounds could I have for saying that any of these possibilities was more or less probable than any other, or that they were all equally probable? In abstracting from *all* my knowledge of the detailed working of the universe and trying to form a judgement on the probability of the universe as a whole, I have deprived myself of all the information in terms of which judgements of probability are made.

A similar point applies to Swinburne's claim that in this position of assumed total ignorance about what does in fact exist, the existence of God, though not very probable, is more probable than the existence of our universe alone would be. His ground is that God is a much simpler kind of being than the universe. But even if he is right about that, why is that a reason for thinking that it is more likely that God will exist than that the universe will exist? In order to form a judgement like that, I would need to know the relative likelihood of simple things existing as against complex things. As in the parallel judgements about the probability of the universe, in a position of assumed total ignorance, I would be unable to form any such judgement.

A parallel objection applies to the claim that since the universe is so unlikely to exist unless God exists, the probability that it exists given the existence of God is greater than the probability that it exists given no evidence either way about its existence. How could one tell that it is unlikely for a universe like ours to exist unless God does? If *per impossibile* one knew of many Gods and knew that the great majority of them produced a universe like ours, then one might have some grounds for saying that the existence of a God would indeed raise the probability that there would be a universe like ours. But of course we do not, and cannot, have any such knowledge; and consequently we cannot make the probability judgements on which Swinburne's version of the argument relies.[7]

Can there be an explanation of the existence of the universe?

We have seen how the cosmological argument in all its forms relies on the claim that the universe as a whole *can* have an explanation, and that it would be very surprising or even impossible for it not to have one. This comes out nicely in some remarks by Swinburne: 'It is extraordinary that there should exist anything at all. Surely the most natural state of affairs is simply nothing: no universe, no God, nothing' (Swinburne 1996: 48). But *could* there have been nothing at all? And if there could have been nothing, is there an explanation of why there is something? Let us consider these puzzling questions in turn.

(a) Could there have been nothing at all?

It is not just defenders of cosmological arguments who think that there could have been nothing. Parfit for example writes: 'It might have been true that nothing ever existed: no minds, no atoms, no space. When we imagine this possibility, it can seem astonishing that anything exists. Why is there a universe?' (Parfit 1992). But the idea that the universe might not have existed is a strange one, so let us proceed more slowly. Let us first try to be clear what is meant by 'the universe', and hence what is meant by saying that the universe might not have existed. 'The universe' covers the whole of space and time, and all their contents. So it certainly includes all material objects, and all their constituents, down to subatomic particles, and all physical forces such as gravity. It includes all processes, events, and states of affairs which happen to or occur in material objects. It will also include non-material minds (if there are any), for even if (as some philosophers have maintained) these do not exist in space, they certainly exist in time. But there may be some entities which exist and yet are not parts of the universe as so far described. If abstract entities like numbers, sets, relations and properties can be said to exist at all, they are not composed of any physical forces or particles, and they do not exist anywhere within the spatio-temporal framework. They exist, but do not exist anywhere or at any time.

And what about God? If he exists, is his existence part of what is meant by the phrase 'the universe'? There is a strong tradition that God is not part of the universe. The existence of this tradition comes out in a number of contrasts (some of which we have already considered) which are often drawn between God and the universe: that the universe exists only contingently, but God exists necessarily; that the existence of the universe is not self-explanatory but the existence of God is self-explanatory; that God is the creator of the universe; that God is 'outside' space and time; and so on. Can we then accept that God is not part of the universe? We shall argue that whether God is regarded as part of the universe or as distinct from it, there is no escape from paradoxes concerning his nature and his alleged activities. But for the moment let us assume that God is not part of what is meant by the term 'the universe'.

Having clarified what is meant by the term 'the universe', let us now ask if it could have been the case that the universe did not exist. We can certainly make sense of the idea that particular objects within the universe might not have existed. The table at which I am sitting would not have existed if some artisan had not made it; the cup from which I am drinking would not have existed if the potter had thrown away the clay instead of fashioning it into a cup. But (it might be said) that is not a radical enough kind of non-existence. For we are not in such cases imagining that some of the stuff of the universe might not have existed, but only that the same stuff could have been differently arranged. The stuff of which the table exists would not have ceased to exist merely because it was not formed into a table; the abandoned lump of clay does not cease to exist merely because the potter does not fashion it into a cup. Can we imagine the non-existence of some of the stuff which the universe contains? It seems that we can. It could have been the case that the stuff of which the table is made did not exist. It could have been the case that the stuff of which the earth is made did not exist. It could have been the case that the stuff of which our galaxy is made did not exist. Could it have been the case that *none* of the stuff in the spatio-temporal universe existed? And are we then imagining the non-existence of the universe?

Let us take this more slowly. There is a gap crossed between imagining the non-existence of this or that piece of matter on the one hand, and imagining the non-existence of the totality of matter (with all its subatomic constituents) on the other. Our best current theories of space and time assume that the size of space is not independent of the matter space contains. Space is curved by massive bodies. So if we think away *all* the bodies which exist in the universe, we should not assume that we will be left with a huge space, the same as before but now empty. With no matter, there would have been no space: a huge space wholly devoid of matter is impossible. So if we are thinking away the totality of matter, we are also thinking away space. Already it becomes less clear what we are envisaging. What does it mean to say that it could have been the case that space did not exist?

It might be objected to this that even if the impossibility of an empty space is implied by Einsteinian relativised space, it could have been the case that space had a nature different from that attributed to it by Einstein. On the Newtonian 'absolute' conception of space, the existence of space and the existence of matter are independent of each other. Had space been Newtonian, as it could have been, it could have continued to exist even in the total absence of matter. But either way, if we are to make sense of the idea that the universe might not have existed, we have to make sense of the non-existence of space. Similarly, we have to make sense of the non-existence of time. It is unclear whether or not we *can* make sense of this: we are close to the point at which metaphysics turns into nonsense.

What about the abstract entities which we mentioned earlier, such as numbers, or qualities, or relations? They hardly seem to be the sorts of things which might not have existed. Is there a possible world in which the number 3 does not exist? It is difficult to see what grounds there could be for saying so – indeed it is difficult to see what could be *meant* by such a claim. So do those who say that there could have been nothing mean rather that apart from the entities, if any, which exist of necessity, there could have been nothing? The trouble with this interpretation of the idea is that it seems a mere tautology: it says that the things which have to exist, have to exist, and the things which don't have to exist, don't have to exist.

(b) Could there be an explanation for the existence of the universe?

Let us assume for the sake of argument that we have fixed what is to be covered by the term 'the universe', and that we can make sense of the claim that the universe might not have existed. Can there then be an answer to the question 'Why does the universe exist?'. We have already touched on reasons for thinking that such a question cannot be answered (which of course may be a reason for saying that the question does not make sense in the first place). Briefly, either there is no explanation, or there is an explanation. If there is an explanation, it cannot refer to anything which is part of the universe, since then we would have a case of self-explanation. In that case, it must refer to something that is not part of the universe, i.e. is not spatial or temporal or material. But even if we could make sense of the idea of there being something non-spatial and non-material, we cannot make sense of the idea of anything non-temporal, if this is meant to cause or bring about the existence of the universe (and hence of time itself). For the idea of a non-temporal cause is self-contradictory. So if there is an explanation of the existence of the universe, it would have to be a non-causal one. What could this be?

Has science discovered why the universe exists?

Speculations about the origin of the universe used to belong to the province of philosophers and theologians. In recent years, and in particular since the development of the Big Bang theory, scientists have thought that they had something useful, and perhaps definitive, to contribute to the debate. Some scientists have spoken as if they have a theory which not only tells us how and why the universe has developed from the Big Bang onwards, but also explains why there is a universe at all. Such scientists seem to regard their theories as a disproof of theism – or if 'disproof' is too strong a word, then as a significant body of evidence against the existence of God.

One example of such a science-based atheism can be found in some of the writings of Stephen Hawking. Discussing the expansion of the universe (which he calls the inflation of the universe), Hawking says

> The inflation was . . . a good thing in that it produced all the contents of the universe quite literally out of nothing. When the universe was a single point, like the North Pole, it contained nothing. Yet there are now at least 10^{80} particles in the part of the universe that we can observe. Where did all these particles come from? The answer is that relativity and quantum mechanics allow matter to be created out of energy in the form of particle/antiparticle pairs. And where did the energy come from to create this matter? The answer is that it was borrowed from the gravitational energy of the universe. The universe has an enormous debt of negative gravitational energy, which exactly balances the positive energy of the matter. During the inflationary period, the universe borrowed heavily from its gravitational energy to finance the creation of more matter. The result was a triumph for Keynesian economics: a vigorous and expanding universe, filled with material objects.
>
> (Hawking 1994: 88)

The first two sentences make a startling claim. They say that science can explain how the universe (matter, energy, space and time) came into existence 'quite literally out of nothing'. That would be an astounding achievement indeed. If it were to occur, it would surely kill stone-dead the cosmological argument. It would show that to account for the existence of the universe (which is what the cosmological argument tries to do), you could start with the assumption that there existed nothing, and from that assumption you could show that a universe like ours would emerge in accordance with a scientific theory.

But if we read further in Hawking's remarks, we see that what he actually delivers is nothing like the initial promise. For he tells us that the particles in the universe were 'created out of energy in the form of particle/antiparticle pairs'; and that *that* energy came from 'the gravitational energy of the universe'. But that is very far from showing that the universe came 'quite literally out of nothing'. It is saying that you can explain some features of the universe (the energy of particle/antiparticle pairs) in terms of other features of the universe (the gravitational energy of the universe). The questions remain unanswered 'Why was there a universe at all, and why did it from the beginning have this very specific feature of negative gravitational energy?'. Hawking here provides no explanation. Indeed, it is difficult to see that his description of the initial state of the origin of the universe is even consistent. He tells us both that the initial state of the universe was one of infinitely dense matter (or perhaps infinitely high energy); and yet also that when the universe was a single point 'it contained nothing'. But how something that 'contains nothing' can also be infinitely dense is far from clear.

Peter Atkins is another distinguished scientist who has argued that modern science can now explain how the universe occurred and can thereby show that a belief in God is superfluous. He tell us that 'the universe can come into existence without intervention, and that there is no *need* to invoke the idea of a Supreme Being in one of its numerous manifestations' (Atkins 1994: vii).

Atkins then tries to tell us not just what happens after the start of the universe, but what it is that brings about the universe. Very often, his descriptions are straightforwardly self-contradictory if taken literally. He speaks, for example, of 'going back in time beyond the moment of creation, to when there was not time, and to where there was no space', of 'the time before time' (ibid. p. 129), of a time 'before time and place were formed' (ibid. p. 133; and cf. also p. 149). But aside from the problem of trying to make sense of such phrases, the hypothesis which he favours is itself self-contradictory. He tells us that at the moment of creation (or perhaps he means just before?), there are 'the points that are to assemble into patterns defining space and time . . . [and] the points that separate from their opposites by virtue of the pattern of time', and he then goes on:

> Time brought the points into being, and the points brought time into being. This is the cosmic bootstrap . . . the universe comes into existence by virtue of self-reference. We have argued that 1 and −1, the points and their absence, constitute time and space when appropriately arrayed. But in order to exist and come into being, point and no point need time, for time separates them, distinguishes them and induces them from nothing. There is the central self-reference:

the emergence of time from its dust; dust brought into being by the act of patterning time.

(op. cit. pp. 142–3)

This tells us that although the points 'constitute' time and space when they are appropriately arrayed, it is time which 'induces' them from nothing. But it is impossible for something to 'induce' its own constituents from nothing. This is not to say that the constituents cannot *arise* from nothing. But it is to say that if they do arise from nothing, as Atkins apparently claims, it cannot be the case that they are *induced* to arise from nothing *by the very thing which they constitute*. If we indeed start from a position of nothing, then (tautologically) there is nothing to do any inducing of anything. Nor can the reason that the first item exists be that it induced itself to exist. Atkins's cosmic bootstraps, like their mundane counterparts, cannot cause their own existence.

The fact that Hawking and Atkins, and modern cosmology generally, cannot explain why the universe began, as opposed to explaining how it developed from the moment after it began, does not in itself prove that science cannot provide such an explanation. The proof of *that* claim lies in the considerations at the end of the previous section. But given those considerations, we should be unsurprised that science is as incapable as theology of explaining why the universe exists.

Further reading

Aquinas's presentation of versions of the cosmological argument is in Aquinas (1963 1a, 2–5), to which Kenny (1969 Chapters 1–3) supplies a good commentary. Reichenbach (1972) and Swinburne (1979) offer modern defences, while Mackie (1982), Martin (1990) and Gale (1991) all provide modern critiques. Rowe (1978) provides a sympathetic but ultimately agnostic rendition of the argument, while S. T. Davis (1999) provides a similarly cautious conclusion which inclines to theism. Craig and Smith (1993) supply a lively debate which invokes the findings of modern scientific cosmology as background. Craig (1980) is a useful collection of historical readings.

5

———•⊙•———

Teleological arguments

although atheism might have been *logically* tenable before
Darwin, Darwin made it possible to be an intellectually fulfilled atheist.

(Dawkins 1986: 6)

Introduction

Teleological arguments in one form or another have probably been one of
the most popular defences of theism. One version was extremely common in
the eighteenth century, and practically every work in natural theology contains an example of it. The then-current versions of it were powerfully
criticised by Hume and Kant towards the end of the eighteenth century.
Hume's critique in particular was important. Contained in the 90 or so
pages of his posthumous *Dialogues Concerning Natural Religion*, his attack
is one of the masterpieces of Western philosophy, and in the judgement of
some, killed stone-dead the claims of one version of the teleological argument. But as with so many philosophical theses, conclusive refutation did
not mean death for the argument. In the nineteenth and twentieth centuries,
the discoveries of Darwin were used to give the argument increasingly heavy
batterings; though John Stuart Mill, writing shortly after Darwin's *The
Origin of Species*, described it as 'an argument of a really scientific character, which does not shrink from scientific tests, but claims to be judged by
the established canons of Induction' (Mill 1874: 167). It has, however sur-
vived and indeed flourished in recent decades, and is currently taken very
seriously by a number of theists. We will distinguish two main varieties of
the argument, which we will call the argument *from* order, and the argument *to* design. For reasons which will become clear, the prepositions in
these names are important. We will not be using the common label 'the
argument from design', since that name embodies precisely the confusions
which we will be seeking to avoid.[1]

The argument from order as such

This argues from the fact that the universe is orderly, or displays regularities, to the conclusion that there must be a cosmic intelligence responsible for creating or imposing and maintaining the order. It is an argument *from* order because it (rightly) takes as unproblematic and uncontroversial the fact that the world does display order, and it sees what can be inferred from that fact. Sometimes the argument proceeds from the mere existence of order as such, and we will call this the simple argument from order. A more recent version proceeds from the *kind* of order in the universe, and we will consider this version under the general heading of the Anthropic Principle.

Swinburne is a thinker who endorses the simple argument from order. He distinguishes two kinds of regularity that we find in the universe, which he calls regularities of co-presence and regularities of succession. We can regard these as spatial regularities and temporal regularities. As examples of the former, he instances a town with all its roads at right angles to each other, and a library with all the books arranged in alphabetical order on the shelves. Here, the order exists *at* a time, in the sense that the orderliness would be detectable at a single instant of time. Of course, the order will persist through time, but it is not in virtue of its persistence through time that it displays the order which it possesses *at* a time. We can leave this sort of order on one side, partly because Swinburne himself does not think that it provides very good evidence for God's existence, and partly because it overlaps with some of the facts that the argument to purpose appeals to. So let us focus on the regularities of succession.

Swinburne means by this that the events in nature do not happen randomly, but occur in accordance with natural laws which determine that a given kind of phenomenon is always followed by a phenomenon of another specific kind. For example, applying great heat to a small quantity of water will always be followed by the water turning to steam; applying a naked flame to petrol will always result in the petrol igniting; striking a thin sheet of glass hard with a heavy stone will always be followed by the glass breaking; and so on. It is true that it sometimes seems as if there are cases where this sort of regularity has broken down: we apply the source of heat, say, but the water does not turn to steam. But when we look more closely, we always find that the apparent irregularity is really an instance of a regularity at a deeper level. The water does not turn to steam, but then we discover that the material of which the container is made is an excellent insulator, and that the failure of the water to become steam is an instance of the regularity described by saying that material of that kind *always* impedes the transmission of heat.

Swinburne wants us to be struck with a sense of amazement at these pervasive regularities, so familiar and yet so striking. As he says:

The orderliness of the universe to which I draw attention . . . is its
conformity to formula, to simple formulable, scientific laws. The
orderliness of the universe in this respect is a very striking fact
about it. The universe might so naturally have been chaotic, but it is
not – it is very orderly.

(Swinburne 1979: 136)

He now raises the question 'What is the explanation of this all pervasive
order?'. Why is the universe so orderly when it could have been so chaotic?
First, he says, we need to note that the orderliness is something science itself
cannot explain. It can explain one sort of order in terms of a second. It can
explain why applying heat to water turns the water to steam, by explaining
that heat (in a liquid) is rate of molecular motion, that greater heat is a
higher rate of motion, and that when water molecules are given a high rate
of motion, they tend to escape in large numbers from the mass of water, and
this is what we call steam. But this explanation of the simple observable regularity utilises a complex unobservable regularity. It explains the regularity
in the behaviour of water and heat by invoking regularities in the behaviour
of molecules. What it does not do (even in part) is explain why there are any
regularities at all. To achieve that, we would need (says Swinburne) some
kind of explanation which explained regularities in terms of non-
regularities, and that is something which science cannot provide. So we face
a dilemma: either we accept that explanation stops with science, and that
there is no explanation at all for the existence of order in the universe, or
there must be some alternative non-scientific kind of explanation. What
Swinburne has in mind when he speaks of an alternative kind of explanation is what he elsewhere calls personal explanation. This is the explanation
of the intentional actions of conscious agents which he regards as importantly different from standard scientific explanations (in particular, in not
involving an appeal to laws or generalisations).

Swinburne claims that we must reject the first horn of this dilemma. He
says that it is simply incredible that there is no explanation for the regularities and order to which he has referred. Recall that he thinks that it is prima
facie very odd that there should be a material world at all (remember how
the cosmological argument invoked that fact as evidence for the existence of
God). But that all these material bodies should throughout all of space display exactly the same general powers and regularities, without there being
any explanation of this fact, would (he implies) beggar belief. So, there must
be an explanation, and that explanation must be in terms of the intentional
actions of a conscious agent. So there must exist some sort of cosmic, powerful intelligence who by his intentional action brings about and sustains in
existence the regularities which we see around us. Invoking again Bayes's
Theorem, Swinburne claims that the existence of order helps to confirm the

existence of God because the existence of order is more probable if there is a God than if there is not.

Swinburne buttresses this conclusion with a few further considerations relating to the kind of order which in fact we find. But we can ignore these supplementary considerations and focus on the primary question of whether there is any plausible argument from the order or regularity in nature to the existence of God. We will level three criticisms against the argument from order: first, that it is wrong to say that the universe, in Swinburne's striking phrase, 'might so naturally have been chaotic'; second, that given that the universe must be ordered, there is no special puzzle about the degree of order which it has; and third, that any Swinburnean explanation of the order in the universe is either circular or question-begging.

First, could the universe have been chaotic? This is an idea that often hovers in the background when philosophers discuss the problem of induction. How can I know that the sun will rise tomorrow, that water was thirst-quenching in the distant past, that hydrogen is the lightest element even in parts of the universe that have never been observed? The implication of these questions is that it is quite possible that the regularities which I can detect in the small part of the universe which I can observe might not hold elsewhere. And from that, it can seem a small step to say that the unobserved parts of the universe could be wholly unordered; and from that, just another small step to say that the universe as a whole could have been chaotic all along.

In considering this possibility, it is important to separate the two questions (a) do unobserved parts of the universe display the *same* regularities which I have detected in the observed part? and (b) do unobserved parts of the universe display *any* regularity at all? Let us take the first of these questions initially. Suppose I am wondering whether bread will continue to nourish me tomorrow. I am then *presupposing* that the world will contain a substance identifiable as bread, about which the question of its nourishing power can be raised. But now we must ask what makes the substance identifiable as *bread*? Broadly speaking, it will be identifiable as bread because of the powers which it has – the powers to interact with and be affected by other bodies, including human bodies. (There may be an intermediate step – for example, the claim that to be bread, a substance must contain flour. But then the question can be raised 'And what makes that substance identifiable as *flour*?'. Ultimately these questions have to be answered in terms of the powers which are characteristic of different kinds of substance and by means of which we identify them.) And what we are here calling the 'powers' of objects are simply another way of referring to regularities in the behaviour of different kinds of substance, or different kinds of object. So, even if it is true that it could come to pass that bread does not nourish me tomorrow, i.e. that there is a breakdown of this particular regularity, we would be presupposing the persistence of a whole range of other regularities whose existence is essential if anything tomorrow is to be identifiable as bread at all.

If we generalise from this example, we arrive at the conclusion that for all kinds of stuff and all kinds of objects, if there is to be a stuff or object of that kind at all, it must display certain regularities in its behaviour. If it didn't, it simply would not be a stuff or an object of that kind. This implies that it could not have been the case that the world contained kinds of stuff or kinds of objects and yet was wholly random. The concept of kinds of stuff (like bread or water, or coal or gold) and of kinds of objects (like trees, or mountains, or telephones) is inextricably linked to the concept of order and regularity, since it is only in terms of the latter that the former can be identified at all. This broadly Kantian point has been very nicely expressed by Strawson as follows:

> Our concepts of objects are linked with a set of conditional expectations about the things which we perceive as falling under them. For every kind of object, we can draw up lists of ways we shall expect it not to change unless . . . lists of ways in which we shall expect it to change if . . ., and lists in which we expect it to change unless . . . concepts of objects are always and necessarily compendia of causal law of law-likeness, carry implications of causal power or dependence.
>
> (Strawson 1966: 145–6)

This means that we cannot coherently envisage a universe which was totally chaotic, any more than we can coherently envisage a circle with four sides. The cosmological argument sought to argue from the existence of the material universe to the existence of God. But since order, as we have seen, is necessarily implicit in the very concept of substances and objects, there cannot be a *separate* argument from order. For there to be a material universe at all is for there to be an *orderly* material universe. The argument thus shows that Swinburne is wrong to say that 'the universe might so naturally have been chaotic'. Given that the universe contains objects and kinds of substance, it is *certain* at once that it displays some order; so it is wrong for Swinburne to say that given the existence of a material universe, the presence of order in that universe is more probable if there is a God than if there is not.

What *is* true is that the universe could have had a different order from the one which it has. We will consider this possibility shortly. It is also true that the universe could have been less orderly than it is. For there is nothing in the argument above to show that the concepts of substances and objects might not display *some* random features. All that the argument shows is that not every feature of a kind of substance or object could be random. So perhaps the theist could beat an orderly retreat at this point and say 'I grant that the universe could not be chaotic. So the question cannot be why it is orderly rather than chaotic. But there remains the question of why it displays as much order as it does, given that it could have displayed much less.' This takes us to the second of the three criticisms mentioned above.

Is there any puzzle about why the universe displays *as much* order as it does? Is it antecedently surprising or improbable that there is as much order as there is? Consider an analogy. I ask you to buy a ticket from a lottery in which 10,000 tickets will be sold. The number you draw at random is 3,333. You might feel surprise that the number you draw should be one, all of whose digits are the same. For, you might reflect, there are relatively few tickets in the lottery all of whose numbers are the same: only nine tickets have four identical digits. How surprising, then, that out of those 10,000 tickets you should have chosen just one of the nine same-four-digits tickets. But of course, there is really nothing surprising here. A number which would not seem noteworthy, like 7,291 or 4,531 or 5,927 would have been no more probable or unsurprising. The probability of your impressive 3,333 and of these other insignificant numbers is exactly the same, namely 1 in 10,000.

Consider again the order of the universe. For all that we know, it is no more antecedently improbable that the universe should have the amount of order which in fact it does, than that it should have somewhat less, or for that matter somewhat more (for example, that events at the quantum level should have been more regular than in fact they are). From the first argument above, we know that the universe must display *some* order. No particular degree of order, as far as we know, is antecedently any less likely than any other. What, then, is so especially in need of explanation about the degree of order which we find that the universe in fact has?

Suppose, however, that the above arguments are mistaken. Suppose that the universe *could* have been chaotic, and that it *is* surprising that it contains as much order as it does. Could God be the explanation for the degree of order? The teleologist who wants to answer 'yes' to this question faces a dilemma: can order arise from the absence of order or not? If she answers 'No', then all that the invocation of God will do will be to explain natural order in terms of divine order – it will not explain order as such. If she answers 'Yes', then she has no reason to say that the order which we find in the universe must have been put there by God, rather than, for example, arising spontaneously. Let us develop the two horns of this dilemma further.

Swinburne denies that there can be a scientific explanation of the order in the universe, because what science does is to explain one sort of order in terms of another. It thus never succeeds in explaining why there is any order at all. But if the order in the world is put there by God, mustn't the behaviour of God itself be another sort of order? God after all is supposed not to be arbitrary or whimsical or to act randomly. He is supposed to be supremely rational, to do nothing except for good reason. That must surely mean that his thought processes display a form of order. So to invoke God to explain natural order is to invoke divine mental order in order to explain natural physical order. It is not to explain order as such. So invoking God gets us no further forward if the object is to explain why things are orderly. The teleologist is in no better position here than the scientist. The scientist is left with the question 'Why is the physical world orderly?', and the teleologist is left with the question 'Why is God's mind orderly?' – or, if it is thought to be some kind of necessary truth that the mind of God is orderly, the question is 'Why is there a mental order which is responsible for the physical order?'.

Suppose then that the teleologist takes the second horn of the dilemma and says that order can emerge from disorder. This would not be saying that order could develop from a situation of total chaos, since we have seen that a totally chaotic universe is an impossibility. It would be saying that a universe with a limited amount of order could develop into a universe with more order. If that is allowed as a possibility, what grounds are there for thinking that the fairly high degree of order which in fact we see in the universe as we know it was put there by God, rather than being a feature which emerged from earlier states of the universe? Of course, this would not be an *explanation* of why the universe displays the degree of order that it does. It would be saying that the degree of order emerged spontaneously, i.e. that it was uncaused. But this result is surely inevitable. Either the degree of order is explicable, in which case it comes from more order, so order as such has not been explained; or order can come from disorder, in which case it emerges spontaneously, so again the presence of order is inexplicable.

The Anthropic Principle: the argument from the kind of order

We have so far argued that the *degree* of order in the universe gives no ground for believing in God. But some writers have suggested that the *kind* of order we find does provide such a ground. It is in connection with this idea that the concept of the so-called Anthropic Principle has emerged. Unfortunately there is no agreement among commentators about what the Anthropic Principle is.[2] We shall use the label 'the Anthropic Principle' for the following claim:

> If intelligent life is to emerge in the world, then a number of fundamental physical forces (gravity, the strong and weak nucleic forces, the electromagnetic force, etc.) must be more-or-less exactly the strength which in fact they are: had they been even very slightly stronger or weaker, the preconditions for the emergence of intelligent life could not have occurred.

The character of the world is largely and perhaps mainly determined by the natural laws which obtain. For many of these natural laws, it seems that we can easily imagine without contradiction that they could have been different. For example, light travels at approximately 186,000 miles per second – but it seems that we can easily imagine that it could have travelled slightly faster or slower than that, or perhaps very much faster or slower. Gravity operates on bodies with a force proportional to their masses and inversely proportional to the square of the distance between them – but we can imagine that the force could have been inversely proportional to (say) the cube of the distance. And so on. To put the point in possible worlds terminology, there is a possible world in which light travels at about 300,000 miles per second, in which gravitational attraction is inversely proportional to the cube of the distance, and so on. It seems, then, that the universe could have been governed by very different physical laws.

However, recent developments in physics have made clear that had the laws of nature been only very slightly different, the universe would have been *radically* different from what we know it to be. Polkinghorne, who combines the twin roles of being an ex-professor of theoretical physics at Cambridge and a professional theologian, gives one example as follows:

> In the early expansion of the universe there has to be a close balance between the expansive energy (driving things apart) and the force of gravity (pulling things together). If expansion dominated then matter would fly apart too rapidly for condensation into galaxies and stars to take place. Nothing interesting could happen in so thinly spread a world. On the other hand if gravity dominated the world would collapse in on itself again before there was time for the processes of life to get going. For us to be possible requires a balance between the effects of expansion and contraction which at a very early epoch in the universe's history . . . has to differ from equality by not more than 1 in 10^{60} . . . [Paul Davies] points out that [the accuracy required] is the same as aiming at a target an inch wide on the other side of the observable universe, twenty thousand million light years away, and hitting the mark!
>
> (Polkinghorne 1996: 57)

So, we are invited to accept that only a highly improbable balance between two physical forces allows for the formation of heavenly bodies like stars. Further examples of such 'fine tuning' abound. The so-called weak nucleic force has to be just as weak as it is, if our sun is to burn gently for billions of years instead of exploding like a cosmic bomb; the strong nucleic force must be no stronger than it is or else all the carbon would be burnt to oxygen. If the electro-magnetic force had been even marginally greater or smaller than it is, the universe would have been radically different in ways which would have prevented the emergence of anything like our planet, let alone life, let alone intelligent, conscious life. (These examples come from Leslie 1996, Chapter 2, from which more details and more examples can be obtained.)

So, the emergence of the world as we observe it, with persisting heavenly bodies, at least one of which is such as to allow the emergence of conscious life, rests not just on one but on a whole series of coincidences (between on the one hand the values for various physical constants which are required if life is to emerge, and on the other the values which we find that those constants actually have). What, then, could explain such coincidences? According to the theist, the most plausible explanation is that those values for the physical constants were chosen by a cosmic intelligence, who chose them *because* they would make possible the emergence of life. The fact that there is a coincidence between the actual values and the values which are required for life is thus rendered unsurprising. If we see a woman whose jacket and skirt and shoes and handbag and gloves all match in colour, we are not surprised at the coincidence because we presuppose that she chose matching items precisely *because* they matched, i.e. because they were coincident. The theist's explanation of the cosmic coincidences on which life depends is similar: the coincidences obtain because they were deliberately chosen, and they were deliberately chosen because they made possible (or likely or inevitable) the emergence of intelligent life.

Does this defence of theism fare any better than the simple argument from order? We shall argue that it does not. However, we can start by agreeing that the anthropic line of argument has noted something for which an explanation may be available. In the case of the simple argument from order, we argued that there was no need for any explanation of the presence of order in the universe, since no matter how different the universe might have been, it was absolutely impossible for it to be chaotic. There is thus no puzzling question of the form 'But why isn't it chaotic?', just as there is no puzzling question of the form 'But why aren't *any* bachelors married?'. But the position with the anthropic argument is different. For both theists and atheists can agree that fundamental physical constants, such as gravity or the speed of light, could have been different. It therefore makes sense to ask why they are as they are. It may be that at the moment, we cannot explain why they are as they are. But it is possible that some super-theory may emerge in the future which synthesises areas of existing knowledge. It may show that there is some more fundamental force in nature which prevents what we now think of as the basic forces from being other than what they are. Thus there might be some physical force of which we as yet know nothing, but which is such that it constrains (say) the electromagnetic force to fall within just those bounds which are necessary for the emergence of life.

It would be a further and much more contestable claim to assume that there would be only *one* further entity which would explain all the coincidences – as if just one further fundamental force could explain why the speed of light is as it is, *and* why gravity is just as it is, *and* why the electromagnetic force is as it is, *and* why the weak nucleic force is no stronger, *and* why the strong nucleic force is no weaker, and so on. Prima facie, it would be just as likely that all these coincidences required different explanations. But in principle, even the stronger claim that a single factor explains them all cannot be ruled out a priori.

But although it makes perfectly good sense for a scientist to look for some more fundamental force in terms of which she can explain why currently accepted constants like the speed of light are as they are, it is important to see that there is nothing surprising or improbable about the constants being such as to allow the emergence of life. Those theists who speak here of '*amazing* coincidences' suffer from misplaced astonishment (see, for example, Craig, in Craig and Smith 1995: 68).

As an analogy, consider a gambler who is about to throw a single die, who reasons as follows:

> The die has six sides – but it also has four corners and twelve edges. So each time I throw it there are twenty-two possible outcomes. So, my chance of throwing (say) a three is one in twenty-two.

The reasoning is patently absurd. You cannot determine the probability of an outcome simply by knowing that it is one out of twenty-two possible outcomes, unless you are *presupposing* that all the outcomes are equally probable. How, then, can we determine how probable a three is, if not by simply counting possible outcomes? The short answer is that we do it by throwing the die many times and seeing what proportion of threes we get in a long run of throws. If the proportion converges on 0.166 recurring (i.e. converges on one-sixth), then we are justified in concluding that the chance of a three on any given throw is one in six. The fact that there are twenty-one possible other outcomes is wholly irrelevant. It is even irrelevant in calculating the probability of a three that there are five other *sides* which could be face up when the die is thrown. For imagine that in our protracted run of throws, half the throws resulted in a three and half in a four. We would then correctly conclude that the die was weighted, and that the probability of getting a three was one in two, i.e. 0.5, whereas the probability of getting any of the other numbers was zero.

In practice, of course, if we are using an ordinary commercially produced die, our belief that the probability of a three is one in six is not based on subjecting that particular die to a protracted series of throws. But that is because we assume that the die has been produced by a method which past experience tells us will produce dice, each of whose sides has a one-in-six probability of turning up.

How does this discussion of mistaken ways of assessing the probability of dice throws apply to the Anthropic Principle? Let us suppose for the sake of argument that the emergence of life depends essentially on ten fundamental forces in nature, and that each of these forces can come with 100 different values or strengths. Then there are 100^{10}, or 1,000 billion possible combinations. Let us suppose that the emergence of life depends on each of those ten forces having one particular value: any other value for any of them and life would be impossible. So only one of those 1,000 billion combinations allows for the emergence of life. How likely is it that the exact distribution of values among the ten forces will obtain? The correct answer is: it is impossible to say. Of course, *if* each combination has the same probability of occurrence as every other, then the combination required for the emergence of life is very improbable. But this is no comfort to the theist for two reasons: first, we have no grounds for saying that each combination is as probable as every other. To determine that, we would need *per impossibile* to observe lots of universes and see in each universe what values the forces took. If we found that the life-allowing combination of values occurred in the great majority of cases, what grounds could there be for saying that in the actual universe, it was improbable that that combination should obtain? Our evidence would show exactly the opposite, that in spite of being one possibility in 1,000 billion, it was an outcome that was very likely to occur. The fact that that combination is one in 1,000 billion does not show that it is improbable, if *all the other options are hugely improbable*; and if *per impossibile* we had evidence from other universes that these other options were hugely improbable, then the emergence of life in this universe would be exactly what we would expect – there would be nothing surprising about it at all. What would then be surprising would be the *non*-occurrence of life.

Second, if we somehow discover that all of the 1,000 billion possibilities are equiprobable, that certainly tells us that the values of the fundamental forces which actually obtain are very improbable. But exactly the same would be true of every other set of values for those forces. There would be no greater improbability in the life-allowing combination of values than in any other combination. Of course there would be greater improbability in the life-allowing values than in the life-preventing values. But that would only be because the phrase 'life-preventing values' groups together many more of the 1,000 billion possibilities.

But suppose the above points were all mistaken. Suppose that it is not just a coincidence, but an amazing coincidence that the fundamental forces all have life-permitting values. Suppose that some explanation is required, and suppose further that this explanation has to be a single explanation for the total set of coincidences. Would a divine 'fine tuner' of these values be a *possible* explanation? Let us assume for the sake of argument that the concept of God is at least self-consistent. How good an explanation would he be for the coincidence of the values? An elegant argument designed to show that he would be a very bad explanation has been advanced by Quentin Smith. Assume that there is a God of the kind postulated by classical theism. Assume that he wants to create a universe in which life emerges; and assume that it is very improbable (say 1 chance in 1,000 billion) that, left to themselves, the fundamental forces will all have the right values for this to be possible. So by a deliberate act of choice, God arranges that something which is very improbable will nonetheless be the case: all the forces will have the values necessary for the emergence of life. But (Smith objects) this means that the theist presents us with an inconsistent picture:

> If God created the universe with the aim of making it animate, it is illogical that he would have created as its first state *something whose natural evolution would lead with high probability only to inanimate states*. It does not agree with the idea of an efficient creation of an animate universe that life is brought about through the first state being created with a natural tendency towards *lifelessness* and through this tendency being *counteracted* and *overridden* by the very agency that endowed it with this tendency.
>
> (Smith, in Craig and Smith 1995: 203–4)

Given that God is a supremely rational being who does not do things arbitrarily, nor change his mind from moment to moment, and given that he does intend to create a life-supporting universe, it would be contrary to his nature to create a universe which would in all probability fail to realise his intention unless he intervened to engage in the requisite 'fine tuning'.

The conclusion thus emerges that even if we focus on the kind of order that there is, rather than the mere fact of order or the degree of order, we are still left without any good ground for postulating a divine architect.

The argument to design: flora and fauna

So far, in considering versions of the teleological argument, we have been considering very general and large-scale features of the universe, such as the fact that it displays order, and that various fundamental physical constants have the value that they do. That the universe does have these features is uncontroversial (philosophically and perhaps also scientifically speaking). Theists can therefore use them in the premises of their arguments without begging any questions against the atheist. The dispute between the two camps focuses on what if anything *follows from* such premises. That is why we have called such arguments, arguments *from* order.

But other versions of the teleological argument have focused on instances of seeming design which are much more obvious to casual observation of the world around us. The theist tries to use such instances of seeming design as a premise, from which to infer that there really is design in the natural world, and thence to the conclusion that there is a divine designer. Here, the existence of *seeming* design is uncontroversial: no atheist need deny that many phenomena in the natural world look at first sight as if they had been designed. So arguments of this sort could certainly be called arguments *from seeming design*. But whether the phenomena which look at first sight as if they had been designed really were designed is a crucial point at issue between the theist and atheist. It is therefore not something that the theist can legitimately assume: it is something which she must argue for. So arguments of this sort are properly called arguments *to design*. The popular label 'argument from design' thus encapsulates the mistaken idea that theist and atheist can agree that the natural world is designed, and that they disagree only over the issue of whether designs require designers. Given that a design is more than just a pattern (for example, because it involves the notion of function, or purpose), it is clear that designs do require designers, and no atheist should be required to prove otherwise. What she can be required to do is to show that seeming design is not real design, or more weakly that we have no reason to think that it is real design.

The best-known version of the argument to design, appealing to the similarity between animals and plants on the one hand, and designed artefacts on the other must surely be Paley's. Paley famously imagines coming upon a watch lying on the ground. He says that he would immediately be able to tell that it been produced by an intelligent designer. Similarly, when he examines an object such as an eye, and sees a similar adaptation of means to ends, he at once is entitled to infer an intelligent designer. Paley was writing in 1802; but throughout the previous century, a number of authors had been drawing the same inference. Here is one charming example in which moles are viewed as displaying design:

> [The mole's] dwelling being underground, where nothing is to be seen, nature hath so obscurely fitted her with eyes that naturalists can scarcely agree whether she hath any sight at all or no . . . But for amends, what she is capable of for her defence and warning of danger, she has very eminently conferred on her; for she is very quick of hearing . . . And then her short tail and short legs, but broad forefeet armed with sharp claws, we see by the event to what purpose they are, she so swiftly working herself underground, and making her way so fast in the earth, as they that behold it cannot but admire it. Her legs therefore are short, that she need dig no more than will serve the mere thickness of her body; and her forefeet are broad that she may scoop away much earth at a time; and she has little or no tail because she courses it not on the ground like a rat or a mouse, but lives under the earth, and is fain to dig herself a dwelling there; and she making her way through so thick an element, which will not easily yield as the water and air do, it had been dangerous to draw so long a train behind her . . . [all of] which being so, what more palpable argument of providence than she?
>
> (Ray 1735: 141–2)

In this passage, Ray is clearly inviting us to view the mole as like an artefact. The mole's features and capacities are to be explained in terms of design and purpose. Thus the mole has been designed with very acute hearing *for the purpose of* detecting her enemies; her legs have been designed to be short *for the purpose* of expediting her way through the earth; her forefeet have been designed to be broad *for the purpose* of scooping a lot of earth quickly; her tail has been designed to be short *for the purpose* of making it hard for her enemies to catch hold of her from behind; and so on.

This location of design in the world of flora and fauna comes very naturally to us. Whereas it takes some effort of imagination to see, for example, the force of gravity or the weak nucleic force as an instance of purpose or design, it takes no imaginative leap to think of the parts and capacities of plants and animals as serving various purposes.

But clearly the designs and purposes which we think we detect in the world of plants and animals are not of human origin. It is not we who have designed the eyes or tail or claws of moles. How then are we to explain the seeming design which we see around us? Typically, the theist has proceeded as if there are only two possibilities: either the seeming design in nature was the effect of a real designer with real purposes, who made the world, as we might make an artefact; or this seeming design was the result of 'blind chance'. Unintelligent atoms, whirling about endlessly in space, had somehow all come together to form living organisms, organisms which displayed in every aspect of their lives the most perfect simulation of purpose. This second option of seeming design originating in 'mere chance' seemed simply too incredible to be taken seriously by most proponents of this argument. So that left only the possibility that the seeming design in the world was indeed real design, that the world of plants and animals was the deliberate product of an intelligent designer; and that designer was of course then identified as God.

Humean criticisms of the argument to design

The argument to design (AD for short) as presented by writers such as Ray and Paley has in the past exercised a powerful hold on the intellects of theists. But, even without calling on any neo-Darwinian thoughts, it is exposed to some powerful criticisms. The most fertile source for these objections is Hume's *Dialogues Concerning Natural Religion*, even though it was actually written some time before Paley's classic exposition. Written over a number of years towards the end of Hume's life, but not published until after his death for fear of the persecution to which it might give rise, the *Dialogues* is a very subtle and wide-ranging discussion of the existence of God. Some of the objections are to the ontological argument, some to the cosmological argument, some are to what earlier in this chapter we called the argument from order. But its most extended treatment is devoted to the argument to design. Hume discusses at least two versions of the AD, the first starting (as Paley does) with an analogy between particular living things and artefacts, and the second with an analogy between the universe as a whole and artefacts. Hume produces a rich array of objections, of differing degrees of plausibility. Because he was writing in dialogue form, and wanted to maintain the dramatic tension of the dialogue, it seems likely that Hume himself would not have endorsed all of the arguments which he puts in the mouth of Philo, the character who most nearly expresses the Humean point of view. But a number of the arguments clearly do carry weight. We can single out for special mention a set of four which all relate to the claim that there is an analogy between artefacts and organisms.

In expounding the AD, Hume emphasises that it is an argument from experience. It tries to extrapolate from cause/effect relations which we find in some parts of our experience, to similar relations in parts of the universe which we have not experienced. We detect a similarity between watches and organisms; experience tells us that a watch is produced by a designer; and relying on the maxim of 'Similar effect, so probably similar cause' (let us call this the Similarity Maxim), the supporter of the AD infers that organisms are probably produced by a designer. Hume's criticisms aim to show that even if we accept this general pattern of argument as legitimate, it will not justify the conclusion that anything like a conventional God is the designer. Such a conclusion would be too rich, in at least four ways.

First, the AD postulates a *single unitary* designer. But the evidence would just as well support a large number of designers, perhaps divided into groups. Suppose we rely on the analogy with the human case (as the AD must). We can then grant to the AD that relatively small and simple artefacts may be wholly produced by one designer. But equally the AD must grant that for large and complex artefacts, a group of collaborating designers and workpeople is essential. One person may design and make a table or a chair. But it takes many collaborating people to build an ocean-going ship. So if we are looking for an explanation for the seeming design of all the objects in the living world, it would be much more plausible on the basis of our experience to postulate many co-operating supernatural designers, rather than just one. In postulating a single designer, the AD is violating the Similarity Maxim.

Second, in all cases of design known to us in our experience, the designer has worked on pre-existing material. The carpenter shapes the pre-existing wood, the watchmaker shapes the pre-existing piece of metal, and so on. So, the inference to a supernatural designer who was *not* a creator but merely a fashioner of pre-existing material, would bring the AD more closely in line with our experience. Certainly the conclusion that the designer was also a creator would have no support from the evidence which the theist adduces. Again, the AD has violated the Similarity Maxim.

Third, the conventional God is supposed to be a non-physical being. But all the designers whom we have ever come across have been physical beings

– indeed, they have had a human form. So to postulate a designer for living things who is non-human in form, even more one who is entirely non-physical, again flouts the Similarity Maxim.

Fourth, the conventional God is supposed to be a moral being, indeed a morally perfect being. But, says Hume, if we take the living world to be the product of a designer or set of designers, there is nothing in it to suggest that the designers have any moral properties at all:

> Look round this universe. What an immense profusion of beings animated and organised, sensible and active! . . . But inspect a little more narrowly these living existences . . . How hostile and destructive to each other! How insufficient all of them for their own happiness! . . . The whole presents nothing but the idea of a blind nature, impregnated by a great vivifying principle, and pouring forth from her lap, without discernment or parental care, her maimed and abortive children!
>
> (Hume 1935: 79)

The first three criticisms above have conceded that there is a similarity between living things and human artefacts (similar effects) and have criticised the theist for nonetheless invoking radically dissimilar causes for these similar effects. This fourth criticism is implicitly saying that there is not even a similarity between the effects. We do not find that artefacts are 'hostile and destructive to each other', and we do not find that they are produced 'without discernment or parental care'. Further, in so far as we could discern any moral qualities in a designer of the living world, the judgement would have to be at best mixed. The flourishing of some forms of life requires the massive, violent, and often painful destruction of other forms. An adequate and enjoyable food supply for the lion requires that numbers of antelope are torn to pieces alive. Birds of prey flourish by pecking to death small helpless mammals. In general, good news for carnivores is bad news for herbivores. But many carnivores also suffer the same fate, since carnivores also eat other carnivores as well as herbivores; and virtually all those creatures who are not eaten alive face death through disease, injury, starvation or dehydration. We do not find in the world of artefacts anything matching this mutual hostility and destructiveness among forms of life; nor would we expect that destructiveness to be displayed by any thing designed by an able and benevolent human designer.

So, Hume implicitly concludes, a proper regard for the inferential principle on which the AD relies would lead to a designer altogether more modest than a traditional theistic God.

Humean criticisms certainly pose problems for the AD, problems which theism to this day struggles to solve. But in historical as opposed to philosophical terms, a more influential line of criticism has come from the work of Darwin, and to this we now turn.

The relevance of Darwin

Some authors have argued that Darwin's discoveries have no bearing on the strength of the AD. Others see them as dealing the AD a fatal blow.[3] Darwin's discoveries are indeed centrally relevant to the AD, as we shall see. But to see exactly why and how this is so, it is necessary to sketch a little background information.

For some centuries, Christian thinkers had taken the creation story of the Bible literally. One part of this story has it that God created the different species of animals and plants separately: from the beginning, the Garden of Eden was stocked with plants and with animals which belonged to different species. It followed that God must have created them separately. This separateness was thought of as fixed and eternal: each species had its own defining essence, given to it by God when he first created it, and which it then passed on to succeeding generations. That thought was then extended, in an entirely reasonable manner, to cover the whole of the living world: wherever there were different species, God must have created them different. No species, in other words, had developed from any other species.

The central aim of *The Origin of Species* was to challenge this belief. Darwin was not primarily seeking to explain why the world of nature displays seeming purpose and design; nor was he seeking to explain the origin of life. It is significant that his work is called *The Origin of Species*, and not, for example, *The Explanation of Seeming Design in Nature*, nor *The Origin of Life*. His main thesis was that some species had developed from others. What we think of today as two distinct species may in fact be linked historically by a chain of intervening life forms which are neither clearly of one species nor clearly of the other. Most famously, and especially in his later work *The Descent of Man*, he argued that humans and other currently existing species such as chimpanzees both developed from a single earlier species of primate. How widely did he think that this mutability of species extended? The main text of *The Origin* has nothing to say about this issue. The thesis it is defending could be put by saying that *a great many species that are now distinct have developed from a common ancestor*. It was not part of his main thesis to show that *all* life forms derive from a single source. However, in his concluding chapter, he addresses the question, and says the following:

> I cannot doubt that the theory of descent with modification embraces all the members of the same great class. I believe that animals have descended from at most only four or five progenitors, and plants from an equal or lesser number.
>
> Analogy would lead me one step further, namely, to the belief that all animals and plants have descended from some one prototype. But analogy may be a deceitful guide . . . [however, all things considered] I should infer from analogy that probably all the organic

beings which have ever lived on this earth have descended from some one primordial form.

(Darwin 1964: 483–4)

That, then, is a thumbnail sketch of the theory of evolution – the claim that species evolved one from one another, rather than being separately created. But there is another essential component to Darwin's overall theory. For he not only maintained that species evolved one from another, he also suggested a mechanism by which this evolution could occur. Various mechanisms are possible in theory. Suppose we wonder how long-necked giraffes could evolve from short-necked herbivores. One possible explanation would be that God intervened in each succeeding generation of short-necked herbivores, making the neck of animals of each generation slightly longer, until the fully fledged giraffe form was reached. (Think of a factory operative who changes the settings on the production machines after each production run.) A second possible mechanism is the so-called theory of acquired characteristics favoured by Lamarck: each generation of originally short-necked herbivores kept stretching their necks, thereby giving themselves slightly longer necks; and this acquired characteristic they then passed on to their progeny who in turn repeated the process.

A third possibility, and the one which Darwin favoured, is the so-called theory of natural selection. This in turn has two components: first, there is the claim that although offspring are substantially similar to their parents, there is some degree of variation between generations; and second, the claim that the environment favours some of these variations more than others. The first of these ideas tells us that offspring are not exactly similar to their parents in all respects. They may, for example, have slightly more acute hearing or larger teeth, or be of slightly heavier or lighter build, and so on. The second idea then says that some of these variations will make the individual better adapted to the environment than individuals who lack the variation. 'Better adapted' here means ultimately 'being more likely to reproduce successfully' – but of course that is a trait that will have many components. Part of being able to reproduce successfully will be having the ability to obtain enough food; another part will be being able to escape from predators; another will be being able to withstand disease; another will be being able to attract fertile mates. And so on. So for example, a cat which belongs to a night-hunting species, but which is born with slightly defective night vision, will have a lower chance of being a successful hunter, a lower chance of surviving in times of food shortages, a lower chance of being in good physical condition for mating, and a lower chance of producing offspring like itself, than the normal cat with good night vision. So the characteristic of poor night vision is ill-adapted to the cat's environment, and other things being equal is more likely not to be passed on to the succeeding generations. Correlatively, cats with good night vision will be better fitted to a night-hunting environment, and over time will reproduce more successfully than other cats, so that ulti-mately good night vision will be a near universal trait among nocturnal cats.

These better-adapted traits thus gradually spread through the whole population. Over a period of perhaps thousands of generations, and many different traits, there thus emerges by a process of natural selection a set of individuals who are sufficiently different from their ancestors to count as a different species.

The theory of natural selection, which was designed to explain how there have come to be a great many different species, thus has as a by-product an explanation of the appearance of design and purpose in the world of nature. The theory explains why, for example, nocturnal cats have all the appear-ance of having been *designed* (i.e. by a conscious designer), without needing to postulate the existence of a conscious designer.

Separating the theory of evolution from the theory of natural selection enables us to see that evolution *per se* is no threat at all to an argument to design. What is ruled out by the theory of evolution (i.e. the theory that the different species evolved from other species) is the theory of special creation (i.e. the theory that the different species were created separately from each other). These are two theories about *the origin of species difference*. They do not provide rival accounts of *why each member of a species seems designed for its own environment*. What *does* put pressure on the traditional AD is the theory of natural selection. AD and the theory of natural selection offer rival accounts of the mechanism which produces seeming design in the living world. The first requires a supernatural designer, the second requires only that in their reproduction, species produce new members who are sub-stantially similar to their parents, but who can differ from the parents in small ways which give their offspring a reproductive advantage over their fellows. So, evidence in favour of the theory of natural selection must tell against the AD.

It would be beyond the scope of this text to provide a thorough assess-ment of the theory of natural selection. That is a task for detailed empirical scientific work, and is something which is anyway admirably performed by a number of other texts. Here we can simply note that there is huge (but not universal)[4] agreement among competent practising biologists (a) that the theory of evolution is correct, and (b) that the theory of natural selection, even if not the whole story, is at least a major part of the story. Further, the majority of those who think that natural selection is only part of the story do not suggest that the rest of the story lies in interventions by a super-natural designer – that natural selection needs to be supplemented (as it were) with some *super*natural selection. Rather, they argue that some other purely physical mechanisms need to be invoked.

We will therefore take as read the biological case in favour of natural selec-tion. There are, however, some broadly philosophical points which seek to limit or undermine the theory; and these we will consider in the next section.

Criticisms of Darwin

There are three points in particular which we will examine: that the theory of natural selection makes the appearance of seeming design a matter of 'blind chance'; that the theory does not disprove the existence of God; and that the theory offers no explanation for the origin of life.

First, hostile critics have sometimes complained that natural selection attributes the development of seeming design in nature to what they call 'blind chance', the implication usually being that this makes a Darwinian explanation for seeming design an absurdly improbable one. How justified is this reaction?

We can note first that the term *blind* chance seems to involve redundancy. Is the critic suggesting that there is an alternative kind of chance called 'sighted chance'? If not, let us speak simply of chance. The question then becomes whether a Darwinian explanation attributes seeming design to the operation of chance. The answer to this will depend on what we understand by 'chance'. Sometimes, we certainly use the term to contrast what happens by prior planning and design with what happens without such design. If two people independently decide to go to a conference, at which they subsequently meet, we could well say that they met by chance, meaning that their meeting was not pre-planned. To say that they met by chance is not itself an *explanation* of why they met – rather it *rules out* an explanation in terms of their prior planning. Nor does their meeting 'by chance' imply that there is no good explanation for the meeting (e.g. in terms of the fact that the conference was on a topic which interested them both, that the conference was fairly small, so that all those attending it would meet each other sooner or later, etc.). In this non-planned sense of 'chance', it is of course true that natural selection says that seeming design occurs 'by chance', for that says no more than that seeming design occurs without being the product of prior planning. In this sense of chance, it is just a matter of chance that every time the temperature rises above $0^{\circ}C$, ice melts; and every time an avalanche occurs on a mountain, the snow slides down rather than up. In other words, even events which are inevitable in the light of the laws of nature can be described as occurring 'by chance' in this 'unplanned' sense of 'chance'.

But the term 'chance' is sometimes used to describe events for which there is no explanation. Heisenberg's Uncertainty Principle, at least as it is often popularly presented, tells us that for some subatomic events, there are no causes: there is no explanation for the occurrence of such events, and in this sense, the occurrence of such events is a matter of chance. But in this sense, natural selection is certainly not saying that seeming design is a matter of chance. Indeed, the theory actually asserts the opposite, since it says there is a good causal explanation for the seeming design.

So, to the charge that natural selection makes seeming design a matter of chance, we can reply 'That is true in one sense of "chance", just as most things that happen are a matter of chance. But it is false in the other sense of "chance", since natural selection says that there is a perfectly good explanation of how and why the seeming design in nature appears and is maintained.'

A second common criticism of a Darwinian approach is to say that it does not prove that there is no God. Kenny, for example, has claimed that 'If the argument from design ever had any value, it has not been substantially affected by the scientific investigation of living organisms from Descartes through to the present day' (Kenny 1969: 188). Kenny's thought is that it is possible to combine an acceptance of evolutionary theory and natural selection with a belief that the *ultimate* explanation of the phenomena must be in terms of the purposes of a designer. A divine designer would, as it were, design the *system* within which species would evolve in accordance with Darwinian natural selection.

But this is a disingenuous criticism. The original form of the AD focused specifically on the features of living things, and said explicitly that those features were very strong evidence for the existence of a divine designer. To the extent that natural selection offers a better explanation of those features than the God hypothesis, it *has* undermined the God hypothesis. The fact that the modern theist can pick on something quite different and say that *that* is evidence for the existence of a divine designer does nothing to show that Darwin's discoveries have not discredited the traditional form of the argument.

Further, the original arguers to design did not merely say that what they could observe in nature was *compatible with* the existence of a divine designer. They claimed that what they could observe was *overwhelming evidence in favour of* the existence of a designer. So even if all Darwin's discoveries could be rendered *compatible with* the AD (and we have implicitly argued above that they cannot be, since they are rival explanations), it would not follow that post-Darwin, the AD could claim the same support from our observations of the natural world. Post-Darwin, the AD no longer provides the best explanation for seeming design, and to that extent its credibility has, *contra* Kenny, been undermined by 'the scientific investigation of living organisms from Descartes through to the present day'.

One final comment is sometimes made to try to limit the power of natural selection. What the theory can do (so the objection goes) is provide a good explanation of how, given one type of organism, or one set of biological features, a further better adapted organism or set of features can develop. Given a creature with a light-sensitive patch on its skin able to detect the difference between light and dark, the theory can provide an explanation of how the creature's distant descendants could come to have a fully functioning eye. But this means that every explanation provided by the theory has to start with some already existing example of seeming design. So the theory can explain one seeming design in terms of another, but what it cannot do is explain seeming design as such (see, for example, Geach 1973). The point is sometimes put by saying that the theory of natural selection cannot explain the origin of *life*. All that it can explain is how, once life exists, it develops in one way rather than another.

The short answer to this comment is that it is true, but that it represents a change of subject. The original AD did not say that the existence of *life per se* (e.g. in bacteria) was good evidence for the existence of a designer. It focused specifically on *certain complicated forms of life* for which it was difficult at the time to find any naturalistic explanation. When the explanation was found (i.e. by Darwin), it remained true that a further question could be raised about life forms which the original proponents of the AD knew nothing about, and which displayed in much less striking form the seeming design on which they focused. But, once that is conceded, there does remain the entirely legitimate question of where and how life itself arises, and whether a good explanation (or even the best available explanation) might be one which called upon a divine designer.

As with the biological evidence in favour of natural selection, so with the state of current biological theorising about the origin of life – detailed assessment is a task beyond the scope of this text. There *is* a real puzzle here, and there is no consensus among biologists. Several radically different theories each have a number of distinguished supporters, and the lay outsider would be unwise to form even a secondhand judgement about which theory was the most credible. All that can be said is that none of the theories which is seriously canvassed by significant numbers of practising biologists invokes any kind of designer. To that extent, although the critic of the AD is right to say that the original theory of natural selection did not provide an explanation of the origin of life per se, he would be wrong to infer from this that by default a designer hypothesis was thereby shown to be more likely.[5]

Modern defences of the argument to design

Versions of the argument to design continue to flourish. Some are simply versions of the argument which are open to the criticisms raised two centuries ago – evidently written by authors who have either not read Hume or have not understood him. Others invoke more sophisticated considerations. Michael Behe, for example, has argued that some biological systems reveal a degree and a kind of complexity, in particular at the biochemical level, which cannot plausibly be explained by anything like Darwinian natural selection. The kind of complexity at issue is what he terms 'irreducible complexity', a concept which he explains as follows: 'By *irreducibly complex* I mean a single system composed of several well-matched, interacting parts that contribute to the basic function wherein the removal of any one of the parts causes the system to effectively cease functioning' (Behe 1996: 39).

The point of calling this 'irreducible' complexity is that the complex whole cannot be viewed as a sum of small-scale changes from a simple whole, if the changes are driven by natural selection. For according to natural selection, *each* change must bring advantages to the organism that has it, if the change is to be passed on to succeeding generations. So a benefit that comes only after a *sequence* of changes has occurred cannot explain why the sequence of development, once started, ever continued to the point at which the benefit would occur.

It is agreed by biologists that many biological systems do display irreducible complexity in this sense. To give a simplistic example: if an organism is to have even a primitive organ of sight (and hence enjoy the increased fitness which that organ can bring), it will not only need some light-sensitive patch on its body, it will also need some primitive form of optic nerve carrying the input from the patch to the brain, and also some kind of optical processing centre in the cortex. Having any two without the third in this set will give it no better visual powers than a creature which has none of the three components. So a visual system with these three components displays irreducible complexity. Therefore, by the argument so far, it cannot be produced by a process of step-by-step natural selection.

What about the possibility that several interacting parts of an irreducibly complex whole should all have come into existence at once, not in sequence? Such a possibility is not absolutely ruled out by the mechanism of natural selection, though it would be a phenomenon for which natural selection could provide no explanation. More seriously, Behe can also reply that if a system does display extensive as well as irreducible complexity, it quickly becomes wildly implausible to suppose that all the interacting parts should have come into existence at once. Perhaps the simultaneous appearance of two, or maybe three, parts which form an irreducibly complex whole is not beyond the bounds of probability. But if an irreducibly complex whole has dozens of such interacting parts, it becomes hugely improbable that they all sprang into existence at just the same moment. So, it is the combination of extensive and irreducible complexity in a single system which presents the problem for the mechanism of natural selection, not either by itself.

There is a second way in which a defender of natural selection may seek to answer the argument. It might be the case that a set of interacting parts which together form an irreducibly complex whole W did emerge in sequence, provided that each of them was selected (i.e. by the processes of natural selection) because of the contribution which each of them made to some other system(s) than W, systems which were not themselves irreducibly complex. This may sound like an unlikely scenario, but a nice example comes from Cairns-Smith (1985). Commenting on the fact that structures within organisms usually have a variety of functions, he writes the cat's way of keeping warm by a furry coat is perhaps only a good one if there is a way of keeping the coat clean. No one would say that the tongue evolved originally for this purpose: but it turned out to be useful all the same as an essential part of a Fur Insulation System. The scratchy cat's tongue is now modified for cleaning purposes, as well as, still, carrying out its more ancient role as part of the Food Processing System.

(Cairns-Smith 1985: 59)

Behe allows that this sort of dual role could in principle allow the parts of an irreducibly complex whole to emerge sequentially. But he again argues that as the number of parts rises, the odds against this happening quickly become astronomical. 'As the complexity of an interacting system increases . . . the likelihood of . . . an indirect route drops precipitously' (op. cit. p. 40). So, the combination of a high degree of complexity with irreducible complexity, which Behe claims that we find all the way down to the cellular level, means that it is hugely improbable that natural selection is the explanation of the simultaneous emergence of all these parts, and hence that natural selection is very unlikely to explain the emergence of creatures like us – or indeed of any known living forms. He concludes that if we have not been produced by the unintelligent, undesigning process of natural selection, we must have been produced at least in part by an intelligent designer.

However, Behe's argument is resistible. First, as Draper has shown in a very careful analysis of the argument, Behe does not really manage to deliver what he initially promises. Some of the undoubtedly complex systems which he refers to do not clearly display irreducible complexity; and some of the undoubtedly irreducibly complex systems do not display great complexity. In fact, he produces no example of a system which is known to be irreducibly very complex. So, he produces no example of a system which is known not to be explainable by natural selection. Since his only ground for accepting the view that 'life was designed by an intelligent agent' (op. cit. p. 252) is the failure of natural selection to explain known phenomena, this must count as a major omission.

Second, even if Behe were correct in saying that no explanation in terms of natural selection is possible for irreducibly and extensively complex systems, there are other explanations possible of an entirely secular kind. Darwin himself at one stage considered whether another mechanism involved in evolution might be sexual selection, and some have even argued that there is evidence for the old Lamarckian theory of the inheritance of acquired characteristics. Nor can we assume a priori that the same mechanism must be responsible for the evolution of every feature of an organism that displays seeming design, every feature that fits an organism to its environment. So even if we were persuaded by the criticisms of natural selection which Behe puts forward, we would still have no reason to think that a divine designer was the only, or the best, explanation of the seeming design which we find in nature.

We will conclude by looking at one last theory which tries to support the AD by invoking some sophisticated mathematical theory which was not available to the AD's earlier proponents. This line of thought has been pressed by William Dembski in particular.

Dembski tells us that, in the past, the scientific respectability of invoking a designer to explain seeming design has been compromised by the lack of any reliable way of drawing the distinction between design and non-design. The recent advances have changed that position: 'There now exists a rigorous criterion – complexity-specification – for distinguishing intelligently caused objects from unintelligently caused ones' (Dembski 1998b). (By a 'criterion', Dembski presumably means a sufficient condition, not a necessary one, since clearly a designed object may display no complexity at all.) By complexity he means 'degree of improbability'; and by specification he means a non-ad-hoc pattern. He then argues that we find in the world of nature, and in particular in the biological world, some very improbable patterning which displays specification. We are therefore entitled to infer that it is caused by an intelligent designer.

But this line of argument is flawed. The only way you can know what designers produce is to find some designers and look at their productions. If you find that all their productions display feature F, then on finding a new object which lacks F, you can reliably (though of course not infallibly) infer that it was not designed. If you find that only their productions display feature F, then on finding a new object which displays F, you can reliably (though of course not infallibly) infer that it was designed. The first problem with Dembski's 'rigorous criterion' for being a designed object is that he gives no grounds for thinking that all and only designed objects meet it, nor even for thinking that most designed objects meet it. (He does not in fact give any grounds for thinking that *any* designed objects do so, although since we can agree that as a matter of fact many will, we can ignore this point.)

But the criterion might still be a good one, even if Dembski fails to show that it is. So, what *would* we find if we tested to see if it was a good way of distinguishing between designed and non-designed objects? We would find that some designed objects (a very large range of human artefacts) did display complexity-specification; and that some non-designed objects (e.g. plants and animals) also displayed the same feature. So we have excellent grounds for saying that to have this feature is *not* a 'rigorous criterion' of design.

In this criticism of Dembski, we have presupposed that plants and animals are not designed; and a follower of Dembski may well object that this begs the question. For the very point at issue is whether plants and animals are designed or not. But what is sauce for the goose is sauce for the gander. What can Dembski mean by a non-designed object? He cannot invoke his complexity-specification, for that would turn his claim that it was a criterion of design into a tautology: the presence/absence of complexity-specification is a rigorous criterion for the presence/absence of complexity-specification. And yet if he turns to the obvious candidates (things known to have been designed by the only designers whose existence we can all agree on, namely human beings), he is bound to discover that his criterion fails to draw the line between designed and non-designed objects.

Mill saw this point very clearly. Commenting on Paley's traveller who finds the watch and infers a designer, he says:

> If I found a watch on an apparently desolate island, I should indeed infer that it had been left there by a human being; but the inference would not be from marks of design, but because I already knew by direct experience that watches are made by men. I should draw the inference no less confidently from a foot print, or from any relic however insignificant which experience has taught me to attribute to man: as geologists infer the past existence of animals from coprolites, though no one sees marks of design in a coprolite.
>
> (Mill 1874, p. 168)

Paley assumed in effect that there was an a priori connection between watch-like construction and genuine design. Dembski assumes in effect that there is an a priori connection between complexity-specification and genuine design. Paley and Dembski make the same mistake – they fail to realise that only experience can tell you what are the reliable indicators of genuine design. Since only experience can tell, it is necessary to look and see if those indicators are present in cases of design and non-design, and that requires you to have a way of identifying cases of design and non-design independently of the indicators in question.

Further reading

The argument from order can be found in Swinburne (1979). The now much more common appeal to the anthropic principle is defended in Polkinghorne (1986), Leslie (1996), and Stannard (1999). Earman (1987) disambiguates some versions of the principle and subjects it to critical scrutiny. Craig and Smith (1995) contains a good deal of relevant material, sometimes given with more scientific detail than many readers will find digestible.

The classic statement of the more traditional argument to design in the world of flora and fauna is Paley's *Natural Theology*, see, for example, Paley (1826); and the classic criticism of such arguments is Hume's *Dialogues Concerning Natural Religion*. (There are many editions of this, but see Hume (1976) for a recent one). Hume's treatment has been widely accepted by many commentators – see, for example, Flew (1961) or Mackie (1982) for typically favourable treatments. But Earman gives a very much more hostile reading of Hume in Earman (2000). Behe's attempt to revive the traditional argument is in his 1996 work, which in turn is meticulously examined by Draper (2002). Dembski's defence of an argument to design can be found in a number of places but is probably best expressed in his 1988a work.

6

———∘◉∘———

Arguments to and from miracles

Introduction

It has been widely supposed that miracles supply one good source of evidence for the existence of God. It is easy to see why people should have thought this. For the ability to perform miracles would immediately reveal a rare and supra-human trait. Such a trait can be a sign of a being who is at least extremely powerful (who can, for example, hold up the waters of the Red Sea), and possibly even omnipotent; and, depending on the miracle in question, it can show this great being to have a concern for the well-being of his followers (e.g. in curing the sick, feeding the hungry, etc.). Thus, asked to justify a belief in the divinity or at least divinely inspired nature of Christ, a Christian might well appeal to the miracles which Christ supposedly wrought. And if these are signs of divinity, then it appears that the occurrence of miracles affords one source of evidence for the existence of God.

We will find, however, that the term 'miracle' is used in several different senses. We will distinguish four main senses, of which there can be a number of sub-varieties, and these will be sufficient for the points we need to consider. We will label the four senses, the violation sense, the directly willed sense, the inexplicable sense, and the coincidence sense; and events which are accurately described in this way we will call violation, directly willed, inexplicable and coincidence miracles.

Hume on violation miracles

The classic discussion of violation miracles is provided by Hume, and it will be convenient to start by considering his view. He begins with a standard definition of a violation miracle: 'A miracle may be accurately defined, a transgression of a law of nature by a particular volition of the Deity or by the interposition of some invisible agent' (Hume 1957: 115 fn. 1).

We shall drop the last clause from this definition (the reference to 'some invisible agent'). It does not figure in Hume's own discussion, nor have later

112

theorists taken it up, and nothing of any importance will be lost if we omit it altogether. Notice that on this definition of miracle, if a miracle is proved to have occurred, it will follow *immediately and obviously* that God exists, since if an event is *produced by* God, God must exist. It would be self-contradictory to agree that a violation miracle had occurred, and yet to deny that God exists. The difficult assertion to establish is that such a miracle has occurred in the first place. A good deal of controversial and unobvious evidence is needed in support of this claim. So in the violation sense of miracle, what is needed is an argument *to* the claim that miracles occur, rather than *from* that claim.

Hume, then, offers us two requirements for being a miracle: first that an event should transgress a law of nature, and second, that this transgression should have been produced by an act of will by God. Some subsequent writers have agreed with Hume that these are two necessary conditions for a miracle, but have wanted to claim that they are not sufficient. Not just *any* violation of the laws of nature by God will do. If, for example, God made a snowflake at the North Pole float upwards instead of falling in accordance with the law of gravity, this would count as a miracle by Hume's definition, even if no one witnessed this event or discovered that it had occurred, and even if its occurrence brought no benefit to anyone. But, according to writers like Swinburne, this conception is too liberal. Nothing could count as a miracle unless it had some religious significance. 'To be a miracle an event must contribute significantly toward a holy divine purpose for the world' (Swinburne 1989: 6). Other thinkers have imposed similar restrictions, requiring for example that to count as a miracle, an event must bring benefits to someone. Another restriction which has been suggested is that a miracle must by definition be something rare or even unrepeatable.

There may well be good grounds for imposing a restriction of the first and second kinds. But a requirement that miracles should be rare *as a matter of definition* seems misplaced, for three reasons. In the first place, there seems no reason in principle why, if God can perform a miracle once, he should not be able to perform it repeatedly (he is after all omnipotent!). Second, if God answers any petitionary prayers, his action is miraculous in the violation sense: he makes something happen which would not have happened had the petitioner not prayed, and had events then taken their natural course; and it would be odd to adopt a definition of the term 'miracle' which had the consequence that prayers could be answered only rarely. Maybe they *are* answered only rarely – but if so, this should not be because of the way we define 'miracle'. Third, we need to recall the Catholic doctrine of transubstantiation (according to which in the Mass, the wine and bread are literally changed in substance into the blood and body of Christ). If such a change should occur, it should surely count as miraculous, notwithstanding the fact that it may happen very regularly and on a very large scale.

Fortunately, we do not here need to take a stand on the issue of what restrictions beyond Hume's two need to be imposed to get a religiously satis-factory definition of violation miracles. All the problems which arise in connection with violation miracles stem from the first two conditions, and it is on these that we need to concentrate our attention.

Hume's discussion falls conveniently into two parts. In the first he tries to show that unless the evidence in favour of a violation miracle is overwhelm-ing, a rational believer should believe that the miracle did not occur; and that even when the evidence *is* overwhelming, the rational believer will always suspend judgement, because there will always also be overwhelming evidence that the miracle did *not* occur. The second part of his argument is designed to show that as a matter of historical fact, the evidence for the occurrence of miracles is never overwhelming. The overall conclusion is then drawn that it is not, and never can be, rational to believe that a miracle has occurred. If that is true, there will clearly be no good argument to be drawn from the occurrence of miracles to the existence of God.

In the first part of the argument, Hume develops in effect a mini-theory about when it is reasonable to believe anything (not just reported miracles) on testimony. First, he says, it is rational to proportion our belief in a propo-sition to the net evidence in favour of it, that is to say, to the total evidence in favour of it minus the total evidence against it (let us call this the Propor-tion Principle). Second, the more antecedently improbable a proposition is, i.e. the more improbable that it is before we receive the testimony, the more evidence is needed to make the proposition rationally credible (let us call this the Antecedent Probability Principle). Thus, if a person tells me that she has seen a brown cow in a field, it is rational for me to believe her, other things being equal. I know antecedently to her report that what she reports is certainly possible, and if she has no motive for lying, if she was in a posi-tion to know the truth of what she reports, and if there was no other evidence against what she reported, it is rational for me to accept her report. Here I am relying on the Proportion Principle. If, however, she tells me that she has seen a three-headed cow in a field, it will probably be rational for me to disbelieve her. Even if I think that three-headed cows are possible, I think that they are very unlikely. It is more likely that the reporter was mis-taken and the cow was not three-headed, than that the reporter was right and the cow was three-headed. Before it would be rational for me to believe *this* report, I would need much more evidence than I did with the report of a brown cow. I might for example want eyewitness reports from a number of expert and independent witnesses. The different response which it would be rational to make to the two reports of the cows is justified by the Antecedent Probability Principle: since a three-headed cow is more improbable than a brown cow, I need stronger testimony in favour of it than for the brown cow before it would be rational for me to believe in its existence.

These two principles governing the rational credibility of every kind of testimony Hume now applies to a belief in violation miracles; and he argues

114

that they create a problem about the credibility of all reports about violation miracles. The problem is that to gain evidence that a violation miracle has occurred, the miracle believer has to establish three propositions of the following form:

(1) L is a law of nature.
(2) Event E (the putative miracle) has occurred.
(3) The statement that E has occurred contradicts the statement that L is a law of nature.

It is obvious that (1) needs to be established: if the miracle believer cannot identify any relevant law of nature, she obviously cannot identify any event as being a putative violation of a law of nature. Equally, some event E has to be identified as the candidate for being a miracle. And finally, if E is to be a miracle, it must not be in accord with L: since it is supposed to 'violate' L, there must be a contradiction between the claim that E has occurred and that L is a law of nature.

To make our discussion more concrete, let us consider a simple example. Suppose the three propositions with the above form are:

(4) It is a law of nature that water cannot be turned into wine.
(5) Some water has been turned into wine.
(6) The statement that water has been turned into wine contradicts the statement that it is a law of nature that water cannot be turned into wine.

Here, I have made it obvious that (6) is true; so we can focus attention on (4) and (5). Why cannot we establish that both (4) and (5) are true? The crucial problem which Hume locates is that any evidence for (4) is also evidence against (5), and any evidence for (5) is also evidence against (4). So it is impossible to gather any evidence which is for *both* (4) and (5). If, at the limit, we could get enough evidence to make it reasonable to believe either, we would necessarily have enough evidence to make it rational to disbelieve the other, and the only rational response would be to suspend judgement. So, under no circumstances would it be rational to believe that a miracle had occurred.

We can put the point in terms of the two principles which Hume has introduced, in the following way. Since a miracle is by definition a violation of a law of nature, it is maximally improbable. So, if testimony in favour of a miracle is to be rationally credible, then the Antecedent Probability Principle tells us that it must be hugely strong testimony – in fact, maximally strong. But even if the testimony were to achieve maximal strength (however we interpret that notion), it would all be cancelled out by the antecedent improbability of anything which contravenes the laws of nature. The Proportion Principle would then tell us that we should proportion our belief to the net evidence for the miracle report, and since the net evidence would be zero (maximal evidence for is cancelled by maximal evidence against), the rational response would be non-belief in the occurrence of the supposed miracle.

This completes the first part of Hume's argument in which he has tried to show that even if the evidence in favour of a violation miracle is overwhelming, it still would not be rational to believe that it had occurred, because there would inevitably be overwhelming evidence against it. He then goes on to argue that as a matter of historical fact none of the evidence which we have for violation miracles is overwhelming. But we can ignore that part of his discussion here, as it depends on the truth of historical rather than philosophical claims. The real destructive power of Hume's critique lies in his philosophical argument that even in the most favourable circumstances possible (favourable, that is, to a belief in theism) it would not be rational to believe that a miracle has occurred. His historical evidence that these most favourable circumstances have never in fact occurred is comparatively unimportant: even if it were wholly controverted, his main argument would remain unaffected.

Would it make any difference if instead of relying on the testimony of some third person, I had observed the putative miracle myself – if, for example, I had been present at the water-into-wine event? Hume does not explicitly discuss this possibility, but the answer implicit in what he says is 'No'. We can grant that there is perhaps a general principle to the effect that eye-witnesses of events have a greater authority than non-witnesses when they are reporting what might loosely be called the observable features of events. But this 'greater authority' is limited in at least two crucial ways. In the first place, an expert *non*-witness may be able to show that it is very unlikely or even impossible for the witness to have seen what she thinks she saw. And second, even if witnesses do have some kind of authority, it clearly cannot extend to the non-observational properties of events. Take the water and wine case again. A witness may be able to report reliably that a liquid which looked and tasted to her like water was changed into one that looked and tasted to her like wine. Whether this is change of *water* into *wine* (which presumably involves a change in the molecular structure of the liquid) is another question. But let us assume that observation alone does tell our observer what is water and what is wine, and that genuine water has been changed into genuine wine. That by itself will not entitle her to say that a miracle has occurred. In order to identify what has occurred as a miracle, she would need to know in addition that it is a law of nature that water cannot be turned into wine; and no amount of close attention to what is going on at the water-into-wine occasion will tell her that. In other words, the concept of miracle is a non-observational concept, and hence eye-witnesses of putative miracles can have no special standing in making claims that a miracle really has occurred.

Assessment of Hume's argument

It is important to be clear what the limits of Hume's argument are. He is not saying that violation miracles are impossible.[1] Nor is the argument saying that the events which are commonly quoted as examples of violation miracles did not occur. His argument does not imply that water has never been turned into wine, nor that five thousand people were never adequately fed on five loaves and two fishes, nor that no one has walked on water or risen from the dead. The real conclusion of the argument is a disjunctive one: either it can be rational to believe that these events occurred but were not violation miracles, or it can be rational to believe that they did not occur. What cannot be rational is to believe both that they occurred and that they were violation miracles. For if the overall evidence makes it rational to believe that these events happened, then that same overall evidence makes it irrational to believe that they were violations of laws of nature (rather than unusual but scientifically explicable events). If, on the other hand, the overall evidence makes it rational to believe that such events, had they occurred, would have violated the laws of nature, then the overall evidence makes it rational to believe that those events did not occur.

This point is worth emphasising because some commentators seem to have misunderstood Hume's point. Davies, for example, claims that Hume has overlooked 'the possibility of corroborating what someone claims to have occurred', for 'past events sometimes leave physical traces which survive into the present' (B. Davies 1993: 204). Davies does not give any examples of what he has in mind when he speaks of 'physical traces'. But a record on film might be an example of the kind of later corroborative evidence which he has in mind. So (Davies seems to be suggesting) if we simply have verbal testimony from people who claim to have seen, for example, levitation, we might be justified in disbelieving them; but if we then found a film of the levitation, this could be further corroborating evidence which would make the original testimony credible after all. But if Davies believes that something like this is a point against Hume, he is wrong. Hume's conclusion does not imply that levitation is impossible, nor that testimony that it has occurred is always incredible. His conclusion is that the more credible the evidence that levitation has occurred (including all the later corroborations which Davies refers to), the less we are justified in believing that levitation is contrary to the laws of nature, and hence the less we are justified in believing that levitation is a violation miracle. Of course, he *does* think that reports of levitation, walking on water, life after death, etc. are incredible. But that is because he thinks that as a matter of historical fact, the evidence in favour of reports of such events is too slender. It is outweighed (he believes) by a great mass of contrary evidence.

Once we are clear about the precise conclusion of Hume's argument, it is decisive in dealing a death blow to the credibility of all reports of violation miracles. But that fact does not settle the whole issue of miracles, for it might well be that with a different definition of 'miracle', the theist could both escape Hume's criticism and identify events of religious significance which pointed to the existence of God. Before we pursue that possibility, however, it is worth pausing to ask if there might not be even stronger objections to violation miracles

Two arguments for saying that violation miracles are impossible

So far, we have been assuming (with Hume and with the great majority of writers about violation miracles) that such miracles are at least possible. Hume's objection has been only that reports of such miracles are never credible. In assuming that violation miracles are possible, we have not of course been assuming that they are *physically* possible, in the sense of being in accordance with the laws of nature. For by definition, they are not physically possible, since by definition they require a violation of the laws of nature, and it is the laws of nature which determine what is physically possible. The question rather is whether violation miracles are *logically* possible, in the philosopher's special sense of that phrase. This is to ask whether the concept is a self-consistent one, or whether (like the concept of round square, married bachelors, and male vixens) it is self-contradictory. In the 'possible worlds' terms introduced in Chapter 3, it is to ask whether there is a possible world in which miracles occur.

Let us first settle on at least one feature which a statement must have to be a candidate for being a law of nature. It must be universal in form, in the sense of saying something about all or every member of a class, or about what always happens whenever something else happens; or about no members of a class, or what never happens. Thus all of the following are at least candidates for being laws of nature by this criterion: all unsupported bodies fall in air; water always boils at 100°C at normal temperature and pressure; no iron can be turned into gold. This beginning of an account of laws of nature of course needs much more detail and sophistication, but it is all that we will need in order to understand the following objections. So let us now turn to consider two arguments, each designed to show that the concept of a violation miracle is logically impossible, and hence that there cannot be any violation miracles.

(a) Argument 1

It is plain that what is incompatible with a truth is itself false. If, therefore, it is a true statement of a law of nature that all As are Bs, it follows that any miracle report which says that there is an A which is not a B is false. It is thus self-contradictory to assert that a miracle has occurred. Suppose, for example, that it is a law of nature that water cannot be converted into wine (all water is non-wine-convertible). If it is true that no water is wine-convertible, then 'Some water was converted into wine' must be false. So any report of an allegedly miraculous conversion of water into wine must be false. Alternatively, if some water was converted into wine, then it cannot be a true statement of a law of nature that all water is non-wine-convertible.

Can this extremely simple objection to the very possibility of violation miracles be evaded? We might try imagining a situation in which the statement of the law is not in fact true. In that case, it will certainly be possible for there to be an A which is not a B. But then the claim that there is an A which is not a B will not violate any law of nature, and hence will not report a miracle. In terms of our previous example: if it is not a law of nature that water is non-wine-convertible, then certainly 'Some water was converted into wine' might be true. But if it is true, it does not contradict any law of nature, and hence cannot be reporting a miracle.

A second possible objection would be to take a different view of laws of nature. Suppose that their form is not 'All As are Bs', but 'All As are Bs unless God intervenes to make an A which is not a B'. If that is what laws of nature are like, they would certainly allow for the existence of an A which is not a B provided it is produced by God. But such an A cannot count as miraculous, because on this understanding of what a law of nature is, the A which is not a B has not violated any laws of nature. For comparison: a black Australian swan does not violate the generalisation 'All swans are white except for black Australian ones'.

It may be that it was something like this second possibility that Mackie had in mind in his defence of the coherence of the concept of a violation miracle. He wrote:

> we might determine that something *is* a basic law of working of natural objects, and yet also, independently, find that it was occasionally violated. An occasional violation does not in itself necessarily overthrow the independently established conclusion that this *is* a law of working.
>
> (Mackie 1982: 21)

But Mackie is simply wrong here. If the laws he is thinking of have the form 'All As are Bs', then there cannot be a true statement of the form 'There is an A which is not a B'. To say that there is only an 'occasional' A which is not a B is no help here. There cannot be any As which are not Bs if 'All As are Bs' is true.

A similar confusion vitiates Swinburne's discussion of this point. He writes: 'To say a generalisation "All As are Bs" is a universal law of nature is to say that being A physically necessitates being B, and so that any A will be

B – apart from violations' (Swinburne 1979: 229). He then explains that by 'violation', he means non-repeatable exception. So a law of nature, on Swinburne's account has the form 'All As are Bs, unless there is a non-repeatable exception'. But what can he think that a non-repeatable *exception* is? Suppose that there is a single case of an A which is not a B. *This* will not be an exception to a generalisation which says that all As are Bs except for a single A which is not B. The generalisation clearly embraces two types of case: (i) All As bar one being Bs, and (ii) one A being not B. Just as (i) is wholly compatible with the law and indeed helps to confirm it, so too is (ii) wholly compatible with the law. We still have been given no understanding of how a law of nature could be violated. So Swinburne's account secures the possibility of there being As which are not Bs only at the cost of making it impossible for them to violate laws of nature. He thus makes it impossible for them to be genuine violation miracles. We still have not been given any understanding of how a law of nature could be violated.

John Stuart Mill gave an excellent brief summary of the argument when he remarked: 'We cannot admit a proposition as a law of nature, and yet believe a fact in real contradiction to it. We must disbelieve the alleged fact, or believe we are mistaken in admitting the supposed law' (Mill 1967: 409; III, 25, ii).

(b) Argument 2

Let us now turn to the second of the two arguments against the self-consistency of the concept of a violation miracle. To understand this objection, we need to be clear that there are two sorts of laws: prescriptive and descriptive. Prescriptive laws are laws which prescribe the way in which things ought to be done, or the things which people ought to do. Statute law is one sort of prescriptive law, but of course there are many others. The laws of etiquette would be another sort, the laws of tennis, or bridge, or football another sort again. If we are thinking of prescriptive laws, there is no difficulty in the thought that there might be a breach or violation or transgression of them. It happens all the time. It happens whenever anyone does not do what the law says she ought to do; or does what the law says she ought not to do; and in many cases there will be some appropriate penalty attached to the violation. In this sense of law, it is really only people (or at least intelligent agents) who can keep or violate the law. If the law prescribes that some state of affairs should hold (e.g. that the football should be placed in the centre spot at the start of a football match), this can mean only that some*one* ought to see to it that the ball is so placed. It is not, as it were, the ball's own responsibility to see that it is placed on the centre spot. So when the law is broken, it is some*one* who has broken the law, not some*thing*. Notice too that in this sense of law, the law cannot be true or false. It may be a good idea or a bad idea to have a law of tennis that permits the first service to be a fault, but such a law cannot be true or false. Similarly with laws against abortion, or drunk driving or failure to vote: they may be good or bad laws, but they cannot be true or false.

But now consider by contrast the laws of nature, which we can label descriptive laws. Consider as an example Boyle's Law, which says that the volume and pressure of a gas vary inversely (i.e. the smaller the volume and hence the more compressed it becomes, the greater the pressure which it exerts). This law does not prescribe to gases how they *ought* to behave – it simply describes how they *do* behave. If it is a genuine law, it will be a true description of how they behave; if it is not a genuine law, but only, for example, an approximation to one, then it will not describe truly how gases behave. Further, suppose that there is a mismatch between the behaviour of gases and the putative law. This would show not that the gases have some-how misbehaved themselves and done what they ought not to have done. It would show that this putative law was at fault: it was not a genuine law at all. Further, laws like Boyle's Law are not just directed at human agents, as we saw that prescriptive laws are. Descriptive laws can be about anything at all, and specifically can be about inanimate objects, as Boyle's Law is.

If we draw together these points, we get the following contrasting charac-terisation of our two sorts of laws:

A. *Prescriptive*
(1) The laws prescribe, they do not describe.
(2) The laws can be assessed as good or bad, but not as true or false.
(3) The laws are addressed to people.
(4) The laws can be violated/transgressed/breached.
(5) If there is a discrepancy between the laws and the real world, it is the world which is at fault.

B. *Descriptive*
(1) The laws describe, they do not prescribe.
(2) The laws (or statements of them) can be assessed as true or false but not as good or bad.
(3) The laws can be about anything at all, not just human action.
(4) The laws cannot be violated/transgressed/breached.
(5) If there is a discrepancy between the putative laws and the real world, the 'laws' are at fault.

The second argument for saying that the concept of a violation is incoherent can now be put. It is that the concept of a violation miracle confuses two different concepts of law, prescriptive and descriptive. The laws of nature are specified in *true* descriptions of how the world behaves; but because they are *descriptions*, it does not make sense to talk of violating them. What can be violated are *pre*scriptive laws – but laws of nature are not prescriptive

121

laws. So since violation miracles by definition involve the violation of a non-violatable type of law, the very concept is an incoherent one.

Assessment of these arguments

How strong are these two arguments? Against their chosen target they are decisive; but, as so often in the philosophy of religion, a fall-back position is available for the theist. The arguments are conclusive in the sense that they show that no coherent concept of a miracle can rely on talk of violating, or suspending, or breaching, the laws of nature. In that sense, they do succeed in showing that violation miracles are absolutely impossible. But what the theist can do here is find a less vulnerable way of expressing the idea which she was trying to articulate in the concept of a violation miracle.

Directly willed miracles

The theist's thought must be like this: God as the creator and sustainer of everything makes happen everything that does happen in the world. Some things he makes happen indirectly, some directly. He makes something happen indirectly when he makes it happen by making something else happen. For example, when he makes the waters on a lake rise and fall in waves, he standardly does so by means of a wind which pushes the waters about; and he standardly makes the wind blow by the rising of large volumes of air; and he standardly makes the large volumes of air rise by raising its temperature; and so on, in a series of regularities stretching back in time. But sometimes, the theist must say, he makes an event happen directly, without using any other natural process as the means. So, if he held back the waters of the Red Sea for the Israelites to pass, the restraining of the waters was not produced by him indirectly (e.g. by some form of whirlwind, which was caused by a combination of low air pressure and high temperature, etc.). Rather, it was caused directly: he simply willed that at a certain time the waters should part and as a consequence, they parted at that time. Similarly with all other miracles: like every event, miraculous or not, they are due to the continuous and on-going sustaining activity of God, but unlike most events, they follow directly an act of will by God.

This way of conceiving of the nature of miracles has several advantages for the theist. In the first place, it bypasses all the problems associated with the idea of violating laws of nature. (It would clearly be silly to suggest that God's direct willings 'violated' his indirect willings.) Second, it allows the theist to develop some empirical criteria for the occurrence of miracles. The search for what we call laws of nature becomes the search for regularities in nature which God indirectly wills. Suppose that we have such a putative regularity, which we express in the form 'All As are Bs'. We then find an A which is not a B. If this particular A (a) occurs in a context which gives it religious meaning (e.g. perhaps in response to petitionary prayer?), and (b) is of significant benefit (e.g. it results in an unexpected curing of the sick), it would be a candidate for being an instance of God's direct willing, and hence for being a miracle. If it occurred without these two conditions being met, it would be a counter-instance to our supposed law, and hence would show only that we had not so far identified correctly the relevant indirectly willed regularity.

But this new concept of a miracle does mean that any proposed argument to miracles takes on a different aspect. On the old conception of a violation of the laws of nature, we were implicitly invited to consider whether an event was produced by the laws of nature or by God. The implication was that events which happened normally and regularly were not potential evidence for God, but events which were rare and impressive were. But what the new way of thinking suggests is that *every* event is equally evidence for the existence of God. If it is a common type of event, it is potentially evidence of God acting indirectly; if it is a rare and impressive event, then it is potentially evidence of God acting directly. But the rare and impressive is no more support for theism than the normal and regular.

Inexplicable miracles

The problems which we have been noting with violation miracles stem from the fact that such miracles, if they occurred, would have to breach a law of nature. But perhaps in spite of being part of a very traditional conception of a miracle, the requirement is superfluous. Perhaps the crucial idea should be not that miracles are violations of laws of nature, but simply that they are inexplicable in terms of the laws of nature. Of course, something that is a violation will also be inexplicable by reference to the laws of nature, but the reverse is not the case. On the face of it, it is possible that although a great many events in the world around are explicable by appeal to the laws of nature, some are not. This suggests that a more promising definition of 'miracle' for the theist to adopt might be that a miracle is an event which is naturalistically inexplicable (and which had religious significance, produced benefits, etc.).

But if we do think of miracles in this way, it at once becomes puzzling to see how we could ever identify them as such. For how are we to interpret the idea of being inexplicable? If it means 'inexplicable to us with our present level of scientific knowledge', then that opens the possibility that something which was a miracle at one time (because inexplicable at that time) is not a miracle at a later time (because explicable at that later time); or a miracle in one place (because inexplicable by the science there prevailing) but not a miracle in another place (because of the more advanced science there prevailing). The point would not be simply that different people would hold different beliefs about whether the event was a miracle or not. Rather, it would *really be* a miracle in one time and place, and also *really not be* a miracle at another time and place. This seems an unpromising line for a miracle believer to take.

It seems then that the miracle believer needs to interpret 'inexplicable' as 'inexplicable in principle'. That is to say, neither present science nor any possible science of the future would be able to provide an explanation of the event. It is not that the event would have a scientific explanation which the human race would never discover. Rather, there would be no scientific explanation to discover. But now the puzzle is to see what evidence there could be that any event *was* inexplicable in this very strong sense. Given the occurrence of any event which we would now find baffling, and which we could not now explain in scientific terms, how could we know that future developments of science would not show that it was explicable after all? For primitive people who first witnessed a total eclipse of the sun, the event might have been utterly unprecedented and mysterious. And yet we now know that it is fully explicable in scientific terms. How could we know now that if we witnessed an unprecedented and mysterious event, it would not similarly be explained by future science? Of course, if we could establish that it had been directly produced by God, we could infer that it was not scientifically explicable. But from the point of view of increasing the probability of theism, that would be to get the cart before the horse: the aim is to see if God can be inferred from miracles, not if miracles can be inferred from God.

Even if such events occurred and could be correctly identified in a non-question-begging way as scientifically inexplicable in principle, what could be inferred from them? If we drop the clause that says that to be a miracle, an event must have been produced directly by God, then it will not follow *immediately* that God exists. Given the premise that a naturalistically inexplicable event occurred, further evidence would be needed before one could infer the conclusion that it was produced by God. If it was rational to think that every event had some explanation or other, and also that a particular event had no scientific explanation, then it would follow that it must have some non-scientific explanation; and from this it might be a plausible inference to the conclusion that God was at least a possible candidate for being the explanation. But those would be two major assumptions, and it is difficult to think of any grounds for supposing either of them is true.

Coincidence miracles

So far, we have been arguing that the theist would be unwise to place any reliance on violation or inexplicable miracles as a way of increasing the credibility of theism. But there is a third way of interpreting the concept which we now need to notice, an interpretation which is sometimes called the 'coincidence miracle' conception, for reasons which will shortly be obvious. It defines a miracle as *a very surprising coincidence with significant beneficial consequences*. Perhaps the most famous (fictional) example of this kind of miracle was provided by R.F. Holland. Holland writes of a child who has wandered on to a railway track. A train is approaching at high speed but because the track is curved, there is no possibility that the driver will see the child in time to stop. The mother is watching from a distance, and can see what is about to happen, but is too far away to intervene. The train hurtles down upon the child, and then suddenly its brakes are applied and it comes to a halt a few feet from the child. Holland continues:

> The mother thanks God for the miracle; which she never ceases to think of as such although, as she in due course learns, there was nothing supernatural about the manner in which the brakes of the train came to be applied. The driver had fainted, for a reason that had nothing to do with the presence of the child on the line, and the brakes were applied automatically as his hand ceased to exert pressure on the control lever. He fainted on this particular afternoon because his blood pressure had risen after an exceptionally heavy lunch during which he quarrelled with a colleague, and the change in blood pressure caused a clot of blood to be dislodged and circulate. He fainted at the time he did on the afternoon in question because this was the time at which the coagulation in his blood reached the brain.
>
> (Holland 1965: 43)

The crucial thing about coincidence miracles from our point of view is what differentiates them from both violation and inexplicable miracles: they are fully explicable in terms of the laws of nature. In this sense of the term 'miracle', there clearly are miracles. There are such events as lucky though unexpected coincidences. There is no need to argue *to* the existence of miracles in this sense – their occurrence is something that can happily be conceded by agnostic and atheist alike. The question is, rather, given the occurrence of coincidence miracles as premise, what can be inferred *from* them?

It seems that the answer to this question is 'Nothing at all', for the following reason. It would be reasonable to infer the (probable to some degree) existence of God from the occurrence of coincidence miracles if such an inference were an essential part of the best explanation for the occurrence of such miracles. In other words, if we could not explain why this particular happy coincidence should have happened, except on the assumption that God had had a hand in producing it, then from the occurrence of coincidence miracles we could draw a more-or-less probable conclusion that God exists. But ex hypothesi, that is not the position. Since a coincidence miracle does not require any violation of the laws of nature, nor is it inexplicable naturalistically, an adequate explanation of such an event can be obtained entirely within the framework of natural law.

Let us apply this point to Holland's own example. A naturalistic explanation is provided of why the train stopped when and where and how it did. There is simply nothing left for an invocation of God to explain: there is no explanatory work for him to do. What should we say about the mother in Holland's example, who continues to thank God for the miracle, even after she accepts the full naturalistic explanation of why the train stopped? Either she is intellectually confused (because she is thanking someone for doing something which she accepts he did not do), or she may be thanking God in the way in which a person thanks her lucky stars, even though she accepts that in sober truth her 'lucky stars' had no causal influence on what happened to her, and indeed that her 'lucky stars' do not even exist. So, as regards coincidence miracles, we can conclude: it is uncontroversial that such miracles occur, but that they occur does nothing to establish the existence of God.

Conclusion

So far we have looked at four ways of defining the concept of a miracle, and we have argued that whichever way is chosen, there are philosophical objections to thinking that an appeal to miracles could provide evidence for the existence of God. But the problems are significantly different on each of the four accounts. On the first definition, in terms of violations of laws of nature, we argued that there were compelling grounds for thinking that a belief in miracles would be irrational, and even that the very concept was self-contradictory. On the second definition, the concept was self-consistent, but it gave us no grounds for looking to miracles rather than to the general orderliness in nature as evidence of God's existence. On the third account, the problems were again epistemological. If miracles are defined as in principle inexplicable, there seems no reason to believe of any event that it is a miracle; nor that if it is a miracle, it is any evidence for the existence of God. On the final definition, it was clear that the concept was self-consistent, and indeed that there really were many miracles in that sense. The problem was that the occurrence of such miracles provided no evidence for the existence of God.

Further reading

Hume's classic discussion is found in Chapter 11 of Hume (1957). Some standard commentaries on Hume's account are provided in Flew (1961),

Penelhum (1975), and Gaskin (1978). A more recent discussion, and one which is very much more hostile, is Earman (2000). Swinburne's defence of the credibility of violation miracles is in Swinburne (1979), and Mackie's hostile treatment of the same in Mackie (1982). Coincidence miracles are discussed in Holland (1965). Swinburne (1989) is a useful collection of articles, which includes pieces by Hume, Mackie, Flew, Holland and by Swinburne himself.

7

---◦◯◦---

God and morality

The existentialist . . . finds it extremely embarrassing that God
does not exist, for there disappears with Him all possibility of
finding values in an intelligible heaven . . . It is nowhere written that 'the good' exists, that one must be honest, or must not
lie . . . Everything is . . . permitted if God does not exist.

(Sartre 1970: 33–4)

Introduction

It is often thought that there is a peculiarly close connection between God
and morality. Whenever Royal Commissions are set up to investigate some
topic that is thought to be a distinctively moral one (prostitution, pornog-
raphy, abortion, etc.) it is thought by many people to be appropriate to
ensure that one or more divisions of theists (Christians, Jews, et al.) are represented. The assumption seems to be that religion (or perhaps theism) has
some especially close connection with morality. Perhaps the thought is that
a theist is more likely to be a moral person than a non-theist; perhaps it is
that a reflective theist will be some sort of moral expert with a hot line to
God.

The idea that theism and morality go hand in hand, and that atheism and
immorality go hand in hand has a long history. We can pick up the story in
the seventeenth century with a remark by Locke. His *A Letter Concerning
Toleration* is a plea for (an extremely limited kind of) religious toleration.
Among those who would be *denied* toleration by Locke's criterion are atheists, of whom Locke says:

> those are not at all to be tolerated who deny the being of a God.
> Promises, covenants, and oaths, which are the bonds of human
> society, can have no hold upon an atheist. The taking away of God,
> though but even in thought, dissolves all.

(Locke 1955: 52)

128

Rousseau in the eighteenth century continues the same line of thought in *Emile*: 'If the divinity does not exist [he writes], it is only the wicked man who reasons, and the good man is nothing but a fool' (Rousseau 1991: 292). Although Rousseau says '*if*' God does not exist, it is clear that he was not himself in any doubt about the matter. His thought is that it is *because* God exists that morality is not an illusion.

A similar thought recurs in the nineteenth century with Dostoievsky's remark that 'If God is dead, everything is permitted'. Dostoievsky of course was convinced that God was *not* dead, and that not everything was permitted. But he clearly thought that whether there was such a thing as morality depended on whether God existed. His point was to underline how catastrophic from a moral point it would be if God did not exist.

It is not theists alone who have accepted the dependence of morality on God. The atheist Sartre gives the maxim a clear endorsement in his book *Existentialism and Humanism*. To elaborate on the quotation at the head of this chapter:

> The existentialist . . . finds it extremely embarrassing that God does not exist, for there disappears with him all possibility of finding values in an intelligible heaven. There can no longer be any good a priori, since there is no infinite and perfect consciousness to think it. It is nowhere written that 'the good' exists, that one must be honest or must not lie, since we are now upon the plane where there are only men . . . Everything is indeed permitted if God does not exist, and man is in consequence forlorn, for he cannot find anything to depend upon either within or outside himself.
>
> (Sartre 1970: 33–4)

The task of this chapter, then, is to examine the relations between morality and the existence of God, and to see if we can find any argument arising from moral considerations which increases the likelihood of God's existence.

God as our creator

Some authors have maintained that because God is our creator, we owe special duties to him. Life, it is said, is a wonderful gift which God has made to us. That life is a wonderful gift is evidenced (so it is claimed) by the fact that the enormous majority of people who are alive are glad that they were born, are glad that they are still alive, and are prepared to struggle hard to stay alive, even when the conditions of their existence seem terrible to the rest of us. God not only gives us this much-valued gift of life – it is by his constantly operating power of keeping everything in existence that we are kept alive from day to day. Without this constantly exerting sustaining power, the whole universe, including us, would collapse into non-existence.

At the very least then (it may be argued) we owe God a duty of gratitude for such a gift.

This line of thought, natural though it is for theism, is highly suspect. In the first place, the very idea of life being a *gift* is incoherent. If A is to make a gift to B, then A and B must both already exist. So if the gift is meant to be the gift of *life*, to whom is the gift made? Either we exist already, in which case we already have what the gift is supposed to give us; or we do not yet exist, in which case there is no recipient for the alleged gift. Either way, the thought that life is a gift makes no sense.

This objection does not show that God did not create us; but it does show that the idea of a *duty of gratitude*, which makes sense if we are thinking in terms of much-valued gift, also makes no sense in this context. The point is not that we cannot have a duty of gratitude to God, but that our having been brought into existence cannot be a reason for gratitude. The reason would have to be some supposed benefit which God had rendered us after we were already in existence.[1]

Suppose, then, that the theist grants that there is an incoherence in feeling gratitude for having been brought into existence, and focuses rather on God's allowing or enabling us to continue in existence, moment by moment, day by day, year by year. Assuming that this is indeed a benefit to us, then it is certainly possible to feel gratitude for it, and perhaps such a feeling is morally required.

But again, this line of thought proves very weak. Although the fact that most people are so eager to stay alive suggests that they do think that being alive is preferable to being dead, we might wonder whether gratitude is the appropriate emotion. For so many lives contain so much pain and suffering – negative features which on the face of it God could have prevented. In such a circumstance, it might well seem that resentment is the more appropriate emotion. Even if God has given *something* valuable, if he could so easily have given something so very much more valuable, it is less clear that gratitude is the right emotion. The appropriateness of gratitude is a function not just of the benefit that accrues to the beneficiary, but also of the degree of sacrifice which is made by the benefactor. It is far from clear how much gratitude we owe to someone who has brought us a benefit at no cost to himself, and who could, also with no cost to himself, have brought us a very much greater benefit. This is a thought which clearly could reasonably cross the mind of someone born with some handicap, such as blindness; but it is also a thought which would understandably cross the mind of anyone whose life turns out as less than wonderful. However, this line of thought raises the large issue of how the existence of evil in a world made by a perfect God is to be understood. We will return to this topic in Chapter 12.

Suppose, then, that we agree that God confers very great benefits on humankind, and that gratitude is the morally fitting response. Given this much, it follows at once that part of our moral duties depends upon the existence of God: you cannot owe a duty of gratitude to a being who does not exist. But establishing this falls a very long way short of anything that would support the dependence of morality on God. In the first place, the truth of the claim 'If God has benefited us, we owe him a debt of gratitude' could hardly be used as a reason for thinking that God exists. The original claim that we do owe a debt of gratitude to God presupposes that God exists, but does not give a reason for thinking that he does exist. Second, there is a large difference between showing (the truism) that duties to God presuppose the existence of God, and showing that morality of any kind presupposes the existence of God. The most that the theist has shown is the claim 'If you are benefited, then gratitude is a morally fitting response'. She has done nothing to show that this claim derives its truth from God, or that had God willed things differently, hostility or indifference would have been the morally fitting response to benefits. In other words, it leaves completely open the possibility that moral values are wholly independent of God: perhaps they can exist even if he does not exist, and they can be known even if he is not known.

God as moral expert: the *Euthyphro* dilemma

A prima facie more promising line of thought focuses on one of God's defining features, his omniscience. If he is omniscient, then he is an infallible expert in every field. For every domain of enquiry, it will be true that if God thinks that something is so, then it is so; and if it is so, then God will think that it is so. In particular, in the moral domain, if God says that something is morally right or is morally wrong, it will follow that it *is* morally right or wrong. God's moral infallibility would be one case of his general infallibility; and his general infallibility would be a consequence of his omniscience, a quality he has by definition. So (the argument would continue) we have grounds for accepting the following claim:

(A) Something is morally right/wrong if and only if God says so.

Thus, according to this line of argument, morality is shown to be dependent on God in virtue of one of his defining features. So, from our prior assurance of the reality of morality, it would follow that God exists.

This is a not uncommon line of thought, and is perhaps initially seductive. But it is mistaken all the same. We need to distinguish two interpretations of claim (A). On the first, the claim says something true (if God exists), but not in a way that shows that morality is dependent on God in the relevant sense; on the second, it *would* make morality dependent on God, but in a self-defeating kind of way.

Let us initially take the first interpretation. It makes the assumption that moral judgements about right and wrong can be true or false, and hence are possible objects of knowledge, and hence fall within the scope of God's omniscience. Some philosophers would want to challenge this assumption, and argue that moral judgements cannot be true or false because, for example, they are really imperative and not assertive in form; or because they are mere expressions of emotion, not statements of fact. But let us leave that complication on one side, and assume with the argument that moral judgements can be straightforwardly true or false. The problem is that far from making morality depend on God, the first interpretation of (A) presupposes the exact opposite. For if you are to be an expert in anything, your expertise must consist minimally in your getting the right answers, where the answers are right independently of your thinking that they are. The rightness of your answer consists in a correspondence between on the one hand what you say (or think), and on the other the range of facts about which you are the expert. And that means that there has to be a realm of facts independent of your beliefs in virtue of which your beliefs count as true and you count as an expert. So on this first interpretation, God can be a moral expert only if moral values exist independently of God. More specifically, even if there were no God, torture would still be wrong, and kindliness would still be morally admirable, for these are truths which are not created by God, and hence do not depend on him for their truth.

On the second interpretation of claim (A), God would not be an expert about a pre-existing set of moral facts. Rather, he would be *creating* the moral facts by divine fiat. Things would become right or wrong solely in virtue of the fact that he had prescribed that we were to do them or refrain from doing them. He would not *accurately report* what is antecedently good and bad, but simply *stipulate* what is good and bad. Just as Parliamentary statutes create the legality and illegality of kinds of actions, and do not simply report on what is antecedently legal or illegal, so God's edicts would create right and wrong, and not simply report (infallibly) on what is right and wrong.

This second interpretation would certainly allow us to say that if morality exists, that is some ground for thinking that God exists (not yet a compelling ground, since we have not yet been given a reason for thinking that God's edicts are the only possible source of morality). But the problem with this interpretation comes when we trace out its consequences. Three consequences in particular are damaging. The first is that this interpretation implies that if God had chosen differently, then, for example, torture would have been morally admirable and kindliness morally wrong (cf. if Parliament had chosen differently, shoplifting would not be a crime, but listening to the radio would have been). That has rightly seemed to many theists an implausible consequence, and has made them shy away from this interpretation.

Could this first objection be blocked by objecting 'But the thought that God could have made such a choice is absurd. It is not possible that God could have chosen to make torture morally right'? It is difficult to see that this objection can work. For why is it impossible that God could have made such a choice? If the answer is that God is by definition morally perfect, and *could not* make evil choices, we seem to be back with the first interpretation. For the answer is assuming that, independently of God's choices, torture is wrong, and that *therefore* a morally perfect being would not condone it. But if we are meant to take seriously the thought that before God makes his choice, torture is morally neutral, then what reason is there for saying that it is impossible for him to make this choice? And anyway, how is this limitation on his choice to be reconciled with another of his defining attributes, his omnipotence?

Second, on this second interpretation of (A), it is hard to see what becomes of the claim that God is morally perfect. We might initially have thought that moral perfection was a very substantive property whose possession by any being would be a ground for us to admire that being. But if morality is simply defined in terms of God's choices, then to say that he is perfect will amount only to the tautology that God chooses what he chooses. We will have deprived ourselves of any means of praising God for his perfection.

The third and ultimately most damaging consequence of the second interpretation is this. Suppose that we accept that God creates morality by edict, and hence could have created differently, so that, for example, torture was right and kindliness wrong. The puzzle would then be to see why we should think that discovering that something is morally right/wrong gives us any reason to do or refrain from doing the action in question.

To understand this objection, we need to backtrack a little. Many philosophers have thought that one of the defining features of a moral system is that it is essentially concerned with what people *do*. A system of judgements that was unrelated to behaviour could not count as a *moral* system at all. How is this connection between moral judgements on the one hand and action on the other to be understood? The standard answer is that moral judgements by themselves give us *reasons for acting*. In this claim, the phrase 'by themselves' is important. If you tell me that the building is on fire, and I accept what you say, that fact *by itself* gives me no reason to leave the building. It is only in conjunction with my desire not to be burnt that the information gives me a reason to act, i.e. to leave. If I had a different desire, for example, to be burnt to death (perhaps I wish to make a martyr of myself), then the very same information, in conjunction with that desire, gives me a reason to do the opposite, and to remain in the building. But if you tell me that it would be morally wrong for me to stay, and I accept what you say, then (so the conventional wisdom goes), by that fact alone, I have a reason to leave the building. Morality gives me reasons for acting that are independent of my desires, and that can even go against my desires.

Some philosophers go further than this and claim that moral reasons are always *overriding* reasons, that they always take precedence over non-moral reasons. So if I have a moral reason to do x (I have promised you that I will, and one ought to keep one's promises), and a non-moral reason not to do x (it is going to inconvenience me), then I have a better reason to do x than not.

We do not have to endorse this more extreme thesis about the dominance of moral reasons in order to accept the weaker claim that acceptance of the rightness or wrongness of an action always gives one *a* reason to do or refrain from doing the action; and the weaker claim is sufficient to undermine the idea that God creates morality. For it follows that not just *any* set of edicts laid down by God could count as moral, since not just any set of edicts could by themselves give us a reason for acting on them. It is only if they have a certain *content* rather than a certain *origin* that by themselves they give us reason to act. If God had decreed that (say) everyone should stand on their head for one minute every morning, then that could not be a *moral* requirement, for there is no reason for me to obey this edict.

But now the theist might object that surely we do have reason for acting on God's edicts no matter what their content; for since God is omniscient he will know infallibly whether we have followed those edicts, and since he is omnipotent, he will have the power to reward the obedient and punish the disobedient. Furthermore, this is a motive to action (a motive for being moral) which can move only someone who believes in God. For the atheist, who does not believe in God, the threat of divine punishment and the promise of divine reward are empty. Thus, the theist can argue that she can defend the claim that morality is created by God, that morality by itself can give us reason to act, and that we have reason to be moral only if we are theists.

But again, this way of bringing God into the realm of morality fails on closer inspection. For there is a contrast between actions which are in accordance with morality, and those which are done *because* they are moral. We draw a distinction between the cashier who is honest *only* because she knows that if she isn't, she will be found out and sacked, and the cashier who is honest because that is the morally right way to behave. The first person would steal if she thought that she could get away with it; the second would not steal, even if she thought that she could get away with it. The actions of the first cashier are in accordance with morality, but she is not moved to action by morality, and she is not acting on moral reasons. The second cashier by contrast is moved to action by moral reasons.

If we accept this distinction, it implies that someone who follows a course of action only because it pays her in terms of divine rewards and punishments is like the first cashier: she is not genuinely moral. So if morality were no more than a set of divine edicts, then although we would have prudential reasons for following them, the edicts could supply us with no distinctively moral reasons for acting. And given that it is a defining feature of morality that it *does* supply moral reasons for acting, it will follow that the set of divine edicts could not constitute a morality after all. It is in this sense that the second interpretation of claim (A) above is self-defeating: if God 'creates morality' or 'is the source of morality', we have no reason to regard what he has created as *morality*. More accurately, the mere fact that God has invented a set of rules gives us no reason to regard the rules as *morality*.

The line of argument which we have rehearsed is in effect the one that arises from the so-called Euthyphro dilemma. The dilemma, which gets its name because it was first posed in Plato's dialogue called the *Euthyphro*, arises from the question 'Do the gods love pious things because they are pious, or are things pious merely because the gods love them?'. Answering 'yes' to either question gives us the two horns of the dilemma. If we take the first horn (corresponding to the first interpretation (A) above), then we are admitting that there is a source of value independent of the preferences of the gods. If we take the second horn (corresponding to the second interpretation of (A) above), then we have to accept (i) that what is now pious would have been impious if the gods had had a different set of preferences, (ii) that we cannot praise the gods by calling them pious, and (iii) that discovering something to be pious gives us no reason to do it.

The Kantian argument

Kant is another author who believes that the existence of God is a kind of presupposition of morality. In his critique of the ontological, the cosmological and the teleological argument (in *The Critique of Pure Reason*), he famously argued that there could be no proof of the existence of God by theoretical reason. In claiming this, he was relying on a distinction between theoretical reason and practical reason (his terminology). Theoretical reasoning is reasoning about what is the case; its conclusions are assertions (i.e. can be true or false); and ideally these assertions will be true. Practical reasoning is reasoning about what to do; its conclusions are prescriptions or imperatives; and ideally these prescriptions will tell you the best thing to do (the best, in either a moral or a non-moral sense). Having argued that theoretical reason cannot provide any grounds for a belief in God, Kant went on to claim in his *Critique of Practical Reason* that there is a sort of argument for the existence of God from the existence of morality. He seems to have thought that this would not be an exercise of theoretical reason, on the grounds that it is an argument from the presuppositions of one kind of practical reason (i.e. from the presuppositions of moral reason). In reasoning thus, he was surely mistaken: there can be a theoretical argument which takes as its premises the existence of moral reasons. But whatever the merits of Kant's own classification of his argument as practical rather than theoretical, his argument from morality to God is worth considering.

He claims that what morality requires is not merely the existence of virtue in as widespread a form as possible, nor merely that there is as much happiness in the world as possible. It requires that the happiness in the world should be proportional to the virtue. A world which contained X amount of virtue and Y amount of happiness in which the virtuous were extremely unhappy and the wicked were extremely happy, would not be as good a world as one which contained the same amounts of virtue and wickedness but in which it was the virtuous who were happy and the wicked unhappy. So what morality requires is not merely the promotion of virtue itself (which Kant, roughly speaking, identifies with having the right motives, and not with performing the right actions) – it requires also the proportioning of happiness to virtue. Since morality requires such a proportioning, it must (says Kant) at least be *possible* to achieve this. It cannot be a requirement of morality that we are under an obligation to do something which is beyond our power. This link between what we ought to do and what we can do is summarised in the famous slogan '*ought* implies *can*'. Next, Kant observes that there is nothing in the natural world as we know it to guarantee such a correspondence of morality and virtue. On the contrary, there seems to be very little correlation between the distribution of virtue and the distribution of happiness. Since there is no *natural* connection between virtue and happiness, Kant says that there must be *supernatural* connection. There must be some supernatural power which is able to achieve this correspondence, and this power is then identified with God. Thus we find Kant saying:

> in the necessary endeavour after the highest good, such a connection [i.e. a correspondence between virtue and happiness] is postulated as necessary: we *should* seek to further the highest good (which therefore must be at least possible). Therefore also the existence is postulated of a cause of the whole of nature, itself distinct from nature, which contains the ground of the exact coincidence of happiness with morality . . . Therefore the highest good is possible in the world only on the supposition of a supreme cause of nature which has a causality corresponding to the moral intention . . . As a consequence, the postulate of the possibility of a highest derived good (the best world) is at the same time the postulate of the reality of a highest original good, namely, the existence of God. Now it was our duty to promote the highest good; and it is not merely our privilege but a necessity connected with duty as a requisite to presuppose the possibility of this highest good . . . Therefore it is morally necessary to assume the existence of God.
>
> (Kant 1949: 228)

If we try to summarise the argument in a perspicacious form, we get the following:

(1) Morality requires us to try and achieve the highest good, the proportioning of happiness to virtue (premise).
(2) 'Ought' implies 'can' (premise). So:
(3) It must be possible to achieve the highest good (from (1) and (2)). But:
(4) The highest good cannot be achieved by beings like us (premise). So:
(5) There must be some supernatural being who is able to guarantee the correspondence of virtue (from (3) and (4)). So:
(6) God exists (from (5)).

But if this is indeed a fair statement of what Kant is saying, the argument looks less than cogent. In the first place, (3) does not follow from (1) and (2). The fact that morality requires us to try and achieve something does not imply that it is in practice possible for us to achieve it. There can be, for example, counsels of perfection, which hold up some mode of life as an ideal to aim at, without it being supposed that it is in practice possible for us ever to attain the ideal. Within Christian morality, such prescriptions as 'Love your neighbour as yourself' or 'Be Christ-like' might be examples of such counsels. It is no doubt important for a moral system also to contain prescriptions which can be fully complied with (such as 'Do not torture', 'Do not rape' etc.), but that is no reason for thinking that a moral system cannot also contain what I am here calling counsels of perfection.

But even without resorting to the idea of counsels of perfection, we can see that (1) and (2) do not imply (3). The most that (1) and (2) imply is that it must be possible for us to *try* and achieve the highest good. The assumption in (3) that our efforts must be successful is unwarranted.

It may be that (1) does not adequately capture what Kant intends. It is true that he says *at least* (1). For example, he says explicitly that 'we should seek to further the highest good' and 'it was our duty to promote the highest good'. So he is certainly committed at least to (1). But perhaps he means more than (1).

To bring this out, compare the following two worlds: in world A, everyone has done as much as possible to bring about the highest good and they have been successful: happiness is distributed in accordance with virtue. In world B, everyone has done as much as possible to bring about the highest good and they have been largely unsuccessful: the wicked are happy and the virtuous miserable. Now in respect of (1), the two worlds are of equal value, inasmuch as both are worlds in which everyone has done what morality requires them to do. But we might well think that in spite of this, world A is better than world B (because, for example, in world A people have got their just deserts, and in world B they have not). Perhaps Kant's point is that if morality is not to seem a sham and illusion, then *ultimately* the virtuous and wicked alike must obtain their just deserts. If that is what Kant means then (1) ought to be replaced by something like: (1a) For morality to have any point, the highest good must ultimately be achieved:

happiness and virtue must be proportioned, people must get their just deserts.

But there are several problems with the idea that (1a) is nearer to what Kant has in mind. In the first place, one of the striking features of Kant's moral philosophy is his belief in the autonomy of morality. One aspect of this belief is that for genuinely moral action, the motive must be disinterested. The agent who acts because she hopes to be rewarded by future happiness, perhaps in a post-mortem state, is not acting morally. She is acting morally only if her sole motive in doing what she does is to do the right thing. It is not clear that this rather austere conception of the preconditions of moral action can be combined with the claim that morality is pointless unless it pays those who follow its precepts.

Second, even if Kant could consistently claim (1a) as well as (1), it seems evident that the original argument is not improved by adding (1a) to (1), or replacing (1) by (1a). At best, (1a) would generate a different argument, as follows:

(1a) For morality to have any point, the highest good must ultimately be achieved (premise).
(4) The highest good cannot be achieved by beings like us (premise). So:
(5) There must be some supernatural being who is able to guarantee the correspondence of virtue (from (1a) and (4)). So:
(6) For morality to have any point, there must be a God (from (5)).

Is this argument any improvement on the first? It hardly seems so, for three reasons. First, (1a) is highly contestable. There could be reasons for thinking that morality had a point, other than the achievement of the highest good. You may well think that there are other virtues than justice, other goods than ensuring that people get what they deserve. Perhaps benevolence is as important as justice. If so, there could be a point to morality even if very little progress is made thereby to the achievement of the highest good. Second, even if you think that justice is the supreme virtue (even, perhaps, the only virtue), you might well think that morality has a point even if it does not ensure the *complete* achievement of the highest good. If, for example, morality makes a substantial contribution to the achievement of the highest good, and no alternative institution could make a greater contribution, you would have a good reason to reject (1a). Perhaps all that is ruled out by (1a) is this combination of views: achieving the highest good is the most important task for humans, and the institution of morality makes either a negligible contribution to that task, or a very much smaller contribution than would be made by some alternative institution. Neither view seems plausible by itself, and their conjunction is therefore even less plausible.

Third, the conclusion of the argument is so weak. If one is interested in lines of argument for the existence of God, (6) gives us at best a conditional reason for accepting theism. But (6) naturally requires supplementing with a further premise, namely:

(7) Morality *does* have a point.

The difficulty is to see what reasons there could be for accepting (7) which were not also reasons for rejecting (6). For the most natural way of seeking to defend (7) would be to show that in some way, morality leaves people better off. Of course, this claim would need to be spelt out carefully. It cannot mean, for example, that morality leaves people *morally* better off, on pain of vicious circularity. (The question would then arise 'And what is the point of being *morally* better off?'.) And it would have to allow for the fact that for some individuals, morality does not leave them better off: as a consequence of doing the morally right thing, they end up worse off than if they had yielded to temptation.[2] But with these and other similar qualifications added, it looks as if the most plausible defence of (7) would by the same token show that (6) was false. And if that is so, then the conclusion must be that the modified Kantian argument is no better than the unmodified argument as a way of inferring the existence of God from the existence of a morality.

In spite of these serious shortcomings, however, the Kantian line of thought has continued to find modern defenders; and in the next section we will consider the views of one of his most recent theistic defenders.

Ward's account

One modern writer who has sought to retread a quasi-Kantian path is Keith Ward. In his *The Divine Image*, he tells us that:

> [a Christian] believes that moral rules are based on the will of God . . . So one thing I want to try to do is to show morality can be founded on the will of God (p. viii) . . . when a Christian says he ought to do something, that it is his duty, he means that it is God's will (p. 1) . . . For a Christian, duty is regarded as God's will . . . God does create the moral law, but not arbitrarily or contingently (p. 2).
>
> (Ward 1976: viii, 1–2)

Similar thoughts are expressed in his later work, *Rational Theology and the Creativity of God*. There, he asserts that:

> For an atheist, there is no objective value which is set before humanity as a possible goal . . . nothing besides oneself determines the course of life one should try to take in the world . . . a person who has such beliefs . . . can still care about the sufferings of others

and work to alleviate them. [But] what it would be irrational for him to do would be to commit his life wholly to the pursuit of an ideal as in any way a 'true' goal of human life.

(Ward 1982: 179)

The picture that emerges is that if there is no God, there are no objective values, and that it would be irrational to think there were any 'true' goals for human actions. This implies that if there are objective values, or rational goals for human action, then there is a God.

Ward tells us that theists and 'liberal secular moralists' can agree on the human desires which ought to be fostered by a moral system, and he then continues:

But without a God to give them objective validity and overriding authority they are transmuted into the sorts of desires that one would choose in the purely hypothetical situation where one was a fully rational agent among others . . . All that is left is a return to the absurdity of moral commitment in an amoral universe . . . or the sort of compromise with reality which makes morality a mere dream of what might have been.

(Ward 1982: 176)

Even more explicitly, Ward remarks:

Things are not . . . good, independently of God . . . [D]oes God make any difference to morality at all? I believe that he makes the most important difference of all, in that only the existence of God can give morality an objective foundation and intelligible fulfilment.

(op. cit. p. 177)

The overall conclusion, then, is that although God is not necessary for the existence of every kind of moral system, he is presupposed by a morality which is to be 'objective', or which is to have a 'rational foundation'.

Unfortunately, Ward is less forthcoming about *how* God gives morality 'an objective validity' or a 'foundation'. It is clear that Ward rejects one standard line of thought, the one that makes God the arbitrary legislator of what is good: 'One cannot satisfactorily ground the finite universe in a God whose values are wholly contingent, like Calvin's God, who could choose anything at all as a value, at the fiat of his arbitrary will' (op. cit. p. 172).

Ward does seem to endorse a second way of linking God and morality (see for example op. cit. pp. 174–6). He suggests that humans have been created by God, and that as part of this creative process, God has given them a certain human nature. Because they have this nature, certain forms of conduct allow humans to flourish, and other forms of conduct lead to their non-flourishing. Ward supplies no details of what he has in mind, but the following might be an example of what he means. In some species (for example, among fish), the offspring can survive and flourish with no help from the parents. In humans, this is not so. Babies and young children can survive only if there are fairly strong bonds between children and their parents (or other adults who are *in loco parentis*). Given, then, that we are humans and not fish, parental care is a virtue in us, in a way in which it would not be in fish. Our God-given nature supplies a 'rational' and 'objective' basis for regarding parental care as a virtue.

But this line of thought is in fact much too weak to sustain the conclusion which Ward embraces. On this account of things, what makes morality objective and rational (if anything does) is human nature, *whatever its source*. Of course, if theism is correct, human nature derives in some way from God. But it would not be its divine origin that enabled it to play the role of moral foundation; rather it would be its content. *Any* species with a nature like ours, wherever that nature came from, would have good reason to value parental concern; and that is a claim that has nothing to do with the existence of God. So no appeal to human nature as God-given is going to support the conclusion that morality is the product of God's will.

Ward also embraces a third line of thought about the relations between God and morality, a view which rather surprisingly makes the existence of God irrelevant to morality. He tells us that true moral propositions are *necessarily* true.

> Morality must connect with rational necessity, because its demands cannot be arbitrary or contingent; what is right could not possibly have been wrong (. . .). What makes [moral] statements true is . . . some fact which is objective and necessary, since moral truths are true by necessity.
>
> (op. cit. pp. 176–7)

But this really gives the game away. If we are asking of something which could have been different why it is as it is, perhaps one possible answer is to be given in terms of God: 'It is thus-and-so because God chose to make it like that'. The implication is that if he had not so chosen then the object would not have been as in fact it is. But if we ask of something which *could not* have been different why it is as it is, there is simply no work for God's choice to perform: it is as it is, *because there is no other way it could have been*; and there is no other way it could have been, *whether or not there is a God*. That is part of the implication of saying that it is necessarily as it is. Thus we do not need God's activity to explain why (say) 2 + 2 = 4. Nothing that God could have done could have brought it about that '2 + 2 = 4' is false; hence nothing that he could have done could have brought it about that '2 + 2 = 4' is true. Similarly, if (as Ward here commits himself to saying) 'Cruelty is a vice' is necessarily true, then nothing that God could have done could have brought it about that cruelty is a virtue; and hence nothing that God could have done could have brought it about that cruelty is a vice.

In summary, Ward's account appears confused and inconsistent. He starts by insisting that God supplies a foundation for morality; he rejects one account of the God/morality relationship, even though it would make intelligible *how* God is supposed to have this role. He accepts an alternative account which invokes human nature, even though this leaves no role for God. And he then accepts a third account, which treats moral statements as necessarily true, even although this again gives God no role to play in providing a foundation for morality. Our conclusion must be that Ward gives us no reason at all to accept his claim quoted above that 'only the existence of God can give morality an objective foundation'. Rather, he accepts a view which is directly incompatible with this claim.

Trethowan and 'apprehending morality as apprehending God'

So far we have concentrated on authors who try to construct an *argument* from morality to God. But perhaps this is to misunderstand the terrain. One author who thinks so is Illtyd Trethowan. Trethowan claims that an awareness of moral obligations *is* an awareness of God – not just *is grounds for* inferring the existence of God, but *is* an awareness of God. However implausible this claim might be, it appears to be exactly what Trethowan has in mind:

> To say that people are worthwhile, that they have value in themselves is to say that there is something about them which makes a demand upon us, that we *ought* to make them a part of our project, identify ourselves with them in some sort . . . I propose to say that an awareness of obligation is an awareness of God.
>
> (Trethowan 1970: 84)

And again:

> [I am not] building an *argument* on the facts of the moral consciousness, but pointing to the presence of God as what we are really apprehending even when we might describe ourselves simply as somehow bound to uphold certain principles.
>
> (Trethowan 1974: 21)

But Trethowan faces a dilemma here. He says that he is simply 'pointing' to the presence of God. Of course he is not literally pointing – what he means is that he is *asserting* that when people feel committed to certain moral principles, they are apprehending God. And in relation to such an assertion, of course we want to know what grounds there are for thinking that it is true, in other words what supporting argument Trethowan has. His disarmingly frank admission that he has none should not blind us to the fact that he *needs* one, if he is to give (either to himself or to anyone else) any reason to think that his assertion is true.

Of course he can win a merely verbal victory here by saying as he does in the first quotation above that he 'proposes' to call an awareness of obligation an awareness of God. But what grounds are there for thinking that this is not an arbitrary and whimsical piece of linguistic revision? I might 'propose to say' that an awareness of obligation is an awareness of Zeus, or Father Christmas, or my grandfather. That would tell you that I was linguistically deviant – but it would not tell you anything at all about Zeus or Father Christmas or my grandfather. Again I could 'propose to say' that an awareness of hunger or of boredom is an awareness of God. This too would be a pointless piece of linguistic revisionism. The attempt to by-pass the need for an argument to take us from morality as premise to God as conclusion is a failure.

The supervenience of the moral

An altogether more serious attempt to derive the existence of God from the existence of morality can be found in the concept of supervenience. In brief, the argument here is that moral properties supervene on non-moral properties, that the best explanation for this is the existence of a supreme being, and that therefore God exists. What does this actually mean?

We can begin to unpack the argument by getting clear about the concept of supervenience. One set of properties supervenes on a second set when the properties are so related that there could not be a difference in the first set without a difference in the second set, but there could be a difference in the second set without a difference in the first set. As an example, consider the distinction applied to a painting. We might distinguish between two sorts of things we say about pictures, or two sets of properties which they have. One sort would concern the precise distribution of pigment across the canvas – which colour of pigment had been applied with which degree of thickness, smoothness, etc., to which precise points and areas on the canvas. Clearly, the whole picture could be described in these terms. In principle, the description could be sufficiently precise for a physically exact replica of the original to be produced. The second sort of description would use such terms as 'harmonious', 'elegant', 'well-proportioned', 'sombre', etc. – terms of aesthetic appreciation. It would then surely be correct to say that the aesthetic properties supervene upon the pigmental properties. Two paintings that were indistinguishable in terms of their pigmental properties would be indistinguishable in terms of their aesthetic properties. It could not be the case, for example, that one painting was elegant and well-proportioned and the other was not. Once the pigmental properties have been fixed, that fixes also the aesthetic properties. The aesthetic properties are in some sense of the word

143

'generated' by or dependent on the pigmental properties. But it would be possible to change the pigmental properties without changing the aesthetic properties. If the distribution of pigment was changed, the resulting picture might still be, for example, elegant and well-proportioned.

This distinction between supervening properties on the one hand, and the properties on which they supervene on the other, can be applied in the area of morality. The thought is that we can divide the properties of an action into the moral (such as whether the action is cruel or kind, honourable or dishonourable, the fulfilment of a duty or an act of supererogation, etc.) and the non-moral (such as who performed the action, why, when, where and how she performed it, and what its consequences were). Then, in parallel with the case of the picture discussed above, it seems plausible to say that the moral properties supervene on the non-moral properties. Once the non-moral features of the action have been fixed, that fixes the moral features too. The moral features are somehow generated by the non-moral ones. So there could not be two actions which were alike in all their non-moral properties but which differed in their moral status. Thus, if an action which is an act of torture is wrong, then any action which was similar in all non-moral respects to that act of torture would also have to be morally wrong. And if an action which is an act of maximising happiness is morally right, then all actions which were like that action in their non-moral features would also have to be morally right. But by contrast, two actions which differed in their non-moral properties might have the same moral properties. Two actions, for example, could be alike in that both were extremely cruel, but be entirely different in their non-moral properties.

Let us accept for the sake of argument that moral properties do supervene on non-moral properties in this sense. What can be made of this fact? How can it be used by a theist to lend support to a belief in God? Here we have to come back to the fact (mentioned above) that it is an essential feature of every system that can count as a moral system that it gives us reasons for acting, even against our own desires. Let us label these 'contra-want reasons'. Let us grant for the sake of argument that it is true not only that moral features give us contra-want reasons, but also that *only* moral features can do this. It is admittedly true, as noted above, that non-moral features of a situation can contribute to giving us reasons to do or refrain from doing certain actions. For example, if I discover that a certain course of action will be hideously painful for me, that contributes to my having a reason not to do it; and if it will be extremely enjoyable, that contributes to giving me a reason to do it. (Remember we are not talking here of overriding or compelling reasons – these are reasons that may be overridden by other considerations. We are saying only more weakly that these considerations provide *a* reason for acting. It is only in the absence of any countervailing reason that the reason would be a strong one and that I would be irrational not to act on it.) But when these non-moral features (being painful, being enjoyable) give me reasons for acting, they do so because they connect with my desires. I have a reason not to do what will be painful for me, because I desire not to inflict pain on myself; I have a reason to do what is enjoyable because I desire to enjoy myself. So, non-moral features of a situation can give us reasons for and against certain actions. What is distinctive about the reasons provided by moral features is that they can be *contra*-want reasons. If something is my duty, that by itself gives me a reason to do it; and it is a reason for me to do it, even if I do not want to do it.

Suppose that we now combine these two facts of the supervenience of the moral, and of the power of morality to supply contra-want reasons. In saying that the moral supervenes on the non-moral, we are saying that features which supply contra-want reasons supervene on features which do not provide such reasons. And the puzzle is to see how the realm which we initially envisage in terms of non-moral features which do *not* supply contra-want reasons can somehow generate a moral realm which *does* supply contra-want reasons. It is here that God appears in the argument. The thought is that the dependence of the supervenient moral features supplying contra-want reasons, on the underlying non-moral features which do not supply contra-want reasons, is so metaphysically strange that only God could have brought it about. Mackie, who expounds the argument although he later goes on to reject it, puts it like this:

> objective intrinsically prescriptive features, supervening upon natural ones, constitute so odd a cluster of qualities and relations that they are most unlikely to have arisen in the ordinary course of events, without an all-powerful god to create them. If, then, there are such intrinsically prescriptive objective values, they make the existence of a god more probable than it would have been without them.
>
> (Mackie 1982: 115–16)

(What Mackie is here calling 'objective intrinsically prescriptive features' is what I called features which supply contra-want reasons; and what he calls 'natural' features are what I called non-moral features.)

The argument has been convoluted, so it will be helpful to set it out in numbered steps:

(1) Moral properties supervene on non-moral properties (premise).
(2) Moral properties supply contra-want reasons (premise).
(3) Non-moral properties do not supply contra-want reasons (premise).
(4) It is unlikely that (1), (2), and (3) would all be true unless they had been made true by an all-powerful god (premise). So:
(5) Probably there is an all-powerful god (conclusion).

What should we make of this argument (let us call it the supervenience argument)? It relies on four premises, and one inference from those four premises.

145

Clearly, then, it will be open to attack if any of the premises is false; or if, although the premises are true, they fail to support the conclusion. In fact, the inference to the conclusion looks to be secure, that is to say *if* the four premises are accepted, then the conclusion follows unproblematically. But should we accept the four premises?

Of the four, perhaps (3) is the least controversial, and can be accepted here without further discussion (although even (3) has been challenged in other contexts). More problematic is (4). We could quibble about why the god in (4) needs to be *all*-powerful, rather than just *very* powerful. But a more serious question to ask about (4) is why it should be thought *unlikely* that moral and non-moral properties should be related in the way described by the argument. Judgements of probability are always difficult to assess, but one standard assumption is that they are always relative to some evidence. So, relative to what evidence is it unlikely that moral and non-moral properties are related in this way? If we find (as we are here supposing that we do) that properties which give contra-want reasons supervene on properties which do not have this feature, then relative to what is it improbable that they are so related? And if the answer is 'Improbable relative to the assumption that there is no God', what grounds do we have for accepting *that* judgement? Why should it be improbable that in a godless universe, moral and non-moral features should be related in the way that the argument supposes? It is difficult to find any plausible reply to this question. But without a reply, we have no reason to accept premise (4), and hence no reason to accept the conclusion which follows from it. Of course, we might agree that there is a *puzzle* in understanding how the supervenience can hold. But the argument supplies no reason for thinking that the puzzle is made any easier to solve by postulating the existence of God.

That gives us, then, one line of attack on (4). A different line is supplied by Swinburne. He argues that it is a necessary truth that the supervenience holds. Using the 'possible worlds' terminology from Chapter 3, we can say that if being morally wrong supervenes on being (say) an act of torture, or more idiomatically, if it is true that torture is wrong, then this is a truth which is necessarily true. Not only is it true, it could not possibly have been false, no matter how different other things might have been. It is in this respect like $2 + 2 = 4$. But if it is necessarily true in this way, then (argues Swinburne) it cannot be improbable (in any possible world) that it is true. And if it is not improbable that it is true, then there is no warrant to postulate the existence of a powerful being who brought about this improbable state of affairs. Just as there is no need to invoke God as an explanation of why $2 + 2 = 4$, so there is no need to invoke God to explain why moral properties supervene on non-moral ones. They do so as a matter of absolute necessity.

Mackie himself supplies a third line of criticism. He accepts that if there are any moral properties at all, they would have to be as premises (1), (2) and (3) describe them. But, he says, moral properties would then be such metaphysically bizarre features, that it would be more plausible to say 'There cannot be any such features', than to say 'There are such features, so there must be a god' (see Mackie 1982: 117). This leads Mackie into his so-called 'error' theory of ethics, according to which morality as commonly conceived is an illusion. If this is right, then of course there is no sound argument from morality to God. Mackie's claim that morality is an illusion might be thought too high a price to pay for rejecting the conclusion of the argument from supervenience, but Mackie is able to show how the idea is more defensible than might at first sight appear.

There are, then, three lines of attack on premise (4) of the supervenience argument. But other premises in the argument are also open to challenge. For example, although we were earlier trying to make plausible the thought that it was an essential feature of morality that it supplies contra-want reasons, that too is an assumption which can be rejected. The assumption derives principally from the moral philosophy of Kant; and for those whose moral thinking derives from a different tradition (such as an Aristotelian way of thinking), the Kantian assumption can appear wholly dispensable. Geach, for example, has denied that *anything*, let alone morality, supplies contra-want reasons. In his view, all reasons for acting depend ultimately on the agent's own wants (see Geach 1969: 121). This would imply that for the person who did not want to act morally, the information that a particular action was immoral would supply no reason at all for him to refrain from performing that action. This seems a perfectly intelligible assumption, which in turn implies that premise (2) is false.

It seems then, that the argument from supervenience is an unpromising way of trying to raise the probability that God exists. It relies on two dubious premises ((2) and (4)); and the reality of the type of morality it presupposes can also be challenged.

What *does* morality rest on?

The comments above, someone might object, have been entirely negative. They have criticised attempts to show how morality rests on, or presupposes, or is derived from, God. But even if this or that particular attempt to articulate the derivation can be criticised, the theist can insist that there still remains a major question: how *can* morality be justified if not by invoking God? Is morality just a snare by which the weak try to entrap the strong, as some Nietzscheans imply? Is it just an instrument of class oppression, as some crude versions of Marxism maintain? Is the generous person ultimately just a fool? The argument from morality to God at least took seriously the need to answer 'no' to these questions. If we are going to reject that argument, how are we going to answer these questions?

One recent defender of theism, who claims that although the moral argument for God's existence is 'inconclusive', it could be on to something important, puts the point like this:

> The real question is whether, in naturalistic terms, such deeds [of moral heroism] can be *justified*, whether it is possible to explain why they are morally warranted. For it would seem that apart from God, such acts are irrational.
>
> (Davis 1997: 149)

The implication seems to be that even if theists have not been wholly successful in establishing that God is in some sense the source of morality, at least they have been struggling in the right direction, while naturalists (i.e. non-theists) have not even recognised that there is a problem.[3]

But this view of the situation would be mistaken. It would take us too far from our present concerns to explore the issue of a non-theistic 'justification' of morality. Part of the problem is that there is much disagreement over what morality is, and there is much disagreement over what a 'justification' would need to be like, or even whether a justification is needed. But without going into detail, and without endorsing either approach, we can note that there are at least two entirely secular accounts of morality which are plausible rivals to a God-based ethic. Both contract theories (of the kind found in such writers as Grice, Rawls, Richards and Gautier), and virtue theories (of the kind found in such writers as Foot and Hursthouse) offer, in one sense of the term, a secular 'justification' for deeds of moral heroism, however unwilling these authors might be to describe their reflections in such terms. So the idea that it is only theists who are taking seriously the need to answer questions about the rational underpinning of morality would be a mistake.

Not only are there non-theistic explorations of the 'justification' of morality: it is also the case, as we have seen, that not all theists think that the binding force of morality has anything to do with God, or with morality having in any sense a divine origin. As we have seen, Swinburne rejects such a claim entirely, remarking: 'I cannot see *any* force in an argument to the existence of God from the existence of morality' (Swinburne 1979: 179, italics added). There could scarcely be a more forthright rejection of the atheist Sartre's insistence that morality does depend on the existence of God, as expressed in the remark quoted at the start of this chapter.

The conclusion we should draw, then, is that there is no currently available justification for morality in terms of God, or his wishes or commands; and that there is no reason to think that any such justification *must* come from an appeal to God. In the light of this, the moral argument for God's existence must be judged worthless.

Further reading

The Kantian argument appears in Kant (1949), with a good commentary by Beck (1960). Quinn (1978) gives a subtle and extended defence of the idea that God underpins morality. Idziak in Quinn and Taliaferro (1997) supplies a brief overview of the same area, with a useful bibliography. For references to some earlier writers who have endorsed some version of the moral argument, see the bibliography in Hick (1964).

8

———•◦⌒◦•———

Religious experience

The spiritual life justifies itself to those who live it; but what can we say to those who do not understand? This, at least, we can say, that it is a life whose experiences are proved real to their possessor, because they remain with him when brought closest into contact with the objective realities of life . . . These highest experiences which I have had of God's presence have been rare and brief – flashes of consciousness which have compelled me to exclaim with surprise – God is *here*! – or conditions of exultation and insight, less intense, and only gradually passing away . . . I find that after every questioning and test, they stand out today as the most real experiences of my life, and experiences which have explained and justified and unified all past experiences and all past growth

(James 1963: 283)

Introduction

It is very rare to find reports of anyone who is converted to theism from a position of agnosticism or atheism purely on the basis of religious experiences. The convictions which religious experiences characteristically produce are of a different kind. In some cases, someone who already accepts the existence of God finds additional confirmatory evidence for their theism in the occurrence of specific kinds of experience. Typically they find confirmatory evidence for some belief more specific than theism itself – for example, a belief that they have won God's favour and will be among the elect. However, it is clearly possible to raise the question whether any of these experiences do by themselves constitute evidence for the existence of God, and if so whether the evidence is strong enough by itself to make it more probable than not that God exists.

Proponents of the view that religious experience can significantly raise the probability that God exists (let us label them the experientialists) often insist that the appeal to religious experience is not simply one more *argument* or *piece of reasoning* for the existence of God, akin to those which we have already looked at. Rather, they insist, it is not an *argument* at all. They *contrast* knowledge of God based on religious experience, with knowledge of God based on argument or reasoning. The point that they are making is that experience gives a *direct* way of knowing about things, as distinct from the indirect, inferential way provided by having to reason our way to knowledge of them. So our first task in getting clear about the appeal to religious experience is to decide whether it constitutes a non-argumentative, non-reasoning, method of supporting or establishing God's existence.

Experience: an alternative to argument?

The distinction which experientialists are here invoking (between what is known just on the basis of experience, and what is known in part by reasoning) is supposed to have a quite general application in areas outside theism. Thus on this view, I know that my computer keyboard is white just by seeing it – I do not have to work out that my keyboard is white by inferring that fact from other propositions which I know or believe. Nor do I have to work out that my telephone is ringing by inferring that fact from anything else – I know just by using my senses, not by using my reasoning capacity. By contrast, if I know that my computer has 512 RAM, that is something that I can know only by inference. I can read that claim in the leaflet that came with the computer, and I then need to infer from the sentences that I see in the leaflet to some facts about the capacities of the computer.

It is this general contrast between what can be known directly by means of the senses, and what can be known indirectly only by using inference, that many defenders of religious experience wish to import into discussions of theism. Thus Alston tells us:

> The thesis defended here is not that existence of God provides the best explanation for the facts about religious experience or that it is possible to *argue* in any way from the latter to the former. It is rather that people sometimes do perceive God and thereby acquire justified beliefs about God.
>
> (Alston 1991: 3)

Similar view are expressed by Gellman (1997: 14) and Plantinga (2000: 258). So the thought is that just as a visual experience of a table can by itself (i.e. without inference) assure me that there is a rectangular table in front of me, so a religious experience can by itself (i.e. without inference) assure me that, for example, God is helping me, or that God forgives me some transgression, or that God disapproves of something I have done. To use the terminology which we came across in Chapter 2, these authors wish to claim that beliefs about God are *properly basic*, in the sense that we can be entitled to accept the beliefs because they are grounded on experience, not because they are inferred from other beliefs.

By contrast, some critics of this defence of theism (and these critics include some theists) often insist on treating any appeal to religious experience as being essentially argumentative and inferential, not direct in the way that its defenders propose (see, for example, Martin 1990, Gale 1991, Bagger 1999). To see whether the experientialist or her critics are right on this issue, we need to think in more detail about what it means for a belief to be properly basic. In the discussion in Chapter 2, we were assuming in effect that a belief would be properly basic if you were fully entitled to hold it without having inferred it from any other beliefs. Relatively uncontroversial examples of such beliefs were the belief '1 + 1 = 2' and 'I am now in pain'. The first you were entitled to hold because it was self-evident, the second because you did not need to infer it from any other belief – you could know that it was true 'directly', just by having the experience of pain. But now we need to sharpen our conception of what is properly basic by drawing a distinction between actually using inference to arrive at a belief on the one hand, and needing to use inference in the justification of a belief on the other. Let us call beliefs of the first kind A-inferential, and beliefs of the second kind J-inferential. We can illustrate the difference with the following examples. If Fred comes in with a frown on his face, I may know without going through a process of inference that he is angry. I may not have to think to myself 'He has a frown; often when people have frowns they are angry; therefore he is (probably) angry'. I may simply look at him and immediately form the belief 'He is angry'. In such a case, my belief is not A-inferential, since I have not actually gone through a process of inference. But if someone asks me 'How did you know that he was angry?', it is clear that the answer 'I saw his anger' would be unsatisfactory. Even if it gives *some* information (e.g. it tells my questioner that my judgement was based on personal experience, and not on a second-hand report), it leaves unclear how what I saw relates to my subsequent judgement 'He is angry'. A better answer would be to say 'I saw his frown, and I know that when he (or perhaps other people) has had a frown like that in the past, he has been angry, so I knew that he was (probably) angry this time'. In other words, to justify my belief 'He is angry' I need retrospectively to show how it could have been legitimately inferred from other things which I was entitled to believe. It is therefore a J-inferential belief, as well as being not A-inferential.

Should the belief 'He is angry' be counted as properly basic? That will depend on whether we think the right criterion for proper basicality is being non-A-inferential, or being non-J-inferential. One reason for thinking that the right criterion is the latter is that those propositions which are uncontroversially properly basic are both non-A- and non-J-inferential. Think back to my belief that I am in pain. When the pain strikes me, and I acquire the belief, I do not actually infer that I am in pain – I just know straight off. So the belief is non-A-inferential. But equally, if someone were to ask me afterwards 'How did you know that you were in pain?' (a very strange question anyway), I would not try to show that my belief followed as the conclusion of a piece of inference or reasoning. I would probably not be sure what to say, because I would not know what kind of puzzle the questioner wanted to solve. In other words, my belief that I am in pain is neither A-inferential nor J-inferential, and hence is properly basic.

If we want to keep our category of properly basic beliefs similar to these uncontroversial examples, then beliefs like 'He is angry' will count as not properly basic and hence as inferred, even though we may not have actually used inference in arriving at them. If we choose to expand the category of the properly basic to include beliefs like 'He is angry', then we will have to recognise that the question 'How do you know?' will be appropriate for some basic beliefs, and will need to be answered in just the same way as it is for beliefs which are not properly basic – by showing how the belief could have been inferred from other beliefs. In what follows, I will follow the first option. In other words, for a belief to count as properly basic, it must be both non-A-inferential, and non-J-inferential. But this is a matter of terminology only – all the points to follow could just as well have been put in terms of the second option.

Now let us come back to the kind of beliefs which theists have thought can be established just on the basis of religious experience. Having surveyed a wide variety of examples, Alston says that in religious experience, God is experienced as having various qualities, and as doing various things, which he summarises as follows:

(A) What God is experienced as being.
1. Good.
2. Powerful.
3. Plenitude.
4. Loving.
5. Compassionate.
6. Wise.
7. Glorious.

(B) What God is experienced as doing.
1. Speaking.
2. Forgiving.
3. Strengthening.
4. Sympathising.

(Alston 1991: 43–4)

Broadly similar lists can be found in other authors (see, for example, Gellman 1997: 13; Plantinga in Sennett 1998: 154, or for a very rich set of examples, James 1963).

When we see lists like these, it becomes clear that religious experiences are insufficient by themselves to ground beliefs about God. Whether the beliefs in question are about God's activities or about his characteristics, they will all be J-inferential. To see that this will be so, consider simply the belief 'God is good'. Here is one example of someone reporting on experience of the goodness of God:

> it began to dawn on me that I was not alone in the room. Someone else was there, located fairly precisely about two yards to my right front. Yet there was no sort of sensory hallucination. I neither saw him nor heard him in any sense of the word 'see' and 'hear', but there he was; I had no doubt about it. He seemed to be very good and very wise.
>
> (quoted in Alston 1991: 17)

The person here reports acquiring the belief (or perhaps having it reinforced) that God is good, and acquiring it on the basis of an experience; and let us assume that it is a non-A-inferential belief, i.e. it was a belief which he acquired solely on the basis of the experience and without actually going through any process of inference. Nevertheless, it is clear that the belief must be J-inferential: to justify the belief, it must in part be shown how it can be inferred as the conclusion of a piece of reasoning. The reasoning would have some such form as the following:

(1) I had some sort of conscious experience.
(2) I would not have had this conscious presence unless God were good. So:
(3) God is good.

Consider a parallel case: I look at Fred and thereby acquire the belief that Fred is good. How is this belief to be justified? On the assumption that I am not actually witnessing Fred *do or say* anything which is good, the justification must surely refer (a) to Fred's visible appearance, and (b) to some correlation between people having that sort of appearance and their being good. In other words, the justification of the belief requires some inference.

It appears, then, that despite the protestations of those who appeal to religious experience to ground a belief in God, we are entitled to treat the appeal to experience as essentially argumentative or inferential in form, on a par with the arguments which we have been looking at in Chapters 3 to 7.

Perceptual v. non-perceptual experience

In reports of religious experiences, the range of kinds of experience is very wide. Some involve straightforward sensory perception (e.g. hearing a voice, seeing light, feeling a warmth, etc.); others involve non-sensory perception; and other involve kinds of experience which are not naturally called perceptual at all (e.g. feeling of security or exhilaration or peace). Most experientialists have regarded non-sensory perception as the most relevant type of experience because most reports of religious experience refer either to non-sensory perception alone, or to non-sensory and sensory experience together; and in the latter case, it is the non-sensory element that is the most important. So our first task must be to see what experientialists take perception to involve.

There is no uniform account which all experientialists accept, but one standard response to this question is that perception involves at least four elements. First, the perceiver must be in a distinctive kind of conscious state, a state with a certain phenomenology. Furthermore, not just any phenomenology will do. Exactly how this phenomenal content is to be described, experientialists have found it difficult to say beyond the fact that the experience must be one in which God *appears to* or *is presented to* the perceiver. Thus Gellman says:

> an experience of God involves a subject experiencing some phenomenal content which is *of* God. And an apparent or purported experience of God involves a subject's experiencing a phenomenal content which seems to be of God.
>
> (Gellman 1997: 13)

Similar claims can be found in Alston (1991) and Yandell (1993). Second, and least controversially, there must be an objective mind-independent entity (i.e. God) who is revealing himself to the perceiver. Third (and this may be simply making explicit something that is implicit in the idea of appearance or presentation in the second condition), the conscious state of the perceiver must be caused by the presence or activity of the mind-independent entity, God. Some experientialists want to add as a fourth condition the fact that on the basis of her experience, the perceiver comes to have certain beliefs about what she has experienced and in particular a belief that God has revealed himself to her. Prima facie, it would be possible to have a perceptual experience of God and fail to notice that it was God whom one was in contact with – just as I might see the Prime Minister, and wrongly believe that it was my next-door neighbour whom I had seen. The fourth condition is designed to block this possibility in the case of religious experience: even if you can believe that your experience is of God when in fact it is not, you cannot have an experience of God and believe that your experience is of something else.

Given this sketch of religious perception, let us call experiences where at least the first condition is met minimal experience; those where only the first condition is met illusory experience; and those where all four conditions are met veridical experience. All experiences will thus be minimal experiences, so some minimal experiences will be veridical, and some illusory.

We can note in passing that most veridical religious experiences would fall within the definition of a violation miracle given in Chapter 6. For they involve someone being in a conscious state which is caused by God, and hence a conscious state which they would not have been in had the laws of nature operated without 'violation'. Veridical religious experiences will thus be open to all the objections which we brought against both the existence of miracles and the credibility of miracle reports. However, as we shall see, they are also open to some problems of their own.

Religious perception

Let us return to the issue of religious experiences used as a support for a belief in God. Suppose that someone says 'I have actually experienced the presence of God, so he must exist'. Should we take the expression 'experience of God' in the minimal sense or the veridical sense? If we take it in the veridical sense, then God's existence would follow immediately from the truth of the experiential claim. For we have defined the veridical sense as one in which if you have an experience of X, then X must have a mind-independent existence. So there would certainly be a secure argument *from* religious experience to the existence of God, if we could take for granted the occurrence of religious experience veridically described.

But of course the non-theist will say that that simply raises the question 'But *did* she have an experience of God, veridically described?'. She will need to produce an argument to show that she really did have an experience of the kind which she thinks she did. She will need to argue *to* the occurrence of (veridical) religious experience before she can argue *from* it.

So it looks as if in order to take religious experience as her starting point, rather than as an intermediate conclusion, the theist must intend her descriptions of experience to be of the minimal kind. She would then be saying:

(1) I had an experience of God (in the minimal sense of 'experience'). So:
(2) It was probably an experience of God (in the veridical sense of 'experience'). So:
(3) God exists.

We might express this more idiomatically as follows:

(4) It seemed to me that I had an experience of God. So:
(5) I probably did have an experience of God. So:
(3) God exists

where the term 'experience' is used only in the veridical sense. We have agreed that the move from (2) to (3) (and equivalently from (5) to (3)) is unproblematic. But what is controversial and in need of justification is the move from (1) to (2) (or equivalently from (4) to (5)).

156

The point of getting the religious argument from experience into this form is this: it is a form which parallels other reasoning from experience which we employ, and hence we can invoke general criteria determining what makes such reasoning good on some occasions and bad on others. For example, I am out walking one day by Loch Ness when, as it seems to me, I see a huge creature rear up out of the deep, and I thereby come to believe that the Loch Ness monster exists. Here I am implicitly reasoning to myself:

(6) It seemed to me that I had an experience of the monster. So:
(7) I probably did have an experience of the monster. So:
(8) The monster exists.

I am moving from a perceptual experience in the minimal sense to a claim about the real existence of a mind-independent something; and this is exactly the move which the theist needs to make in the case of God. So, under what conditions is it legitimate to move from beliefs like (6) to beliefs like (8)?

There are no doubt many conditions which are relevant here, but we will focus on just three. The first is that my experience must cohere with other experiences which I myself have. Suppose for example that I have a visual experience of an apple, and I wonder whether there really is an apple which I can see, or whether I am just hallucinating (is the description 'experience of an apple' true only in the illusory sense, or in a veridical one?). One test I will apply will be whether I get further visual experiences of the kind which I would expect to get if an apple really were present. For example, how does my experience change if I move my position, or if I increase the illumination, or come closer to where it seems that the apple is? If it is a real apple which I am experiencing, then my experience of it will change in predictable ways as I conduct these tests. But if it is just a hallucination, then my experience may be unaffected, for example, as I change my position. I will also test to see if I can get some non-visual experiences of the apple, for example, by trying to touch it. If it turns out that I cannot get any further visual experiences of the apple, and that when I go to touch it, my fingers simply pass straight through the space where the apple seemed to be, I will be justified in concluding that there was no real apple there. It was just a play of light or a momentary hallucination.

The second sort of factor that would justify me in treating my experience as veridical and not merely illusory would be a causal interaction between the supposed object and other real objects. Suppose, for example, my seeming apple is on a cushion. Does it make a genuine depression in the cushion? If I shine a torch on it, does it cast a shadow? If I pick up another apple and roll it towards the seeming apple, does the second apple bump into the seeming apple and displace it or does it just pass through where the seeming apple seems to be? These tests reflect the fact that we think that for something to be a real object, it must interact causally with the rest of the environment. If it does not interact, then it was not a real object.

The third test is corroboration by other people. If there is a real apple in front of me, then other people ought to be able to obtain perceptual experiences of it just as well as I can. But if no one else can obtain such experiences, the right conclusion for me to draw is not that I am extra sensitive in detecting things which they cannot detect, but that I have made a mistake: on the basis of my minimal perceptual experience, I wrongly concluded that there was a real apple there for me to see when really there wasn't.

In some situations, I will not be able to apply any of these tests. If, for example, I am alone, I obviously cannot rely on the third test. If what I experience is a sound, and I do not have any sound-recording equipment fitted up, there is no way in which what I experience will interact with the other things around me. And again, if it is only a momentary sound, I will not be able to check it against my other auditory experiences, or against experiences from other senses. How in such circumstances can I tell whether my perceptual experience is hallucinatory or real?

I must then rely on the background information that I have. This will be information about (a) the reliability of my senses in particular situations, and (b) the likelihood of there being some real object for me to perceive of the kind which I seem to perceive. Suppose, for example, that I am lying alone in bed late at night. I seem to hear a door bang. Was there really a banging door? If I know that my hearing is averagely good, that it is a windy night, and that a shed door was left unfastened, it is not unreasonable for me to assume that there really is a banging door which I am hearing. Suppose on the other hand that I seem to hear a baby crying. I know that neither I nor any of my neighbours have any babies, nor any visitors with babies. It is then reasonable for me to assume that I am mishearing or simply hallucinating. Perhaps I am continuing into waking life a fragment of a dream.[1]

Note that with all these tests, and with the reliance on background information, what is being demanded is not certainty, but only probability. I am asking what it is reasonable for me to believe in the circumstances, not what is indubitably true. In a parallel way when we are considering whether religious experience can support a belief in God, the relevant question is not whether such experience can *prove* that God exists, but whether it can *help to support* the belief that he does.

Let us apply these considerations to the experience (in the minimal sense) of God. Suppose someone has an experience of having God speak to her. Might this be an experience in the veridical sense? Let us apply the three tests which we have elicited above. Immediately we come upon a problem. Whereas in the case of an experience of an apple, we know what other experiences would count as confirmatory or disconfirmatory, in the case of God we do not. Because apples are the kind of independent object which we regularly come across in our experiences, we know what does and does not

158

count as an apple-confirming experience. Similarly, there is a known, standard set of ways in which apples interact with other mind-independent objects in the world, and hence we can use our knowledge of these interactions as confirmation of apple status. By contrast, it is very unclear when someone has an experience (minimally described) of God, what other experiences would count as confirmations that the experience is veridical. Whereas we have some idea of what falls within the cluster of possible experiences of apples, we have no comparable knowledge of experiences of God.

If unresolved, this problem would be a major stumbling block to accepting religious experience as a basis of theism, for it amounts to saying that we can have no grounds for saying that any religious experiences can justifiably be described as veridical, i.e. no grounds for saying that any of these experiences give us reason to believe in the existence of God. What is the theist to say in response?

The first move would be to say that the three tests which we have mentioned above *can* be used with religious experience, although not as straightforwardly as in the case of experience of mundane objects such as apples. For when we look at accounts of religious experience, characteristically the subjects do report having a cluster of mutually reinforcing experiences. Nearly always when a voice is seemingly heard, it says something profoundly important to the subject. For example, it gives guidance on some important life choice, or it offers comfort or reassurance. It never comments on the price of houses, or asks for the time, or complains how hot it is for the time of year. Second, these auditory experiences are accompanied by feelings of exhilaration, delight or uplift. Often there are reports of the subject being bathed in light and/or warmth. Subjects never report other feelings which prima facie they might just as well feel, for example, amusement, disdain, boredom, etc., nor do they say that they were aware of, for example, the humidity rather than the warmth, or that the light became crepuscular rather than bright and glowing. Further, the theist may say, although religious experiences characteristically befall people in isolation, on occasion they may be shared by a group of people, in which case it is possible to confirm one person's experiences by references to those of other people.

The atheist, however, will be unimpressed by these replies. She will say that viewed dispassionately, all we have is a collection of people saying that they have funny experiences, and believing as a consequence in the existence of a being whom no one else can detect. So (the atheist will continue) we have no grounds for saying that any of those experiences is a veridical experience of a mind-independent object, nor consequently that any of these beliefs is true. Can the theist do any better? In the following sections, we will consider two attempts, one by Swinburne and one by Alston, to show that there is more to be said in defence of religious experience.

Swinburne's additions

Swinburne puts his discussion of religious experience in the context of ordinary sense experience as a whole; and in connection with such experience, he advances what he calls the Principle of Credulity. He says this:

> I suggest that it is a principle of rationality that (in the absence of special considerations) if it seems (epistemically) to a subject that x is present, then probably x is present: what one seems to perceive is probably so.
>
> (Swinburne 1979: 254)

By the expression 'It seems (epistemically) to a subject that x is present' Swinburne means 'The subject is inclined to believe, on the basis of his current experience, that x is present'. In other words, Swinburne is saying that there is a standing presumption that our minimal sensory experiences are veridical as well. But it is a presumption which can be rebutted if special factors are present. If, for example, I am drunk or drugged or in a highly emotional state, or the viewing conditions are very bad, or I am very tired, we know that my experiences may be misleading. But in the absence of such factors, Swinburne says, it is reasonable to assume at once that our experiences are veridical. And he goes on to say

> From this it would follow that, in the absence of special considerations, all religious experiences ought to be taken by their subjects as genuine, and hence as substantial grounds for belief in the existence of their apparent object – God, or Mary, or Ultimate Reality, or Poseidon.
>
> (op. cit. p. 254)

Let us be clear exactly what Swinburne is saying. He is not saying that all religious experience is a proof of the reality of God, or Mary, et al., nor even that all religious experience makes it reasonable to believe that God exists, or that Mary exists, etc. He is not denying that there can be hallucinatory religious experiences, nor that people can misidentify ordinary natural objects as being divine. What he is saying concerns the onus of proof. If I have the (minimal) experience of there being a table in front of me, reason requires me to believe that there really is a table there, *unless* there are special reasons for thinking that my experience is illusory. Someone who wants to deny that there really is a table in front of me cannot *simply* say 'But you have only had an experience of a table, and that experience *might* be illusory, so it is not reasonable for you to think that there is a table there'. She has to show grounds for thinking that experience *is* illusory; and if she cannot do this, then the Principle of Credulity entitles me to assume that there is a table there. I do not have to give special reasons every time for thinking that my experience was veridical. The Principle of Credulity relieves me of that necessity. In a precisely similar way, Swinburne is saying, if I have a minimal experience of God talking to me, reason requires me to believe that it really is God talking to me, unless there is some special reason for thinking that my experience is illusory. Someone who wants to deny that it was God talking to me cannot simply say 'But you have only had an experience of God, and it might have been an illusory experience, so it is not reasonable for you to think that there is a God'. She has to show grounds for thinking that my experience is illusory; and if she cannot, then the Principle of Credulity entitles me to assume that God exists.

Why should we accept the Principle of Credulity? Swinburne's defence is indirect. He says that if we do not accept it, there will be no way to avoid scepticism about the external world. If one's minimal experience of an X is no ground *at all* for thinking that there is a real X which I am experiencing, then nor will two minimal experiences, nor twenty, nor a hundred. Accumulating experiences which are no grounds at all for beliefs about what really exists will leave me with no grounds at all for what really exists. Since only experience can give me grounds for believing that mind-independent objects exist, if scepticism is to be avoided each (minimal) experience must carry some probative force unless there is some reason to think otherwise.

There is one other move which Swinburne makes to strengthen the argument from experience. He draws a distinction between what he calls public and private perceptions (op. cit. p. 248). His terminology here is potentially misleading and we will re-label the distinction as being that between publicly and privately perceivable objects. It is a distinction between two kinds of mind-independent object. A publicly perceivable object is one which will cause all persons who are rightly positioned and with the appropriate sense organs and paying attention to that object, to have an experience of its seeming to them that the object is present. Thus, the great majority of objects which we know of are publicly perceivable. A table, for example, is the sort of object which will cause any suitable observer who is paying attention to it and who is in the right conditions, to have experiences as of a table. But, Swinburne says, there may be another kind of object, the ones that I am calling privately perceivable objects, and he describes them in this way:

> There may be objects *o* which cause certain persons to have the experience of its seeming to them that *o* is there without their [i.e. the objects] having that effect on all other attentive persons who occupy similar positions and have similar sense organs and concepts.

(ibid. p. 248)

There are, Swinburne says, two possible ways in which this might come about. The first rests on the laws of optics being probabilistic, not deterministic, and is not here relevant. But second, and relevantly for our purpose it could be because *o* is a person who can choose whom to cause to have experience of its seeming to them that *o* is there. *o* may be a normally invisible man with the power of letting you but not me see him.

(ibid.)

He then points out that the objects or religious experience are generally privately perceivable objects not publicly perceivable.

Swinburne's thought, then, is that there could be really existing objects which had the unusual power of making themselves perceivable by only one person, or by two, or by some other selected numbers. Swinburne in effect is showing that the theist can undercut the three tests mentioned earlier as part of what we rely on in deciding whether our perceptions are veridical or illusory. I said that if the supposed object of an experience failed the three tests, then my experience was illusory not veridical. But Swinburne can say that an experience can fail the three tests and still be veridical provided that we recognise that the object of the experience is a strange kind of object. The fact that my experience is not corroborated by other people will not show that my experience is illusory, if what I am experiencing is a (real, mind-independent but only) privately perceivable object. Other people's non-corroboration of my own experiential reports thus has two interpretations: I might be having an illusory perception of a publicly perceivable object, or I might be having a veridical perception of a privately perceivable object.

In a similar way, if the object I am perceiving is a being who can control whether he is perceivable by other observers than myself, presumably he will be able to control his perceivability by me. So if I fail to get confirmatory experiences of him, that does not show that he was not really there, but only that he was a privately perceivable object who was choosing not to make himself continuously perceivable by me. So my perception could fail the first test and still be veridical not illusory.

If we can make sense of the idea of this being making himself visible to some people and not to others, there will be little difficulty in imagining him able to control his causal interactions with other parts of his environment. So if I, for example, shine a light in what I take to be his direction, and he casts no shadow, this need not be because my experience is illusory – it could be because he is making himself totally transparent to light rays. It could be that I am having a veridical experience of a privately perceivable being. So the second test of whether a perception is veridical can be circumvented.

We can thus see that if we accept Swinburne's distinction between publicly and privately perceivable objects, there will be fewer grounds on which it could be argued that religious experiences must have been illusory; and he can then use the Principle of Credulity to claim that since there are fewer grounds for saying that religious experiences are illusory, there is a corresponding greater likelihood that they are veridical. Of course, this does not show that any religious experiences *are* veridical. But it clears away objections to saying that they *could not* be veridical, and severely limits the grounds on which they could be argued not to be veridical.

Should the Principle of Credulity be accepted?

Should we accept the Principle of Credulity? It is worth noting that it has an appeal far beyond its use in connection with religious experience. We have already seen how Swinburne thinks that it is the only way we can avoid scepticism about our knowledge of the external world. And certainly other philosophers with no religious preconceptions invoke it as acceptable. Thus we find Chisholm saying:

> *anything* we find ourselves believing may be said to have some presumption in its favour . . . [This] principle may be thought of as an instance of a more general truth – that it is reasonable to put trust in our own cognitive faculties unless we have some positive ground for questioning them.

> (Chisholm 1982: 14)

And again, Lycan maintains that every spontaneous belief is prima facie justified, and says: 'I want to propose the following Principle of Credulity: "Accept at the outset each of those things that seem to be true"' (Lycan 1988: 165). If these authors are right, there are important consequences. If the principles which they invoke have to be accepted by agnostics and atheists as well as by theists, and if these principles are all that is needed to justify interpreting experience as veridical, it will obviously be much harder for agnostics and atheists to claim that religious experiences cannot give any grounds for belief in a mind-independent object, God.

But that is only a reason for accepting the Principle if you already have a reason for thinking that such scepticism is false – and a reason, moreover, which does not presuppose the truth of the Principle itself. Deep questions in epistemology are raised here, but it is probably enough for the theist to rely on an ad hominem argument at this point. She can say to her opponents 'You do *in effect* accept the Principle of Credulity when dealing with the great majority of perceptual experiences – that is how you are able to escape scepticism about the physical world. So it would be inconsistent of you to refuse to accept it when dealing with religious experiences in particular.' This, of course, is a point that cannot be made against someone who is willing to accept scepticism about the external world, or who alternatively thinks that there is a way of avoiding such scepticism without having to rely on the Principle. But it will probably be cogent against most of the theist's opponents. So let us at least provisionally accept the Principle.

Can there be privately perceivable objects?

What should we make of the concept of privately perceivable objects, that is to say of entities which have the power to make themselves detectable only by selected people at selected times and in selected ways? We have seen that the existence of such entities could give the theist a powerful tool. It would enable her to undermine claims that experiences of God must be illusory because they all fail the types of checks referred to on pp. 157–8 above.

The sceptic can here point out first that our current understanding of the laws of nature does not permit the existence of such privately perceivable objects. We know of no mechanism, either actually existing or constructible from any known material or by any known process, which would enable a being to make itself detectable to only one person, or to suspend its normal causal interactions with its environment. So there is no reason to believe that any such being(s) exist.

Such an objection, however, will seem question-begging to the experientialist. She may say that there *is* reason to believe in the existence of such an entity, if we make the assumption that other arguments for the existence of God show that it is at least probable that he exists. She would interpret the fact that science does not recognise the possibility of any such objects as revealing the fact that there is more to reality than science reveals. The weakness of this reply is that it does make the argument from experience (at least as supplemented by Swinburne's idea of privately perceivable objects) depend for its evidential value on the cogency of other arguments for the existence of God. Alternatively, the theist may say that the reason to believe in the existence of such an entity is provided simply by religious experience itself. To require that it should be able to validate itself by reference to scientific canons would be to appeal to irrelevant criteria. To put the point in an Alstonian vocabulary which we will shortly be explaining, it would be to try to judge one cognitive practice by another.

In the face of these replies by the theist, the sceptic might do better to argue for a stronger conclusion: not just that privately perceivable entities are implausible in terms of existing science, but that they are absolutely impossible. How might such an argument go?

First, the sceptic needs to concede that even if science does not currently recognise the existence of any privately perceivable objects, it is at least logically possible that there could be a being which had some power to make itself undetectable in certain ways. It might, for example, have the power to affect the light in its vicinity in such a way that no light rays were reflected from it to an observer. It might be able to emit a special sort of sound wave which did not spread from its source in all directions, but which could be directed like a beam of light to a single perceiver's ears. But the Swinburnean concept goes beyond this. It envisages a being who can control not just this or that of its perceivable properties, but every property by which it could be detected in any way at all. The sceptic might well try to argue that it is not logically possible for there to be any such objects.

The argument would begin with some ideas that were introduced in Chapter 5 (see pp. 88–9). There it was argued that the concept of a mind-independent entity and the concept of causality were so deeply connected that a universe containing such mind-independent entities but obeying no causal laws was impossible. The very being of an object was partially constituted by the causal powers and limitations that it had. It could not lose all its existing causal powers and limitations in favour of another set, and yet still remain the same object; and it could not lose all its causal powers and limitations and remain an object. If therefore a being has the power to make itself differentially perceivable (as envisaged in the previous paragraph) that causal power must be in virtue of its nature, where its nature will inevitably also impose causal limitations on it.

This line of thought clearly raises some deep, controversial, and puzzling metaphysical assumptions, and as sketched here is plainly at best inconclusive. But it may nevertheless repay the sceptic to pursue it as potentially the strongest line of objection to the concept of privately perceivable objects.

Alston's appeal to 'mystical perceptual practice'

Alston provides a different approach to solving the problem which we identified above (p. 159), the problem that we have no grounds for saying that religious experiences are of a mind-independent object. He first demarcates something which he calls 'mystical perceptual practice'.[2] This is centred on that segment of human life which is concerned with religious experience, both veridical and illusory. It includes centrally the having of such experiences, and the beliefs to which they give rise. But it also includes reflection on those experiences and beliefs, for example, in comparing, classifying and analysing them. Most importantly, it also includes what Alston calls a system of overriders. These are criteria which determine for us which experiences are veridical and which illusory; and which beliefs arising from those experiences are justifiable as probably true, and which not. This mystical perceptual practice is an epistemic practice, i.e. one that is ostensibly concerned with knowledge and belief, with justification and reason, with truth and falsehood. Alston's thought is that the right question to ask is whether this whole practice is epistemically defensible, in the sense of being directed at a real, mind-independent entity, and our knowledge of that entity; or whether it is simply an exercise in psychopathology, an investigation into the psychological states of various people, states which are admittedly intensely felt but which reveal nothing about a mind-independent reality. If the experientialist can show that the practice *as a whole* is epistemically defensible, then it could be reasonable to take *particular experiences within it* as veridical and hence as being genuine experiences of God.

How, then, is a whole epistemic practice to be shown to be legitimate? The history of philosophy is full of discussions of this question in relation to our normal reliance on sense experience to give us veridical experiences and hence true information about the mind-independent world around us. From the time of the Ancient Greeks, philosophers have discussed arguments seeking to show either that sense perception as a whole is unreliable, or that conversely it is reliable. Alston's strategy is to see how defences of our sense perception practice (SP for short) have fared, and then to see if the defence of mystical perception practice (MP) fares any worse.

His conclusion about SP is that there is no non-circular justification for the reliability of the practice as a whole. We can confirm or disconfirm the beliefs about external objects which we acquire from particular sensory experiences – but only by relying on other beliefs which we acquire from other sensory experiences. In terms of the example which we considered earlier, I can confirm my sense experience belief that there is an apple in front of me by reaching out my hand and getting tactual experiences where the apple appears to be. But that presupposes that the tactual experience I have is veridical, in the sense of giving me a true belief that there is a solid object where the apple appears to be. I can in turn check up on the belief from my sense of touch, for example, by asking other people whether they too can feel an apple where I thought that I felt one. But that test presupposes that their tactual experiences will be veridical, and also that the auditory experience I have when they (as I think) speak gives rise in me to a true belief about what they have said. At every stage, in checking one sensory experience, I rely on another.

After further investigation, Alston concludes that a similar circularity affects a range of other cognitive practices (he mentions introspection, memory, rational intuition, and reasoning). For example, we can certainly check particular memory beliefs which we have – but only by relying in part on yet other memory beliefs. What we cannot do is stand back from our memory practice as a whole, and give a non-memory-based reason why we should ever trust *any* of our memories. Alston's claim is that MP is in the same position as all these other cognitive practices: particular claims made within MP (for example, to have had an experience of God) can be justified within that practice, but there is no non-circular justification of the practice as a whole.

So far, then, Alston believes he has established what we can call a parity thesis: MP is no worse epistemically than other practices (such as SP, or reasoning) which atheists and agnostics are willing to accept. So, in consistency these sceptics ought to accept MP as epistemically legitimate. However, this is only an ad hominem argument: it does not tell against a really thoroughgoing sceptic who is prepared to extend her scepticism from MP to SP and beyond. Alston therefore seeks to undermine such an extreme position by arguing that it is rational to accept any of these practices if they are socially well-established, unless we have positive reason to think them unreliable. After arguing that MP is a socially well-established practice, and that there is no good reason to think that it is unreliable, he draws the conclusion that MP is a rationally defensible practice and hence that its deliverances in the form of beliefs grounded in religious experiences ought at least in principle to be accepted.

Assessment of Alston

Does Alston's talk of cognitive practices provide any more secure defence of the idea that religious experience can reveal the existence of God? We will argue that it faces objections of increasing seriousness. We might first question whether MP is a genuine practice, analogous to sensory practice, memory practice and so on. One point to note here is that all of the other practices are non-optional: every human being of any cognitive competence relies on her senses, on her memory, on her power of introspection, and on her reasoning power. A creature who did not rely on these cognitive practices would quickly become completely helpless to secure its own survival, and would either die or become passively dependent on others. This suggests (to put it no more strongly) that those who rely on these cognitive practices are, in however approximate a manner, latching on to a part of reality.[3] Those who steer their course through the world relying on (for example) their sense-generated belief that an angry bull is approaching, or that there is a sheer drop beside the path, or that there is a fire in the hearth, are more likely to survive and flourish than those who think there is no reason to think their senses reveal anything independent of their own minds. The same is true for reliance on memory. A person who placed no reliance on any of her memory beliefs would be as helpless as a baby, and would quickly perish.

By contrast, the supposed MP is entirely optional. It is possible to lead a long, healthy and flourishing life without participating in MP at all. And those who do participate in MP are not noticeably more successful by such criteria than those who do not. This is some reason, though admittedly not a strong one, for thinking that MP is not a practice which connects with any real mind-independent reality. The experientialist might reply that it is no reason at all. She might object that the criticism presupposes that everything mind-independent is crucial for an organism's survival and flourishing. But (she will continue) this is clearly not so. For example, if a strange sensory deficit had left humans unable to detect moonbeams, it seems unlikely that anyone's well-being would be seriously affected. And yet moonbeams are clearly mind-independent objects.

However, even though this reply is well-made in general, as applied to the case at hand, it misfires. For God is precisely unlike moonbeams in that he is supposed to make a huge difference to a person's well-being. How strange, the critic will then say, that there seems to be no difference in the well-being of those who allegedly have and those who lack the ability to detect something whose existence supposedly hugely affects our well-being. But again the theist will have a reply. She will say that what matters is our acceptance of God's existence (and of various more specific religious claims), and whether we accept them on the basis of experience, or on the basis of, for example, one of the other arguments at which we have looked in Chapters 3 to 7 is comparatively unimportant. So the fact that some people, including some theists, lead flourishing lives yet fail to have any religious experiences, would not tend to show that no religious experiences were of a mind-independent divine being.

Second, we might wonder whether MP is really an independent practice at all. For the crucial question about religious experience is whether it is ever veridical. Does it ever provide a ground for beliefs about a mind-independent entity? MP is supposed to be a practice directed at mind-independent entities – but so is SP. Why then count MP as a separate practice? Surely MP should be classed as simply one branch of SP, analogous to VP (visual perception practice), AP (auditory perception practice), etc. It might be thought this is a trivial point of terminology – why should it matter whether MP and SP are called two distinct practices, or whether the former is a subcategory of the latter. But something important does turn on this question, since Alston thinks that different practices have their own standards (Alston 1991: 199). In particular he thinks that there is no justification for judging MP by the standards appropriate to SP. This is a point which will be important in what follows.

A third objection which the sceptic will want to raise is that there is no reason to believe that there is a mind-independent object associated with any religious experiences. She will say that all religious experiences are illusory, and fail to reveal the presence or attributes of anything veridical at all. It as if all religious experiences had the same status as mere hallucinations.[4]

In seeking to meet this objection, experientialists will point to the fact that they are very aware of the distinction between illusory and veridical religious experiences, and have been very concerned to draw up lists of criteria to distinguish one from the other. It is true that different theists come up with different lists of distinguishing criteria, but it is also true that there is substantial overlap between the different lists, enough to make Alston's claim that they 'say essentially the same thing' a reasonable one (Alston 119: 202 fn.). The real problem arises when we look in detail at the criteria which theists offer. Here is a list, which Alston quotes with approval, of the marks distinguishing 'true' and 'false' religious experiences.

	True	False
	Intellect	
1	Not concerned with useless affairs	Futile, useless, vain preoccupation
2	Discretion	Exaggeration, excesses
	Will	
1	Interior peace	Perturbation, disquiet
2	Trust in God	Presumption or despair
3	Patience in pains	Impatience with trials
4	Simplicity, sincerity	Duplicity, dissimulation
5	Charity that is meek, kindly, self-forgetful	False, bitter pharisaical zeal

(Alston 1991: 203)

The problem with this list arises when we ask why we should think that any items in the left-hand column have anything to do with *veridical* religious experience. If the answer is that they have been found by past observation to be correlated with such experiences, and hence can now be treated as reliable signs of these experiences, that presupposes that there is some way of picking out which past experiences have been veridical, so that a correlation could then be noted between those veridical experiences and the correlated signs. And the sceptic will ask by reference to what criteria *that* initial identification of veridical experiences is supposed to have been achieved. If the answer is that the left-hand list is not a list of mere correlates, but itself supplies the criteria for veridicality, that claim looks very implausible, if a criterion is a fundamental way of judging whether something is so. For a theist could display all of the states in the left-hand column without having a religious experience, and indeed an atheist could display all of those states bar the trust in God. So the features cannot be a set of more-or-less sufficient conditions for veridical religious experience. Nor do they fare any better as a set of more-or-less necessary conditions. Why should experiential sensitivity to a mind-independent object require me to be charitable? Why should that sensitivity require me to be sincere (sincere about what?) The strangeness of these ideas is apparent when we imagine analogous claims in relation to other cognitive practices. Is being meek a necessary condition of spotting logical fallacies? Is enjoying interior peace a necessary condition of seeing a flash of lightning? Is being kindly a necessary condition of hearing someone asking me the time? Why then should any of these character traits and dispositions be necessary for having veridical experience of God?

This is where Alston will insist that we cannot judge one cognitive practice by reference to another. He asserts that since MP and SP are distinct cognitive practices, the fact that certain traits and dispositions are neither necessary nor sufficient for successful activity within SP is not a good reason to deny that they are necessary and/or sufficient within MP. Here, the sceptic needs to make two points, apparently pulling in opposite directions. On the one hand, she needs to concede that there can be some great variations between legitimate cognitive activities. For example, there are great variations between the preconditions for successful seeing and successful tactual perception (the former requires good light, the latter doesn't; the latter requires contact between the perceiver's sense organs and the object perceived, the former requires that there is no such contact; etc.). In a similar way, it may be that there can be some major differences between the successful exercise of MP and the successful exercise of other forms of SP, without that fact by itself discrediting MP as a cognitive practice. Just as perceptions via each of the senses can differ among themselves, so mystical perceptions may differ in other ways again from sensory perception. But on the other hand, the sceptic also needs to insist that there are limits to how different MP can be from other kinds of SP and still count as giving perceptions of a mind-independent reality. If the only criteria which the experientialist can offer for veridical religious experience are the sort suggested above in the quotation from Alston (see p. 169), those limits have been transgressed.

Fourth, the sceptic will insist that there are better explanations available of the religious experiences than the theistic claim that they are veridical experiences of God. There are of course naturalistic explanations of the phenomenon of religion in general, such as those offered by Marx or Freud. But what the sceptic needs here is something more specific: a naturalistic explanation of religious experience in particular. Such an explanation lies readily to hand. It seeks to explain such experiences in terms of psychological dispositions for which there is already very considerable empirical evidence. The first of these dispositions is a tendency for the subject's expectations to influence what she takes herself to perceive. If I expect to hear the word 'collision', then I am more likely to think that I have had a veridical auditory experience of the word, even if the acoustical signal I received was much closer to 'collusion' than to 'collision'. If I expect to see Fred rather than Jim, I am more likely to believe that I have had a veridical visual experience of Fred and not Jim, even though my ocular irradiation would have led me to think the opposite if my expectation had been reversed. Expectation, then, is a partial determinant of what we take ourselves veridically to perceive. Effects like this can be replicated in the laboratory and measured by experimental psychologists. For one early example, see Bruner and Minturn's paper 'Perceptual Identification and Perceptual Organisation' reported in Vernon 1966: 279). Other instances abound in the psychological literature.

Do those who have religious experiences *expect* to have experience of God? It might seem implausible to say so, especially as one theme which experientialists stress is the unpredictability of divine activity, and the impossibility of specifying any circumstances when it can be more or less guaranteed that a normal perceiver will perceive God. Nevertheless, it is not implausible to think that expectation does play a part in religious experience. Although the experiences are not predictable, and in that sense may not be expected, they do tend to occur at times when believers would most expect them, for example, at times of prayer, when they are actively seeking support and guidance from God and hence would be at least half-expecting some response from God.

The second disposition which would feature in a naturalistic explanation of religious experience is a tendency for the subject's wishes or hopes to influence what she takes herself to perceive. If I very much want to sight the Loch Ness monster, I am more likely to interpret an experience as being of the monster than if I am coolly indifferent about its existence. The football fan who wants her team to score will believe that she actually saw the ball cross the goal line, when the more impartial referee rules that it was deflected back into play without ever having crossed the line. Again, this effect of desire on perception is well established independently of its use in a religious context.

That theists in general and experientialists in particular would like or hope to have experience of God is undeniable. Since they take God to be the most important entity in existence, the one who created and sustains them, who has boundless love and care for them, and whose plans are of the greatest import for every individual, it is no surprise that they have a very welcoming attitude towards any divine response directed at them individually. So they have a powerful predisposition to interpret experiences as being revelatory of God.

So, the sceptic will argue, there is available a naturalistic explanation of the occurrence of religious experience (minimally construed), and this explanation is superior to a theistic explanation in two related respects. First, it invokes only psychological dispositions for which there is a great deal of independent evidence. Second, it provides a much simpler explanation than the theistic explanation. It does not invoke any new entities or processes or mechanisms, but relies solely on ones which we already accept. The theistic account, by contrast, postulates a unique and completely unprecedented sort of being, with an amazing range of properties and powers which are in conflict with all that science tells us about what is possible, what is impossible and what is necessary; and about whom theists often say that he is to a greater or lesser degree unknowable.

There is a further fact here which harmonises with the naturalistic rather than the theistic account. We have already said that the distribution of religious experiences is suspiciously biased towards those who expect and want to have such experiences. It is also biased towards those who antecedently believe in the existence of God. Prima facie, one might expect that God would appear in roughly equal measure to believers and unbelievers – to believers to maintain their faith and to unbelievers as a warning or exhortation. How strange then, that the distribution should be so hugely in favour of believers! Why would God have so little to say to those who (one would have thought theism would say) have greatest need of having their eyes opened to him? But on a naturalistic account, this imbalance is precisely what one would expect. For a prior belief in God underpins the prior expectation that God will appear, and the prior expectation contributes to the belief that he has appeared.

The oddity of experiencing God

But now we need to face something which we have so far been avoiding. We have been speaking as if God might be one experienceable object among many – a being whom it would certainly be *possible* to experience, and about whom the only question was whether this or that supposed sighting of him was a genuine sighting or not. We have been assuming in other words that he is rather like the Loch Ness monster. If there is no Loch Ness monster, then all putative sightings of it are mistaken. But a Loch Ness monster is at least the sort of thing which certainly could be sighted if it existed. And if someone wondered whether the monster existed, one sensible way of trying to find out would be to try and get an experience of the monster.

But however bizarre a creature the Loch Ness monster might turn out to be, we know that God (if he exists) is not remotely like the Loch Ness monster. The Loch Ness monster, if it exists, will be a finitely sized physical object, located in space and time, with a characteristic visual appearance. It will have a colour, a shape, a size; it will have identifiable features such as a head, a body and limbs. It will have a mouth, and almost certainly eyes; and so on. God by contrast (if he exists) will be non-physical, and omnipresent. He will have no colour, no shape, no size, no discernible features. Furthermore, he will have no features detectable only indirectly, like electric charge, gravitational attraction, or chemical composition. He will have no characteristic appearance whatever to sight or to any other of our senses, even with the use of instruments. God, in other words, is not even a *possible* object of sensory experience.

There is a correct way of understanding this point, and an incorrect way. To clarify the difference, let us spell out what is not being said. It is sometimes objected to the idea of an experience of God that an experience could not tell you whether the object of experience was, for example, the creator of the universe, or was omnipotent, or omniscient, or morally perfect. Since these are defining characteristics of God and they could not be detected in any object by any sensory experience of that object, no sensory experience could be an experience of God. So (the bad argument concludes) religious experience cannot help to establish that God exists.

This objection is a mistaken one. Suppose an object X has certain properties F, G, etc. – perhaps it even has them by definition. It does not follow that if I am to experience X, my experience must reveal to me the F-ness, the G-ness, etc. of X. All that is required is that my experience is of the entity who, perhaps unknown to me, has these properties. Thus if I am to see the Prime Minister, all that is required is that I see the person who is in fact the Prime Minister. It does not have to be the case that his (or her) Prime Ministerial status is itself a visually detectable feature of him (or her). Nor does it have to be the case that my visual experience by itself assures me that the person is the Prime Minister. What assures me that it is the Prime Minister whom I see is a combination of my visual experience and my prior knowledge that the person who is in fact the Prime Minister has a certain visual appearance. Similarly, if I am to see an omnipotent being, all that is required is that I see a being who is in fact omnipotent. It is not necessary that my visual experience itself tells me that he is omnipotent.

Does it make any difference if I am trying to *identify* the object I am seeing as so-and-so? No – again an example will make clear why. When I see the Eiffel Tower, I can know that I am seeing the tallest building in Paris, even though when I look at the Eiffel Tower, there is nothing in my visual experience to tell me about the relative height of other buildings in Paris. As long as I know what the Eiffel Tower looks like, and also know that the Eiffel Tower is the tallest building in Paris, when I see the Eiffel Tower I can identify it as the tallest building in Paris. In a parallel way, as long as I know what God (as it were) looks like (how he would appear perceptually to someone like me), and as long as I know that God is (say) omnipotent, omniscient and the creator of everything, then I can know when I experience God that I am doing so, and hence know that I perceiving an omnipotent, etc. being, even though his omnipotence is not and perhaps cannot be perceptually presented to me.

So the point to be made here does not turn on the fact that this one or that one of God's defining characteristics is not perceptible. The point rather is that *none* of his properties is perceptible, either directly or indirectly by mean of instruments. There is no characteristic appearance which he has, which could give a sense to an expression like 'It seemed to be God' or 'It looked like God' or 'It appeared to be God'. Recall Gellman's remark quoted above that religious experience must have a phenomenal content in which 'God appears to us or is presented to a subject'. The problem is that God is not the sort of being who has an appearance which could be presented in experience. There is in effect a twofold problem with the very idea of religious experience. In the first place, the supposed object, God, lacks any properties that are perceivable, either directly or indirectly (i.e. by instruments); and second, as a consequence, religious experience cannot have the phenomenal content which theists have wanted to claim for it.

This fact has important implications for Swinburne's Principle of Credulity. The Principle, it will be remembered, told us that: '(in the absence of special considerations) if it seems (epistemically) to a subject that x is present, then probably x is present: what one seems to perceive is probably so' (Swinburne 1979: 254). But we now have reason to think that *all* alleged perceptions of God fall within the scope of the 'special considerations' clause. For God is the sort of thing that is in principle not experienceable. As an analogy, suppose it is the case that someone is inclined to believe that she is currently perceiving the square root of 2. We know at once that she cannot invoke the Principle of Credulity and claim that the square root of 2 is probably present. For the square root of 2 is in principle not a perceptible object, and consequently her belief is certainly false. The same goes for someone who claims to have a perception of God: God is not a perceptible object, and therefore her claim is false.

In response to this line of thought, Alston has objected that 'the way an object phenomenally appears may not correspond exactly to the way it is' (Alston 1991: 19). He instances objects which appear to us to be coloured when (perhaps) modern science shows us that colour is not an objective property of objects. So even if God does not possess perceptible properties F and G, there is no reason why he should not *appear* to possess F and G. But Alston here overstates a reasonable point. An object may lack some of the properties which it seems to us to have, but it could not lack all of them, for then there would be nothing to link the properties which we seemed to perceive to the object which did not have any of them. Confronted by a cube that appears to be blue, we can agree that the cube is not really blue, because we can fix the reference of 'the cube' in terms of the properties which it appears to us to have and which it really does have. It is, for example, and appears to be, to the left of us, to be on top of an oblong, to have a corner pointing towards us, and so on. But if the cube had none of these features, nor any others of those which (as we thought) 'it' appeared to have, we would have no grounds for thinking that we had successfully referred to anything with our words 'the cube'. More generally if an object really has none of the features which it appears to us to have, there are no grounds for saying that it is *that* object which is appearing to us. Similarly, if none of the features which are presented to us in our experience belong to God, there is no ground for saying that it is God who is being presented via those features.

Gutting has raised a different objection. He says that the claim that God is in principle not perceivable assumes that we can tell a priori that some properties can be directly experienced by us and others cannot be. It assumes in particular that such properties as omnipotence, omniscience, being the creator of everything, etc., are not perceivable. But, he objects, it is an empirical question which properties are perceivable. So to claim that the divine properties cannot be perceived begs the question against those who claim that as a matter of empirical fact they have been perceived (Gutting 1982: 154).

In reply we can agree that it is an empirical fact that by touching an object, human beings can perceive its temperature but not, for example, its magnetic field. It is also true that there could turn out to be a correlation between our sensations and any mind-independent fact at all – and hence a correlation between our sensations and any set of properties instantiated by some mind-independent state of affairs. But it does not follow that such a correlation is sufficient for those properties to count as perceivable. It may be that when-ever I think of a number, I get characteristic sensations if and only if the number is a prime number. I could then use my capacity to have sensations of this sort to check whether hitherto unclassified numbers were prime or not. But that would not mean that I was *perceiving* the primeness of any numbers. The concept of perception imposes constraints on how our internal sensa-tions are related to mind-independent objects, if we are to count as perceiving those objects at all. Philosophers of perception usually say that the internal states must 'present' the mind-independent object to awareness. Exactly what this means is obscure. But if the condition is dropped, as Gutting's objection implicitly does, he leaves unclear how the correlation between sensations and divine properties could be discovered in the first place. For it is presumably an empirical fact that there is a correlation, and this requires that we should be able to identify the presence of the relevant divine features independently of the sensations. But neither he nor any other theist has ever suggested how this might be done.

Let us review the position. We have looked at five objections to religious experience viewed as an exercise of Alstonian MP.

(1) MP is suspicious because it is not universal.
(2) MP is really a subcategory of SP.
(3) Religious experience is never veridical.
(4) There are better explanations of religious experiences than the theistic one.
(5) God is in principle not a possible object of experience.

These objections, even if correct, have different forces. The theist might con-cede the first and say that a practice can be suspicious in the sense of initially arousing suspicion, even if there is nothing wrong with it. She might say that the second objection comes down to a dispute about terminology; and that the fourth is an empirical objection and its cogency will depend on the detailed empirical facts. The third objection, even though it says that in fact religious experience is never veridical, allows that it could have been. But the fifth says that in principle religious experience is not and could not have been veridical. The fifth objection is thus (if correct) the most damaging to the idea of religious experience.

A more liberal conception of experience?

At this point, the theist may make a tactical retreat and say that she has tied the idea of religious experience too closely to the concept of perception, and in particular to the idea that experiences of God must have a particular phenomenological content. All that is needed for veridical experience of God, she may now say, is the existence of a reliable correlation between kinds of minimal experience on the one hand, and the presence or activity of God on the other. Since there is no a priori limit to what can be reliably correlated with what, this manoeuvre would enable her immediately to sidestep the final objection above, the objection which said that in principle, perception of God is impossible. So what we now have to envisage is that some people have strange, hard-to-describe experiences which are very closely correlated with divine activity, and which allow the experiencer legitimately to form such beliefs as 'God forgives/loves/supports me'.

Let us look at some examples where perhaps this kind of non-perceptual experience is being invoked. Here is one example quoted by James:

> As usual, on retiring I prayed. In great distress, I at this time simply said 'Lord, I have done all I can, I leave the whole matter with thee'. Immediately, like a flash of light, there came to me a great peace, and I arose and went into my parents' bedroom and said 'I do feel so wonderfully happy'. This I regard as the hour of conversion. It was the hour in which I became assured of divine acceptance and favour.
>
> (James 1963: 253 fn.)

What is striking here is that the subject does not report that his senses revealed anything new or distinctive to him. What he reports is a sequence of non-perceptual changes: distress, followed by great peace, followed by wonderful happiness. It is clearly possible for a sequence of such states to be correlated with the presence of various kinds of mind-independent objects, such that the experiencer can use those states as more-or-less good evidence that the relevant object is present. It may be that I feel the sequence distress-peace-happiness if and only if (very nearly) there is falling air pressure. In that case, I could use my internal experiences as good evidence for falling air pressure. But before I could do that, I would have to know that such a correlation exists, and that would require me to be able to identify falling air pressure independently of the occurrence of my trio of internal states.

Precisely the same is true of James's subject. He can use his trio of emotional states as evidence of 'divine acceptance and favour' only if he has independent evidence that correlates his states with such acceptance and favour. James's subject does not produce any such evidence and, in its absence, the sceptic will rightly doubt that there is any such evidence to be produced.

Here is another example which again construes religious experience non-perceptually. The subject had been feeling in some religious confusion and depression, and at family prayers, he reported the following experience:

> At that instant of time . . . redeeming love broke into my soul with repeated scriptures with such power that my whole soul seemed to be melted down with love; the burden of guilt and condemnation was gone, darkness was expelled, my heart humbled and filled with gratitude and my whole soul that was a few minutes ago groaning under mountains of death and crying to an unknown God for help, was now filled with immortal love, soaring on the wings of faith, freed from the chains of death and darkness, and crying out, My Lord and my God; thou art my rock and my fortress . . . etc.
>
> (op. cit. p. 220)

Here we find the same evidence of a series of powerfully felt emotional states (confusion, depression, love, joy, exultation), and the same deficit from the evidential point of view. If these states are to be used as evidence for the existence of anything outside the subject's own mind, it must be because there is a reliable correlation between states of that kind and the mind-independent object. But the subject appeals to no such correlations, but seems to leap directly from his emotional experiences to a completely unrelated claim about mind-independent reality (that God is his 'rock and fortress').

Further reading

James (1963) is a still unsurpassed record of the variety of religious experience, interwoven with a sympathetic commentary. Contemporary influential defences of the claim that religious experience can be a source of rational belief in or even knowledge of God are in Swinburne (1979) and Gutting (1982), while more recent defences are in Davis (1989), Alston (1991), Yandell (1993), and Gellman (1997). In the tradition of scepticism, C.B. Martin (1959), Mackie (1982), Michael Martin (1990), Gale (1991), and Bagger (1999) all supply important contributions.

9

---◦◯◦---

Naturalism, evolution and rationality

Introduction

All the arguments which we have looked at so far have been directly supporting theism, and one direct consequence has been that if they are sound,
then atheism is false. The argument which we consider in this chapter has a
different form: it is an argument for the conclusion that atheism and agnosticism are untenable, which (if the argument is sound) has as a consequence
the conclusion that only theism is tenable. Although versions of the argument can be found in several writers, the most detailed presentation of it is
by Plantinga, and we can therefore usefully take his version as canonical.[1]
Plantinga has produced a number of versions of the argument. Some of them
are clearly different arguments, some are clearly different versions of the
same arguments, some include what appear to be merely stylistic or rhetori-
cal differences. In what follows, I will expound a simplified version of what I
take to be the main version.

The argument against naturalism

The argument starts with some reflections on our capacities as cognitive
beings. All of us are equipped with a range of cognitive faculties which allow
us to acquire, store and manipulate information about a huge variety of subjects. Our sensory equipment enables us to know about our perceptual
environment; our memory enables us to store information both about specific events in the past and about general truths; and our reasoning capacity
enables us to see the implications of the information which we have and to
draw sometimes long and complicated inferences. We all assume that these
cognitive faculties are substantially reliable. When they are operating properly, they reveal to us truths, or probable truths, or near truths. They are, we
might say, truth-directed. Of course, on occasions we arrive at falsehoods.
We are careless in our inferences, our observations, or the viewing conditions are not ideal, or there is some malfunction in the relevant organs. But

in general, we take it that our cognitive faculties succeed in giving us truths (or probable or approximate truths – for the sake of brevity, I will omit this qualification in what follows). Not all our faculties are like that. Most obviously, the faculty of wishful thinking is not truth-directed. Nor is the faculty of imagination. But our cognitive faculties we do take to be truth-directed. What, then, is the origin of these faculties? How has it come about that human beings have this set of reliable truth-directed cognitive faculties?

According to naturalism, the explanation must lie entirely within the realm of natural processes. Exactly what is covered by the term 'naturalism' here is unclear, but Plantinga tells us that it would be fair to take it to be 'the view that there is no such person as God, nor anyone or anything at all like him' (Plantinga 2000: 227). It later emerges that the term is being given a rather wider sense than this, to cover, for example, agnostics. In practice, naturalism in this context means simply non-theism. So a naturalistic explanation of how we come to have reliable cognitive faculties will be one which does not invoke God. Accordingly, it is fair to assume that of the available natural explanations, the most plausible and certainly the most widely accepted is neo-Darwinism, and so Plantinga raises the question of what naturalism-with-neo-Darwinism can say about the origin of our cognitive faculties. He assumes that this is currently the most plausible version of naturalism, and that if it turns out to be untenable, then so will every other form of naturalism. How, then, does the defender of Darwinian naturalism answer the question about our cognitive faculties? The answer in brief will clearly be that our cognitive faculties evolved through the operation of 'blind' processes, in particular the process of natural selection. This process selects the creatures[2] who are better adapted to their environment, and part of that better adaptation can consist in having better information about the environment. An animal that is better at detecting such features as food, danger and mates is, other things being equal, more likely to survive and reproduce than its less fortunate conspecifics. It will thus be more likely to pass on its genes than those conspecifics. So the forces of natural selection would favour the development of better and better perceptual systems. Again, an animal that engages in some problem-solving will, other things being equal, be better able to cope with novel situations than its dimmer-witted cousins. It will therefore be to that extent better adapted to a changing environment, and thus be more likely to reproduce successfully and pass on its genes to succeeding generations. So natural selection could favour the emergence of creatures with beliefs, who could engage in reasoning from one belief to another. Of course, all of these likelihoods have to be set against a background of other contingencies. The animal whose perceptual system has the edge over its rivals might be wiped out by an event in relation to which it has no comparative advantage: a lightning strike incinerates it without warning, a meteor strikes it and all other life for miles around with a colossal explosion. But, other things being equal, these improvements in an animal's cognitive system will give it an advantage, and hence will be more likely to be spread in the next generation. (For details on evolution and natural selection, see Chapter 5.) Such is likely to be the account which the naturalist offers of how and why we developed reliable cognitive faculties.

The Plantingan objection can now be set out in the following argument (A):

(1) If our cognitive faculties had developed entirely by naturalistic process like natural selection, it would be improbable that they are reliable (premise).
(2) If it was improbable that they were reliable, we would have no good reason to rely on any of their deliverances (premise). So:
(3) We would have no good reason for trusting our reasoning powers (from (1) and (2)).
(4) We would have no good reason for trusting the reasoning that led us to accept naturalism in the first place (from (3)). So:
(5) We could have no reason to accept naturalism (from (4)). So:
(6) Even if naturalism is true, we can have no good reason for accepting it (from (5)).

The believer in naturalism (let us call her the Naturalist) is thus caught in an impossible position: if naturalism is false, then she ought not to accept it (because it is false); and if naturalism is true, then she ought not to accept it (because of Argument (A)). But is the theist in any better a position? Plantinga has less to say on this issue, but he clearly thinks that the theist *is* in a better position, for reasons which we can capture in the following Argument (B):

(7) If God exists, then as an omnipotent and benevolent creator who has designed us in his own image, he will have equipped us with a set of cognitive systems that are reliable (premise). So:
(8) If God exists, we have reason to believe that the deliverances of our cognitive systems will be at least broadly correct (from (7)). So:
(9) If God exists, we have no reason to think that any arguments we produce (e.g. rebutting objections to theism or criticising naturalism) are unreliable merely because they are the product of our cognitive faculties (from (8)).

Although Plantinga formulates the argument first as an attack on an atheistic naturalism based on Darwinian natural selection, it can clearly be adapted to aim at a much wider target. Suppose for example that like pre-Darwinian agnostics (Plantinga has Hume in mind), you are entirely uncommitted to the truth of Darwinism. Suppose that like Hume himself, you simply have no beliefs at all about our origins. You think that a wide variety of non-theistic origins for humanity is possible. You can then have no reason to think that our cognitive faculties are reliable, and you hence fall prey to an argument closely parallel to (A).

The controversial claim here is (1): why does naturalism imply that it is improbable that our cognitive mechanisms are reliable? In defence of this claim, Plantinga points out that what evolution selects are organisms (or perhaps genes – the argument would be the same either way) that are successful at reproducing themselves. This requires that their behaviour should be well-adapted (in the sense of their being able to produce future generations that are copies of themselves). But whether this has any implications for the reliability of their cognition is a further question, and will turn on how we think that their cognition and their behaviour are related. The normal view of our cognitive systems is that they yield mainly beliefs that are true or probably true or nearly true, and that these beliefs can guide our behaviour in ways that conduce to our surviving and flourishing. For example, my visual system enables me accurately to detect the approach of a dangerous predator, my resulting belief that an angry bear is coming towards me then combines with my desire to live, and the resulting belief/desire combination causes me to take evasive action. Or again, my olfactory sense enables me to acquire the true belief that the fruits in my hand are malodorous; my memory accurately tells me that in the past, malodorous fruits have proved fatal for those who have consumed them; my reasoning faculty enables me to draw the inference that (probably) these fruits will be bad for me to eat; and all of this cognising then combines with my desire to survive and be healthy, to cause me not to eat poisonous fruits. Let us call this the Normal view of how the reliability of our cognitive faculties is meant to contribute to our survival and hence could be favoured by natural selection.

Plantinga accepts that this Normal view is possibly true, even if naturalism is true. But he also says that consistent with naturalist and evolutionary theory, our cognitive faculties could have developed in other more peculiar ways. It could have been the case that we were so constructed that these true beliefs had no effect on our actions. We might have had beliefs about predators, about food sources, about mating opportunities, etc. and we might have acted successfully in respect of these aspects of our lives, but there might have been no causal connection between our cognitions and our actions. It could have been that we had some other adaptive system that ensured our actions were appropriate, and hence that it did not matter from the point of view of survival that our beliefs never affected our actions, and because our beliefs did not affect our actions, it did not matter whether these beliefs were true or whether our cognitive faculties were reliable. To borrow a term from the philosophy of mind, our beliefs could have been epiphenomenal, that is to say, caused by physical changes in our bodies, but not themselves having any effect on the state or actions of our bodies. Plantinga is not saying at this point that this is likely – that is a further question which he will shortly address. The claim here is merely that given naturalism, this strange lack of linkage between our cognitions and our actions is a possibility. It is one of a range of possible ways in which, given naturalism, our cognitive system could have developed in ways that do not accord with the Normal view. Let us group all these abnormal cases together under the general heading of the Abnormal view of our cognitive faculties.

So, there are two rival views about our cognitive systems, the Normal view and the Abnormal view. Given the assumption of naturalism, on the Normal view, it is reasonable to think that our cognitive systems are reliable, since their reliability contributes indirectly to our survival and reproduction (because it affects our actions) and hence will be favoured by natural selection. Given the same assumption of naturalism, on the Abnormal view, there is very little reason to think that our cognitive systems are reliable; for since their reliability does not affect our actions, it will not contribute to our survival and reproduction and hence will not be favoured by natural selection.

To assess the probable reliability of our cognitive systems, given naturalism, we therefore need to combine two sets of probabilities: the probability that the Normal rather than the Abnormal view is correct, and the probability that our system is reliable given the correctness of each of the two views in turn.

Plantinga argues that, given naturalism, the Abnormal view is a good deal more probable than the Normal view. The reason for this is that given naturalism, it is very difficult to see how our beliefs *could* influence our actions in the way in which the Normal view assumes that they do. The naturalist is likely to assume that beliefs are either just physical states of the brain (a standard form of materialism), or are non-physical states somehow associated with events in the brain (a standard form of dualism). On the first assumption, it is difficult to see how the content of the belief (what it is about and in virtue of which it can be true or false) can be part of the causal chain leading to the agent's behaviour. Surely if the behaviour is caused by a physical state of the brain, then that physical state would have caused that behaviour even if the state had been linked to a quite different belief content. On the alternative assumption (that the belief is a non-physical state), there is a puzzle which has haunted the philosophy of mind since the time of Descartes: how can non-physical events produce physical effects? How could a non-physical belief produce physical behaviour, or even a physical response in the brain? So, given naturalism, it is difficult to see how the Normal view can be correct. Plantinga quotes with approval a remark by Robert Cummins that 'epiphenomenalism is in fact the received view as to the relation between belief and behaviour' (Plantinga 2000: 236). Consequently, the probability that the Normal view is correct, given naturalism, is low, and the probability that the Abnormal view is correct is correspondingly high.

We have already seen how the Normal view implies that our cognitions are probably correct, and the Abnormal view that they are probably incorrect. So, given that on the assumption of naturalism, the Abnormal view is more probable than the Normal view, the overall upshot is that, given naturalism, it is probable that our cognitive systems are not reliable, and hence that premise (1) (that naturalism implies that it is unlikely that our cognitive faculties are reliable) of argument (A) is correct.

Plantinga gives a helpful analogy to this line of reasoning (see Plantinga 2000: 239). Suppose you have a barometer, which you believe can be in one or other of two states C1 or C2. If it is in state C1 then it is very likely that it accurately measures the air pressure. If it is in state C2 it is very unlikely that it gives accurate measurements. You don't know whether it is in state C1 or state C2. As far as you know there is a roughly 50 per cent chance that it is in either state. Given this position, it is obvious that you would not be entitled to rely on the measurements provided by the barometer. The analogy is clear: the barometer is the analogue to our cognitive faculties, its accuracy is the analogue to the reliability of our cognitive faculties. The analogy is designed to illustrate how, just as you would not be entitled to rely on the barometer readings, so, given the assumption of naturalism, you would not be entitled to rely on your cognitive faculties. The argument could be summarised in the form shown in Figure 9.1 (overleaf).

What about the rest of Argument (A), the argument for the conclusion that even if naturalism is true we can have no good reason for accepting it? Premise (2) seems unexceptionable, and step (3) follows directly from premises (1) and (2). Premise (4) is entailed by (3), and in turn entails (5), from which (6) follows. So it seems that in Argument (A), it is only premise (1) which is really controversial. What about Argument (B), the argument for the conclusion that theism escapes the self-refuting character of naturalism? Here, the naturalist will query (7), the claim that if God exists then our cognitive systems will be reliable. Premise (7) is not asserting that God does exist, but only what he will have done, if he does exist. In his latest discussion of the argument, Plantinga has very little to say about how the theist escapes the problems which he believes are raised by naturalism, but in earlier discussions of the topic, he treated (7) simply as a starting point. The implication seems to be that different theists will have different justifications for accepting (7). Some may regard it as a properly basic belief, in the sense explored in Chapter 2. Others may accept it on the basis of some reasoning of the kind explored in Chapters 3 to 9. Either way, they take themselves to be justified in asserting (7); and given (7), (8) follows and in turn entails (9).

This completes the defence of the claim that naturalism is in a certain sense self-refuting (its truth would undermine all reason for believing that it was true) whereas theism is not self-refuting. Given that we are going to accept that either naturalism or theism is true, it follows that we should accept theism.

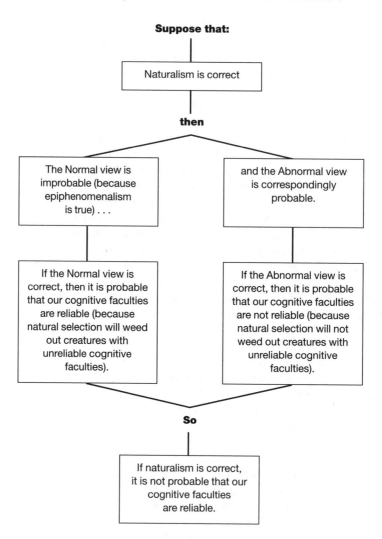

Suppose that:

Naturalism is correct

then

The Normal view is improbable (because epiphenomenalism is true) . . .

and the Abnormal view is correspondingly probable.

If the Normal view is correct, then it is probable that our cognitive faculties are reliable (because natural selection will weed out creatures with unreliable cognitive faculties).

If the Abnormal view is correct, then it is probable that our cognitive faculties are not reliable (because natural selection will not weed out creatures with unreliable cognitive faculties).

So

If naturalism is correct, it is not probable that our cognitive faculties are reliable.

Figure 9.1

Before we consider this line of argument critically, let us remove some possible misconceptions about what Plantinga is saying. First, he is not saying to his opponents that they are not entitled to rely on their cognitive faculties unless they can first prove that those faculties are indeed reliable. He is not requiring of them that they start from a position of neutrality about whether their faculties are trustworthy, and that they then produce a proof of this trustworthiness; nor is his criticism of naturalists based on the fact that they do not succeed in doing this. As he clearly acknowledges, this would be an impossible task for any view to accomplish. For any supposed proof of this trustworthiness would be question-begging: the 'proof' would be produced by the very faculties whose reliability was supposedly in question. Rather, he is saying that any thinker must be able to answer this question 'Given as premise the reliability of my faculties, what are the presuppositions of this reliability? What else must I take to be the case, for example, about the origins of these faculties, if this reliability is to be explicable?' Plantinga's claim is that theism can provide a self-consistent answer to this question, but naturalism cannot. Second, Plantinga is not himself endorsing the Abnormal view, nor saying that it is more probably true than the Normal view. He does think that the Abnormal view is possible, in the sense that there is at least one possible world in which it is true. But he does not think that it is remotely probable. His claim is only that it is the naturalist who is committing to thinking the Abnormal view more probable than not.

Assessment of the argument

What reply can the Naturalist make to this attempted proof that she cannot rationally believe that our cognitive faculties are reliable? The first criticism to make concerns the idea that naturalism makes the Normal view improbable. Plantinga is right that there is a philosophical puzzle about how the content of our beliefs can be causally effective in producing behaviour. Although it seems obvious to commonsense that our beliefs do affect our actions, and that the effect is essentially determined by the content of the beliefs, it turns out to be very hard to explain in detail how this can be so. But to say that there is a puzzle about how is it possible for something to occur is by itself a weak ground for saying that it (probably) does not occur at all. The fact that there is no philosophical consensus on the explanation of how the content of our beliefs influences our actions is a weak ground for saying that the Normal view is probably wrong. It is hence a weak ground for saying that the Abnormal view is probably right, and hence a weak ground for saying that given naturalism, our cognitive faculties are probably unreliable. So whether or not premise (1) in Argument (A) (the premise that says that if naturalism is true, then it is improbable that our cognitive faculties are correct) is true, we have been given no reason to believe it.

Second, the problem of how beliefs and actions can be linked is not one which naturalism *in particular* gives rise to: it is just as acute if one is a non-naturalist. The theist does not solve the problem by saying 'We have been designed by God in such a way that the content of our beliefs makes a difference to our actions'. The problem of *how* that is possible remains just as acute. The theist of course can say that since God is omnipotent, he can bring it about that the content of our beliefs makes a difference to our

185

actions. But this will be an empty move unless the theist can provide an explanation of *how* this is possible. She cannot fairly criticise the naturalist for being unable to say how something is possible, and then refuse to explain how in *her* view it is possible (and saying that God does it by a miraculous power is not to explain how it is possible). The problem therefore does not tell against naturalism more than against theism, and so cannot be a good reason for giving epistemic preference to theism over naturalism.

Third, the problem of how minds affect the material universe is if anything even more acute for theism than for naturalism. The problem for the naturalist is how finite human minds (possibly non-physical) can affect the material world, in particular how they can affect human brains. Theism faces both this problem, and also a cosmic-sized version of it. For according to theism, a divine (non-physical) mind caused to come into existence, and causes to remain in existence, the whole of the material world. If there is a puzzle about how *my* thought at a given time can produce changes in *my* brain at that time (or momentarily thereafter), how much greater a puzzle there must be about how another mind can produce changes anywhere in the whole of the material world – and indeed can produce literally out of nothing the material world itself. It is as if the theist says to the naturalist 'You have an unsolved problem explaining how a particular phenomenon is possible. I take that failure to be a refutation of naturalism, and a vindication of theism, even though theism faces the same problem on a much greater scale.'

Fourth, the Naturalist is likely to be unpleasantly surprised by the theist's use of premise (7), the claim that if God exists, he will have given us reliable cognitive faculties. There are two forms which her displeasure might take. If the theist claims that (7) is a properly basic belief for her (the theist), the Naturalist will reprise the reservations expressed about Reformed Epistemology in Chapter 2. In that chapter, the issue was whether a belief in theism *per se* could be regarded as properly basic. Premise (7) differs from theism in two respects: it does not *assert* the existence of God, but only considers it conditionally; and it makes very specific claims about what God would or would not do if he existed. Nevertheless, the Naturalist will think that (7) has if anything even less claim to be properly basic than theism itself.

Suppose however that the theist claims to know or rationally accept (7) on the basis of argument. The Naturalist will then want to see that argument properly displayed. This requirement is particularly pressing because (7) claims some very specific knowledge about what God will do if he exists. How is this knowledge obtained? The Naturalist can allow the theist any claims which say that if God exists, then anything derivable from his defining characteristics (say, omnipotence, omniscience and goodness) must also hold; and can also allow the theist any claims which both sides accept independently of the issue of God. But that means that the Naturalist will be willing to concede:

(10) If God exists, then anything derivable from his defining characteristics will also be real.
(11) Human beings exist

and from those, she can concede that it follows:

(12) If God exists, he is by definition the creator and sustainer of human beings.

But that is a very long way from accepting:

(13) If God exists, he will equip human beings with a set of cognitive faculties which enable them to discover truths, and which are appropriately connected with their actions (i.e. that he will equip them in such a way as to make the Normal view correct).

And it is (13) which Argument (B) requires. Even if we think that God exists, we simply have too little information about why he would have created human beings at all to know whether he would have created them in accordance with the Normal view. What divine purposes would explain, for example, why different humans have these faculties to such different degrees? Some are, for example, brilliant mathematicians, others are congenital idiots and half-wits; some have perfect pitch while others are born deaf. Most humans experience a deterioration in their cognitive powers with aging. How does all this variation fit in with the picture presented in (13)? Again, our best investigations suggest that most humans are comparatively bad at reasoning involving probabilities. Why would God have made us with this species-wide weakness? The point here is not that there are no theistic answers to such questions. Rather the reverse – there are too many, with no principled way of choosing among them. The data that we have about human cognition radically underdetermine any hypotheses about what God's purposes would be, if he existed. As a consequence, the theist's use of premise (7) is vulnerable, and with it the whole of Argument (B).

The same point can be brought out by a line of argument put forward by Lehrer (in Kvanig (ed.) 1996: 29–30). As Lehrer points out, theists standardly regard God's goodness as compatible with huge amounts of evil in the world, in the form of huge and hideous and wholly undeserved suffering. (This gives rise to the problem of evil, which we will be exploring in Chapter 12.) The theist uses various strategies to explain away the apparent discrepancy between a benevolent creator and creation containing evil. But now the naturalist can advance an *ad hominem* argument against the theist, using the same approach. Even if (she will say) the theist can establish that God is essentially truth-loving or knowledge-loving, that would be fully compatible with his allowing huge amounts of cognitive error in the universe at large, and in human beings in particular. So, the theist cannot make any decent estimate of the reliability of our cognitive faculties, given theism, and she hence has a defeater for her belief (delivered by those same cognitive faculties) that theism is true.

Plantinga's response to this (see op. cit. pp. 335–8) is to claim that the theist wishes to judge the reliability of our cognitions not against theism per se (i.e. simply the belief in the existence of God) but against 'the *whole* message of Christianity, the *whole* of what the Holy Spirit testifies to' (op. cit. p. 337). Against this larger package of ideas (let us call it theism-plus), he says, it *is* plausible to think that God will have equipped us with some faculties which allow us to discover the truth, even if he has also made us as creatures in whom 'the fall into sin has damaged the image of God in us, and damaged our cognitive faculties' (op. cit. p. 336).

The naturalist is likely to find this an unsatisfactory reply, for several reasons. First, and more generally, the appeal to 'what the Holy Spirit testifies to' seems to imply that theism-plus is being given the status of a properly basic belief (see Chapter 2). So the doubts that were raised in Chapter 2 will here return, alongside a further suspicion. For it now seems that the Reformed Epistemologist is using the category of the properly basic as a kind of epistemological dumping ground for any belief which she cannot defend, but which she nevertheless wants to hold on to.

Second, the naturalist might well wonder why what is sauce for theism cannot also be sauce for naturalism. If the theist is allowed to say that the probability that our cognitions are reliable is to be judged against theism-plus, not against just theism, why can't the naturalist say that she wants the probability of reliability judged against naturalism-plus, where the latter is naturalism with some extra doctrines which boost that probability?

Third, Plantinga's reply here has some implausible implications. One of the claims which he says is implicit in theism-plus is that 'sin . . . has damaged our cognitive faculties' (op. cit. p. 336); and he uses this claim to explain why there is so much error in a world which is supposedly made by a truth-loving God who has given us reliable cognitive faculties. But this mining of the resources of theism-plus to explain away error can quickly be seen to be wildly implausible. If it means that sin has damaged our cognitive faculties indiscriminately, we would expect sinners to display cognitive unreliability across the board – in all three areas of perception, memory and reasoning. But on the assumption that atheists form one class of those whom Plantinga would regard as especially sinful,[3] we do not find that this is so. Atheists do not suffer from blindness, deafness, etc. more than do theists; nor are atheists more prone to amnesia than theists; nor are they in general worse at reasoning than theists. So how is it that some - non-sinners do have damaged and hence unreliable cognitive faculties, and some sinners do not? There must be some other explanatory factor at work than just sin. And once one starts a *serious* investigation of cognitive mal-

function, sin would simply drop out of the picture as a worthless explanatory concept. When you go to the optician for glasses, you expect her to tell
you that your sight is defective because the lens in one eye has become
cloudy, or the eye muscle is too weak to tighten the lens properly and bring
objects into focus, etc. If you visit the hospital to discover why your memory
is playing up, you expect to be told that you suffer from a deficiency of some
neuro-transmitter, or you have a tumour on the brain. And so on. In no serious investigation of the cause of a cognitive malfunction would any
properly informed person say 'You are red/green colour blind because you
are sinful' or 'You are poor at detecting the fallacy of affirming the consequent because you are sinful'.

At one point, Plantinga seems to forestall this criticism. He says in a foot-
note that we should not assume that:

> damage to the *sensus divinitatis* [the sense by means of which we
> detect facts about God] on the part of a person is due to sin on the
> part of the same person. Such damage is like other disease and
> handicaps: due ultimately to the ravages of sin, but not necessarily
> sin on the part of the person with the disease.
>
> (Plantinga 2000: 214 fn. 22)

But with this admission, the whole account of sin as the source of a cognitive disability which prevents us seeing what would otherwise be obvious,
simply unravels. Just as we cannot explain my malfunctioning memory by
reference to neural deficiencies in your brain, or my red/green colour blindness by reference to the cones in your eyes, so we cannot explain any
deficiency in my supposed *sensus divinitatis* (if I had one) by reference to sin
in you. There is no underlying causal mechanism in terms of which we could
understand a supposed explanation of the one phenomenon in terms of the
other. Nor does it help Plantinga's case that he thinks that everyone is born
with sin (op. cit. p. 207). It seems that although you and I are both sinful,
and sin is the cause of damage to one of our cognitive faculties, your sin
may be the cause of the damage to my faculties, and my sin may be the
cause of damage to yours. One must be thankful that Plantinga became a
philosopher and not an epidemiologist.

This assessment of the argument from naturalism has been convoluted
and it may be helpful to summarise it. Five objections were raised to the
argument: first, Plantinga was wrong to say that the existence of a puzzle
about mind–body interaction gave the naturalist a strong reason to reject
the Normal view; second, theism does not make the Normal view any easier
to accommodate; third, theism faces in addition a cosmic version of the
problem raised by the Normal view; fourth, the theist is not entitled to
premise (7) (the claim that if God exists, he will equip us with reliable cognitive faculties); and finally, the Lehrer objection, that if the theist believes a
benevolent God is compatible with huge amounts of evil in the world, she

must think that a truth-loving God is compatible with the existence of huge amounts of cognitive error in the world. In response to this final criticism, we considered Plantinga's reply, namely that the reliability of our cognitive faculties is to be judged in relation to theism-plus (where theism-plus includes information about God's intention to give us reliable cognitive faculties and about how sin can impair the functioning of these faculties). And in relation to that Plantingan reply, we raised three objections: first, that theism-plus is being given the status of a properly basic belief, and this is implausible; second, that if the theist can appeal to theism plus, the naturalist could appeal to naturalism-plus; and third, that the explanation offered by theism-plus of cognitive malfunction in terms of sin is implausible.

In consequence of the above arguments, the Naturalist will claim, both halves of Plantinga's argument against naturalism fail: we have been given no reason to think that if naturalism is correct, our cognitive faculties would be unreliable; nor any reason to think that if theism is correct, these faculties would be reliable (even less reason to think that only if theism is correct would this reliability hold). So this line of thought gives us no reason to think that reason requires us to embrace theism.

Further reading

The argument discussed in this chapter first appeared in Plantinga (1991) and is reprinted in Sennett (1998). Another version appeared on the web with some replies by Plantinga to his critics at http://www.homestead.com/philofreligion/files/alspaper.htm. Parts of this web paper were then printed in Plantinga (1995). The latest full published version is in Plantinga (2000), although there is a brief summary of the argument in Plantinga's introductory essay in Beilby (2002). The rest of the Beilby volume contains critical discussions of the argument, with a long reply by Plantinga. The argument is also criticised by O'Connor (1994) and Ginet (1995), who both argue that naturalism can add a further claim to naturalism to the effect that our faculties are reliable. Nathan (1997) challenges the claim that if the naturalist has no reason to trust her faculties, she is condemned to epistemic incoherence.

10

———•◉•———

Prudential arguments

It is wrong always, everywhere, and for anyone to believe anything upon insufficient evidence.

(Clifford 1879: 186)

When I look at the religious question as it really puts itself to
concrete men, and when I think of all the possibilities which
both practically and theoretically it involves, then this command that we shall put a stopper on our heart, instincts and
courage, and *wait* – acting of course meanwhile more or less as
if religion were *not* true – till doomsday, or till such time as
our intellect and senses working together may have raked in
evidence enough – this command, I say, seems to me the queer-
est idol ever manufactured in the philosophic cave.

(James 1918: 123)

Introduction

We have so far been concerned with a number of arguments which attempt
to show that a belief in God is *justified* – justified in the sense that there are
good reasons for thinking that the belief is true. These good reasons are supposed to arise either from some argument which has the existence of God as
its conclusion, or from the fact that God is known directly by experience.
But we now need to consider a cluster of arguments which try to show that
a belief in God is justified in a quite different sense of the word. So our initial task must be to clarify what the distinction is between the two sorts of
justification.

The first sort of justification is what I will call *epistemic* justification. This
is justification for a belief, and consists in producing some argument, or reasoning, or evidence, or grounds which support (to some extent or other) the
belief in question. They are grounds for thinking that the belief is true (or
probably true, to some degree or other). A belief can thus be epistemically

justified, without there being any implication that it will *benefit* you to believe it, or to come to believe it if you do not believe it already. You might be epistemically justified in holding a belief, where your holding it had bad or even disastrous consequences for you. You might, for example, have very good evidence that you suffer from a fatal disease, and in that case you would be epistemically justified in holding that belief. But it might also be the case that your holding that belief made you feel very depressed, made you more sensitive to pain, and even hastened your death. So you would have been better off if you had not held a belief which you were epistemically justified in holding. Or, to give another example, it may be that you have good evidence that you are socially maladroit (you forget people's names as soon as you have been introduced to them, you misremember who their partners are, etc.). If so, then you would be epistemically justified in believing that you were socially maladroit. But it might be that your holding this justified belief simply reinforces the social maladroitness from which you suffer, and prevents you from becoming socially competent. Again, then, it is a belief which you are (epistemically) justified in holding, even though holding it leaves you worse off than if you did not hold it.

The second sort of justification is what I will call *consequential* justification. To call a belief justified in this sense is not to say anything about grounds or evidence for its truth. It is to say something about the beneficial consequences of someone's holding it. Thus, in the two examples above, you would not have been (consequentially) justified in believing that you had a fatal disease, since it left you worse off than you would have been without that belief. And you would not have been (consequentially) justified in believing that you were socially maladroit, since that too left you worse off. As an example of when you *would* be consequentially justified, consider the following possibility: you are an athlete who can achieve your best performance *only if* you believe that you are the best in the field (the county, the region, the country, etc.). There may be no good evidence that you are the best (so you are being epistemically irrational in holding the belief), and the belief may not even be true. But if you did not hold this (epistemically) irrational belief, your actual performance would be worse. So you are consequentially justified in holding this (epistemically) irrational belief.

Given this distinction between the two sorts of justification, it will be obvious that the arguments for a belief in God's existence which we have been looking at so far have all been invoking epistemic justification. They have all been trying to produce grounds, or evidence, or justification for believing that it was *true* that God exists (or probably true). By contrast, the arguments to which we now turn ignore questions of epistemic justification and focus entirely on consequential justification. They thus fall under the heading of what Gale calls 'pragmatic' arguments, and what Mackie calls 'belief without reason'.

Pascal's Wager

The first argument of this type that we shall consider is probably the most famous: Pascal's Wager. Pascal was a seventeenth-century mathematician, a Jansenist who himself believed in God for reasons quite other than those put forward in his Wager. He was also the friend of some gambling aristocrats, who persuaded him to lend his mathematical talents to calculate the odds of certain combinations of cards turning up in play. He thus became interested in the question of what the rational course of action is when the costs, benefits and probabilities of the outcomes of different courses of action can be calculated in advance.

From this basis, he developed an argument which was designed to appeal specifically to convinced hard-nosed, self-interested gamblers who thought that neither the existence nor the non-existence of God could be established, and that therefore the rational egoist would not waste any time on theism, or any moral constraints which supposedly owed their bindingness to the truth of theism. This background is important. In particular, we need to bear in mind that in its basic form, the argument presupposes two points. The first is the failure of all epistemic arguments for and against the existence of God: neither the existence nor the non-existence of God can be shown to be in the least probable. Second, the Wager is addressed to persons motivated entirely by self-interest. It thus operates with restrictive background assumptions, and is targeted at a restricted audience. In what follows, I will not be concerned primarily with Pascal's own version of the argument, which is relatively undeveloped. Instead I will consider some arguments which are based on Pascal's approach, but which go beyond what he himself says. Accordingly, I will speak in what follows not of Pascal, but of a 'Pascalian'.

The basic argument consists in a simple piece of games theory, designed to show that whether or not God exists, the consequentially rational person will believe that he does. There are, says the Pascalian, only two possibilities: either God exists, or he does not exist. And in each of these situations, you might either believe that he exists, or not believe this. So we can give an exhaustive list of all the possibilities:

(1) God exists and you believe that he does.
(2) God exists, but you do not believe that he does.
(3) God does not exist but you believe that he does.
(4) God does not exist and you do not believe that he does.

The Pascalian then assumes that each of these possibilities will have consequences for the person concerned. The person will either benefit or suffer, according to which of the four options applies. Thus if God exists, and you believe that he does, the Pascalian assumes that God will be very pleased with you, and you will get infinite bliss in the afterlife. If God exists, but you do *not* believe that he does, the Pascalian assumes that God will be extremely wrathful, and that you will suffer endless torment in hell. If God does not exist, but you believe that he does, then you suffer no costs but receive no benefits. If God does not exist, and you do not believe that he does, then again you have no costs but no benefits either.

We can now represent the possible pay-offs as shown below. We can see that the pay-offs for belief are much better than the pay-offs for non-belief. The best pay-off under belief is infinitely better than any pay-off under non-belief; the worst pay-off under belief is no worse than the best pay-off under non-belief but infinitely better than the worst pay-off under non-belief. So the non-believer cannot possibly do better than the believer, and may very well do infinitely worse; and correlatively the believer cannot do worse than the non-believer and may do infinitely better. So the consequentially rational person will be a believer.

	God exists	God does not exist
You believe that God exists	Infinite bliss	No benefit, but no cost
You believe that God does not exist	Infinite torment	No benefit, but no cost

That gives us the basic version of the Wager, and the Pascalian then adds various refinements to it, designed to meet some objections. It might be objected for example that believing in God does have some significant costs. It requires you, let us suppose, to spend time in church, to go to Mass, to do penance, to give alms to charity when you could be spending the money on riotous living, and to say prayers, when you could be out enjoying yourself with wine, women (or men) and song. So, the person who believes does suffer some costs, and these will be outweighed only if God does exist. If God does not exist, then the believer has incurred these costs in vain. What these complications do in essence is to alter the expected costs and benefits, as follows:

	God exists	God does not exist
You believe that God exists	Infinite bliss, less the minor inconveniences of being pious	Minor inconvenience of being pious
You believe that God does not exist	Infinite torment	No minor inconvenience, but no benefits either

The Pascalian seeks to show that this complication makes no difference to the conclusion of the calculation: it is still consequentially rational to end up with a belief in God. Why? Because the best possibility under belief is better than the best possibility under disbelief; the worst possibility under belief is only slightly worse than the best possibility under disbelief; and the worst possibility under disbelief is hugely worse than the worst possibility under belief.

Again, perhaps you do not accept the initial assumption of the argument that the chances of God's existence and non-existence are exactly evenly balanced. Perhaps you already think that it is very improbable that God exists. And if that is so, then the weight that you attach to the nasty consequences of wrongly believing that he does not exist, and the weight you attach to the nice consequences of rightly believing that he does exist, must correspondingly diminish.

However, again the Pascalian seeks to show that this complication will still leave it consequentially rational to believe in God. Since the expected benefit/cost is (the probability of the outcome × the benefit/cost if the outcome occurs), those outcomes where the cost/benefit is infinite will always outweigh those where it is finite, even if in the former case the outcome is hugely improbable. The same point applies if the probabilities are other than as supposed in the Pascalian's original argument. The smaller the probability, the smaller the expected cost/benefit, except where the cost/benefit would be infinite if it occurs. If we assume that any number multiplied by infinity gives infinity, changing the probabilities really makes no difference to the argument, as long as there is a finite probability, no matter how small, that God exists. In other words, the argument requires only that the audience should agree that the existence of God is at least *possible*. Suppose we think that it is say 75 per cent probable that God does not exist, and only 25 per cent probable that he does exist, our pay-off matrix would then look like this:

	God exists	God does not exist
You believe that God exists	(Infinite bliss, less the minor inconveniences of being pious) × 0.25 = infinite bliss	(Minor inconvenience of being pious) × 0.75 = very minor inconvenience
You believe that God does not exist	(Infinite torment) × 0.25 = infinite torment	(No minor inconvenience, but no benefits either) × 0.75 = no costs and no benefits

Given all the Pascalian's assumptions, i.e. given the pay-off matrices which are implicit in what he says, it follows fairly uncontroversially that belief in God is consequentially rational. The controversy surrounds the assumptions which he needs to make in order to get to his pay-off matrix in the first place. Let us look at two of those which can be questioned.

The first assumption we might challenge is the idea that we can simply choose to believe in God when we see that it will pay us to do so. This could be put briefly by saying that belief is not subject to the will. We cannot *choose* what to believe. We simply find ourselves forced to believe something, or forced to disbelieve it, or perhaps in some situations, forced to suspend judgement. So the idea that I could choose to believe in God because to do so would have beneficial consequences for me is false; I cannot *choose* to believe (or not to believe) in God at all.

The Pascalian, however, has a ready reply to this objection. He will say that his argument is not committed to saying that we can choose our beliefs, in the way in which, for instance, we can choose our actions. It is not saying that we can choose them *directly*. What his argument assumes is the much less contentious claim that we can directly choose courses of action that will *affect* which beliefs we acquire and retain, and in that way we can *indirectly* choose our beliefs. We are familiar with the thought that people often come to believe what most suits their own interests. The rich generally think that they *deserve* to be rich, the unsuccessful often believe that they would have been successful if only they had not been obstructed by some unlucky or malicious force. Without saying that humans are incapable of epistemically rational and unbiased thinking, we can accept that we are all subject to the dangers of wishful thinking. I might know my own intellectual limitations well enough to be able to judge that, given the sort of person I am (e.g. intellectually suggestible), if I went to live with New Age travellers, I would willy-nilly come to acquire some of their beliefs which I currently reject. So if I want for some reason to hold those beliefs, even though I cannot directly produce them in myself by an act of will, I can choose to follow a course of action which I know will indirectly produce those beliefs in me. Similarly, although it is true that I could not think to myself 'It will benefit me to believe in God, therefore I will start believing in God', I can think to myself 'It will benefit me to believe in God, therefore I will pursue a course of action which will very probably have the consequence that I believe in God'. The course of action might include, for example, mixing with lots of intellectually able theists whom I anyway find morally admirable, avoiding atheists, attending church/synagogue/mosque, reading theistic tracts and avoiding atheistic tracts, and so on. I could go through the outward motions of the believer, for example, in praying. At the start, I might well think to myself that my prayers were ridiculous. But it could well be that as I persevered, and as I mixed constantly with other people who took praying seriously, I would gradually find myself taking it seriously too. I would move from thinking that in prayer I was merely communing with myself, to thinking that I really was communicating with another presence, a spiritual force who heard me and who from time to time responded to me. I would come to think that a course of action which I had embarked on in a somewhat cynical and self-interested fashion had, by very great good fortune, brought me to accept important truths which I would otherwise have missed. I would be a genuine believer.

A number of commentators have thought that this reply to the objection that belief is not subject to the will is adequate. But we might well doubt whether the issue is quite so favourable to the Pascalian. It is one thing to concede that the causes of our beliefs are often not (epistemically) rational. It is another to think that we can deliberately manipulate our own beliefs in the way in which the Wager requires. Even if we agree that, *in principle*, a person can in some cases deliberately induce in herself beliefs which initially she finds incredible, using the indirect methods described above, there are still doubts about whether the Wager can be practically effective. How many people can manipulate their beliefs in the required manner? In relation to which beliefs can they do this? Can they really know beforehand whether they are likely to succeed in inducing in themselves any particular belief? It would be entirely reasonable for someone to think that for deeply held beliefs, nothing of the kind envisaged by the Pascalian would lead her to change her mind. Even if she thought that some such change was *possible*, she might quite reasonably also think that there are significant costs to trying to engineer the change in herself. She might well feel some measure of self-contempt at seeking to bypass her own rational faculties in order to induce in herself a belief which she initially regards either as unsupported or as false. These points do not of course show that the Pascalian's Wager is not a good argument for anyone at all, but only that there are empirical reasons for thinking that at best, its application could only be very restricted.

The second point at which the Pascalian is vulnerable concerns the assumptions which the Wager makes about God's nature and possible future behaviour. In particular, the Wager makes some questionable assumptions about what would please and displease God, about the rewards and punishments which he would hand out, what the grounds would be for such rewards and punishments, and so on. These raise problems which are much less easily dealt with by the Pascalian. In particular, why should we make the following assumptions:

(1) If I disbelieve in God, then he will condemn me to infinite torment.
(2) If I believe in God, he will reward me with infinite bliss.

Such a view surely implies a conception of God as being morally shallow and egotistical. It attributes to him the bizarre view that the *only* thing that matters to him is that we should believe in him. But surely a more plausible view from the perspective of traditional theism is the following: let us accept for the moment the assumption of the argument that if God exists, it is certain that he is going to reward and punish us in an afterlife. Then, given the traditional conception of God as a being who is morally perfect, who is concerned with human well-being, etc., he will consider the moral quality of our lives as a whole, not just the single question of whether we believe he exists. If we have led honest, compassionate, industrious lives, then it would be reasonable for us to expect that God (as traditionally conceived) would look with favour on us, even if we have been atheists. If we have led mean, cruel lives, God will look with disfavour on us, even if we have been theists. Perhaps we gain (or lose) a few merit points for being theists (or atheists). But the idea that we get *infinitely* many merit points just for being theists, no matter what quality the rest of our lives display, or that we get *infinitely* many minus points just for being atheists, no matter what quality the rest of our lives display, portrays God as a megalomaniac simpleton, a kind of cosmic Joseph Stalin. Given the idea that God is morally perfect (which is indeed usually regarded as a defining feature of God) we could say that any being who behaved in the way in which Pascal's Wager supposes God to behave would just not be God. And whether we call such a being 'God' or not, he/it would deserve our utter contempt and defiance, and not our kowtowing to him in the way that the Wager recommends.

William James and 'The Will to Believe'

Although Pascal's Wager is the most famous of the consequentialist arguments for the existence of God, it is not the only one. William James famously offers another in his essay 'The Will to Believe'. In that essay, James claims that in general we ought to believe or disbelieve propositions if and only if we have adequate evidence in favour of them. Using the terminology we introduced above, we can say that he urges us to be, in general, epistemically rational. Sometimes, however, the evidence does not allow us to come to a conclusion either way about the truth of a proposition. It may be that there is some evidence for it, but it is exactly balanced by evidence against; or it may be that there is no evidence either way. In such a case, the proposition is what James calls 'intellectually unresolvable'. What should our attitude be towards propositions which are unresolvable? Should we simply suspend belief in them? According to James, although the answer is in some cases 'Yes', in a significant number of cases the answer is 'No'. For some (but not all) unresolvable propositions, James implies that assent is intellectually *permissible*, and even rationally *required*.

The subclass of unresolvable propositions which James says we are entitled to believe concerns those where the decision whether to give or withhold belief is what James calls *living, forced* and *momentous*. What does James mean by these three preconditions? A choice is a living one if it is between two propositions each of which 'appeals as a real possibility to him to whom it is proposed' (James 1918: 100). That is to say that each of the two propositions must stand some chance of being credible. A choice is a forced one if it is one which you cannot avoid making. James's example of a non-forced choice is 'Choose between going out with your umbrella or without it'. The choice is not forced because you can avoid it by staying indoors. By contrast the choice 'Either accept this proposition or go without it' is forced because there is no third alternative: the person who suspends judgement, just as much as the person who rejects the proposition, must 'go without it'. And a choice is momentous if it is more-or-less unrepeatable, more-or-less irreversible, and if something momentous to the person might come from it. Let us call the propositions which are intellectually unresolvable and about which our choice whether to believe them is living, forced and momentous, open propositions.

James now declares that our 'passional nature' is entitled to decide whether to accept or reject open propositions. But what is our 'passional' nature? The title of James's paper ('The Will to Believe') suggests that James is saying that in at least some cases, we can legitimately *choose* what to believe; and this interpretation is supported by a number of other things that he says in the paper.[1] But as the discussion proceeds, it becomes clear that he has in mind something wider in scope than the will, and indeed something that in some ways is opposed to the will. At one point, he tells us that by our passional nature, he means more than just our emotions or our will – he means 'all such factors of belief as fear and hope, prejudice and passion, imitation and partisanship, the circumpressure of our cast and set' (op. cit. p. 106). So if, for example, I find myself believing something just because I have been brought up to accept it, my belief is due to the 'circumpressure of my set', and hence falls under the general rubric of being based on my passional nature, even although my will had nothing to do with either the acquisition or the retention of the belief. Again, if I find that my partisan commitment to a political party leads me to think that its manifesto promises are more credible than those of any other party, my belief is due to my passional nature, although again there is no suggestion that I have chosen my belief.

Not only *may* such factors legitimately decide our acceptance of open propositions, James says that they *must* decide, since each of the three possible decisions of rejection, acceptance and suspension of judgement relies on such factors. '*[F]or to say under such circumstances* [i.e. choosing between two intellectually unresolvable propositions], *"Do not decide but leave the question open", is itself a passional decision – just like deciding yes or no and is attended with the same risk of losing the truth*' (op. cit. p. 108, italics in original).

This implies that recourse to passional decisions is absolutely unavoidable with open propositions. It is not simply that it would be irrational never to accept an open proposition. The claim here is that whatever your reaction to an open proposition, whether you accept it or reject or suspend judgement, the decision is bound to be a passional one. The tacit implication is that the agnostic, i.e. someone who always suspends judgement on open propositions, is in no position to criticise the believer for having relied on passional factors to prompt his assent; for the believer can reply in turn that the agnostic has placed a similar reliance in arriving at *his* suspension of judgement.

There is nothing in James's discussion so far which implies that only theism will fall within the class of open propositions. Indeed, he gives several non-theistic examples of open propositions, such as moral propositions, and even propositions saying that a particular person does or does not like me. However, he now extends his line of thought to a belief in theism. (He actually speaks of a belief in 'religion' rather than in God, but we will here treat his discussion as if it were concerned with the God of traditional theism.) He explains what he takes religion/theism to be, in two theses: (1) the best things are the more eternal things, and (2) we are better off even now if we believe (1). He does not explain what he means by (2), but charitably we could take him to mean that a belief in God can, for example, provide inspiration in times of hope, consolation in times of darkness, and a feeling of companionship in times of loneliness. Those are respects in which a theist might plausibly claim that her belief makes her life go better for her.

Given that explanation, James now tries to show that a belief in God is indeed an open proposition. He starts with the tacit assumption that it is an intellectually unresolvable proposition, presumably taking for granted that the evidence for it and the evidence against are evenly balanced. Next, he assumes that it is a living option for his audience – insofar as it is not, he says that he is not addressing that section of the audience. Third, he claims that theism is a momentous choice: 'We are supposed to gain, even now by our belief, and to lose by our non-belief, a certain vital good' (op. cit. p. 120). Finally, theism is a forced choice: we lose the good which belief will bring, if with the atheist we reject the belief; but we also lose it if with the agnostic we suspend judgement. So, James concludes that theism is an open proposition; hence, even if there is no evidence in favour of it, and even if the evidence in favour of it is wholly counterbalanced by the evidence against it, we are fully entitled to believe it.

So far, James has argued that it is permissible and indeed unavoidable to rely on passional factors in responding to open propositions. But that of course leaves open which passion-backed response is the appropriate one. For all that James has said so far, one might accept a passion-backed rule that said 'Always suspend judgement in open propositions' (call this the agnostic rule). One might accept an alternative passion-backed rule that says 'Always accept one of a pair of rival open propositions'. How should we choose between rival open propositions? What James does is not advance a rule of his own, but offer an objection to the agnostic rule, in the following terms:

> a rule of thinking [such as the agnostic rule] which would absolutely prevent me from acknowledging certain kinds of truth if those kinds of truth were really there, would be *an irrational rule*. That for me is the long and short of *the formal logic* of the situation.
>
> (op. cit. p. 122, italics added)

So, although James seemed initially to have trimmed the wings of reason in favour of a non-rational appeal to passional factors, it now appears that some passional responses are more rational than others, and that in particular 'formal logic' dictates that the agnostic rule is an irrational one. And he seems to think that adoption of this (i.e. the rule which tells us always to accept one or other of a pair of rival open propositions) will underwrite an acceptance of religion/theism. The acceptance is rational in the sense that it is the only conclusion which can be arrived at without violating any consequentially rational rules for the acceptance/rejection of open propositions.

There is now a complication in James's account which we need to note, although it is strictly extraneous to his main line of argument. He claims that in at least some cases, if you believe an open proposition, then that can put you in a position to discover some hard evidence in favour of it, evidence that you could not have discovered if you had not initially believed it. Since this is a claim independent of his main line of argument, we will ignore it in what follows.

So the argument that James arrives at is:

(1) That God exists is an open proposition (in the sense defined above) (premise). So:
(2) It is unavoidable that we should rely on our passional nature in deciding whether to assent, dissent or withhold belief in open propositions (from (1)).
(3) In deciding how to let our passional nature guide us in relation to open propositions, we should not accept any rules which would prevent us from accepting as true any open propositions which are in fact true (premise). So:
(4) We should not assent to an agnostic rule which tells us always to suspend judgement in open propositions (from (3)). So:
(5) We are entitled to assent to the proposition that God exists (from (1) and (4)).

How strong is this as an argument for believing in God's existence? We can note first of all how it differs from the Pascalian argument of the previous section. First, the Wager at least in its extended versions can be applied to the belief in God's existence even if there is some good evidence that God does not exist. So, the Pascalian maintains that even if it is epistemically irrational to believe in God, it can simultaneously be consequentially rational to believe. James, by contrast, invokes the permissibility of accepting a belief which is consequentially rational *only if* the belief is unresolvable, i.e. undecidable in terms of evidence. This means that the potential target audience for the Jamesian argument is to that extent much smaller than for the Wager: the Wager applies equally to those who think that 'God exists' is intellectually resolvable, and to those who deny this. But the Jamesian argument applies only to those who think that the belief is intellectually unresolvable, and who further think that the choice whether to accept the belief is living, forced and momentous.

Second, the Wager assumes that you will reap the benefits of believing (and the penalties of disbelieving) only if God exists; for it is only in the afterlife (if there is one) that the pay-offs of the Wager are forthcoming. James, by contrast, locates the benefits and losses in the here-and-now. Even if there is no God and so your belief is false, you will benefit now from holding the belief: it will help make your life go better. The atheist and the agnostic are losing out *now* through not believing. James makes no assumption about any benefits accruing in an afterlife to believers.

Third, the Pascalian, as we saw, has to make some very implausible assumptions about the nature of God and his likely response to belief and disbelief among his creatures. James, on the other hand, makes no explicit assumptions about the nature of God, and all his argument requires are some commonplaces of traditional theism, such as that God cares for us, responds to our needs, helps us in times of difficulty, and so on. And his argument does not require that these commonplaces be true, but only that they be believed, for the benefits come from the belief, whether or not it is true.

There are, then, some important differences between the Pascalian and James. But does James mark an improvement on the Wager? It is difficult to think so, for every step in his argument is open to challenge. First, and perhaps least importantly, we can question whether the existence of God is really intellectually unresolvable. Many people have, of course, thought that it was – but they are generally those who are ignorant of the immensely detailed argumentation that surrounds the claim. It would be a reasonable empirical assumption that the great majority of people who have seriously considered the issue of God's existence have thought that the evidence did favour either belief or disbelief. In other words, they have thought that belief was epistemically rational or irrational, and hence would have denied that a belief in God was the kind of belief to which James's line of thought could apply. To say this is not by itself, of course, to say that they think that the evidence is *overwhelming*, or that it justifies *certainty*, but only that it justifies belief.

Suppose, however, that James is right in his assumption that the existence of God is intellectually unresolvable. A second objection then arises, about

James's assumption that a person's passional nature is involved in deciding how to respond to open propositions. James is caught in a strange lack of consistency here. In respect of intellectually resolvable propositions, he accepts that our passional nature has no legitimate role to play: the requirement to believe propositions for which there is overall good evidence, and to disbelieve those for which the evidence is poor, he accepts is a requirement of reason. But if that is so, why is the requirement to suspend judgement in all those cases where the evidence is lacking or evenly balanced not also a requirement of reason? Given that he rightly thinks that reason is the guide in the first two cases, why does it suddenly cease to be so in relation to the third? James provides no explanation or justification for this strange asymmetry.

The third problem focuses on James's negative rule concerning how our passional nature should guide us. He tells us that we should not accept a rule which would prevent us from accepting as true any propositions which in fact are true, i.e. even when we have no evidence that they are true. But on the face of it, the rule he rejects sounds an excellent negative rule to accept! If there are any propositions which are in principle unresolvable, they are propositions for or against which we cannot get good evidence; and in that case, it sounds eminently reasonable to withhold both assent and dissent. Certainly from the point of view of epistemic rationality, a suspension of belief would be the only possible rational response. If it is to be different for consequential rationality, then it has to be shown that there are beneficial consequences from believing propositions in relation to which one has no evidence. What James really needs is a much more restricted thesis than the one he advances. He rejects a rule which would prevent him from accepting propositions in relation to which he has no evidence. But the most that his argument requires him to reject is a rule which would prevent him from accepting propositions in relation to which he has no evidence, *where the acceptance of the propositions would bring him some benefits.*

More seriously for James's argument, his negative rule does not have the application to theism which he supposes. His actual words were:

(A) 'a rule of thinking which would absolutely prevent me from acknowledging certain kinds of truth if those kinds of truth were really there, would be an irrational rule.'

Differently expressed, this says:

(B) It would be irrational of me to adopt a rule about belief formation which would forbid me from believing any proposition that is in fact true.

Applied to theism in particular this says:

(C) It would be irrational of me to adopt a rule about belief formation which would forbid me from believing that God exists if in fact he does exist.

But if (C) is true, so presumably is (D):

(D) It would be irrational of me to adopt a rule about belief formation which would forbid me from believing that God does not exist, if in fact he does not exist.

If there were any grounds for accepting (C), they would surely equally be grounds for accepting (D). So if the theist can appeal to his passional nature to justify his acceptance of theism, it seems that the atheist can appeal to *his* passional nature to justify his acceptance of atheism. In other words, what principle (A) licenses is the acceptance of one *or other* in a pair of open propositions: it has no means of picking out which proposition the passionally moved believer should accept.

It might be thought that James does have good grounds for distinguishing between accepting the existence of God, and accepting the non-existence of God. For he tells us that 'we are better off even now' if we believe in religion. Although he himself does not elaborate on this claim, a friendly reading of his position could take this to be an omission which can easily be remedied. All that has to be done is to point to the benefits which a belief in God brings to the believer.

However, this reply on James's behalf does mean that his argument is committed to giving further hostages to fortune. For he then needs to supply empirical evidence that belief rather than disbelief does have this beneficial consequence. For some people, no doubt it is belief which makes their life go better; but for other people, it may well be disbelief. And if this is so, the potential audience for James's argument is diminished yet again.

The argument from solace

So far we have looked at arguments from Pascal and James, and found both of them wanting. But is it possible to construct a stronger version of a prudential argument than either Pascal or James presents us with? In what follows, I will try to construct such an argument (in fact a cluster of related arguments) and I will call it the argument from solace. It utilises some thoughts from James's account but steers clear of the serious weaknesses which we have found in what James says. The argument goes like this: my belief in God helps me to get through life. It reconciles me to the pain and suffering which I and others undergo; it provides solace in times of distress; it provides inspiration in moments of weakness; it gives me purpose by assuring me that there is a cosmic plan of which I am an essential part. Without such a belief, I would be unable to think that anything ultimately mattered, I would be unable to cope with the traumas of daily life. So my life as a whole would be immeasurably worse, if I did not have this belief. So, I am (consequentially) justified in holding the belief, and I am also consequentially justified in resisting any attempts to persuade me out of it. So it would be rational of me not to read anti-theistic books, or listen to anti-theistic arguments, in case, rightly or wrongly, they might destroy my belief.

That gives us the basic version of the argument from solace. It is what we might call the individual version of the argument from solace. But we can clearly also envisage what we can call the social version of the argument. For, insofar as I judge that other people are similar to me, and I have a concern for their welfare, I have good (consequentialist) grounds for trying to bring it about that they too hold this belief, even if this bringing-about process is not a rational one. (One obvious circumstance where this is a very real issue for me will concern how I am to bring up my children. If I am a believer in whose life religion plays the central role I have described, I may well hope to bring up my children so that they are both committed theists, and also open-minded and critical thinkers. But suppose that these are not mutually compatible objectives. Suppose that I also had good grounds for thinking that my children would lead happier and more fulfilled lives if they were theists than if they were critical thinkers. It then seems that it would be consequentially rational of me to bring up my children in whatever manner will secure that they end up as theists, even if this involves bypassing normal canons of epistemic rationality.)

As well as distinguishing between an individual and a social version of the argument from solace, we could also distinguish *within* each version two further sub-species, which may be importantly different. In the argument as I presented it above, I was assuming that I *already* had a belief in God, so the only question was whether I should *retain* it or not. Let us call this the *retention* version of the argument. But there is a different scenario we can imagine, namely the position of an agnostic who starts with an entirely open mind on the issue of whether God exists, and is wondering whether to accept the belief. Suppose he is then told that he ought to accept that God exists because there is good consequential justification for this belief. Let us call this the *acquisition* version of the argument. We can summarise these possibilities as shown in the matrix on the next page. In each case, the rationality in question is of course consequential rationality.

We can note first some similarities to and differences from Pascal's Wager in several ways. First, like the Jamesian argument but unlike the Wager, these arguments make no assumptions about God's nature and his propensities to reward and punish. In particular they do not assume a God with the shallow, vindictive and megalomaniac nature which the God of the Wager would have to have. Second, again like the Jamesian argument but unlike the Wager, they do not depend on importing any infinities into our pay-offs matrix. Third, as a consequence of this, a change in what you take to be the

205

	Acquisition version	Retention version
Individual version	It is rational for me to try to acquire the belief.	Given that I have the belief, it is rational for me to ensure that I keep it.
Social version	It is rational for me to try to ensure that other people (family, friends, citizens) acquire the belief, insofar as the consequences will be the same for them as they are for me.	Given that other people have the belief, it is rational for me to try to ensure that they retain the belief insofar as the consequences will be the same for them as they are for me.

probability of God's existence will make a (possibly enormous) difference to the expected costs/benefits of belief. Fourth, the cluster brings into a much sharper focus than either the Wager or the Jamesian argument the distinction between using consequential considerations to acquire and to retain a belief. Fifth, however, they share with the Wager the assumptions that our beliefs are under our control at least indirectly.

Assessing the argument from solace

What should we make of this little family of arguments? The first point to make is that if they are to be any good, the causal claims on which they are based must be sound. By the causal claims I mean this: the arguments all claim that there is a causal connection between on the one hand a person's belief in the existence of God, and on the other, various benefits to that individual in terms of (loosely speaking) mental welfare. Establishing such connections is not easy, even (perhaps especially) for the person concerned. The person may well feel convinced that their high level of mental flourishing is causally dependent on their belief in God; but they may simply be mistaken about this. They may be convinced that if they lost that belief, their mental welfare would suffer badly; but again, they may be wrong about that. In saying that they may be wrong, I am not simply making an unthinking sceptical remark which could be made about virtually everything which we claim to know. Rather, I am saying that tracing the causal dependencies between different parts of our mental life is something that is very difficult; and our claims in this area need to be cautious and provisional. It may well be that someone who has a sunny disposition articulates their sunny outlook in theistic terms (God cares for me, the world is a wonderful

206

place, everything will be all right in the end, etc.). But it may well be that if they did not believe in God, exactly the same sunny disposition would be articulated in terms of some alternative non-theistic world view (a Buddhist one, a humanist one, a Marxist one, or some analogous world view). Knowing whether a sunny disposition is essentially dependent on a belief in God is not something which it is easy to discover.

Of course, there is the evidence of past theists who have 'lost their faith', as it is rather question-beggingly put. But the evidence here is equivocal. Some certainly do experience their change of belief as a *loss*, and a loss after which their life became less satisfactory (to put it rather blandly). And the more cases there are like this, the more one might be justified in believing that there was not just a regular *sequence* here (loss of belief followed by loss of quality of life), but that there was a *causal* connection. But on the other hand, there are some erstwhile theists who report their loss of faith as a liberation, as a weight lifted from their lives. Hume famously lost the misery-inducing, sin-intensive Calvinist faith of his upbringing, and having thrown it off, went on to lead a happy and very fulfilling life. Of course, agnostics' and atheists' claims that there is a causal connection between the loss of their belief in God and subsequent benefits to their lives have to be viewed with the same caution as I was urging on those who found their loss of faith depressing. So the essential point to insist on here is the difficulty of knowing whether anyone's belief in God does have the beneficial consequences that the argument from solace alleges. It may not be impossible for us to have good evidence that this is so, even less that it is impossible for it to be true. But we should not simply take for granted the causal claims on which the argument relies.

That first point about the need to *establish* and not simply to *assume* the causal connections was more a caution than an objection. But the second point is more of an objection. It is an objection which can be raised especially in connection with both types of the social version of the argument, although it can also apply to the retention version of the individual case. This is that the argument requires some unacceptably illiberal attitudes. One standard liberal view is that you should let people form their own opinions, at least insofar as they are sane adults. One corollary of this is that if you are bringing up children who do not have the intellectual equipment to form their own views, a central aim of education should be to foster intellectual autonomy in the child, to get them to think for themselves. This involves in part exposing them to the relevant evidence bearing on whatever question they are considering. Hiding relevant evidence, whether it is done by governments or individuals, is a form of manipulation and a violation of the individual's autonomy.

But, so it might be argued, the argument from solace, particularly in its social version, *does* involve precisely such manipulation. For it involves deciding that it would be good for other people to be kept in ignorance of anti-theistic arguments if these might weaken or destroy those people's belief in God. It thus involves both elitism (I know what is good for you, perhaps better than you do yourself); and also censorship (I will prevent you gaining access to evidence which is relevant to the beliefs which you hold).

A slightly different version of the objection could also be raised against the individual version of the argument. For in deliberately not allowing *oneself* to become aware of factors which could undermine one's belief, one is in a sense manipulating oneself. It is perhaps worth noticing that the degree of censorship required might be quite considerable. For of course a person cannot know antecedently to hearing an objection whether the objection would indeed undermine her belief in God. So in order for the censorship policy to be *effective* (i.e. definitely to prevent her becoming aware of factors which would undermine her belief), it will have to be a policy which will also censor material which would not *in fact* have undermined her belief. So to be effective, it will involve the censorship of a lot of quite innocuous material, simply because she cannot know that the material *is* innocuous.

What should we make of this as an objection to the argument from solace? It is not clear that the argument is really much damaged by the objection. Let us take first the social versions of the argument. In saying that I have reason to prevent other people's theism from being undermined, the argument is not committed to saying how high a priority I should attach to this, nor what steps I am entitled to take in pursuit of my aim, nor what institutional measures (if any) I would be entitled to set up and/or support. Thus supporting the social version of the argument is entirely compatible with also opposing any legal censorship of anti-theistic material. My concern to protect other people's theism might extend only to, for example, not giving them copies of pro-atheist texts, not recommending them to watch or listen to pro-atheist radio and television programmes, etc. It is entirely compatible with thinking that there are other social values than the protection of theism in the public at large, and that very often these other values take precedence over the protection of theism.

By analogy, consider the following: I may think it not in the best interests of other people that they should use heroin. If I am concerned for their welfare, I then have a reason to direct their attention in other directions. But this does not commit me to thinking that information about the practicalities of heroin use (where to get it, what to pay for it, how to inject it, how much to inject, where to inject, etc.) should be legally censored. I will simply not suggest to other people that they attend meetings where information like this is provided, I will not give them books containing this information and so on. It is very far from clear that this would be unacceptably elitist or censorious on my part; and the same could be true (*mutatis mutandis*) of a supporter of the social version of the argument from solace.

What about the implications for the individual version of the argument? Here again, it is difficult to see that the objection has much weight. It might force on me a certain intellectual timidity, in that I would seek to shield myself from all those influences which would undermine my belief in God. But it is difficult to believe that this would have very bad consequences for the rest of my intellectual life. Again as an analogy, consider the claims made by some artists and performers (perhaps comics in particular) that they do not want to know what the psychological source of their inspiration is, for fear that understanding the source would destroy the inspiration. Operating a form of self-censorship of that kind is not noted for leading to intellectual timidity in general. So my conclusion is that this second point against the argument from solace is not a strong one.

Third, as with the Wager arguments, we might well wonder whether the argument from solace is not making unrealistic assumptions about the degree to which we can control our own beliefs and other people's beliefs. Do we really have a good enough understanding of human psychology to be able to create the very specific belief, or tight little cluster of beliefs, which is theism? Here, the distinction between the acquisition and the retention versions of the argument may be important. Simply as a matter of empirical fact, we have better understanding of how to retain a belief which we already have, than to bring about acceptance of a belief which is not epistemically justified and which we do not currently accept. So we will probably succeed in our attempts to retain a belief more often than in our attempts to acquire one.

There is also, however, a logical point of difference between retention and acquisition. If you are considering acquiring a belief of the relevant kind, it is *ex hypothesi* one which you do not antecedently think is true. You think that it *may* be true, but that it may well be false. So you are in a relation of neutrality with respect to it. It has no initial hold over you in terms of its credibility, and it will be correspondingly hard to implant in you, and easy to keep at arm's length. By contrast, a belief which you are considering whether to retain is a belief which you already have. And since to believe something is to believe it to be true, you already have some commitment to it. It is not that the truth is a *reason* (in the epistemic sense) for you to hold the belief. It is rather that you are already committed in favour of the belief. It will be part of your network of beliefs, in terms of which you, for example, assess the credibility of further beliefs, interpret possible evidence, and so on. It will have a vivacity for you which will not be possessed by the neutral propositions about which the question of acquisition arises. So, it is likely to take very little psychic effort or manipulation to retain the belief, and certainly less than would be needed to dislodge it.

If this line of thought is correct, then retention versions of the argument look to be better arguments than acquisition versions, simply because retention is probably more under our control (direct and indirect) than is acquisition. And the individual versions look to be better than the social versions, for the same reason.

So, are any of the little family of arguments which we are calling the argument from solace any good? Certainly, they avoid some of the more objectionable claims of the Wager and the Jamesian argument. Equally, they do have to rely, like those two earlier arguments, on some claims about human psychology (about the benefits of theistic belief and about the possibility of belief manipulation) which can be doubted. But if these claims are correct then they do provide, for a limited range of people, good arguments in favour of holding theistic belief. They are not, of course, reasons for thinking the belief is *true*; but they are good (consequential) reasons for holding the belief.

Combining consequential and epistemic rationality

So far, we have looked at various consequential arguments for believing in God, and have concluded that for some people they are good arguments for theistic belief: it really is (consequentially) rational for such people to believe in God. Hence it is rational for such people to control as far as they can their exposure to the evidence and counter-evidence about the truth of theism. In coming to this conclusion, I have concentrated on consequential rationality in isolation from any epistemic reasons. But people who are sufficiently reflective to enquire into the rationality of their acceptance or rejection of theism are very likely to want more than this. They want to know whether the belief which they have good consequentialist reasons for holding is true. They will want to know whether the belief is supported by epistemic reasons. This will require them in some way to integrate their consequential and epistemic reasons, and this, combined with their efforts to shield themselves from undesirable epistemic reasons, can lead to some philosophical puzzles.

Let us focus on the retention version of the argument. So we are thinking of someone who already believes in God, who secures from this belief net benefits which she could not secure in any other way, and who therefore takes steps to ensure that her belief is not destroyed by exposure to counter-arguments. We now need to distinguish different scenarios. The believer can think of the counter-arguments to the epistemic rationality of her belief along two dimensions: are they epistemically good arguments, and would they persuade her to give up her theism? So there are four possibilities (see the next matrix overleaf).

Consequential rationality requires the believer to ensure that she is not exposed to anything in A or B, but that exposure to anything in C or D would be innocuous. Epistemic rationality requires the believer to ensure that she is exposed to anything in A or C. So someone who is interested in

	Epistemically good reasons to reject theism	Epistemically bad reasons to reject theism
Reasons that would (rightly or wrongly) make the believer abandon theism	A	B
Reasons that would (rightly or wrongly) not make the believer abandon theism	C	D

both the consequential and the epistemic rationality of their current belief needs both to secure and to avoid exposure to anything in A. Let us see in detail how this conflict might work out in practice.

We are imagining a believer who thinks that the counter-arguments from which she hides herself *are* good arguments, at least good enough to show that her current theistic belief is epistemically unreasonable; and further that if she were exposed to them, they would be causally efficacious in undermining her theism. She is caught here in an incoherent position. For she is implicitly saying 'Although I believe that p (that God exists), there is evidence, of whose details I am currently ignorant but which is such that if I came to know of it, it would show that my belief that p is epistemically unreasonable, i.e. is more probably false than true'.

The puzzle about this position is that to believe something is to believe that it is true (or probably true): you cannot believe that p, and also think that your belief is false (or probably false). Having this directedness-at-the-truth is part of what *constitutes* the phenomenon of belief. So if you are considering some proposition p, you cannot think to yourself without contradiction:

(i) p, but p is false or:
(ii) p, but p is probably false or:
(iii) p, but my overall evidence is that p is (probably) false.

Now the theist in our second scenario is not saying exactly (iii), but she is saying something extremely close, namely:

(iv) p, but there is some evidence of which I do not have the details, which would show that p is (probably) false.

Really to think that the balance of evidence shows p to be (probably) false logically requires you to think that p is (probably) false.

These reflections do not show that the argument from solace by itself is caught in any incoherence or contradiction. Nor do they even show that anyone who tries to integrate their epistemic and consequential rationality is bound to be caught in contradiction. For all that has been said in this chapter, it might be that there are no arguments against theism which fall in A. If all the arguments against theism fall within B and D, and the believer can know this to be true, then she will be caught in no contradictory attitudes when she ensures that she is not exposed to any arguments from B. The problem arises if there are any arguments in A. If there are, and the consequentially rational believer tries to shield herself from them, she is then caught in the contradiction outlined in (iv) above. So if there are any arguments in A, someone who is to make use of the argument from solace must be sufficiently enquiring to be interested in the rationality of holding the beliefs she holds, but not sufficiently enquiring to be interested in the epistemic rationality of those beliefs. Whether this constraint means that in practice the argument from solace is an impotent weapon in the theist's armoury can be left to the reader to decide.

Further reading

Pascal's Wager is outlined in Pascal (1995: 150–1). The starting point for serious modern discussion of it is in Hacking (1972), reprinted in Craig (2002), and both Martin (1990) and Gale (1991) supply lengthy and thorough critiques. Scheslinger (1994) gives a modified defence. Matson (1965) supplies useful background information about James's pragmatist conception of truth and belief in general, as does Ayer (1968). Matson goes on to examine 'The Will to Believe', and Ayer also has some brief but useful comments. As before, Martin and Gale give sharp critiques, although much of Gale's is somewhat idiosyncratic.

11

————•◦⊙◦•————

Arguments from scale

No argument I know of for the conclusion that it is irrational
to believe that God exists has any force whatever.
>   (Van Inwagen 1995: 41)

Introduction

The first argument against theism which we consider is a modest science-based argument, and it aims to show that the picture of the universe with which modern science presents us constitutes evidence against the truth of theism. The evidence by itself is not very strong, certainly not overwhelming, but it is nonetheless significant. Traditional theism presents us with a certain picture of God and of his intentions in creating the universe at large, and in creating human beings in particular. In general, if someone hypothesises that there is an agent with a certain nature and a certain set of intentions, then we can form some idea of what the agent is likely to do – in what respect things will be different just in virtue of the hypothesised agent's having that nature, those beliefs, and that intention. If we then discover that the world is not as we have predicted, then we have evidence that the initial hypothesis that there was such an agent is mistaken. The argument thus has the form:

(1) If there is an agent with nature N, beliefs B, and intention I, then he will produce change C in the world.
(2) The world does not display C. So:
(3) There is evidence against the hypothesis that there is an agent with N and I and B.

As an example of the argument at work in an uncontroversial context, consider an updated Robinson Crusoe. Suppose he considers the hypothesis that elsewhere on the island with him is another survivor of the shipwreck similar to Crusoe himself in his physical and mental capacities, including his beliefs, and with the intention of making contact with any other survivors,

213

such as Crusoe. Even given as vague and impoverished a hypothesis as this, Crusoe can make *some* predictions about what the hypothetical survivor will do. He can formulate in his mind a range of what he might call apt behaviour, and a range of inapt behaviour, which the survivor might display – apt and inapt relative to the intention with which Crusoe has tentatively credited him. It would be apt if, for example, the survivor left visible signs of his presence on the island (marks on trees, scratchings on rocks, carefully arranged pieces of wood or stone). It would be apt if he emitted characteristically human noises (whistling, singing, shouting, etc.). It would be apt if he lit a fire and tried to send smoke signals. These would be apt pieces of behaviour because they are just the sorts of things which a Crusoe-like survivor would do if he were trying to let other possible survivors know of his existence on the island. By contrast, it would not be apt if the hypothetical survivor, for example, found some deep undergrowth and lay in it, quiet and still, for the greater part of each day. It would not be apt if after being in any location on the island, he carefully removed all signs of his presence (footprints, ashes from fires, etc.). And so on. These are not apt ways of realising the intention of making your presence known to another human who might be in the vicinity. They are not the kind of actions which it would be reasonable for Crusoe to expect another survivor to pursue, given the intentions and beliefs with which Crusoe is crediting him.

So, even before starting his empirical investigation of the island, Crusoe can formulate to himself a description of what evidence would help to confirm his initial hypothesis, and what evidence would help to disconfirm it. If he looks hard and carefully for evidence of what we have called apt behaviour, and finds none, that constitutes some evidence against his initial hypothesis that there is another survivor. It is evidence for saying that either there is no actual survivor, or if there is one, the initial hypothesis was wrong about either his capacities or his intentions. In saying that some kinds of behaviour by the hypothetical survivor would be 'inapt', we do not mean that it *absolutely disproves* the initial hypothesis about the survivor's capacities and intentions, but rather that it constitutes *evidence against* the hypothesis. The evidence is defeasible in that it is possible that there is some factor of which Crusoe is unaware which would explain away its initial anti-hypothesis import. (Perhaps the survivor is injured or even unconscious.) But if he does not discover any such factor, he would be justified in concluding that the initial hypothesis is to some degree disconfirmed.

Let us see now how considerations of this kind can be applied on a cosmic scale, and how the nature of the universe as revealed by modern science gives us reason to reject traditional theism.

The argument from scale

Consider, first, the account of God's nature and purposes with which theism presents us. Theism tells us that God is a being who is omnipotent and omniscient, wholly self-sufficient, with no needs, or lacks, or deficiencies of any kind. For reasons that are not entirely clear, God decides to create a universe in which human beings will be the jewel. Although he will have a care for the whole of his creation, God will have an especial care for human beings. He will give these creatures the power of free choice. Exactly what this power is, no one can agree. Some think that it is a capacity the possession of which is incompatible with the truth of determinism; others think that it is a kind of freedom which is compatible with determinism, and which perhaps even requires determinism. Because humans are the jewel of creation, the rest of the universe will be at least not unremittingly hostile or even indifferent to human flourishing. Even if the universe will not make such flourishing immediately and easily and painlessly accessible, it will make it at least accessible in principle for humanity at large. The question then to ask is: given this much information about God and his nature and his purposes, what sort of a universe would you expect to find? Which of all the possible worlds that God could create would you expect him to create, given this much knowledge of his nature and of his overall plan?

As with our example of Robinson Crusoe, it is difficult to answer this question in any great detail. The description of God is so sketchy, and in particular the theistic hypothesis gives us so little information about his aims, that a large number of possible worlds are left equally likely. But among the more likely scenarios is a universe somewhat like the one presented to us in the story of Genesis. In particular, traditional theism would lead you to expect human beings to appear fairly soon after the start of the universe. For, given the central role of humanity, what would be the point of a universe which came into existence and then existed for unimaginable aeons without the presence of the very species that supplied its rationale? You would expect humans to appear after a great many animals, since the animals are subordinate species available for human utilisation, and there would be no point in having humans arrive on the scene needing animals (e.g. as a source of food, or clothing, or companionship) only for them to discover that animals had not yet been created. But equally, you would not expect humans to arrive *very* long after the animals, for what would be the point of a universe existing for aeons full of animals created for humanity's delectation, in the absence of any humans? Further, you would expect the earth to be fairly near the centre of the universe if it had one, or at some similarly significant location if it did not have an actual centre. You would expect the total universe to be not many orders of magnitude greater than the size of the earth. The universe would be on a *human* scale. You would expect that even if there are regions of the created world which are hostile to human life, and which perhaps are incompatible with it, the greater part of the universe would be accessible to human exploration. If this were not so, what would the point be of God creating it?

These expectations are largely what we find in the Genesis story (or strictly, stories) of creation. There is, then, a logic to the picture of the universe with which the Genesis story presents us: given the initial assumptions about God, his nature, and his intentions, the Genesis universe is pretty much how it would be reasonable for God to proceed. Given the hypothesis of theism and no scientific knowledge, and then asked to construct a picture of the universe and its creation, it is not surprising that the author(s) of Genesis came up with the account which they did. It is not that God would have *had* to proceed in the Genesis way (just as there is not just one kind of behaviour which a possible island survivor would need to produce to confirm Crusoe's initial hypothesis), and it is not that *every* non-Genesis way would be extremely puzzling. There is in fact a wide range of possible universes which God could have created and about which there would not be a puzzle of the form 'But how could a universe like *that* be an expression of a set of intentions like *those*?' Nevertheless, we can still draw a distinction between universes which would be apt, given the initial hypothesis, and universes which would be inapt. The Genesis universe is clearly an apt one, given the theistic hypothesis; but a universe in which (say) most humans could survive only by leading lives of great and endless pain would be a surprising one for God to choose, given the other assumptions we make about him.

The question now to raise is 'Is the universe as it is revealed to us by modern science roughly the sort of universe which we would antecedently expect a God of traditional theism to create? Is it an apt universe, given the admittedly sketchy conception we have of his nature and his intentions?'

The short answer to this is 'No'. In almost every respect, the universe as it is revealed to us by modern science is *hugely* unlike the sort of universe which the traditional thesis would lead us to expect. Although the bare quantitative facts will be familiar to many readers, it is worth repeating them. First, in terms of age: our best estimates are that the universe itself is very roughly 15 billion years, and the Earth is roughly 5 billion years old. How long humans have existed will depend partly on what we take a human to be. But if we take humans to be homo sapiens, and if we take them to be creatures with some sort of language and some sort of social culture, then realistic estimates would allow that they have existed for no more than 100,000 years. So if we imagine the history of the universe represented by a line which is roughly 24 miles long, human life would occupy only the last inch. Or if we imagine this history of the universe represented by a single year, humanity would emerge only in the last few seconds of the last minute of the last hour of the last day of the year. So for something more than 99.999 per cent of the history of the universe, the very creatures which are meant to be the jewel of creation have been absent from it. The question that at once arises is 'What, given the hypothesis of theism, was the point of this huge discrepancy between the age of the universe and the age of humanity?'. How very inapt a creation of that kind must strike us.

The same story recurs if we turn to the size of the universe. Suppose we take the size of our solar system to be within the expectable parameters of the theistic hypothesis. (This might seem over-generous to theism: why would God need a solar system as big as ours to achieve any of his purposes? Why does he need a sun that is 93 *million* miles from earth? Why wouldn't 93 thousand miles have been enough? Of course the laws of physics would then have had to be different if the sun were to make earth habitable – but as an omnipotent being, God could easily have adjusted the laws of physics. However, let us overlook this and allow that a distance of 93 million miles counts as intelligible – it is intelligible, that is, that a God with the nature and intentions ascribed by traditional theism should create a universe that big.) But of course, we know now that the universe is staggeringly larger than any such intelligible size. The sun is about 8 light minutes from us, the next nearest star is about 4.3 light years, the next nearest galaxy to the Milky Way is scores of light years away. Current findings indicate that the furthest star visible from earth is about 3 billion light years away. In other words, the most distant star is very roughly some 200,000,000,000,000,000 times (two hundred thousand trillion times) as far from us as the sun. This sort of scale to the universe makes no conceivable sense on the theistic hypothesis. Nor should we assume that the most distant visible star is the most distant detectable entity. The furthest galaxy, detectable only by radio telescopes, is reckoned to be about three times further away – 9 billion light years. The possible limits of the universe lie further away still. If the Big Bang occurred about 15 billion years ago, and if the expansion had occurred at the speed of light, the limits of the universe would be about 30 billion light years. Assuming that the expansion was at less than the speed of light, that still leaves the possibility of a universe whose overall size is between 10 and 30 billion light years across (i.e. up to two million trillion miles). Why would a God make it that big?

Further, astronomers tell us that there are about 100 trillion galaxies, each with a billion stars (giving us something of the order of 100,000,000,000, 000,000,000,000 stars) (Woodward 2000: 25). It could count as apt if a creator created a universe with one star or perhaps a few dozen or even a few hundred, so that the night sky were as beautiful as we now find it. But what could be the point of the huge superabundance of celestial matter, especially given the fact that the very great majority of humanity will never be aware of most of it? Again, given the theistic hypothesis, it is strikingly inapt.

If we confine our attention to the earth, the same extraordinary inaptness confronts us. The Genesis story presents God's actions as apt in relation to the non-human creatures who share the planet with humans: they all emerge at about the same time; and all the creatures which surround humanity in that story share a human scale – none are so tiny that it is impossible to detect them by the senses, and none are so huge (e.g. thousands or millions of times larger than humans) as to be unrecognisable as organisms at all. But again, modern science reveals this to be deeply wrong – not just in points of detail, but in almost every major respect. Life has existed on the planet for something like 3 to 3.5 billion years. For roughly half of that time, it has been solely bacterial in form. Given that humans have emerged only in the last 100,000 years, that means that for 99.99 per cent of the history of life on earth, there have been no humans. How very bizarre, given the theistic hypothesis! Further, from a biological point of view 'On any possible or reasonable or fair criterion, bacteria are – and always have been the dominant forms of life on earth' (Gould 1996: 176). In terms of their numbers, their longevity, their ability to exploit the widest variety of habitats, their degree of genetic variation, and even (amazingly, give how tiny they are individually) their total biomass, they outstrip every other kind of life. If God had intended any species to flourish, the obvious candidate for divine favour would be bacteria, not humans.

In short, then, everything that modern science tells us about the size and scale and nature of the universe around us reveals it to be strikingly inapt as an expression of a set of divine intentions of the kind that theism postulates. Let us emphasise that the claim here is not that there is a logical incompatibility between these modern scientific findings and traditional theism. It is not that the findings *disprove* theism. The claim is weaker than that. The claim is only that the findings of modern science *significantly reduce the probability* that theism is true, because the universe is turning out to be very unlike the sort of universe which we would have expected, had theism been true. However, before accepting this conclusion, let us see what responses the theist might make.

Reply 1: modern science is fallible

A first reply would complain that the argument places too much reliance on modern science. This is a mistake, the theist may say, for two reasons. First, all of the figures used in the above arguments are subject to huge margins of uncertainty. For example, although it is customary for the age of the universe to be given as 15 billion years, estimates by wholly reputable experts range between 12 and 18 billion years. Similarly with the other figures for the size of the universe, the amount of matter it contains, the age of life on earth, and so on. All of the figures have a 'back of an envelope' quality to them. They are, the theist may complain, little more than ballpark figures, on which no reliance can be placed. Second, even if the figures could be made more precise, they are derived only from current scientific theories;

218

and scientific theories, the theist can rightly point out, change constantly. They do not constitute secure knowledge, they are fleeting 'best bet' guesses all of which will probably be rejected in time as science advances. So, in the light of these two objections, the theist might conclude that the argument from scale is built on sand.

The atheist, however, should be unmoved by these objections. She can concede the essence of what they say, but reject the conclusions which the theist draws from them. Take first the uncertainty about the numbers employed. Even if the numbers are inaccurate, even if they are hugely inaccurate, the atheist's argument is largely unaffected. Suppose, for example, that the universe is not 15 billion years old but only one tenth as old or one hundredth or one thousandth as old. That would still leave it at 15 million years old. That may not sound much to modern ears, accustomed to the huge dimensions which cosmology introduces. But it still gives us a universe that is still *massively* inapt on the theistic hypothesis. One way of seeing how this is so, is to reflect on the estimates of the age of the universe provided by those who did not have access to modern science. From Scaliger and Spanheim in the fifteenth and sixteenth centuries, through the famous Ussher discussion of the seventeenth, and on to a number of competent and respectable Victorian scientists, the consensus figure was that the universe began in about 4000 BC. Reflective thinkers clearly believed that a universe with roughly this sort of timescale is what the theistic hypothesis would lead one to expect. That would be an apt universe in terms of age, given theism. So even if current estimates of the age of the universe were out by a factor of a thousand, that would still give us a universe that was roughly 3,000 times older than prescientific theists thought made sense from a theistic point of view. So the power of the argument from scale does not depend on the figures it uses being correct, or even approximately correct. They could be a thousand times too big, and the argument would still be a good one.

The theist's second objection to reliance on science was that science presents us with a set of constantly changing, constantly refuted hypotheses; it does not give us knowledge. This again the atheist can concede, while denying that it carries the implications which the theist supposes. For in the first place, although theories are constantly being superseded, the *general picture* of which they are a transitory part does not fundamentally change. Although it is possible that future estimates of the age or size of the universe may be greater or smaller than those which we now accept, there is no possibility that we will return to the scales which would deprive the argument from scale of its force. There is no possibility that future scientific theories will tell us that the universe started in about 4000 BC. There is no possibility that future theories will tell us that it is only about one million, or ten million, or a hundred million, or a thousand million miles across. In short, there is no possibility that future theories will tell us that the scale of the universe is what it would need to be, to be apt for the theistic hypothesis. So even if the details of current scientific theorising cannot be taken as secure knowledge, the general picture which science presents can be so taken; and it is that general picture which presents us with a universe inapt for theism.

Reply 2: theism is not committed to what science has disproved

A second natural response would be for the theist to deny that she is committed to what the argument is attacking. The theist might, for example, point out that theism per se has no commitment to any specifically Christian doctrines, even less to the truth of any specifically Biblical claims. To believe in God is not to be committed to any claims about prophets or messiahs, or any empirical or quasi-empirical claims about the age of the universe, the origin of humanity, or even God's special and unique concern for humanity. As a matter of historical fact, the theist may be willing to concede, the vast majority of theists *have* accorded special status to the Bible – but that was in virtue of their acceptance of further claims which were not entailed by theism itself. It is possible to be a theist without being a Jew, or a Christian, or a Moslem. So, whatever may be the relations between Biblical claims on the one hand, and the doctrines of these specific religions on the other, is completely independent of theism. Modern science is incompatible with, for example, a literal reading of Genesis – but that is a problem for Fundamentalist Christians and Jews (the theist may say) and not for theism per se.

There is a sense in which this theistic response is correct and a sense in which it is wrong. It is correct in the sense that it is of course right to say that theism is not committed to the literal truth of the Genesis creation story. But it is wrong to think that the argument from scale makes this assumption. Rather, what the argument from scale assumes is that the theist is committed to the universe being an apt expression of the nature and intention of God, where it was allowed that a wide variety of possible universes would count as apt. The point was only that some universes must count as inapt (such as the universe in which every human being could survive only by leading a life of great and ceaseless pain); and that the universe that modern science reveals falls into the inapt category.

For surely the theist must concede that her assumptions about the nature and purposes of a creator and sustainer of all things carry *some* empirical implications, however vague and however defeasible. She surely does not want to say that the character of the universe would have been just as it is if there had been no God, or if there had been a creator with a very different nature, and with very different intentions. Once the theist concedes that her theistic hypothesis does carry *some* empirical implications, then we can test those empirical implications, and when we find that they are false, carry the disconfirmation back to theism itself.

Even so, the theist may reply, the argument as presented assumes that theism is committed to more than in fact it is. Certainly theism is committed to the view that God is benign, and hence will have a concern with human welfare. But it is not committed to the view that God is concerned only or even specially with humanity. It is not committed, as the Genesis story is, to the claim that life appears only on earth. So it is not committed to there being anything surprising in the fact that the universe is very much bigger than it apparently needs to be for specifically human flourishing; or in the fact that specifically human life has appeared very late in the history of the universe, and indeed very late in the history of life.

This response has some force – but not much. First, it seems that theism *is* committed to certain evaluations on God's part. One of his defining attributes is omniscience; and this suggests that God thinks knowledge is a valuable attribute. (We saw in Chapter 9 how this assumption formed one essential premise in Plantinga's argument against atheistic naturalism.) So, all other things being equal, he will think that species which are capable of knowledge are better than species which are not capable of knowledge. So, given that humans are the supremely knowledge-possessing species as far as we know, theism must think that God will regard them as especially valuable. And in that case, the puzzle for theism returns: why in the three billion year history of life have intelligent, knowledgeable humans existed only for the last 100,000 years? To use the same analogy we used above: if the history of life on earth is represented by a year, humans have appeared only in the final few seconds of the year. Why the delay, given that theism must think that humans are the most valuable species created so far? Who or what has gained, and how, from that colossal delay?

Similar puzzles return if we look out to the stars. The theist could plausibly say that God places no special value on humans, if it were the case that when we scanned the heavens we found it teeming with intelligent life comparable to and perhaps greater than ourselves. But that is exactly what we do not find. What we find are unimaginably huge volumes of space with no sign of intelligent life at all – in fact, no sign of any kind of life. Of course, there *may* be life elsewhere, and conceivably there may also be intelligent life elsewhere. But we have as yet nothing but the barest circumstantial evidence for thinking that there is. So, of everything which we know to exist in the universe, it seems that theism is committed to saying that humans are the most valuable things in creation. They are the nearest to God – they are made in his image.

Reply 3: there *is* a divine purpose in the scale of things

A third theistic response would allow what the second response denied, namely that theism does carry some implications about what the universe will turn out to be like. But it would deny that the universe as we find it is different from the universe as theism would predict it to be. It would seek to show that the universe as we find it is very much as theism would predict it to be – or at least, even if theism could not have predicted that God would choose to create the universe which he has created, it would try to show *ex post facto* that it is not surprising that God has chosen to create a universe of this kind. How might such an argument go in detail? The theist might point to the fact that God's omniscience is a sign that knowledge is a valuable commodity. So, God would want his creatures to acquire it, so it is explicable that he would create a world of relatively high complexity. The world would be complex enough for the pursuit of knowledge to be a taxing and worthwhile human pursuit, but not so taxing that it was wholly or largely beyond human power. And that is just the degree of complexity which we find the world to have. Cosmology, physics, chemistry, biology and other sciences studying the natural world *are* intellectually challenging: they do require discipline, imagination, and rational thought; but they are to some degree within the compass of a significant and expandable proportion of humanity.

There are, however, several problems which the atheist will find with an *ex post facto* justification such as this. She might point out in the first place that it is a purported justification of *complexity*, rather than of *scale*, and that a universe on a human scale could certainly display plenty of complexity (in such domains as say, mathematics and history, biography and literary criticism – and even philosophy). But second and more importantly, the weakness of all such *ex post* justifications is revealed in the very fact that they are *ex post*. Those early theists (in fact, right up to the nineteenth century) who never thought that God might make such a colossally huge universe knew perfectly well that omniscience was one of God's defining properties, that he was therefore likely to regard knowledge as a good thing, and that he would therefore create a universe in which human knowledge would be attainable, albeit with some effort. Why did it never cross their minds that given these initial assumptions, God might create a universe billions of times bigger and older than their contemporary cosmologists were contemplating? Surely, the atheist will claim, it is because it is simply arbitrary to try and connect any supposed value placed by God on knowledge on the one hand, with the huge dimensions of the universe on the other.

Reply 4: science uses the wrong criterion of significance

A different line of reply for the theist is to challenge the significance of the findings of modern science, at least as they have been used here by the atheist. What the atheist has implicitly been doing (the critic will allege) is asking us to be impressed by sheer size – either temporal or spatial. Thus, the atheist draws our attention to the fact that the universe is very big by human standards; or to the fact that the duration of humanity compared with other life forms is very small; or to the fact that in numbers and variety, lowly species of life like bacteria show much greater richness than humanity. The implication which the atheist wants us to draw is that human beings are insignificant in the cosmic scheme of things. But, the theist will object, this conclusion cannot be drawn. What gives value to something is not how big it is, or how long it has lasted, or whether it exists everywhere, or exists in huge numbers. What gives value to it is a set of qualities such as intelligence, creativity and morality. These are qualities which are found uniquely, or to a unique degree, in human beings. For that reason, no findings about the huge size of the universe or the vast age of the earth, or the biological success of lowly life forms could in any way undermine the importance and significance of human life. Human life would not become more significant if science were to discover that the universe was very much smaller or younger than we now take it to be; nor would it become less significant and less valuable if we were to discover the universe to be larger and older than we now take it to be. In short (the theist will say), the atheist has been over-impressed by big numbers, and ignored the fact that these have no necessary connection with significance or value.

However, the atheist can object that this misrepresents his position. The point about the argument from scale is not that it shows human beings to be unimportant or insignificant, even less that they are unimportant or insignificant *because* they are small in space and time. Rather, the aim of the argument is to show that there is a mismatch between the kind of universe which one would expect, given the theistic conception of God and his purposes, and the kind of universe which modern science reveals to us. The atheist can happily concede all the theist's claims about the value of humanity, and how that is unaffected by the scale of the universe within which it finds itself. The inaptness which the atheist wants to insist on concerns the size of the universe (in space and time) and the position of humanity within the domain of life, given the hypothesised existence and purposes of God. Given that God wants to create beings akin to human beings, with certain features which give them value and significance, why does he set these beings in a universe whose spatio-temporal dimensions are so hugely in excess of what is needed? Why does he precede these human beings with vast multitudes of life forms, most of which simply become extinct, and none of which display any intrinsically admirable features?

Reply 5: God is inscrutable

The final line of reply which the theist might make is to concede that there *is* a prima facie inaptness about the scale of the universe, given the nature and purposes which theism attributes to God, but to claim that this is wholly inconclusive. We should not presume, the theist may say, to understand *everything* about God's reasons and purposes. We may be unable to see why God should make a universe as big or as old as the one in which we find ourselves, a universe in which so much of what has existed and does now exist has nothing at all to do with humanity – or indeed with life. But that just shows, the theist may say, that God surpasses all human understanding. It is wholly unsurprising, given what theism tells us about God, that we should find him largely inscrutable. Clearly, he will have had his reasons for creating a universe as big and as old as the one we have, and the fact that we have no idea what those reasons are simply reflects our own limited intelligence: it does not discredit the doctrine of theism at all.

But again, the atheist should be unmoved. In the first place, she can legitimately press the theist for some details of what these further divine purposes might be. The point here is that it is not enough for the theist to say 'There *could* be some intention which would render the scale of the universe intelligible to us'. Whether or not we have any grounds for thinking that God has any of these intentions is a further question: the prior question is whether the theist is right to say that there could be some such intentions. If she cannot actually specify what intentions she has in mind, then her claim that there are such intentions is simply frivolous.

Let us assume that the theist can specify what these possible intentions are. The atheist will now ask what grounds there are for thinking that God actually has any of them. She will object that there is no independent evidence for thinking that God *does* have these extra inscrutable purposes, purposes which would explain the otherwise puzzling features of the universe. This extra hypothesis which the theist is forced to adopt is thus entirely ad hoc and unreasonable. And if the only way to prevent considerations of scale from reducing the probability of theism is by adopting a further hypothesis for which there is no evidence, then the theist is unreasonable in adopting that further hypothesis. So, the atheist will conclude, she is either unreasonable if she denies that considerations of scale reduce the probability of theism, or she is unreasonable because in trying to block that charge of unreasonableness, she accepts a hypothesis which there is no reason to accept.

We can think again here of the Crusoe analogy with which we started. Suppose that in spite of careful searching, Crusoe finds no evidence of a survivor (no rock scratchings, no smoke signals, no shouts, whistles, etc.), and infers that this reduces the probability of his initial hypothesis that there was another survivor who was trying to contact him. It then occurs to him that if he attributed some further strange intentions to the hypothetical survivor, then the lack of obvious signs on the island of another person would be exactly what he would expect. Suppose, for example, that the survivor does not simply want to make contact with Crusoe, but to make contact *by using a method which would initially lead Crusoe to think that there was no survivor.* This would be a strange intention for the survivor to have, and there is no reason for Crusoe to think that the survivor, if there is one, has such an intention. But if there were a survivor, and if he had this strange intention, then the absence of signs on the island of the survivor would precisely be an apt expression of the survivor's strange intention. But we can see that in such a situation, Crusoe would be unreasonable in adding to his initial hypothesis this further unsupported hypothesis, just to make the original hypothesis square with the lack of evidence which he found for the existence of the supposed survivor. And in a similar way, the atheist can insist, the theist who attributes arbitrary further intentions to God, in order to square the hypothesis of God's existence with the scale of the universe, is being unreasonable.

The atheist might also note in passing how an appeal to divine inscrutability appears as a *deus ex machina* argument. Historically, theists have claimed to have a very detailed knowledge of God's intentions and preferences. They have claimed to know, for example, that he does not want humans to consume certain sorts of foods and drink, that he objects to some specific kinds of contraception but not to others, that he has firm views on the cutting or non-cutting of (some) hair of (some) people, that it matters to him on which days of the week people perform certain tasks, and so on. How very strange that God's mind should be so transparent on such small-scale and local issues, and yet opaque on much larger issues.

Conclusion

The upshot of this line of thought, then, is that there is indeed a mismatch between the universe as revealed to us by modern science and the universe which we would expect, given the hypothesis of theism. Utilising the argument schema with which we started, we can say:

(1) If the God of classical theism existed, with the purposes traditionally ascribed to him, then he would create a universe on a human scale, i.e. one that is not unimaginably large, unimaginably old, and in which human beings form an unimaginably tiny part of it, temporally and spatially.
(2) The world does not display a human scale. So:
(3) There is evidence against the hypothesis that the God of classical theism exists with the purposes traditionally ascribed to him.

We need to notice the limited nature of this conclusion. We have already emphasised that it is not a *proof* of the falsity of theism. We can also add that as presented, it does not even claim that theism is *probably* false. For it could quite well be the case that there was evidence against theism, but not of such a weight as to make the falsity of theism more probable than not. On the other hand, the argument is not negligible. It shows that those who think that science and theism can be kept wholly insulated from each other are mistaken. Science *does* reveal to us unobvious facts about the nature of the universe; the nature of the universe *is* relevant to the question of whether theism is a possible, or a good, or the best explanation of the existence and nature of the universe; and the argument of this chapter shows why the findings of modern science tell against the truth of theism.

Further reading

The argument of this chapter is not one which has been discussed in the philosophical literature about the implications of science for theism – such discussions have focused instead on Big Bang cosmology or the Anthropic Principle (see Chapter 5). But accessible introductions to the science-based assumptions on which the argument in this chapter rests can be found in authors such as Calder (1985), P. Davies (1992), Gribbin (1993) and Ferris (1997).

12

—◦◖◗◦—

Problems about evil

Introduction

The argument from evil is an objection to theism as old as theism itself. A version of it can be found in Epicurus (341–270 BC); it was employed by Hume in his *Dialogues*; supported by Mill; endorsed by Russell; and in the past century supported by a wide variety of atheists, such as Flew, Mackie, Rowe and Martin. It tries to show that theism is in conflict with certain obvious features of the world, in particular with the existence of evil in the world. (We can note in passing that Mackie is mistaken to say that 'The problem seems to show . . . that some of [theism's] central doctrines are, as a set, inconsistent with one another' (Mackie 1982: 150). The claim that there is evil in the world is not one of theism's doctrines at all, central or otherwise. Rather, the problem of evil attempts to show not that theism is inconsistent with itself, but that it conflicts with indubitable facts about what the world is like.)

The evils that are invoked here are often divided into natural and moral evils. Natural evils are those that flow from the mere operation of the laws of nature, without the intervention of any human agents. Thus the prevalence of crippling and agonising diseases; and the huge cost in pain and distress which can be caused by natural disasters (the term itself is significant) such as earthquakes, tornadoes, tidal waves, blizzards, droughts, floods, forest fires, etc. would both count as paradigms of natural evil. Moral evil would cover the evil found in a wide variety of human acts and practices – acts which are cruel, deceitful, dishonourable, selfish, mean, etc. Central to both kinds of evil is the presence of physical pain, but the evil goes beyond physical pain in both cases. Sometimes the evil is more like mental pain (distress, grief, despair, depression), sometimes it is not a form of pain at all, but simply the awfulness of what someone has done, whether or not their action has caused either physical or mental pain.

Most discussions of the problem of evil focus exclusively on the evil as it is experienced by human beings. But in this context, we should bear in mind the existence of animal pain. Whereas human beings have existed for at most a million years, other animal species capable of suffering have probably existed for upwards of 100 million years. During that huge length of time, most of the colossal number of sentient animals who then lived will probably have had a more or less dreadful death – being torn to pieces and eaten alive, dying of thirst or starvation, burnt or frozen to death, drowning or being engulfed by lava flows from a volcano, etc. It is important to remember all this non-human suffering. Some proffered solutions to the problem of evil do not take account of this suffering and provide explanations and justifications only for evil as it relates to humans. Such 'solutions' are necessarily defective, for the problem of evil is not just about the comparatively small amount of evil perpetrated and endured by humans, but also about the colossal suffering which the world saw before the arrival of the human species.

Theism has generated a huge range of responses to the problem of evil. A representative range, briefly summarised would include the following suggestions:

(1) God's goodness, etc. passes human understanding.
(2) Evil is unreal – evil is the absence of something.
(3) Evil may be the work of the devil or of fallen angels.
(4) God is not omnipotent.
(5) Evil is a punishment for human wrongdoing.
(6) The evil is required for some good.
    (a) Evil is a test of faith.
    (b) Evil is required for 'soul-making'/moral growth.
    (c) Evil is a product of the human mis-use of the gift of free will.
    (d) We cannot know that there is not some counterbalancing good.
(7) The divine attributes need a special interpretation.
    God does not know about future free actions by humans.
    God cannot bring about free actions by humans.
    God's goodness requires us to make our own mistakes.
    God is not *morally* good.

It is now conventional to distinguish two main forms of the problem of evil. The so-called *logical problem of evil* tries to show that 'the existence of evil is logically inconsistent with the existence of a being which is all-powerful, all-knowing and perfectly good' (Stump and Murray 1999: 153). So, if there is evil in the world, it follows with certainty that there is no God. The so-called *evidential problem of evil* tries to show 'not that the existence of evil is *logically inconsistent* with God's existence, but simply that the existence and amounts and types of evil in the world makes it *very unlikely* that there is an all-knowing, all-powerful, and perfectly good divine being' (ibid., second italics added). Some authors then distinguish different versions of the logical problem, and also different versions of the evidential problem according to whether the focus is on the existence of evil per se, or on the huge total amount, or on the distribution, or on the awfulness of the worst evils, etc. It has become customary to call theistic responses to the logical problem, defences; and theistic responses to the evidential, theodicies. A defence needs only to find a *possible* reason for the existence of evil (i.e. possible given God's defining attributes), a reason which need not be God's actual reason, for if there is a possible reason, this will show that the non-existence of God is not necessitated by the existence of evil. By contrast, a theodicy aims to show with at least a fair degree of probability, what God's actual reason for permitting evil is.

In fact, the distinction between the logical and evidential lines of objection is not as clear-cut as this suggests. Some formulations which are normally classified as evidential are clearly logical.[1] And some lines of reply by theists are equally available in response to both versions of the problem. Further, both versions of the problem present the theist with a conclusion which she must find unacceptable. But because the distinction has become so entrenched in modern discussion, it will be useful at least initially to follow it, even if we subsequently depart from it.

The logical problem

The basic form of logical problem of evil which is put to the theist is this. She will have to accept

(1) the world contains evil because the presence of evil is so obvious.
    But she also wants to accept
(2) God is omnipotent
(3) God is omniscient
(4) God is morally perfect

since these are defining features of God: God, if he exists at all, must have these features. But (so the problem goes) (1)–(4) form an inconsistent set, so if the theist asserts (1), she has to give up (2) or (3) or (4). But since (2)–(4) ascribe defining features to God, to give up any of them would be to agree that God does not exist. So the existence of evil shows that there is no God.

What is distinctive about the logical problem is that it asserts that (1)–(4) form a *self-contradictory* set. But that is an assumption which has been famously challenged. Plantinga argues that there is no sense of 'inconsistent' or 'contradictory' in which (1) to (4) as they stand form an explicitly contradictory set. If they are contradictory at all, they will be at most *implicitly* contradictory, where that means that if further premises are added, which are themselves necessarily true, an explicit contradiction can be inferred. And Plantinga argues that the atheist who is relying on the problem of evil cannot find any such premises, and hence that the logical problem of evil does not show that God does not exist (see Plantinga 1967 Chapter 5; 1974 Chapter 9; 1977 Part I a 1–3). Other authors have followed Plantinga's lead.[2]

There is clearly a sense in which Plantinga is right here. Premises (1)–(4) do not form an *explicitly* contradictory set; and it would be difficult to find any atheist who thought that they did. Do they form an *implicitly* contradictory set? Or are they perhaps best viewed as a rough and informal pointer to what the inconsistent set would be? If so it would not be the existence of evil by itself which entails the non-existence of God, but the existence of evil, together with some further true premises. The interesting debate about the logical problem of evil is about what these further premises might be. It turns out to be surprisingly difficult for the atheist to find further propositions which the theist has to accept, and which when added to (1)–(4) give an explicitly inconsistent set. Correlatively, it is difficult for the atheist to extract from (1)–(4) a sound deductive argument for the non-existence of God. Suppose, for example, he tries something like the following:

 (5) God is morally perfect (premise).
 (6) God is omnipotent and omniscient (premise). So
 (7) God will prevent all the evil that he can (from (5)) and
 (8) God can prevent all evil (from (6)). So
 (9) God will prevent all evil (from (7) and (8)). So
(10) the world will contain no evil (from (9)). But
(11) the world does contain evil (premise).

Plantinga shows convincingly that no sophisticated theist need accept that (5) implies (7), nor that (6) implies (8) as they stand. For example, if there are very large goods which cannot exist without some comparatively small evils, a morally perfect being might well allow the small evils in order to secure the greater goods. (This is a thought to which we shall have to return shortly.) In that case (5) does not imply (7). Again, and less obviously, it may be that God's omnipotence does not require him to be able to do everything, so it may be the case that (6) does not imply (8). This is something which we will be exploring later, in the discussion of the divine attributes. If either of these criticisms of the argument is correct, the conclusion (10) will not have been shown to follow from premises which the theist is committed to.

How should the atheist respond? One of the most promising lines of reply has been developed by Rowe. Rowe focuses not on the existence of evil per se (as the above argument does), nor on the total amount of evil in the universe. Instead, he concentrates on a single instance of what seems to be a very great evil where there is absolutely no corresponding good. He imagines a forest fire in which 'a fawn is trapped, horribly burned, and lies in terrible agony for several days before death relieves its suffering' (Rowe in Stump and Murray 1999: 159). As far as we can tell, such suffering is utterly pointless: it is not a necessary precondition of any greater good, it is not a means of avoiding a greater evil. With that type of example in mind, Rowe advances the claim that:

(12) There exist instances of intense suffering which an omnipotent, omniscient being could have prevented without thereby losing some greater good or permitting some evil equally bad or worse.

To that he adds a second premise about what sort of behaviour could be expected from God as traditionally conceived:

(13) An omnipotent, omniscient, wholly good being would prevent the occurrence of any intense suffering it could, unless it could not do so without thereby losing some greater good or permitting some evil equally bad or worse.

Given those two premises, the conclusion then follows deductively that:

(14) There does not exist an omnipotent, omniscient, wholly good being.

Since the argument is deductive, the only line of objection for the theist is to reject one or other of the premises. In fact, both premises have come under attack. Let us consider them in turn.

Some critics have argued that even if (12) is true, we are not in a position to know that it is, because we are not in a position to know whether or not there are some greater goods which counterbalance any given instance of intense suffering. It may seem to us that there are no such goods, because we cannot discern any. But, the critic will say, the fact that we cannot find such goods in the world around us is a poor ground for thinking that they do not exist. It would be a good ground only if some such principle as the following were true:

(15) We are in a position to form rational beliefs about all the goods which the world does and does not contain

and (the critic will continue) there is no good reason to accept (15). So, we have no reason to accept (12), and hence no reason to accept the claim in (14) that God does not exist.

In response to this, the sceptic is probably best advised not to argue that we can know all the goods which the world contains. But that leaves the question of what goods the theist thinks *would* if they existed counterbalance the evil. Is there any conceivable good which could only be achieved by the occurrence of (say) the millions of people tortured and killed, and which is so great that it would somehow more than counterbalance all that suffering? If the theist thinks that the problem with the sceptic's argument is just that it is possible for the world to contain goods which we do not know exist, then she ought to be able to say what possible goods she has in mind to counterbalance the evils. It is true that the sceptic is here presupposing a further principle, namely:

(16) Every logically possible good is such that we can describe what it is like.

But unlike (15), this principle looks defensible, and if it is, then although it will not rescue Rowe's agonised fawn example, it will leave the theist in the unsatisfactory position of saying that it is logically possible for a good to have various properties (being a precondition of a given evil, counterbalancing that evil) even though she cannot think of even a *possible* good which has them. If she cannot think of even possible candidates, how can she claim that it is possible for there to be such candidates?

This discussion of the logical problem reveals how one resource of theism is to argue not just that the evil in the world is more than counterbalanced by the good, but more strongly that the evil earns its place in the world (as it were) by being a necessary precondition for the good which then counterbalances it. But we need now to notice that the concept of a necessary precondition can be taken in one or other of two ways, causally or logically, and that these are of very different value to theism.

Evil as a causal presupposition of good

On the causal interpretation, 'necessary precondition' means 'causally necessary'. It means that the laws of nature being what they are, it is possible to achieve a certain good only at the cost of some evil. A familiar example of this is going to the dentist. We accept that a relatively small amount of pain suffered when the dentist drills a tooth is a necessary precondition of the long-term good of healthy teeth; and that the good outweighs (or absorbs) the evil. Again, an athlete may religiously (!) do her training, although she finds it boring and unpleasant. She does it because although to her it is an evil, it is a necessary means to what she regards as a greater good, namely athletic pre-eminence.

It is implicit in this interpretation of 'necessary precondition' that had the world been different in imaginable ways, what is *now* a necessary precondition would not have been one. The world could have been such that people became top-class athletes not by doing boring and exhausting training but by eating a particularly delicious food, or having a really relaxing massage, or by pleasantly lolling about in the sun. Similarly, the laws of nature could have been such that in order to get good teeth, we did not need to have our teeth drilled at all, but could simply sip a tasty healing drink, or have totally painless rays directed at our teeth.

Clearly, for us, who are bound by the laws of nature, it is often reasonable to endure a certain amount of evil in the form of pain or distress in order to gain the good in such circumstances. We reckon that the evil will be totally absorbed by the consequent good. And because of this fact, we are willing to inflict the pain not only on ourselves but also on other people. The parent who is getting the splinter out of her child's finger will think it permissible to inflict pain on the child because of the subsequent good of avoiding an infected finger, even though the same amount of pain, if inflicted wantonly or gratuitously, would be morally evil.

The first interpretation of the idea that evil is a necessary precondition for good assumes that by analogy with such human cases a justification for the evil in the world can be found which will show it to be compatible with the existence of a morally perfect and benevolent God. Take a natural disaster, such as freak tidal waves or cyclones. They are the product of meteorological forces and the laws of nature. Considered in themselves, some of these natural phenomena are evil (in terms of the pain and misery which they cause). But the overall effect of having those laws of nature is beneficial, because they help to render much of the earth habitable. The rain waters our crops, the sun makes them grow, the wind disperses the seeds, and so on. So (the theist continues) if we set the natural disasters in a wider context, we can see that they are a necessary part of a wider scheme of things, and that the wider scheme of things is a good one. Its goodness absorbs the local pockets of evil, such as destructive tidal waves and cyclones.

As an attempted justification for the existence of evil, such a line of argument is worthless. It is worthless because God is not bound in the way that we are by the pre-existing set of natural laws. God as omnipotent could have made the laws of nature such that we had beneficial amounts of rain, sun, wind, tides, etc. but never had cyclones, tidal waves, earthquakes, etc. If natural evils like these are supposed to be explained and justified by saying that they follow inevitably from the operation of God-given laws of nature, the question must arise of why God did not make a 'better' set of laws, 'better' in the sense of yielding the benefits but not the harms of the actual laws of nature.

It is clear that this criticism of the 'good presupposes evil' maxim applies also to all attempts by theism to utilise a biological justification for pain. It is sometimes argued that, in general and overall and in the long run, it is good for us (and for other kinds of sentient life) to have a pain sense. For our pain sense serves as a valuable warning of danger to our bodies. Mild pain distracts our attention from other matters and draws our attention to some current problem. Severe pain tells us that an emergency is occurring, and demands our immediate attention. Without such a sense, our bodily ailments and injuries could go unattended and become much worse. And after all (the proponent of this view might conclude) don't empirical studies show us that those very few unfortunate people who have no capacity for pain lead lives that are difficult and dangerous?

As part of a theistic justification for the occurrence of physical pain, such reasoning is strikingly weak. In the first place, there is a significant mismatch between degree of pain and degree of attention required. Some actions which can be extremely dangerous are relatively painless (such as slitting one's skin with a razor blade); other actions which are not particularly injurious can be very painful (having one's hair pulled). Some pain is unrelievable, so the information that it gives, that something is wrong, is unusable. But second, and in this context conclusively, if the laws of biology could have been different, it could not have been beyond the power of an omnipotent designer to create beings which had a 'better' pain sense. It would be better in two respects: first it would more accurately indicate the severity of the damage or injury, and second, it would motivate us to act on the information received but without causing the sometimes agonising distress which we can currently suffer.

So, if the idea of evil as a precondition of good is to be of any use in defusing the problem of evil, the evil and the good have to be much more tightly enmeshed than simply by the laws of nature. They have to be so tightly enmeshed that not even an omnipotent being could secure the good without the concomitant evil. The evil, in other words, has to be thought of not as a causally necessary precondition, but as a logically necessary precondition. It has to be the case that there is no possible world in which the good is achieved and yet the evil is absent. And it is this idea which takes us on to the second interpretation of evil as a precondition for good.[3]

Evil as logically presupposed by good

Just as God could not have made a world in which being male was not a necessary precondition of being a brother, so (according to this second interpretation) he could not have made a world in which current goods exist without making it one in which the current evil also exists. To explain how this can be so, even although God is omnipotent, let us distinguish between what (following Mackie) we can call first and second order goods and evils. First order goods and evils are those whose occurrence does not presuppose the occurrence of any other goods or evils. They include, for example, pain, suffering, misery, depression, etc. on the one side; and happiness, health, pleasure, enjoyment, etc. on the other. Second order goods would be those goods whose occurrence is logically impossible without the occurrence of some first order evil; and they would include such virtues as charity, sympathy, mercy, etc. The point here would be that it is logically impossible for me to extend sympathy to someone unless they have suffered some kind of misfortune. I could behave *well* towards someone who was not the victim of misfortune; but unless they are such a victim, my good behaviour will not count as sympathy. Similarly, if my action is to be charitable, the recipient of my generosity has to have suffered. If he has not suffered then although my treatment of him may be kind, it will not count as charitable.

What this second interpretation does, then, is to retain the instrumental view of evil (evil as a necessary precondition of good) and so construe the kind of necessity as to block the objection 'But why didn't God make the world in such a way that the good could have been achieved without the

234

accompanying evil?'. If the defence is to work, it has to be shown that all the evil in the world is counterbalanced by good (absorbed by good, in Mackie's nice metaphor) which is such that it is logically impossible that the good could have occurred without the evil. If this is not so, then a perfectly good and omniscient God would have known that the universe which he could create would contain gratuitous evil, and hence would not have created it in the first place. How then is the counterbalancing of evil by good to be calculated?

There is clearly no possibility of any precise quantification of the good and evil in the universe and of the balance of one over the other. But we can make a number of observations. First, we need to notice that not only do the first order evils make possible some second order goods, they also make possible some second order evils. It is because people can feel pain and suffering (first order evil) that it is possible to be cruel to them (second order evil). If there were a species incapable of suffering, it would be logically impossible to be cruel to them (vegetables would be one group of such species). It is because some situations are dangerous and terrifying (first order evil) that it is possible to be cowardly (second order evil). So what the second order goods have to outweigh is not just the first order evils which make them possible, but also the second order evils which the first order evils also make possible. So, if they do not outweigh the second order evils as well, there will be unabsorbed evil in the system as a whole, and hence it would not have been created by a morally perfect God in the first place.

Second, it is important to be clear exactly which goods are available to absorb the evils in the universe. Given someone who has suffered a great misfortune, we can behave towards them in all sorts of ways which are good. We can treat them with sympathy, with kindness, with generosity, with tact, with patience, with understanding, and so on. Perhaps the Good Samaritan displayed all of these virtues in his dealings with the man who had fallen among thieves. But of these virtuous modes of behaviour, only the first can count as a second order good, since only the first logically requires the existence of suffering. To someone who had suffered nothing at all, the Good Samaritan could have displayed exactly that range of virtues, bar sympathy. We can agree that his kindness, generosity, tact, patience and understanding were morally admirable features of his behaviour. But none of them is available to absorb any of the evil of the attack on the victim. Although the sufferings of the victim may have been a *causal* precondition of the Samaritan's kindness, benevolence, etc., they could not have been a logical precondition, and are therefore not available in any absorption equation. So, in general, when we are considering any situation, our question is not whether on balance its occurrence adds to or detracts from the goodness in the universe. Rather, our question is whether the evil which the situation contains is absorbed by *that good in the situation whose existence logically presupposes the evil*. Unless this condition is met, the world would have been a better place without the occurrence of that situation, and therefore God would not have produced a world in which such a situation occurred.

Third, notice that what we have to consider is not just potential second order goods but actual ones. It is no doubt true that the existence of suffering is a logically necessary precondition of the occurrence of sympathy. Suffering by one person *makes possible* sympathy by another. That logical point has to be conceded by the atheist. But what is needed to absorb the evil of suffering in the world is not merely the *possibility* of sympathy, but the actuality of sympathy. It may be that a world which contains suffering, and therefore the possibility of sympathy, but which lacks the actuality of sympathy is nevertheless on balance a good world (we will consider this in a moment). But if it were overall good, it would not be good because the second order goods had absorbed the first order evils, but because it contained something else of value, something which was of sufficient value to outweigh the suffering-unabsorbed-by-sympathy which it contained.

As an application of this third point, we need to remember that many first order evils are *not available* for absorption by second order goods. Clearly, if someone is to sympathise with the unfortunate, to bring succour to the needy, etc., the benefactor must know about the sufferings of the person towards whom her virtue is directed. And certainly, great swathes of suffering are apparent in the world around us. But equally, a good deal of suffering occurs privately, or at a time or place which makes it unknowable by other people, and which thus is not even a candidate for being absorbed. It is, as it were, pure loss in the imaginary balancing book, and hence would not have occurred in a universe created by a morally perfect God.

Fourth, we need to reflect on an aspect of the world's evil that has already been referred to – the extent of animal suffering. The significance of this is that it seems that very little of the evil of animal suffering is absorbed by second level goods. Although some few species of animals show some limited sympathy with a small number of their conspecifics, more particularly towards their kin, the great majority themselves show little or no sympathy with other suffering animals. And although some humans show some sympathy with some animals, it is no more than a scratch on the huge rockface of animal suffering. Why would a perfect God create a universe in which such huge amounts of suffering occur, when such suffering does not bring into existence any of the goods required to absorb the suffering and make the situation on balance a good one?

For these reasons, any appeal to the idea that the evil in the world can be explained away as necessary to the good faces a number of limitations on its effectiveness. But there is anyway surely something absurd in the whole approach. Of course, given that there is some evil, it is desirable if some good can come from it and someone can surmount or overcome or absorb it. But it is surely ridiculous to think that the good for whose existence the evil is a logically necessary precondition is *so* valuable that it is worth bringing into existence the evil so that it makes possible the occurrence of the good. If evil E is a logical precondition of good G, and the theist judges that G more than counterbalances E, is she really saying that we make the world a worse place by removing evil E? Given that I am badly injured by a vicious thug, it is a good thing (let us assume) that there are surgeons who can repair my badly damaged parts. And certainly the good of the surgeon's extensive repairs logically presupposes that I have been extensively damaged. But it would be absurd to say that the good of the surgeon's repairs is so great that it justifies the original infliction of injuries on me; or that someone who had intervened to prevent the thuggish assault (and hence the subsequent surgical repair) would thereby have made the world a worse place.

However, given all the above reservations about the 'good presupposes evil' move, it is nonetheless true that some theists would say that they had done enough to defuse the atheist's appeal to the problem of evil. They think, as they survey the world, that there *are* enough second order goods to absorb all the first and second order evils, with some to spare. Atheists who rely on the problem of evil will disagree. And given the impossibility of any quantification of the good and evil in question, it is unclear how the debate can continue further along the same lines.

Must God create the best possible world?

But now a new line of criticism opens up. Suppose that the theist is right to maintain that the world as it is, with its past and current evils, is on balance a good thing, and could not be made any better by removing any of the evil. Is this enough to secure theism? Is it enough for theism to show merely that *the world contains more good than bad*? Or does she not rather need to show why the world is not a great deal better than in fact it is? For on the face of it, even if some evil is necessary for the maximisation of the good in the world, there is far more evil than is required in order to achieve that purpose. Perhaps even more strongly, theism implies that *the world is the best possible*? After all, the God to whom the theist ascribes the origin and maintenance of the universe is not simply a *good* God, but a *perfect* God. Should not then his creation be not merely *good*, but the *best possible*? We will find that some theists answer this by saying 'Yes, God's perfection does require him to produce the best possible world; and the world around us is not only good, it *is* the best possible'; while others reply by saying 'No, it is not the best possible, but this is not a reason for saying that it is not the product of God, since God's perfection does not require that he produce the best possible world'. We will consider each of these responses in turn.

Leibniz, following Plato (*Timaeus* 29–30A), famously declared that 'this universe must be in reality better than every other possible universe' (Leibniz

1997: 378), or, in the phrase made more familiar by Voltaire, that this is the best of all possible worlds. Leibniz in fact understood this maxim in several ways, not all of which have anything to do with the problem of evil, but certainly he also deployed it in connection with the argument from evil.

Let us assume, then, for the sake of argument that Leibniz is right in thinking that if God creates a world at all, he must create the best possible. Can the atheist use this Leibnizian claim to argue to the non-existence of God? Here is one simple argument which the atheist might deploy:

(17) If God created a universe at all, he would create the best possible (premise).
(18) The universe is not the best possible (premise). So:
(19) God did not create the universe (from (17) and (18)). But:
(20) If God exists, he created the universe (premise). So:
(21) God does not exist (from (19) and (20)).

It is prima facie plausible to claim (17), given God's perfection, and the logical possibility of a best possible world; the extent and distribution of evil, even if not its mere presence, makes (18) prima facie plausible; and (20) is surely common ground to theists and atheists, at least given the existence of the universe. Since (17) and (18) entail (19), and (19) and (20) entail (21), the atheist can construct an argument which has prima facie plausibility. How is the theist to respond?

Not surprisingly, both (17) and (18) have come under attack. Leibniz offers a rather skimpy attack on (18). But what he says does not really support the claim that the universe is the best possible, rather than the much weaker claim that some of the evils in the universe are justified by their role in making possible some actual greater goods.

A more interesting attack on (17) comes from Adams. Adams argues that (17) would be true only if God's perfection is properly thought of in a maximising consequentialist way. If God's perfection consisted in God always bringing about the greatest amount of good, then indeed the universe which he created would have to be the best possible. But (says Adams) within the Judaeo-Christian tradition of theism at least, God's perfection is not standardly understood in maximising consequentialist terms. So the prima facie plausibility which the atheist claimed for (17) disappears. Are there any other non-consequentialist grounds which could be provided for accepting (17)? Adams claims that there are only three possible non-consequentialist grounds for doing this. The first is that if God did not create the best possible world, he would *wrong someone (violate their rights)*; the second is that if he did not create the best possible world, he would be *less kind* to someone than a perfect agent would be; and the third is that if he did not create the best possible world, he would reveal himself to have a defect of character. Given that these are the only three ways in which a perfect being might be obligated to produce the best possible world, Adams undertakes to describe a possible world which is not the best possible but in which none of these constraints is violated. All we have to do is to imagine a world in which:

(A) None of the individual creatures in it would exist in the best of all possible worlds.
(B) None of the creatures in it has a life which is so miserable on the whole that it would be better for that creature if it had never existed.
(C) Every individual creature in the world is at least as happy on the whole as it would have been in any possible world in which it could have existed.

Given (A), the creatures in that world would not have been wronged by being brought into existence in an inferior world rather than in the best possible, since ex hypothesi they would not have existed at all had the best possible world been created. Nor are the creatures who would have existed in the best possible world wronged by not having been created. For you do not wrong possible persons by not creating them – you can wrong only persons who actually exist, or who will exist no matter what you do. Further, given (C), there is no other possible world in which any of the creatures of this world would have been happier, so none of them have been treated with less than perfect kindness. So in creating such a world, God has not wronged anyone, either those whom he created or those whom he did not create; nor has he treated with less than perfect kindness either those whom he created or those whom he did not create. So, it is fully compatible with the divine attributes that God should have created a world which is less than perfect. In other words (16) is false.

There are however, two responses open to the atheist. First, he could point out that Adams has only said that there is a *possible* world which is not the best possible, the creation of which by God would not impugn his perfection. If the argument is cogent, it successfully undermines any proof of atheism from the two claims that this is not the best possible world, and that God if he existed would have to create the best possible world. But Adams does not show that that possible world which he describes is our actual world. And it takes only a moment's reflection to see that the actual world is not Adams's possible world. For in the actual world, precondition (C) of Adams's possible world is not met: it is not the case in the actual world that 'every individual creature in the world is at least as happy on the whole as it would have been in any possible world in which it could have existed'. So even if Adams's argument is sound, it leaves open the possibility of a sound argument from the evil which we find in the actual world to the non-existence of God.[4]

The second response by the atheist would be to challenge Adams's argument itself. Taking for granted a non-utilitarian stance, Adams says that God would have to create the best possible world only if that was the only way for him to avoid wronging someone, or the only way for him to treat them with perfect kindness, or if it would reveal a character defect in him if he did not create the best possible world. The puzzle is to see why it is not a character defect to refuse to create the best possible world, when you could have done so with absolutely no cost of any kind to anyone. What does it mean to say that a world is the *best possible* if not that it is better that it should exist than that any other should exist? How could a world be the best possible, and yet it be better (or even just as good) that a quite different and inferior world should exist? Further, if God is indeed perfect, why would he knowingly choose to create a worse possible world than he need have done? To say that his perfection does not consist in his acting like a utilitarian maximiser is not sufficient. For there is middle ground between rejecting utilitarianism (which tells us that it is *always* obligatory to maximise the production of goodness), and thinking that a perfect being *never* has an obligation to maximise goodness. If we add in the traditional theistic assumption that God is not arbitrary or whimsical, but always has excellent reasons for what he does, what reason could there be for him deliberately to choose the inferior? The standard theistic move in discussions of evil, that the evil is a precondition of realising a greater good, is not available here, since we are comparing total possible universes, and have therefore already taken account of any greater long-term goods that might be actualised only by the presence of some evil. In such circumstances, choosing what is known to be the worse looks merely perverse.

A more compelling criticism of (16) (the claim that if God creates a world at all, he has to create the best possible) is provided by Swinburne. He believes contra Adams that God is a maximiser: his perfection requires that he does the best possible thing whenever there is a best possible thing to do ('if there is a best action, he will do it; or, if there are alternative equal best possible actions, he will do one of them' (Swinburne 1994: 135). But he also believes that often, there is no best action which is possible for God. This will be true when God is confronted by a situation in which there are infinitely many actions open to God, each of which is inferior to some other. Let us call this an 'ascending infinity' of possible actions. Apply this thought to God's situation as he contemplates creating a world. Then (says Swinburne) there will be no best action open to God, since for any world of conscious agents which God could have created *ex nihilo*, there is, plausibly, a better one – for instance, one obtained by adding one more person. So Swinburne continues, for any world, A, which God could create, there would be a better one, B, which he did not create. But this will not derogate from his perfection, since if he had created B instead, there would still be a better world C; and had he chosen C, there would have been a better world D; and so infinitely. So, God's perfection does not require him to create a best possible world, and hence does not require him to create a perfect world (ibid.).

Swinburne's position might be questioned on two grounds. I shall reject both grounds, but I think that they are worth mentioning because they raise issues which have an independent interest. The first criticism challenges his claim that when God has to choose between an infinitely large range of possibilities, there will be no best choice for him to make. The second criticism questions his 'the more the better' assumption (let us call this the maximising assumption).

Let us consider the first objection. Suppose we grant Swinburne's implicit assumption that for any finite number of persons whom God creates, he could have created a larger number. And let us accept also for the moment Swinburne's assumptions that the existence of some conscious agents is good, and that the more conscious agents there are, the better. Let us express this (of course, much too crudely) by saying that a world with one person has one unit of value; with two people, two units of value; and in general, for n people, the world has n units of value. Swinburne's point is then that for any n people whom God could create, he could always have created n + 1. So for any world with n units of value which he creates, there is always a world with n + 1 units of value; so there is no best possible world which he could create. The first objection to Swinburne's position can now be put: it is that his argument holds only if n is a finite number. But if God creates an infinite number of people (so the objection goes), the argument collapses. The best possible world for God to create (given Swinburne's other assumption) is one with infinitely many people (always bearing in mind Swinburne's thoughtful requirement that they do not crowd each other!).

How should Swinburne respond to this first objection? Not by taking the seeming obvious line of denying that God could create infinitely many people. No one has ever argued that it was logically impossible for God to create an infinite space, or that if it had turned out that space was infinite, the non-existence of God was an immediate corollary. So if God could have created a space, divisible into arbitrary units (say feet) of which there were infinitely many, he surely could also have created humanity, divided into units (i.e. individual people) of which there were infinitely many. So to the question which must arise for Swinburne 'If more means better, why didn't God create infinitely many people', the right reply cannot be 'Not even an omnipotent being can create an infinite number of people'.

A reply on behalf of Swinburne which is possibly better but also more contentious comes from an appeal to Cantorian mathematics. The objection to the idea of a best possible world trades on the thought that God could have created infinitely many people. Swinburne can reply that even if he had, there would still be a better world which he could have created, for he could have created more than infinitely many people. For, as Cantor showed, infinities come (to express the point somewhat loosely) in different sizes. The infinity we have been speaking of so far is the number (or cardinality) of the natural numbers, known as $\aleph_0$ (aleph 0). As Cantor showed, there are infinities larger than $\aleph_0$ – in fact, if the continuum hypothesis is correct, there are infinitely many infinities larger than $\aleph_0$, and no largest one. So even if God had created a world with a population whose cardinal number was $\aleph_0$, and which hence had $\aleph_0$ units of value, there would still be other possible worlds, whose population had cardinality $\aleph 1$ or 2 or 3, etc. which he could have created and which would have had greater value. So, Swinburne can still maintain that it cannot be incumbent on God to create the *best* possible world, since whichever one he creates (even one that contains infinitely many people and hence is infinitely valuable), there will always be a more valuable one which he could have created. And if the objector asks why if God, as an omnipotent being, has the power to create a world whose value has the cardinality $\aleph_0$, is it beyond his power to create a world whose value has the cardinality $\aleph_n$, where n is some suitably large and impressive number, Cantor supplies Swinburne with a compelling answer: there is no greatest cardinal number which can serve as the subscript to $\aleph$ itself. If the continuum hypothesis is true, then even if n (the subscript to $\aleph$) is itself infinity (i.e. $\aleph_0$), there will be yet greater numbers. From this it will follow that *whatever* the cardinal number of the people whom God has created, he could always have created more. And if we add in the assumption 'the more the better', then for any world which God could have created he could always have created a better one. So the first objection to Swinburne fails: given his other assumptions, he is right to say that there could be no best possible world for God to create.

The second objection focuses on Swinburne's assumption that the more people the better, as long as God considerately spaces them so that no one is crowded. The problem here is that even if we add in the assumption that everyone enjoys high levels of utility (interpret that term as a variable, and give it whatever values you like), it is unclear why we should agree that a world with 5 billion persons is to that extent better than one with 4 billion and worse than one with 6 billion. Of course, if these persons already exist, it is better that they have high levels of utility than not, and better that more of them rather than fewer have these high levels of utility. But if the point of comparison is whether it would be better to *bring into existence* 5 billion persons rather than 4 billion, many people might think that there is no reason to suppose that it would be better. And if it would not be better, then Swinburne's argument against the possibility of a best possible world will at least need reformulating and at worst will fail altogether. For he will not be able to say that God could always have created a world with more people, and *hence* with more value, than exist in any world which he actually creates; and hence Swinburne will not have *this* reason for saying that there cannot be a best possible world.

This objection will be found less than compelling to some people, and Swinburne and others who agree with him may well find it *wholly* without force. Many people may find it obvious that other things being equal (such as the satisfaction of the spacing condition) the more persons the better, perhaps precisely on the Swinburnean ground that the existence of persons is a good thing, and that the more you have of a good thing the better. Support for this intuition may come from considering the opposite scenario. If we think of the existence of deeply wretched people, it does seem worse for there to be 6 billion wretched people than 5 billion, and worse again for there to be 6 billion + 1. In the case of misery, increasing numbers *do* make the situation worse. So, by parity of reasoning, it seems that in the case of fulfilled lives, increasing numbers should make the world better. So we have no good reason to reject the maximising assumption that the more the better, and hence that as a matter of logic there could not be a best possible world. And of course if there could not be such a world, the fact that this world is not the best possible is no evidence at all against the existence of God.

Must God create a *perfect* world?

But now the atheist needs to reformulate his attack. While recognising that creation is not properly construed as a temporal notion, we can for ease of exposition put his argument in temporal terms. Creation can then be interpreted in terms of different kinds of dependence by different kinds of theist. Let us use the term 'world' to refer to the totality of contingently existing things that have actually been created by God. And let us use the term 'cosmos' to refer to *everything* that exists, including any platonic entities, including God, and including the world. Since platonic entities will play no further part in the argument, I will omit mention of them, and speak as if the only things which the cosmos might consist of are either God by himself, or God plus the world.

So, putting the story in temporal terms, the theist is envisaging a succession like this. First the cosmos consisted of just God (let us call this cosmos 1). Then God decided to create a world, as a consequence of which the cosmos consisted of God plus the world (let us call this cosmos 2). The question we need to raise is whether the theist can consistently say either that the change from cosmos 1 to cosmos 2 was a change for the better, or that it was for the worse.

The change cannot have been for the better. For since God is by definition fully and infinitely perfect in every respect, and the cosmos initially consisted only of God, the cosmos could not have been improved from its initial state. To say otherwise would imply a lack or deficiency in God, a falling short of genuine perfection which could be made up only by God's creating a world; and that would surely be incompatible with divine perfection.

Nor can the change have been for the worse. Again God's perfection surely blocks a 'Yes' answer. For suppose that the answer were 'Yes'. That would be to imagine God comparing the two possible cosmoses (one consisting only of him, the other of him and the world), recognising (since he is omniscient) that the latter is worse than the former, and freely choosing what he knows to be the worse option. That would surely be incompatible with his divine perfection.

But if the change from cosmos 1 to cosmos 2 could not be a change for the better nor a change for the worse, the implication must be that cosmos 1 and cosmos 2 are of equal value. But if they are of equal value, it follows that the world must itself display the same kind of full and infinite perfection that God does. For suppose it did not. That would be to say that starting with something perfect, something imperfect could be added to it, and yet the resulting whole end up perfect, even while the addition itself remained imperfect.

So, if God created the world, it would not merely be *the best possible*, it would be *as perfect as God* himself. Since it is clear that the world is not as perfect as God himself, it follows that God did not create the world. But since the world exists, and if God existed, he would be the creator of the world, it follows that he does not exist.[5]

We can see then that Leibniz was half-wrong and half-right to invoke the concept of the best possible. He was wrong, inasmuch as there cannot be a best possible *created universe*, nor a best possible combination of *God-and-a-created-universe* (for Swinburnean reasons). But he was right, inasmuch as theism must regard God alone as perfect and must regard cosmos 1 as the best possible. What he did not see was that the sense in which he is right, combined with the fact that the created world is not perfect, entails that God does not exist.

Is there any incompatibility in accepting that God does not have to create the best possible universe, but insisting that he must create a perfect universe? Perhaps surprisingly, there is not. If an item X is perfect, then there is none better, but there could be other items which were just as good (they too would be perfect). But if X is the best possible, not only is there none better than X, but also X is better than any other. In other words, the concept of the best possible has a uniqueness requirement built into it, and the concept of perfection does not. So something can be perfect even if it is not the best possible, provided that the reason that the only reason that it is not the best possible is not that there is something better than it, but that there are others which are just as good. Hence, although the fact that this is not the best possible world does not disprove the existence of God, the fact that this is not a perfect world does.

The free will defence

Suppose the previous line of argument for atheism is incorrect, and that the theist is right to say that God need not create either a perfect or the best possible world.

This still leaves the theist with a major problem. For the kind of falling short of the optimum which the world displays is quite different from the kind of falling short which the maximising assumption can explain away. The difference can be captured in the two following claims:

(a) The world is not the best possible because although it is filled entirely with admirable, fulfilled and flourishing people, it could have contained even more such people.
(b) The world is not the best possible because it contains huge amounts of apparently gratuitous pain, distress and misery.

The maximising assumption shows how theism can accept a less than best world if it is like the world described in (a), but not if it is like the world described in (b). But it is (b) and not (a) which describes the actual world. So the kind of sub-optimality which our world displays cannot be reconciled with divine omnipotence and perfection by the maximising principle.

The theist then faced the original problem of how this can be reconciled with the fact that this world seems to contain a great deal more evil, both moral and natural, than it needs to. The first theistic move to solve this problem was to say that evil is a precondition for a greater good; and in previous sections above, we explored some ways in which that might be so. The most promising line tried to find specific evils which could be seen to be logically required if specific goods were to be possible (as your sympathy for my misfortune logically requires that I should suffer a misfortune). But now we need to turn to another kind of good which has been invoked by theists as explaining and justifying the evil in the world, the good of free will.

The thought here is that the existence of free choice, even the free choice to act wrongly, is itself something of moral value. It is sometimes described, using the terminology which we introduced above, as a third-order good. But this is a mistake – or at least, freedom is not a higher order good in the sense of that phrase as we used it earlier. For it was crucial to second order goods that they were goods which it was logically impossible to produce without a corresponding first order evil. But even if we agree that freedom is a good, and that because it is sometimes misused, it sometimes produces evil, it is not the case that freedom is logically impossible without evil. The idea of a being who is both free and also embodies moral perfection is not self-contradictory – indeed, according to theism, God is precisely such a being. So, to avoid confusion with the earlier terminology of first and second order goods and evils, let us simply call freedom a *further* good.

Of course this further-order good brings with it some possible evils, for people can freely choose to act wrongly as well as to act rightly. But the claim by the theist would be that there is a logically necessary link between the two: you cannot have the power to act freely without also having the power to act both rightly and wrongly. So the existence of free will explains at least some of the evil in the world (it has been caused by humans misusing the divine gift of free will, and hence has not been caused by God); but according to the free will defence, free will is itself so valuable that it is better for humans to have and misuse it as often as they do than not to have it at all.

We can note first of all that the free will defence could at best explain only how *moral* evils can exist in a God-created universe. Since natural evils are not brought about by any misuse of human free will, the theist who takes the existence of evil seriously needs to find an independent justification for the existence of natural evil: the free will defence is at best incomplete. Further, it appears to rest on three questionable assumptions:

(22) that the value of free action is sufficient to outweigh the otherwise unabsorbed evil in the world;

(23) that this further good of free choice could not have been achieved without bringing with it the further evils of bad free actions; and

(24) that if the evil is produced by humans misusing their free will, the resulting evil is not evidence against the existence of God.

Let us examine these more closely.

Assessment of the free will defence

First, then, what *is* so good about free action? We can supply one answer to that question in terms of instrumental value. Sometimes the things that I need and want can be achieved without my needing the power of free choice, and sometimes they cannot. For example, I do not want foreign bodies entering my eye, and I am born with an eye-blink reflex which ensures that by and large my eyes remain intruder-free. If a fly hovers near my eye, I do not freely choose to blink, nor do I need to choose. The eye-blink movement is instinctive and reflex, and its effectiveness would not be improved by bringing it under my conscious control. By contrast, I do want food entering my mouth, and I am not equipped with any instincts or reflexes which ensure that this happens. It happens only if I exercise my power of free choice to gather food, prepare it, and lift it to my mouth. Without the power of free action in such a case, I should perish. So we can say that in those areas where we do not have an instinctive or reflective mechanism which guarantees the satisfaction of our desires and needs, there is an instrumental value in having the power of free choice.

But this instrumental defence of the value of free will is a very long way from declaring it to have absolute or unconditional value of the kind needed to support the free will defence. If it were such a good, then presumably *any* increase in it would make the universe a marginally better place; and any decrease would make the universe marginally worse. But is this really so? Consider the case of a man who, by dint of practice, manages to bring under his direct control something that in the rest of us functions perfectly well on an instinctive or non-conscious level. Suppose that he gains control of his heart-beat. He can freely choose whether to speed it up or slow it down, just as he can freely choose to help someone or freely choose to ignore their needs. Is this *in itself* an accomplishment of any value? It may be that as part of some larger project (such as bringing himself a new self-confidence, or perhaps as becoming a circus performer) it has some value for him. But in the absence of any such wider setting, it is surely impossible to think that this increase in free choice in the universe has made the universe a better place in even the most marginal way. Correlatively, if the man then loses that capacity, it is impossible to think that the universe then becomes, however marginally, a worse place.

It is true that many exercises of our power of free choice are valuable, and indeed morally valuable. But such freely performed actions are valuable not principally because they are free, but principally because they are the doing of something good. And bad actions do not have their badness offset by the fact that at least they are free – if anything, the fact that they are free makes them worse. In these absolute scales, freedom will be neutral. And if that is right, the addition of freedom to the universe could be an improvement to the universe only if the freedom was exercised in a particular way. So if there are any evils in a world in which there is no freedom, they cannot be removed *merely* by adding to the universe the power of free choice. What would also be necessary would be that the power of free choice should be exercised in some ways and not in others.

But, it may be said, this is to misunderstand the appeal to free will in the context of the problem of evil. What is of value and is able to absorb otherwise unabsorbed evilss is not the power of free choice itself, but rather a set of particular uses of this ability, those uses when the power is being exercised in morally significant contexts, contexts in which the successful exercise of our free will can bring us a deeper understanding of, for example, temptation, moral conflict, moral heroism, sacrifice, steadfastness, etc. This is a line of thinking which is associated with the 'soul-making' theodicy of John Hick.

But two problems bedevil the soul-making approach. First, it must surely imply that we have been created as deficient beings who need to go through a process of moral growth in order to become, if not perfect, as least as excellent as we can become. And this leaves soul-making wide open to the question we posed in the previous section: why would a perfect God deliberately choose to make the cosmos worse than it need have been by creating some deeply flawed beings? Second, the soul-making perspective approaches the problem of evil too late as it were in the process of creation. Given that God is going to create creatures *just like human beings*, it is obviously important that those creatures do undergo moral growth. It is important that they develop an understanding of moral dilemmas, a capacity of moral courage, a set of character traits such as benevolence, compassion, fairness, honesty, etc. But the reason these are so very important to creatures like us is that we have been created as beings who have to live together and who have the capacity to inflict enormous suffering on each other. Morality is a way (the best way we have so far found) of limiting the colossal harm which people can do to each other. So, given that God has created us, it is very important to us to ensure that a sense of morality is a major determinant of people's conduct. But that does not mean that morality in itself has any special value – that it is, for example, so valuable that it is a good idea to create creatures with such mutually destructive power that morality is a precondition of their survival. If we were beings of a completely different sort, we would have no need of morality. The insect world presents us with many species who enjoy highly social, highly co-operative forms of existence, with no morality at all. And as soon as one contemplates the world of science fiction or theology, it becomes clear that God could have created beings of an intelligence and understanding superior to that of humans, who simply had no need of morality. Suppose, for example, each of us had a cloud-like existence, drifting about the universe, unable to be harmed or benefited by anything in our environment, simply thinking beautiful or intellectually exciting thoughts. No doubt there are many people for whom (given that they are already human beings with our typical tastes) that would be a prospect with only modest appeal. But if the choice was between such an existence, and, for example, being burned alive, starved to death, crippled by a paralysing and fatal disease, or any of the other fates that await so many of us, the alternative form of existence would doubtless seem very much more attractive.

But there is a second point at which the free will defence can be attacked. Suppose we grant that freedom is in itself a good in the universe, irrespective of how it is exercised. Given that free will is a good thing, and that God therefore wished (some of) his creatures to have it, why did he not make us so that we all freely choose to do the right thing all the time? Some theists have argued that this is not logically possible, and that if it is not logically possible, then we cannot sensibly ask why God has not done it. If, on the other hand, it is logically possible to make creatures who always freely choose the best, then God could have made the world so that it contained moral dilemmas, opportunities for self-sacrifice, etc. without also containing the truly terrible things which it does contain, and theism would still be in serious trouble. So, *could* God have made creatures in such a way that they always made the right choices, but made them of their own free will?

We need to be clear what this question amounts to. On the assumption that it is logically possible for everyone freely to make the right choices, it is presumably logically possible for God to make everyone in such a way that, as it later transpires, they all freely make the right choices. God as an omnipotent being can presumably bring about any state of affairs that is itself logically possible. But our question is a different one. It could be put informally like this: when God was first setting up the universe and arranging for there to be agents with the power of free choice, could he tell *then* that some ways of making the universe would result in agents who always freely choose correctly, and that other ways of making the universe would result in agents who sometimes did and sometimes did not freely choose correctly; and did he knowingly choose to make a universe of the second kind rather than the first kind?

It seems that theism is in trouble whether the answer to this question is 'Yes' or 'No'. If the answer is 'Yes', then the theist is saying that God could have made a better universe than this one, but he freely and knowingly chose to make an inferior one. In such a case, even if we do not say that God is the *direct* cause of the evil in the universe, he is the cause of the cause (he causes the people who freely choose to cause the evil, and he knows as he makes this choice that that is what they will do); and he certainly *permits* the evil to continue. So a 'Yes' answer presents a direct challenge to the theistic belief in the perfection of God, and hence to the belief that God exists.

But suppose that the answer is 'No', that is, that God did not know at the time he was making the universe and its contents whether the people in it would always or sometimes or never make the right choice. This view presents theism with a problem for different reasons. First, it seems to undermine another of God's defining attributes, and hence to entail the non-existence of God. If an omniscient being knows of every truth that it is true, and of every falsehood that it is false, then surely an omniscient being will know the future free actions of all agents. Second, suppose that God did not know what the future free actions would be of the agents he created, and that this fact can somehow be reconciled with his omniscience. Given the *huge* amounts of evil which humans could bring about (vastly more than we find in the actual world), it would seem amazingly irresponsible for God sto bring such beings into existence. It would be a kind of cosmic Russian roulette, where the possible outcomes would range from an absolutely appalling world, perhaps through a world like ours, to a world that was all sweetness and light.

However, the theist need not be moved by the first of these points. As we will see when we examine the divine attributes in more detail (see Chapter 15 in particular), many theists want to construe omniscience more narrowly than the above criticism assumes. If, for example, we think of omniscience as knowing every truth which is *knowable* (rather than every truth which is true), and we add the thought that there are some truths (e.g. about future free actions) which are unknowable in advance, it would be possible to maintain that God could be omniscient, while remaining ignorant of the future free choices of his creatures.

There are at least two points at issue here. The first is the possibility of different conceptions of omniscience. But the second, and more central issue here, is that there are two rival conceptions of free action. Very broadly, theists embrace one, and their opponents the other. According to the *compatibilist* tradition, which embraces Hobbes, Hume, Mill, Ayer, Flew and Mackie among others, an action can be both free and also wholly caused by prior events. According to one basic formulation of this view, you act freely if you choose to act in accordance with your own wants, and your action is brought about by your own choices, desires, etc. This basic version can then be enhanced with further subtleties and refinements in different ways by different compatibilists. But according to all versions of compatibilism, to say that you act freely is compatible with saying that your action had a cause, provided that the cause was of a certain sort (e.g. your own choices, wants, etc.). In particular, it is not assumed that to be free an action must be uncaused. On this conception of free action, it is clearly possible to know in advance of what someone does what their free action will be. All we need to know are precise events which precede that action and which in accordance with the laws of nature will cause them to perform that action. For us mere humans, with our limited knowledge, it may be practically impossible to gather all the information required to make such a prediction. But for a being who is omniscient, there is no problem. God will be able to predict down to the last detail every future action of every free choosing creature in the universe. And the fact that he will have this foreknowledge in no way derogates from the status of the actions as *free*.

According to the rival *incompatibilist* view which is favoured by many theists, an action cannot be both free and caused by prior events. For it to be sgenuinely free, there must not be anything in the situation leading up to the action which guarantees that the person will perform or refrain from the action in question. It is generally conceded that prior events can *have an influence* on the agent, or predispose her one way or the other. But if the action is to be free, then at the moment of choice, it must still be entirely up to her which action she performs.

The significance of this contrast between different conceptions of free actions is twofold. First, if the compatibilist is right, then God could secure the good of human free choice, and also know in advance how that free choice would be exercised. So he could perfectly well have foreseen all the moral evil in the world, even if it is brought about by human free action. Even if we do not want to say that God brought it about directly, he brought it about indirectly; and he certainly foresaw that the world which he was choosing to create would contain all the evil which it does contain. Why then did he not create a better world than this? Why not, for example, a world in which all the free agents always freely make morally the best choices? The fact that our world is not like that is evidence that it was not created by the God of traditional theism, and hence evidence that God does not exist.

There is a further problem faced by the compatibilist theist which is to do not with divine *foreknowledge* of morally objectionable free actions, but rather with God's *involvement in the doing* of free actions. God both creates the universe, and keeps everything in it in existence moment by moment. So when you go to perform a free action, God has been involved in the production of all the causal antecedents of your free action. He has been involved in producing exactly those hopes and fears, wants and aversions, convictions and opinions which collectively cause your action (or, in more materialist mode, those brain states, muscle states, etc. which bring about the action). It can be difficult on this conception to see how there is any room left for *you the agent* to do anything. It seems as if nothing has been left up to you – God does it all. From a compatibilist perspective it seems that from God creating everything, and sustaining everything, to his *doing* everything is a very short step. This is a problem to which we will return in discussing divine omnipotence (see Chapter 13).

It seems then that the compatibilist is not well-placed to invoke human free will as a possible explanation for the evil in the world. Divine foreknowledge of the evil choices that will be made, and divine participation in the events leading up to and causing those free choices would make God responsible for the evil.

If then, the theist is to rely on the free will defence, he evidently needs to combine it with an incompatibilist account of free will. And this is exactly the line which we will find taken by many able theists. Here is such a defence as deployed by one of its subtlest and ablest supporters:

> A world containing creatures who are sometimes significantly free (and freely perform more good than evil actions) is more valuable, all else being equal, than a world containing no free creatures at all. Now God can create free creatures, but he cannot *cause* or *determine* them to do only what is right. For if he does so, then they are not significantly free after all; they do not do what is right *freely*. To create creatures capable of *moral good*, therefore, he must create creatures capable of moral evil; and he cannot leave these creatures *free* to perform evil and at the same time prevent them from doing so. God did in fact create significantly free creatures; but some of them went wrong in the exercise of their freedom: this is the source of moral evil. The fact that these creatures sometimes go wrong, however, counts neither against God's omnipotence nor against his goodness; for he could have forestalled the occurrence of moral evil only by excising the possibility of moral good.
>
> (Plantinga 1982: 166–7)[6]

251

But here we need to notice a division within the camp of those who rely on an incompatibilist conception of freedom to support a Free Will Defence. Some (such as Ward, Tennant, Lucas, Swinburne) draw the conclusion that God could not *foresee* how the free agents whom he had created would exercise their free will. Others (such as Plantinga) insist that God does foresee how the agents will use their free will, but also that he is in no way responsible for the resulting evils. We can briefly explore these in turn.

According to the first position, from the range of possible worlds, God chooses to create a world of a certain sort. In particular, he chooses to create a world containing free creatures, because he attaches enormous value to free choices. But in creating creatures who are free (in the incompatibilist sense), he is creating creatures whose free actions cannot be foreseen, even by God in his omniscience. So, if the free choices are exercised badly, God cannot be blamed for them; and correlatively, the fact that the world contains enormous amounts of moral evil is not evidence that it was not created by a perfect God, but evidence only that the God-created free creatures have exercised their freedom in ways that God would condemn.

In this way, some theists seek to construct an explanation for moral evil, based on a combination of a particular interpretation of what free action requires and a willingness to accept severe restrictions on divine foreknowledge. But the atheist can well wonder whether the theist has here said enough; and it is here that the third objection to the free will defence comes to the fore. For it seems that the moral culpability will attach to God, whether we construe free will à la compatibilism or à la incompatibilism. On the compatibilist account of the matter, God could know before creating anyone precisely what evil they would perform. He is therefore actively involved in creating foreseen evil. Given that this would make God partially evil, and given that perfection is one of his defining features, it follows that God does not exist. On the incompatibilist account of the matter, the theist has a choice. If she allows that incompatibilist-style free actions can be foreknown by God, the objection is the same as for compatibilism: God would be actively involved in creating foreseen evil, and it would follow that God does not exist. If she says that incompatibilist-style free actions cannot be predicted by God, then God can certainly plead initial ignorance of the evil he helped to create. But he is then open at once to the charge of cosmic irresponsibility: if he had no idea at all how his creatures would exercise their freedom, then given the huge amounts of evil which they could produce, it was reckless to go ahead and create them. Second, even if God had no idea at the outset how anyone would exercise their freedom, surely after a time he would be able to acquire the ordinary sort of inductive knowledge which humans can acquire about each other's future free choices. Even if we do enjoy an incompatibilist kind of freedom whose exercise is in principle unpredictable with certainty, we nevertheless can have very reliable probabilistic predictions about each other's free choices. If we can acquire such knowledge, why can't God? And if God can acquire such knowledge, why does he not use the knowledge to intervene to prevent at least the most awful consequences of his 'gift' of free will? Further, although it is true that the perpetrator of the moral evils is the human agent concerned, not God (since we are granting that what free actions are performed are 'up to the person concerned'), it is also true that God *as sustainer* of the world and its contents keeps the evil agent going throughout the duration of his evil acts.[7] For often, the evil is spread out over a period, not concentrated in a single unpredictable moment. The torturer who lays out his implements in front of his victim, and lays aside several hours of his time for torture, has to be kept going throughout that period by God's continuing sustaining power. While the atheist can agree with the theist that the torturer remains fully responsible for the evil which he does throughout that period, he can also surely insist that God's role as described would be morally outrageous. And this fact, combined with the fact that God by definition cannot be morally outrageous, entails the conclusion that God does not exist.

Conclusion

The discussion in this chapter has been long and convoluted, so it may be helpful to summarise the main conclusions as follows:

(1) God does not have to create the best possible world, since there cannot be a best possible. But he does have to create a perfect one. The fact that the world is not perfect entails that God does not exist.

(2) The evils which are logically necessary preconditions for certain goods can be ameliorated by those goods. But it would always be better for there to exist neither evils nor goods, so the existence of evil cannot be justified by saying that evil is necessary in order to make the goods possible.

(3) Free will is not an especially valuable capacity to have, and certainly not so valuable that it is worth having if it is the source of great evil in the world.

(4) If the previous point were mistaken, and free will was especially valuable, God could have created beings who had compatibilist free will whom he foreknew would always choose well. The fact that he did not tells against his existence.

(5) If free will has to be construed in an incompatibilist way, but God could still foreknow how created beings would exercise their free will, the objection is as in (4). If he could not initially foreknow how they would exercise their free will, then (a) he would have been reckless in creating them, and (b) he would in due course have been able to gain the ordinary inductive knowledge we have of each other's future actions, and

his non-intervention would then be culpable. This again implies that he does not exist.

(6) In all of this, animal suffering is left unexplained by the 'greater good' defence of (2) above, and by the free will defence of (3)–(5).

Further reading

There is a huge amount of material on the problem of evil. An excellent introduction to the issues is provided by Peterson (1998), who uses the contrast between the evidential and the logical problems to structure his discussion. Standard atheistic deployments of the problem of evil can be found in Flew, Mackie, Martin and Gale. Mackie (1982) argues that God could have made human beings so that they always freely choose the best. Martin's discussion (1990) considers in detail the Rowe probabilistic argument, and also has an extended critique of the free will defence. Gale focuses exclusively on the logical problem of evil, giving a very detailed critique of Plantinga in particular. Plantinga (1974, 1977) argues contra Mackie that God cannot bring about every state of affairs – in particular he cannot bring it about that an agent freely does one thing rather than another. Stewart (1993) is an extended defence of the 'greater good' defence, with good discussions of Plantinga and the free will defence.

13

---◦◯◦---

Omnipotence

Introduction

The first of the atheist arguments which we considered (the argument from scale) took for granted that the concept of God was internally coherent, and that it was offered in a quasi-scientific (albeit supernatural) way as part of a hypothesis which explained a range of phenomena which were otherwise inexplicable (why there is a universe at all, why it is as orderly as it is, why certain violations of the laws of nature appear to occur from time and time, why people report so-called religious experiences, and so on). And the argument from scale objected that even if the God-hypothesis had once provided a reasonable explanation of these phenomena, the universe as it is being revealed to us by modern science makes the theistic hypothesis decreasingly credible. The second atheist argument (the argument from evil) claimed that irrespective of any extension of our scientific knowledge, common sense and reason alone would tell us that the God of traditional theism was ruled out by what the world is like. In the deductive form, the problem of evil said that God and the evil which we find are logically incompatible; while in the evidential form, the argument was that the evil which we find makes the existence of God highly unlikely.

All of those arguments conceded to the theist that God, considered in himself, was at least a *possible* being: even if he did not exist, he was the sort of being who could have existed. But the range of considerations which we are now about to explore argues that God is not even a possible being. Quite aside from whether his existence would be compatible with anything else, such as modern science or the existence of evil, it is not even compatible with itself. The claim is that the concept of God is, in a wide sense of the term, self-contradictory, just as the concept of a highest prime number is self-contradictory. In neither case is the self-contradiction obvious, which is why intelligent people can believe of each of these concepts that it applies to something. But in both cases, so an atheist may claim, there is a hidden contradiction.

How is the atheist to pursue this line of argument? What she will do is take the defining attributes of the God of traditional theism and seek to show either that the attribute itself is self-contradictory, or that it is in contradiction with another of God's defining attributes. If she can succeed in either of these tasks, in relation to any of the divine attributes, she will have *proved* that God does not exist. It will be showing not just that it is very unlikely that God exists, but that it is absolutely impossible. Thus if God is by definition omnipotent, and the atheist can prove that no being could be omnipotent, it will follow at once that God does not exist. Similarly with the other divine attributes. Even if it turns out that each attribute taken by itself contains no hidden contradictions, the atheist may still succeed in showing that no one being could possess all the attributes together. Thus it might turn out, for example, that although it is possible for there to be an omnipotent being, and also possible for there to be an omniscient being, no one being could both be omnipotent and omniscient; so if God by definition has to have both of these characteristics, it will follow that God does not exist.

All of the defining attributes of God raise serious philosophical problems, but in the following chapters we will concentrate on only a handful of the most discussed ones: omnipotence, omniscience, eternity, omnipresence and non-physicality.

Divine power

Leaving on one side for the moment the question of God's omnipotence, how should we understand God's power in general? The reason for asking this question is that it seems clear that our power to act and God's power to act are importantly different. In general, when we do things, we do one thing by doing another (or by doing a range of things). For example, Charles is a revolutionary who wishes to foment a revolution. He decides to do this by assassinating the President. He assassinates the President by shooting him with a gun. He shoots the gun by pulling the trigger. He pulls the trigger by squeezing his index finger. And so on. And he has to achieve his aims in this indirect way because he cannot control directly (by the mere power of thought, as it were) the course of events. If he simply wills a revolution to occur, or the President to be assassinated, or the President to be shot, etc., nothing happens. He can perform one of these actions only *by* performing another.

Theists are generally agreed that God's power is not essentially like that. Although he could choose to operate in the world in this indirect manner, he does not have to. He can by-pass all the indirect methods which humans per-force use to achieve desired states of affairs, and he can bring into being, or actualise *directly*, whatever states of affairs he wishes to. If he wishes to make the President die, he does not have to bring it about that the President is shot (or poisoned, or incinerated, or savaged by hungry lions, or struck by lightning, etc.). He can simply make the President drop dead, without there being any intervening causal chain between his (God's) will and the end at which it aims. If he wishes the gun to fire, he can simply make the bullet shoot out of the barrel – he does not have to make that happen by making the trigger move or the hammer strike the head of the cartridge, or the charge explode.

This may sound at first like a completely mysterious kind of power about which the sceptic should indeed be sceptical. But the theist can urge that on a more modest scale, a similar sort of power is familiar to us all from our own experience. Although in general, we do one thing by doing another, this cannot be the case *universally*, for that would generate an infinite regress. If everything has to be done by doing something, then nothing can be done unless infinitely many things are done. At some point, the theist will say, we all recognise that we have a divine sort of power to do things directly – direct in the sense that merely by our willing something to be, it comes about. Exactly what sorts of actions are of this kind has been a disputed question. Some authors have thought that squeezing your finger is one kind of action of this kind. Other have argued that you squeeze your finger *by* contracting your finger muscles. But even if that is true, how do you contract your finger muscles? Perhaps the only thing we do directly is to put our brain in such a state that it will bring about the contraction of our finger muscles. But at some point in this regress (the theist will insist), we all have to recognise that anybody who can do anything at all can do at least some things in this direct way. As it is sometimes put, every agent can perform some *basic* actions. The distinctive thing about God's capacity for action, then, is not that it has absolutely no parallel with the capacity of humans. It is simply that his capacity for basic action is very much more extensive than ours. It is no doubt this fact that Descartes has in mind when he says in his third Meditation that although God's will has greater scope than Descartes's own, 'it does not seem any greater than mine when considered as will in the essential and strict sense' (Descartes 1984 vol. II: 40).

The theist is therefore able to point to something in human experience which renders intelligible to some degree the kind of power that God has. Although this is a limited achievement (because the relevant kind of human power is also philosophically very puzzling) it is a real and worthwhile achievement. For although a puzzle remains about how basic action itself is possible, and a further puzzle about how God's power can be so extensive, the theist can plausibly claim that it is not *utterly* mysterious to us what kind of power it is.

The concept of omnipotence

Let us turn then to the concept of omnipotence. What does it mean to say of any being that it is omnipotent? Here is one natural definition that seems initially obvious:

Definition 1 X is omnipotent = X can do everything

Some writers have accepted this simple definition. Descartes, for example, thought that God could even do something which was inconsistent with the laws of logic. God could have made the universe in such a way that 2 + 2 = 5, or triangles had four sides. That Descartes should have believed this helps to explain how it is so important to his epistemology that he should be able to prove that God exists, and that God is no deceiver, and why he thinks that an atheist mathematician cannot achieve any certainty even in mathematics. However, most writers have thought (surely correctly) that God cannot break the laws of logic (or alternatively, that he could not have made the laws of logic to be other than they are). (Notice how this thought fits nicely with the idea that God is a supremely rational being, who does nothing arbitrarily or whimsically.) But most writers have also thought (again surely correctly) that this is not a genuine incapacity or limitation in God's power, since this does not imply that there is (as it were) a realm of the do-able from which God is excluded. To say that something is logically impossible is precisely to exclude it from the realm of the do-able. So to say that God cannot do what is logically impossible is not to say that his power is limited in any way.

This leads us naturally to a second understanding of divine omnipotence:

Definition 2 X is omnipotent = X can do everything which it is logically possible to do

Although it might seem that the move from Definition 1 to Definition 2 is a small one, and a move which is forced on us by the obvious faults in Definition 1, it provides the theist with a powerful resource. Whenever the atheist finds an example of something which God cannot do, the theist can try to argue that the task in question contains some hidden logical impossibility, and hence that God's incapacity is not proof of his lack of omnipotence.

A range of problem cases

Let us see how the debate might proceed from Definition 2. What possible actions can the atheist provide which God will be unable to perform? Prima facie, there is a range of things which are possible, because humans actually do them, but which are ruled out for God by God's other properties. One set of examples concerns actions which humans can do because they are not morally perfect. Humans can behave in a mean, cowardly, cruel, selfish, hypocritical way, etc. But since God is by definition morally perfect, it seems to follow that he cannot act in any of these ways.

A second set of examples concerns actions which humans can do but God cannot, and comes from the fact that humans have bodies and God does not. For instance, it is logically possible for humans to walk, since they have legs. It is not logically possible for legless beings to walk. Since one of God's defining properties is that he is immaterial, i.e. has no body, it follows that he has no legs, and this in turn implies that he is unable to walk. Clearly, there will be many things which humans can do which logically presuppose that they have a body, and hence which will be logically impossible for a being without a body to do, such as winking, standing up, sitting down, running around, coughing, spluttering, kissing, hugging, scratching one's nose, and so on.

A third example of a limit on God's omnipotence is raised by a very traditional though frivolous-sounding question, namely 'Can God create a stone which is too heavy for him to lift up?' (let us label this a superheavy stone). The thought here is that the answer must be either 'yes' or 'no'. But either way reveals a limitation on God's power. If the answer is 'yes', then there can be a stone too heavy for God to lift, so he is not omnipotent; if the answer is 'no' then there is a superheavy stone which God cannot create, so he is not omnipotent. Since omnipotence is a defining characteristic of God, and we have just shown that the concept is self-contradictory, it follows that *no* being can be omnipotent, and hence that God does not exist.

A fourth class of actions which promises to create difficulties for the theist concerns humans' ability to end their own existence: they can commit suicide. But can God commit suicide? It would be natural (even if ultimately indefensible) to say that an omnipotent being must be able to do everything which we (as *non*-omnipotent beings) can do, *and more*; so that if we can commit suicide then so too can an omnipotent being. Certainly, if we accept Definition 2, it will follow that an omnipotent being can commit suicide. But many theists would find this conclusion unacceptable. They have wanted to say that if God exists at any time, he exists at all times.

On the face of it, then, there seems to be a range of things which it is logically possible to do (since *we* do them), and hence which an omnipotent being ought to be able to do; and yet which God cannot do. So, if to be God a being would have to be omnipotent, it would follow that God cannot exist. How is the theist to reply to this pro-atheist argument?

Some possible replies

The theist, however, has a range of possible replies, different replies to different lines of attack. Let us consider first the superheavy stone, the one which is so heavy that not even God can lift it. Rather surprisingly, it seems that the theist can find a consistent line of defence for either a 'yes' or a 'no' answer. Consider first the case for a 'yes' answer, i.e. for saying that God *can* make a stone too heavy for him to lift up. The theist has at least two lines of argument here. According to the first, he could say that God *can* create the superheavy stone, and that as long as he does not do so he remains omnipotent. Of course if he were to create the stone, there would be something that he would not then be able to do, and he would then no longer be omnipotent. But if he never creates such a stone, he is, was and will be omnipotent for all time.

The problem with this first line of reply is that if omnipotence is one of the defining characteristics of God, then a being who is not omnipotent at any time cannot at that time be God. But could a being exist as God at one time, and while continuing to exist, cease to be God because he had deprived himself of one of God's defining propersties? We considered this issue in Chapter 1, when we looked at whether 'God' could be interpreted as a title. We accepted there that theists were entitled to impose a constraint on the interpretation of 'God', namely that if God exists at all, he could not continue to exist while ceasing to be God. It was this consideration which ruled out the idea that 'God' is a title. Similarly, in this context, the idea that God could destroy his own omnipotence and hence his divinity, while continuing to exist, will be unacceptable. So, the theist cannot solve the problem of the superheavy stone by saying that God has an unexercised power; for this would be saying that God *could* cease to be omnipotent (if he were to exercise the power), whereas we are agreeing that God *cannot* lose any of his defining properties.

However, there is a second line of defence for giving a 'yes' answer. Suppose that God when he creates the superheavy stone intends that it shall be too heavy to be lifted by anyone, even by himself. If this is a logically possible task, then he can indeed do it. If it is not a logically possible task, then he cannot do it – but by Definition 2, the fact that he cannot do it does not show him not to be omnipotent. Further, if it is logically possible for God to create the stone, and he does create it, the theist need not then concede that since God cannot lift it, God cannot be omnipotent. For by Definition 2, God's omnipotence requires only that he be able to do whatever it is logically possible; and (so the theist can argue) *it is not logically possible to pick up a stone which an omnipotent being has made unliftable.* For if it were possible to lift the stone, that would have shown that the omnipotent being had failed to achieve a logically possible task – and *that* would surely be self-contradictory. (Alternatively, if the omnipotent being had failed in the task, that would prove that the task is not logically possible, contrary to hypothesis.)

It seems then that the theist can consistently allow that God can create the superheavy stone. Could he also consistently take the other option and deny that God could make the stone? If the idea we sketched above is correct, then it seems he could. For the argument would then be that although God could not make the stone, this does not show that he is not omnipotent, since making such a stone is not logically possible. It is not logically possible to make something which is too heavy to be lifted by an omnipotent being, i.e. a being who can lift up anything which it is logically possible to lift up.

In brief, the theist can argue either that it is logically impossible to *make* the stone (because it is logically impossible to make something too heavy to be lifted by a being who can lift anything which it is logically possible to lift); or that it is logically impossible to *lift* the stone (because it is logically impossible to lift something which has been made by an omnipotent being with the intention that no one should be able to lift it). Either way, the incapacity in God is no evidence that he is not omnipotent, since it involves something which it is *logically* impossible to do. The theist would be in difficulty only if there was something which it is logically possible to do but which God cannot do, and no such possibilities are raised by the superheavy stone.

Although this problem of the superheavy stone is in a way trivial, we have pursued it at some length partly because it is one of those problems which naive atheists think is sufficient to convict theism of paradox, and partly because it reveals how difficult it can be to find an example which will allow an alert theist no room for manoeuvre. On reflection, we can see that the problem of the superheavy stone is an unlikely candidate to put Definition 2 under pressure. What will put Definition 2 under pressure are examples of actions which are uncontroversially logically possible (e.g. because we perform them) yet which God cannot perform. Creating superheavy stones is not something which we do, and it is far from obvious whether it is logically possible either to create or to lift such a stone. The atheist does better to stick to a range of obviously possible actions, such as sinning, or ending one's own existence, and ask whether those possible actions are possible for God.

Can God sin?

What about the thought that humans can act immorally and God cannot? One mistaken way for the theist to reject this claim would be to challenge the view of divine perfection which the objection is implicitly resting on. Let us agree that God is by definition morally perfect, i.e. that no being could count as God unless it were morally perfect. Would this mean that God *could not* act immorally? Or would it be enough to say, more weakly, that although God *could* act immorally, he never does, and it is that fact which makes him morally perfect?[1] If this is a tenable interpretation of moral perfection, then moral perfection and omnipotence would be compatible.

Although this may sound like a neat solution for the theist, in fact it quickly leads him into an untenable position. Suppose he grants that God does have the power to act immorally (since he is omnipotent). We then have to ask what the position would be if God exercised this power. It would surely follow that he was then no longer perfect; and since moral perfection is a defining feature of God (i.e. he *must* have it if he is to be God), this means that he would have deprived himself of his divine status. He would have brought about his own non-existence as God. This is precisely the position which the theist hoped to avoid when he denied that 'God' was a title which could be laid aside.

Clearly, then, the theist needs to say that God's perfection consists not in the fact that he never does wrong, but in the fact that he *cannot* do wrong. But how can this be reconciled with the claim that God can do anything which is logically possible? Some theists at this point simply add to Definition 2 a further clause saying that something counts as omnipotent only if it does not believe of anything which it does that it would be better if it did not do it (see, for example, Stewart 1993: 28). But by itself, this is a poor response for two reasons. First, it is simply arbitrary to add to a definition of omnipotence a clause (namely about what it would be *better* to do) which has no intuitive connection with omnipotence. Surely an omnipotent being ought to be *able* to do X even if it does believe that it would be better if it did not. Perhaps its belief has the consequence that it does not actually *do* X – but this does not show that it is unable to do it. Second, it still leaves God unable to do things which any human can do, namely perform an action while believing that it would be better not to perform it.

There is however a more promising line of reply for the theist, which we will shortly explore in connection with Definition 3.

God's lack of a body

What then about the second category of cases produced by the atheist of things which God cannot do, namely those which depend upon the fact that humans have bodies and God does not? One possible line of reply here for the theist is to argue that God can perform such actions, because God can have a body.

What this means is not that God *standardly* has a human body, for he is by definition an omnipresent spirit, and both of these characteristics are incompatible with being a human body. The thought is rather that on particular occasions, God could assume a human form. If this is so, then God *could* do that range of things whose performance by us depends essentially on the fact that we are embodied beings, and indeed beings with a very particular type of body (we have arms, legs, toes, fingers, etc.).

It is unclear what force this line of reply has. Let us assume that it is possible for God to create (maybe *ex nihilo*) a human form, and to speak and act through this human form. Would that mean that if that human form did something (e.g. scratched its nose) that was *literally* God scratching his nose? If this line of argument is to be effective against the claim that we can do things which God cannot, the answer must be 'Yes, that would literally be God scratching his nose'. But we might well be uneasy with this response, for the following reason. When I scratch my nose, it is indeed *I* who am scratching *myself*. It is not just that I am bringing about a scratching of something which I own or control: it is I who am being scratched. The person who does the scratching is *identical with* the person who is scratched. But when the God-created human form scratches *his* nose, it seems that what is happening is that God is bringing it about that a being who is not identical with God scratches his nose. For this reason, it is not clear that this line of reply to the objection (that we can do things which God cannot) is really compelling.[2]

Can God destroy himself?

We considered above whether God's omnipotence implied that he could bring about his own non-existence *as God*, by envisaging his doing something as a consequence of which he loses one of his defining Godly properties. We were there presuming that although before the change he was God, and after the change he was not, he was the same individual before and after the change. And we accepted then that such a conclusion would be unacceptable to theism. This might make it seem otiose to consider the related question whether God's omnipotence implies that he can bring about his *total* non-existence. The question is not just whether he can produce a change as a consequence of which he loses his divinity, but whether he can produce a change as a consequence of which he ceases to exist altogether. Clearly the theist who denies that God's omnipotence extends to the first alternative will also deny that it extends to the second. But there may be certain logical costs to such a denial, which we now need to explore.

We can certainly say that God could not have the power to destroy himself if he exists necessarily, i.e. if some versions of the ontological and cosmological arguments are sound. For the conclusion of all versions of the ontological argument, and at least some versions of the cosmological argument is not merely that God exists, but that he necessarily exists – he could not *not* have existed. Now *if* the impossibility of God's non-existence is logical impossibility, then the theist can rightly claim that God's omnipotence under Definition 2 would not require (and indeed would not permit) that he could bring about his own non-existence. For his omnipotence (we are assuming) requires only that he can do everything which is logically possible;

and if his own non-existence is not logically impossible, the fact that he cannot bring it about does not show that he is not omnipotent.

In fact, if we take God's existence to be logically necessary in this way, it means that he cannot lose *any* of his defining properties (not merely that he does not or will not lose them, but that he cannot). This means, for example, that God not merely never has done and never will do anything immoral, but that he *cannot* do anything immoral. But these incapacities will not undermine his omnipotence, since it is logically impossible to do anything which will bring about the non-existence of a logically necessary being. We see here how a line of argument (namely the ontological argument) which might at first glance seem unpromising, can nonetheless be one which theists would hope could be patched up; for it has helpful consequences of a remote kind for the theistic enterprise.

However, most theists would be willing to concede that whatever kind of existence God has, it is not logically necessary: atheism is not actually self-contradictory. If that is so, then, the problem for theism returns: given that committing suicide is a logically possible action, why cannot an omnipotent being commit suicide?

Omnipotence relativised to God

The problems which we have been exploring reveal how Definition 2 allows the theist to cope with a range of initially problematic cases, actions which we can perform but which God cannot. The general technique of the theist is to show that when ascribed to God, the action contains some hidden logical impossibility, and hence is excluded from the scope of his omnipotence. But nevertheless, there remain some problem cases. In particular, if God's existence is not logically necessary, why can't he bring about his own non-existence, and why can't he sin?

To resolve these problems, the theist is likely to relativise omnipotence to the being in question as follows:

> *Definition 3* X is omnipotent = X can do everything which it is logically possible for X to do (i.e. everything which is logically consistent with X's other defining properties)

Relativised to God, this gives us:

> *Definition 3a* God is omnipotent = God can do everything which it is logically possible for God to do (i.e. everything which is logically consistent with God's other defining properties)

The new definition immediately gives the theist the ability to deal with cases which were problematic under Definition 2. It explains at once why God cannot sin: it is logically impossible *for God* to sin, since he is by definition perfect, so his inability does not compromise his omnipotence. Another of the defining features of God is that he is immaterial, or pure spirit. This means that it is not logically possible *for God* to scratch his nose, cough, etc. and hence his inability to do so will not be a limitation on his omnipotence.

Definition 3 also enables the theist to cope with a range of cases which otherwise threaten to be a threat to divine omnipotence, namely human free actions. We noted in Chapter 12 how theists often seek to solve the problem of evil by relying on the free will defence; how the sceptic challenges the free will defence by asking 'Why didn't God make humans with free will, but make them so that they always freely choose to do the best?'; and how theists tried to answer that sceptical question by appealing to an incompatibilist account of freedom. According to an incompatibilist, if agent A freely decides at time t to perform action X, there does not exist at any time before t a set of conditions which guarantee that A will decide to do X. The only person who can bring it about that A freely decides to do X is A herself. Although God can bring it about that conditions propitious for or hostile to A's decision prevail, he cannot bring it about that A's free decision is made. Putting the matter slightly differently, in creating free agents, God is exercising his omnipotence to bring it about that there are some further states of affairs which he cannot bring about: the free actions of the beings whom he has created. This move is essential to the free will defence because it explains why if God gives humans freedom, he *cannot* ensure that they use it properly. He cannot ensure this (according to the incompatibilist) because an action cannot be both freely performed by person A and also brought about by God. Does this mean that after creating free agents, God is no longer omnipotent? Definition 3 enables the theist to answer 'no'. Although A's freely doing X is certainly logically possible (and hence is something which an omnipotent being by Definition 2 could bring about), it is not logically possible *for God* to bring about, so God's limited power in this respect does not count against his being omnipotent.

Strictly speaking, this theist argument is not that performing A's free actions is incompatible with one of God's *defining* properties, but that it is incompatible with one of God's *necessary* properties, namely God's non-identity with any of his creatures. It is because God is not A that he cannot perform A's free actions. But we can charitably allow the argument through, by interpreting 'defining' widely to include 'necessary'.

However, a further source of complication comes from the fact that there may be some kinds of action that are, as we might put it, possible at one time but not at another. In 1754, God had the power to cause or to prevent the earthquake which hit Lisbon in 1755. In 1756, given that he had allowed the earthquake to occur, he no longer had the power to bring it about that the earthquake had never occurred. Is it then logically possible for God to prevent the 1755 earthquake? Given the meaning which Definition 5 attaches to that question, i.e. would be it be consistent with God's other defining properties, we would have to say 'yes'. But we can now see that this answer is too simplistic. The theist needs to relativise God's power to a time: something can be logically possible for God at one time and not at another. So Definition 3 needs to give way to

> *Definition 4* X is omnipotent = at every time, X can do everything which it is logically possible for X to do at that time (i.e. everything which is logically consistent with X's other defining properties)

There are, however, some doubts which one can raise about Definition 4 omnipotence, stemming from the very undemanding nature of the conception of omnipotence which it provides. First, it opens up the possibility of there being great numbers of omnipotent beings. Of course there would be a great many things which these omnipotent beings were powerless to do; but as long as their powerlessness was a logical consequence of some of their defining properties, it would not show that they were really not omnipotent. Certainly there could be a *sequence* of different omnipotent beings. Provided omnipotent being A exercises his power to limit his omnipotence, he could be followed by omnipotent being B, who in turn limits his own omnipotence, making possible the emergence of omnipotent being C and so on. So a sequence of omnipotent beings is possible. But it looks as if the *simultaneous* existence of many omnipotent beings is possible too. Suppose we define perfectrons as beings who by Definition 4 are omnipotent (i.e. can do anything which is not logically excluded by their other defining properties); and whose dominant preference is never to thwart the preferences of any other omnipotent beings. Then it seems that the universe could contain many perfectrons. For if we make it one of their defining characteristics that they wish not to thwart the preferences of other omnipotent beings, it follows that if they are unable to thwart those preferences, this is not a limitation on their omnipotence. For by Definition 4, any powerlessness in a being B which is implied by the defining features of B does not count against B being an omnipotent being.

We can even, it seems, imagine an absurd case which is consistent with this definition of omnipotence. Let us define a nullipotent being as a being, one of whose defining features is that he cannot do *anything*. He will then count as omnipotent by the revised definition. For it will be true of him that he can do everything which it is logically possible for a nullipotent being to do, i.e. nothing at all. It would clearly be absurd to describe a nullipotent being as omnipotent, so any definition of omnipotence which allows us to do this, as Definition 4 does, must also be absurd.

Is there any way forward for the theist? Can he amend Definition 4 to avoid the absurdity which it would allow? Some theists have suggested:

> *Definition 5* X is omnipotent = at every time, X can do everything which it is logically possible for X to do at that time (i.e. everything which is

logically consistent with X's other defining properties); and no being, Y, greater in overall power than X, can be conceived[3]

Although nullipotent beings qualify as omnipotent by Definition 4, they do not qualify by Definition 5 because they fail the final clause: we *can* conceive of beings greater in power than nullipotent beings. Does this provide the theist with a satisfactory account of omnipotence?

The revised definition still leaves the theist with some problems. There is first a problem about precision. The definition uses the notion of one entity being 'of greater power than another'. But how are different degrees of power to be measured? Do we really have a sharp enough grasp of this concept to be able to make use of it in a definition? If one being A can do only X, and a second being B can do both X and Y, then clearly B is more powerful than A. But often the capacities of agents do not bear this simple relation. We find that A can do X, Y and Z, and B can do R, S and T. How are we to judge whether the power to do the former is greater or less than the latter? No doubt in some cases we will have some strong intuitions about the matter, but in other cases it will be very unclear which power is the greater. Suppose A can work out in his head all the prime numbers up to 10,000,000, and B can compose elegant sonnets in his head. Which power is the greater?

More seriously, from a theistic perspective the definition is both too lax and too demanding. It is too lax in that it allows that an omnipotent being could commit suicide (at least on the assumption that the ontological argument fails), whereas most theists would prefer to avoid having to accept this consequence. On the other hand, it does not let in enough, for it will exclude God from being omnipotent. To see that this is so, compare what God can do, with what a semi-God-like being (call him Semigod) can do. Semigod is omniscient, eternal, omnipresent, etc. In fact, he has all of God's properties except for moral perfection. In terms of power, he can do everything which is logically consistent with his other defining properties. Since his actions are subject to fewer constraints from his other defining properties (no moral constraints, for example) than God's actions are constrained by *his* defining properties, Semigod can do everything that God can do, *and more*. He can sin and God cannot. Semigod would therefore be greater in overall power than God; hence God would fail to meet the final clause of Definition 5; hence God would not count as omnipotent by Definition 5. Nor does the definition entail that there can be only one omnipotent being. For all that the definition tells us, there might be a set of omnipotent beings, all of very great but equal power, and no other being could be conceived of with greater power than each of them had.

Conclusion

We have now reprised, in Definitions 1 to 5 the main course which is followed in discussions of this topic.[4] The conclusion that emerges is that the very idea of an omnipotent being, in the most natural reading of that term, is logically impossible. The most natural reading of that phrase is given by Definition 2; and all the subsequent amendments which we have considered have been attempts to find a sense of omnipotence which (a) allows that an omnipotent being is logically possible, and (b) renders consistent the thesis that God is omnipotent with a variety of other theistic claims about God. What can we conclude from the discussion?

The atheist may well conclude that there cannot be an omnipotent being; that God (if he existed) would be omnipotent; and therefore that God cannot exist. The theist is likely to reply to this, 'It is we who are defending the claim that an omnipotent God exists, so it is up to us, not up to you the atheist, to say what we mean by "omnipotent". And by our definition of the term, it *is* logically possible for there to be an omnipotent being, and an omnipotent being moreover who can have the other divine attributes.' This is in one way a reasonable response, and in another way unreasonable. It is reasonable that anyone arguing for any thesis should have the right to specify what the thesis is. In that sense, it is indeed up to the theist and not the atheist to say how the concept of omnipotence is to be interpreted. But it is unreasonable in the sense that if the defence of the thesis in question requires extensive semantic deviance, then a more straightforward and perspicuous expression of the theist's position would be to say 'God of course is not omnipotent – because no being could be. Nor is he the most powerful being consistently describable – because he is constrained in his power by, for example, his essential goodness. He may not even be describable as the most powerful being that there is – since some ranges of power are simply incommensurable. All we can honestly claim is that he is indeed very powerful.'

Further reading

Many sources provide helpful accounts of debates over omnipotence. Plantinga (1967) is an old but still useful guide. More recent contributions which lead the search for a definition into the present century are Swinburne (1986), Martin (1990), Gale (1993), Stewart (1993), Rosencrantz and Hoffman in Quinn and Taliaferro (1997). For a sophisticated modern analysis which tries to accommodate the points made in this chapter, see Flint and Freddoso in Craig (2002).

14

---o☺o---

Eternity and omnipresence

Introduction

The second of God's defining properties to raise some serious problems for theism is his omniscience. What the theist can coherently say about divine omniscience will, however, be constrained by the interpretation which she accepts of two further defining properties of God, namely his eternity and his omnipresence. Accordingly we will first explore how these two properties can be interpreted, and then in the next chapter consider how they generate problems about omniscience.

A. Eternity

That God is eternal is agreed by all mainstream theists. But there are two significantly different interpretations of what is meant by this claim. According to one interpretation, God's eternity consists in the fact that he always has and always will exist – he exists at every time there ever has been or ever will be. He is, like us, a temporal being, that is to say, a being for whom some times are past, some times are future, and for whom every time either was or is or will be the present. What differentiates God from us in respect of time is that whereas we exist for very short periods of time, preceded and followed by enormously long periods of time when we do not exist, God continues to exist through every moment of time. He has an infinite past existence and an infinite future existence. There is no past time at which he began to exist, and there will be no future time at which he will cease to exist. To use a potentially dangerous but possibly useful metaphor, God is 'in' time. Let us call this the temporal conception of eternity. According to the second interpretation, God's eternity means that God is a timeless being. He is a being for whom no time is (or has been or will be) past, present or future. No truths about him are essentially tensed. To mirror the previous metaphor, we can say that on this conception, God is 'outside' time. Let us label this the timeless conception of eternity.

The timeless conception dominated in Western thinking about God from Augustine to Aquinas, and is still well-represented among modern theists. But before Augustine, and after Aquinas, the temporal view also had considerable support, and has able defenders today. We will consider the two conceptions in turn, starting with the temporal conception. We will find that what generates the problems for theism is not so much the issue of whether God exists at *all* times or not, but rather whether God exists at *any* times or not.

The temporal conception of eternity

The temporal conception of God's eternity has certain consequences for what else can be intelligibly said of God. Since he is thought of as a very long-lived person, a whole range of mental predicates which can be applied to us as creatures who have a short temporal existence can also be applied to God – or rather, there will be no objection to the application of such predicates based simply on the fact that God is eternal. Thus God will be able to *expect* future events, to *foresee* them, to *plan* them; and he will be able to *remember* past events. He will be able to *interact causally* with his creatures in the sense of responding to, for example, their prayers, their hopes, their fears. He will be able to *intervene in the course of world history* by causing the occurrence of some events and preventing the occurrence of others. It will be possible for him to *be an agent* in the sense in which we are agents, i.e. beings who do things in time, who form intentions, and then subsequently carry them out. He will of course be vastly more powerful as an agent than we are, but this is a difference in scale and not of kind.

Further, although I shall call this into doubt later, this temporal conception of eternity might seem to make the doctrine of creation capable of a literal interpretation. That is to say, God having existed for an infinite past time, decides to create a material universe at a certain point in time (say about 15 billion years ago, and say by means of a 'Big Bang'). He then keeps it in existence moment by moment throughout its lifetime, and perhaps at some time in the future decides to end its existence, which he then does, while he himself continues to exist for an infinite future time.

All of this might seem to make the temporal interpretation of God's eternity attractive to a theist. It at least seems to allow God to be a person (in the sense of being a subject of mental or personal predicates), a person who can be in causal interaction with his creatures, and who can thus display a responsive care and affection for them. However, in spite of these attractions, defenders of the temporal conception have faced some problems. The principal one has been the one which we will look at in Chapter 15 on omniscience: on the temporal conception of eternity, God is 'in' time. So, he has foreknowledge of our future actions, and this has been thought to make it impossible for us to be genuinely free. We will argue that in fact there is no real problem here, and that theists have been unduly worried. But there are other more serious problems which face the temporal conception, and we shall look at two of them in the next section.

The temporal conception, infinite time and creation

The first problem with temporal conception is that the doctrine sits uncomfortably with the findings of modern science. The temporal conception can maintain that God, as eternal, always has existed and always will exist: if he exists at all, there is no time at which he does not exist. But this is very different from saying that he has *infinite* temporal existence: that at every moment in time, he has an infinitely long past behind him and an infinitely long future ahead of him. If time itself is of only finite duration, then God has existed for only a finite time, and has only a finite future ahead of him. Now in fact, our best available cosmological theory (the Big Bang theory) tells us that the universe began very roughly 15 billion years ago. That was not simply the point at which matter began to exist in a pre-existing spatio-temporal framework. Since relativity theory ties the existence of matter and time and space inextricably together, the Big Bang marks the beginning of space and time, as well as of matter. So, if the theory is correct, there has not been an infinite past time in which God could have existed. If he exists at all, and his existence is of the eternal temporal kind, then he began to exist about 15 billion years ago. Further, if the universe should end (e.g. in a so-called Big Crunch), and time come to an end, then God will cease to exist. If this were to happen, it would still be true that he had existed at every moment of time – but if time has a start and an end, then God's existence as a temporal being would have a start and an end, and would not be of infinite temporal duration.

It is important to be clear that it is not open to the theist to protest 'But perhaps God existed before the Big Bang and will exist after the Big Crunch (if there is one)'. To say that something happened before the Big Bang is to say it happened before the beginning of time – and this is to say that there was a time before the first time, a claim which is patently self-contradictory. So, if the theist accepts our best available cosmological theory, and if she adopts the temporal conception of God's eternity, she will be forced to the conclusion (unacceptable to theism) that God's existence had a beginning and that it might have an end.

This is not so far to say that the concept of an eternal God, when this is understood in the temporal sense, faces any *logical* problems. It is not to say that it is self-inconsistent, or in conflict with God's other defining properties. It is a straightforward scientific argument against the existence of God, *if* his eternal existence is taken to mean that he is a temporal being who never came into existence and will never go out of existence.

The second problem with the temporal conception of divine eternity concerns God as the creator. He is standardly thought of as the creator of everything, and indeed this is another of his defining attributes. But, as with the other divine attributes, creation needs to be understood in a special way.

First, it is almost universally agreed among theists that God's creation applies only to things which have a contingent existence. Things that exist of necessity (i.e. things which exist in every possible world) were not created by God, but have an independent existence. As possible examples of such things, we could mention numbers (see below). (Note how this restriction on God's creative role goes hand in hand with a parallel restriction in his omnipotence: he cannot do what is logically impossible. So if there are entities such that it is not logically possible that they do not exist, then their existence cannot be due to the fact that God has created them.)

Second, creation is usually taken to be something that need not be a once-and-for-all act of bringing something into existence. Theists have characteristically asserted that the same creative power which brings something into existence is needed to keep it in existence moment by moment. The instant that God ceases to exercise his creative power in respect of any created object, it ceases to exist. This conception is clearly expressed by Descartes in his 3rd Meditation:

> . . . a lifespan can be divided into countless parts, each completely independent of the others, so that it does not follow from the fact that I existed a little while ago that I must exist now, unless there is some cause which as it were creates me afresh at this moment – that is, which preserves me. For . . . the same power and action are needed to preserve anything at each individual moment of its duration as would be required to create that thing anew if it were not yet in existence. Hence the distinction between preservation and creation is only a conceptual one . . .
>
> (Descartes 1984 vol. II, 33)

One way of putting this Cartesian idea would be to say that creation is an on-going *process*, not a single event. Suppose, for example, contrary to the Big Bang theory, that the universe has existed for an infinite past time, so that there is no past moment when God brought it into existence. It could still be the case that the universe is, in Descartes's phrase, being 'created anew' moment by moment.

Creation thus conceived is clearly a causal notion. The created universe either in its original existence or in its continued existence, or both, is something that is brought about by the creator. The universe is caused to exist, or caused to continue existing, by the activity of the creator. So to understand creation, we need to think about what is involved in the concept of causation.

Following Hume, we standardly think of causes as *preceding* their effects. If the window broke because the stone hit it, the stone must have struck *before* the window broke. If you are to die as a result of my stabbing you, you must be alive at the time I stab you – in other words, your death must occur *after* I have stabbed you. Kant objected to this Humean conception of causation (which we might call sequential causation) that sometimes a cause and its effect may be simultaneous. He gave the example of a heavy ball resting in a cushion and forming a dent in the cushion. The dent, he said, is simultaneous with the pressure from the ball, even though the pressure causes the dent. Let us assume for the sake of argument that Kant is right about this, and so add to our recognition of Humean sequential causation the idea of Kantian simultaneous causation. So, one thing can be the cause of another only if the cause precedes or is simultaneous with the effect, in other words if both of them are located in time. If A is neither before nor simultaneous with B, then A cannot be the cause of B.

How do these thoughts about causation in general apply to creation and conservation in particular? If God is to create something (in the sense of bringing it into existence) his creative act must precede the beginning of existence of the thing he creates. If he conserves in existence something which already exists, his creative power must be simultaneous with its effect. Suppose, then, we think of God as being the creator of the whole of the material universe. This must include the creation not just of its material aspects, but also of its spatial and temporal aspects. God must have created time. But clearly God cannot *precede* the existence of time, for that would be to say that there was a time when he existed, a time which was before the first time – and that would be simply self-contradictory. So God cannot be related to time by the concept of sequential causation. Could it be the case, then, that God's relationship with time is that of simultaneous causation? That would be to say that he causes the existence of something whose existence is a precondition of the possibility of all causation. Is that something which is possible?

It is difficult to be sure. Here is an analogy: suppose that in order for anything to count as a legally binding rule, it has to be passed by a legitimate body; and the first rule which a given body passes is one which declares that that very body is indeed a legitimate body. Here we can say that if the body *is* legitimate, then all its rules are, including the one which says that it is legitimate. Could God's relation to time be of a similar bootstrapping kind? Even if we admit the existence of simultaneous causation, it is not clear that the answer must be 'Yes'. But whether or not it is possible, as a matter of metaphysics, for a cause to cause the existence of something which is a precondition for the possibility of any causation, there is a further epistemological problem here. If we are thinking of sequential causation, there is a temporal difference between the two events which allows us to pick out one as the cause (the earlier event) and the other as the effect (the later event). If we are allowing simultaneous causation, how do we know which of the two events is the cause and which is the effect? The answer has to be 'By an

273

appeal to what happens on other occasions'. As Kant observes, you can make dents in cushions by lowering heavy balls on to them, but you cannot make heavy balls appear on cushions by making dents in the cushions. This means that in cases of simultaneous causation, we can have grounds for identifying one of the events as the cause and the other as the effect only if on other occasions we can use the one to bring about the other. But this is a test which clearly cannot be applied in the case of God. Suppose God's existence and the beginning of time are simultaneous, and we wonder whether God created time, or time created God. There is clearly no possibility of finding out on other occasions whether we can bring about the existence of time by bringing about the existence of God, or can bring about God by bringing about the existence of time.

It seems therefore that the theist who opts for the temporal conception of God's eternity will face three problems. First, she will be in conflict with modern cosmological theory. Second, she will have the metaphysical problem of explaining how a cause can bring about something which is a precondition for all causation. Third, if God and time are related by simultaneous causation, she will have the epistemological problem of how to discover whether God causes time or time causes God.

The timeless conception of eternity

According to the rival timeless view of eternity, God is not a temporal being at all. He exists, but he does not exist 'in' time. He has no past and he has no future; it is not true that as each day passes, God has existed for a longer and longer period of time. He does not age with the passage of time. No times are past, or present, or future to God.

Timeless existence immediately sounds philosophically suspect. Are there other examples of things which uncontroversially exist timelessly? The answer to that is probably 'No'; but two examples which come closest to being uncontroversial would be numbers and truths. Consider, for example, the number 7. We might well be convinced that 7 exists (if someone asks 'Is there a whole number between 6 and 8?', the answer is 'Yes, it is 7', whereas if they ask 'Is there a whole number between 6 and 7?', the answer is surely 'No'). But did 7 begin to exist at some time in the past? Might it cease to exist in the future? It is true that there was a time in the past when no one spoke or thought of the number; but we are familiar with the idea that whether something exists does not depend on people thinking or speaking about it. It is also true that there was a time when the *numeral* '7' (the symbol by means of which we currently denote the number 7) did not exist; and no doubt there will be a time in the future, when the human race has become extinct, when the symbol will cease to exist. But just as we distinguish between the word 'dinosaur' and what the word refers to, so we must distinguish between the symbol '7', and what the symbol refers to. Numbers, then, are one fairly plausible candidate for being timeless entities.

Another possible candidate would be truths. Consider the truth 'If something is made of solid iron, it will sink in water'. As with numbers, we must distinguish between the symbols (words) used (in current English) to express the truth, and the truth which those words currently express. The words are certainly temporal entities, but arguably the truth that they express is not. It is not a truth which requires any temporal facts at all. It does not even require, for example, the existence of iron and water, for in a waterless and iron-free universe, it could still be true that if something were made of solid iron, it would sink in water.

There is, then, *some* independent plausibility in the idea that a non-temporal but real existence is not a self-contradictory concept. We need, however, to guard against a natural but mistaken understanding of this non-temporal existence in the case of God. Boethius, an early defender of the position, famously commented:

> Eternity, then, is the complete, simultaneous and perfect possession of everlasting life . . . [Something eternal] lacks nothing of the future, and has lost nothing of the past . . . Of necessity, it will always be present to itself . . . and have present the infinity of fleeting time.
>
> (Boethius 1999: 132–3)

An unkind but possible reading of Boethius here would say that he is claiming that all times are present to a timeless being. If nothing future and nothing past are absent from such a being, it would be natural to conclude that future and past are both present to it. This reading seems confirmed by the final claim that 'the infinity of fleeting time' (all past and future times?) is 'present' to such a being.

Whether or not Boethius meant his words in such a way, we need to be clear that on this interpretation, they represent a hopeless account of timelessness. There is *no* time at which past and present could be 'present' to any being: different times by definition are not simultaneous but successive. It is therefore logically impossible for God (or any other being) to possess simultaneously the different temporal stages of a life.[1]

Why should a theist find the timeless reading of divine eternity appealing? One consideration springs from a further aspect of God's existence which we have not so far mentioned but which has seemed important to many theists, namely that God is immutable. Like so much else in this area, the concept of immutability can be variously interpreted.[2] But if we take it to mean that an immutable being cannot change at all, only a timeless being can be incapable of change. To change is to have one set of properties at one time and a different set at a different time, so everything in time is potentially open to change.

To someone viewing the issue as it were from the outside, the issue of divine immutability seems a side issue. Although of course theists are free to define God in whatever way they choose, there does not seem any obvious rationale for including immutability in the list of defining features. There seems no compelling reason for thinking that a being worthy of worship must be unchanging. One bad line of argument would be to say that change and perfection are incompatible. For (the argument would go) a perfect being cannot change for the better, since it is initially perfect, so any change would have to be for the worse, which again would be incompatible with perfection. But this argument overlooks the obvious possibility that the change might be from one state of perfection to another state of perfection.

A second argument in favour of the timeless conception is this: God creates everything, including time. Since his creation is wholly free, he could have *not* created time, so he could have existed even if time did not. So his existence must be timeless (see Leftow 1991: 259). This is an intriguing little argument. But as we will argue below, when traced out fully, it reveals hidden contradictions in the very idea of God as a creator of time, on any conception of God's eternity.

Could a timeless God be a creator?

We saw above that the temporal conception of divine eternity faces some serious problems with the thesis that God is the creator of all that exists contingently. In particular, it could give no clear and coherent account of God's relation to the start of time. But it now seems that the timeless conception is bound to be in an even worse position. For it denies that God precedes or is simultaneous with anything, and hence makes it impossible for God to stand in *any* causal relations with the universe. This will exclude him not just from being a creator, but also from performing miracles, and from appearing in religious experiences.

Is there any way to avoid this conclusion? Perhaps the theist who wants to maintain the timeless interpretation of God's eternity has the following line of defence. The crucial idea for theism (she might say) behind the thought that God is the creator and sustainer of everything is not that God is the *cause* of the universe but rather that everything *depends upon* God for its existence. The universe exists, but has only dependent existence; God exists, and has independent existence, that is to say he depends on nothing else for his own existence. He is self-existent. One kind of dependence is causal dependence. We rightly think that effects depend upon their causes. This causal dependence can be cashed out in different ways. Effects depend on their causes in the sense that effects would not have existed if the causes had not existed (at least if we ignore those cases of over-determination). Effects also depend on their causes in the sense that effects can be explained in terms of their causes, not vice versa. But, the theist might continue, we must not think that that general idea of dependence is the same as the more specific idea of causal dependence: there can be non-causal dependences. What would be an example of such non-causal dependences? One example might be found in the case of an argument. We naturally think of the conclusion of an argument as *depending on* the premises, in a way in which the premises do not depend on the conclusion. Often, we also think that if the premises had not been true, the conclusion would not have been provable either. And very often at least, we also think that the premises *explain* the conclusion, although the conclusion does not explain the premises. Can the theist put forward some non-causal kind of dependence which the universe might bear to a timeless God, and which could be an understanding of how a timeless God could nevertheless be called a creator of the universe?

One possibility is this: suppose that a timeless God timelessly wills that there should come into existence a universe with such-and-such a character, and that such a universe does indeed come into existence. (The universe does not come into existence *after* God has willed it, since the willing is timeless. For the same reason, God's willing is also not simultaneous with nor subsequent to the creation of the universe.) This by itself would not show a dependence of the universe on the will of God. All we have imagined so far is a correlation between the content of God's (timeless) willing on the one hand, and the emergence of a physical universe on the other. This could just as easily show the dependence of the former on the latter, as of the latter on the former. But suppose the theist now adds the assumption 'The universe would not have come into existence if God had not (timelessly) willed that it should do so'. This at once appears to establish an asymmetry between the divine willing and the existence of the universe. If we could know it to be true, we could know that the universe depends on God in a way in which God does not depend on the universe. But is it enough to provide the theist with an interpretation of the idea that a timeless God could be a creator?

There are four problems with such a suggestion, one epistemological and three logical. We can start with the epistemological. How could the theist know to be true the claims which he is here making? How could he know what willing a timeless God had done, and how could he know the truth of the conditional sentence which is supposed to give sense to the idea that God created the universe, rather than the universe causing God?

Second, we said that the assumption 'The universe would not have come into existence if God had not (timelessly) willed that it should do so' introduces an asymmetry between God's willing and the coming into existence of the universe, an asymmetry which allows the theist to say that it is God who creates the universe, not vice versa. The problem with this idea is that the appearance of asymmetry is spurious. The assumption says in effect that God's willing is a necessary condition of the coming into existence of the universe. But since God is omnipotent, his willing the existence of the universe is also a sufficient condition of its coming into existence. This in turn entails that the coming into existence of the universe is a necessary condition of God's willing. In short, God's willing and the coming into existence of the universe are both necessary and sufficient for each other: there is no asymmetry. It follows that there is nothing to distinguish one as the dependent factor and the other as the independent factor, and hence nothing to make it true that God is the creator and the universe his creation, rather than vice versa.

The third problem is this. Suppose we accept the Big Bang theory: the universe began about 15 billion years ago. What is it that God timelessly wills, in virtue of which the universe began about 15 billion years ago. Clearly his willing cannot be expressed as 'Let a universe with such-and-such a character exist *now*', willed 15 billion years ago, since for a timeless being there is no 'now' at which he could have willed anything. Is it simply 'Let there be a universe with such-and-such a character'? The problem then is that there is nothing to connect God's willing with *this* universe, rather than with any one of a range of other possible universes, duplicates of our own, peopled by doppelgangers of ourselves. The theist wants to say that God's creativity explains the existence of *this* universe, not just the existence of any universe at all which resembles this one in its general characteristics. This point will become clearer after we have discussed the role of indexicals in Chapter 15.

Fourth, what is it that makes true the conditional 'The universe would not have come into existence if God had not (timelessly) willed that it should do so' which the theist is here appealing to? In normal cases we understand what is meant by saying that something would not have happened if someone had not willed that it should. Suppose you want me to go to London, and this leads you to ask me to make the trip. I agree, and consequently travel to London. We can say in retrospect that I would not have gone to London if you had not willed or wanted me to go. But our understanding in such cases is based on the fact that there is a causal connection between the willing and the event in question. In the example above, your willing that I should go precedes and causes your asking me to go; and your asking me to go precedes and causes my going. If we are asked to envisage the truth of a claim which says that something would not have happened if someone had not willed it to happen, and then we are told that the connection is not a causal one, and that the willing stands in no temporal relation to the event, although the occurrence of the event depends (in a non-causal sense) on the willing, we must lose all grasp of what the relation between the willing and the event is meant to be.

The upshot is that if God's existence is non-temporal, it is impossible to understand how he can play his traditional role of being creator and sustainer of contingent reality.

And now it seems that we can combine our reflections on God's relation to time and to creation in an argument which shows that however the theist conceptualises the matter, theism will be in trouble. Suppose we start the two theist assumptions:

(1) God created everything (theist assumption).
(2) God's creation is wholly free, i.e. for everything which he created he could have not created it (theist assumption). So:
(3) God created time (from (1)). And:
(4) God might have not created time (from (2)). So:
(5) God might have had a timeless existence (from (4)). But:
(6) What is timeless cannot be a cause (by the definition of 'cause'). So:
(7) If God's existence had been timeless he could not have created anything, or sustained anything in existence (from (6)). But:
(8) A being who can create nothing and sustain nothing cannot be omnipotent (by the meaning of 'omnipotent'). So:
(9) If God's existence had been timeless, he would not have been omnipotent (from (7) and (8)). But:
(10) It is a necessary truth that God is omnipotent (by the definition of 'God'). So:
(11) God's existence could not have been timeless (from (9) and (10)). So:
(12) If God exists, he had to create time (from (11)).

But the conclusion (12) contradicts one of the premises, namely (2). It seems therefore that however the theist tries to conceptualise the relations between God's relation to time and to creation, there is no consistent interpretation which will accommodate all that she wants to claim.

Could a timeless God be a person?

Philosophers customarily distinguish between humans and persons. To be a human is to be a member of a particular biological species, homo sapiens. So being a human depends on whatever biological characteristics determine membership of the species. Minimally, and wholly uncontroversially, we can say that being physical organisms is a precondition of being a human: non-physical beings (if there are any) will not count as human. By contrast, being human does not absolutely require the possession of any mental faculties at all. A severely mentally handicapped child, who is born unconscious, and dies before ever gaining consciousness, is still a member of the species. Similarly, someone who has a normal adult life but then lapses into an irreversible coma late in life does not then cease to be a member of the species. They are still human, in this sense of the term, even if they lack those faculties which we most value in humans.

By contrast, being a person is often defined in mental terms. A being is a person if it is conscious of itself and of its own past states. This requires that it should have thoughts not just about its environment ('The cat is black', 'It is raining', 'The orrery is on the atlas'), but also about itself ('*I* can see the black cat', '*I* am feeling gloomy', etc.). Furthermore, some of these thoughts must relate to its own past: it must be aware of itself as a being that is extended in time, a being with a history. It must be able to make judgements of the form 'I *was* so-and-so' or 'I *did* such-and-such'.

The concepts of human and person, then, are different concepts: being a person is different from being a human. But there is no reason why an individual cannot be both: most humans are also persons. But it also seems clear that not all humans are persons, and quite possible that not all persons are humans. To take the first possibility: how much thought babies are capable of is a disputed question, but it seems improbable that they have thoughts about themselves, let alone about their past selves. Those suffering from the mental disabilities of old age (extreme senility, Alzheimer's, etc.) may well cease to be persons, through ceasing to have any conception of themselves as beings with a past. It is less clear that there are any persons who are not humans. Some philosophers have argued that the higher primates are persons, and many also agree that extra-terrestrials could be persons, even though they would clearly not belong to the species homo sapiens.

Of more relevance in the present context is the fact that in specifying the preconditions for being a person, no explicit mention was made of any physical requirements. If it is possible for a being who is wholly non-physical to be the subject of conscious states, to have thoughts about its environment, about itself, and about its own past, then it too will be a person. Thus, God (if he exists) will count as a person: a non-physical mind of huge power, knowledge, etc., able to have thoughts both about its environment and about its own present and past states. Nor is this aspect of God's existence incidental to the role which he plays in most religions. For he is portrayed as *caring* for us, *listening to* our prayers, *offering guidance* in return, sometimes as *making promises* or *giving assurances*; and all of these aspects are manifestations of his being a person. His status as a person also underlies his more conventional defining attributes. His omniscience gives him (in superabundance) the degree and kind of knowledge which persons must have; his omnipotence presupposes that in the exercise of his power, he is guided by knowledge of exactly what he is doing. It is, then, crucial to theism that God should have the status of a person.

Although it was conceded above that not all humans are persons, and that possibly not all persons are humans, it is nevertheless true that our best understanding of what it is to be a person comes from our grasp of the idea of human persons; and of course all human persons are physical persons. If we are to make sense of the idea of God as person, we have to be able to make sense of the idea of non-physical person; and if we are to make sense of the idea that God has a timeless existence, then we have to be able to make sense of the idea of a timeless person. Can we achieve this understanding?

There is a range of powerful arguments which have the effect of showing that we cannot make sense of the idea of a non-physical person.[3] But even if they are all wrong, it is a further question whether we can make any sense of the idea that this non-physical person might also be timeless. When we discuss omniscience, we will argue that a timeless being could not be omniscient, and would in fact be very largely ignorant. This is because the possibility of knowledge rests on a grasp of indexicals, and a timeless being would have no grasp of temporal indexicals. Further the possibility of a wide range of beliefs also rests on a grasp of indexicals, so a timeless being would be debarred from all such beliefs. Given that such beliefs are central to being a person (because they underpin the possibility of a wide range of other mental states, such as desires, intentions, hopes, fears, emotions, etc.), it will follow that a being who is incapable of such beliefs has a very poor claim to be regarded as a person. The timeless conception of God, then, undermines another central claim of theism, the idea that God is a personal being.

Could we combine the two views of God's eternity?

Would it be possible to circumvent the objections to divine eternity which have been raised above by claiming that the two conceptions of eternity can be combined? Suppose, for example, that God had a timeless existence *until* he created the temporal universe, but that once he has created the temporal universe, and for as long as he keeps it in existence, his own existence is temporal. Because his existence is then temporal, he can enter into temporal and hence causal relations. His temporal existence allows him to hear prayers and respond to them, allows him to foresee the future, and remember the past, etc. The knowledge he can then have of his own current and past states enables him to fulfil the criteria for being a person.

Attractive though this scenario might initially sound for the theist, it is in fact self-contradictory. If God exists timelessly, no part of his existence *precedes* his creation of a temporal universe. To suppose otherwise would be to assume that God *first* exists timelessly, and then *subsequently* creates time, and exists temporally. But this requires that his timeless existence precedes his temporal existence, i.e. that there is a time before the start of time. This is the problem which we raised earlier for the idea that a timeless God could also be a creator. The problem is not made any easier to solve by imagining that after creating time, God becomes a temporal being himself. For a similar reason, if he and the universe both have a temporal existence, his temporal existence cannot *follow* his timeless existence. Nor, for the same reason, can God's existence be *simultaneously* timeless and temporal. To suppose otherwise in any of these three cases is to fail to take seriously the idea that a timeless being stands in *no* temporal relations (precedence, sequentiality, simultaneity) to anything. There is no possibility of a being switching from a timeless to a temporal mode of existence, and there is no possibility of a being combining the two modes of existence.

B. Omnipresence

The concept of divine omnipresence presents some choices and problems for the theist parallel to those which we have seen arise in connection with divine eternity. Just as we saw that divine eternity can be interpreted to mean either that God exists at all times successively or at no times at all, so his omnipresence can be interpreted to mean that he exists in all parts of space, or that he is nowhere in space. And just as we saw that the theist encounters problems in reconciling God's eternity on either interpretation with his role as creator and sustainer, so there are parallel problems in relation to that role and his omnipresence.

Let us label the idea that God exists in all parts of space the spatial conception of omnipresence, and the idea that he is nowhere in space the non-spatial interpretation. Both conceptions have proved attractive to theists, sometimes (inconsistently) to a single theist. For example, in successive chapters of his *Monologion*, Anselm came to the two conclusions that God 'exists everywhere and always (i.e. in every place and time)' and also that he exists 'in no place or time' (Anselm 1998: 34 and 37). It easy to see how a theist could be tempted in both directions, and we will use Anselm's two contradictory conclusions to sketch out possible lines of theistic thought.

God as non-spatial

There are two positive reasons and several negative ones why theism should be attracted by the idea of God as non-spatial. First, God is thought of as being a purely spiritual being. Exactly what this means is not clear, but one entailment which would be widely recognised by theism is that it means that God is not a physical or material being. It is not clear whether being spatial has to be regarded as a physical property; but if it is a physical property, then theism can claim that God's spiritual existence requires that he has no spatial properties. Second, God is standardly regarded as simple, that is to say as having no parts. Traditionally, simplicity has been regarded as a reliable sign of indestructibility (because destruction consists in the radical rearrangement of parts, perhaps going all the way down to the subatomic level). If God had parts, it seems that in principle the parts could split off from one another and God might cease to exist. Since theism has regarded that as inconceivable, it has had a reason to say that God cannot be composed of parts. But if he were a spatial being, then he would certainly have parts, for space is precisely one of the things which has parts. So God's simplicity gives theists a second reason for wanting to say that God is non-spatial.

Further, this conclusion is apparently buttressed by the problems which arise if God is thought of as having a spatial existence. If God is in space, it would seem arbitrary and limiting to say that he is in one region of space but not in another. What grounds could there be for his occupying, say, one half of space but not the other? So if he is in space at all, it seems that he ought to be in every part of space. But some parts of space are already occupied: how could God be in the very same region of space as, say, my table? Doesn't my table exclude all other things from simultaneous occupancy of that very region of space? Further, if God is the creator of everything, including space, and his creation is wholly free, it must have been within his power not to create a spatial universe at all. But since he would still have existed himself, he would then have had a non-spatial existence. So, given that his mode of existence is not changed by what he has created, his existence now must be non-spatial.

God as spatial

There are however some equally weighty reasons for theists to opt for the spatial interpretation of divine omnipresence. God is by definition the creator and sustainer of all things. This means that God must be in constant causal connection with the whole of creation – with the creation and all its contents. How then could God's constant causal activity be exercised? As we saw when discussing omnipotence, some theists have thought that it is direct in this sense: God does not use one item A as a means of achieving another thing B. Rather, all the effects he wills, he achieves directly. If he wills that B should come into existence, then his will alone brings it into existence; and if he wills that it should remain in existence, then it is his will alone that keeps it in existence. Further, many theists have been persuaded that God must be wherever his causal power is exercised. As Aquinas tells us, 'God is in every place giving it existence and the power to be a place, just as he is in all things giving them existence, power and activity . . . so God fills all places' (Aquinas 1975: 115. 1a.8.2). However, the very same considerations which speak in favour of the non-spatial conception must count as objections to the spatial conception. How can God's spirituality and his indestructibility be reconciled with his spatiality? How can God be everywhere in space when parts of space are already occupied by other things?

Perhaps there is available to the theist here a resource which was not available in the case of time. With time, we argued that it is impossible for God to start as a non-temporal being, then for him to create time, and then for him to have a temporal existence. As a putative sequence of causation or dependence, this is simply incoherent. But no similar incoherence infects the idea that God starts as non-spatial, creates space, and thereafter has a spa-tial existence, at least as long as space lasts. For since (at least as we have treated it here) causation does not involve a spatial requirement (e.g. that cause and effect should be spatially related), no paradoxes arise from the idea of a non-spatial being creating space, nor from the idea that a being might at one time have a non-spatial existence and at a later time have a spatial existence. There does not have to be an answer to the question 'But *where* does he change from being spatial to being non-spatial?' as there would have to be an answer to the question 'But *when* does he change from a non-temporal being existence to a temporal existence?'. Necessarily, changes require time but do not require space.

Omnipresence and omniscience

Immediately after claiming that God's creativity requires him to be every-where in space, Aquinas added the further thought that God's omniscience, as well as his creative role, requires him to be everywhere: 'God exists in everything . . . by presence, inasmuch as everything is naked and open to his gaze' (op. cit. 121, 1a.8.3). Later theists have tried to use the thoughts of Anselm and Aquinas not so much as reasons for making the further claim that God is everywhere in space, or is wholly non-spatial, but rather as ways of explicating what it *means* to say that God is omnipresent. Thus Swin-burne tells us that the doctrine of divine omnipresence *is* the view that: 'God controls *all* things directly and knows about *all* things without the informa-tion coming to him through some causal chain, for example, without light rays from a distance needing to stimulate his eyes' (Swinburne 1986: 104, italics in original).[4]

So construed, the doctrine of omnipresence is really a modification of the doctrines of omnipotence and omniscience. Divine omnipotence tells us that God can do everything, and omnipresence adds 'and do it directly'; and divine omniscience tells us that God knows everything, and omnipresence adds 'and know it directly'. But although this is a possible construal of omnipresence (theists are free to specify how they intend their words to be taken) it clearly leaves out something which most theists have thought important. It makes it puzzling, for example, why an early thinker like Anselm should have gone through the dialectical contortions which we find in the *Monologion*; or why he and many subsequent thinkers should have thought that there is a close parallel to be drawn between God's omnipres-ence (his relationship to space) and his eternity (his relationship to time).

Accordingly, we will assume that theism does indeed need to give a non-reductionist sense to omnipresence – that is, not to reduce it to an aspect of omnipotence or omniscience. As we will see in the next chapter, this does present theism with some major problems.

Conclusion

It seems, then, that however the theist interprets eternity and omnipresence, she faces serious problems. If God's eternity is temporal, then he cannot be the cause of time. If his eternity is temporal, *and* our best confirmed cosmological theory is correct, then if God exists at all, he must have come into existence about 15 billion years ago, and will go out of existence at some time in the future if a 'Big Crunch' should occur. If God's eternity is timeless, then again God cannot cause time – in fact, he cannot cause anything, and hence cannot be the creator and/or sustainer of contingent reality. Further, as we will argue in the next chapter, if he is timeless, he could not be omniscient. If God's omnipresence means that he is everywhere, the theist faces the problems first that God will have parts, and second, that God cannot be in places which are already occupied by other things. If God's omnipresence means that he is not spatial at all, then as the next chapter will argue, he cannot be omniscient. If his omnipresence means (rather curiously) that he is in some places and not in others, then even if this does not conflict with his omniscience, it does imply that God has parts.

Further reading

Anselm (1998) provides a very lively discussion of God's relation to both space and time, concluding that 'the supreme essence . . . is always and everywhere and never and nowhere' – and calmly claiming that he has 'got rid of the rumble of contradiction'! Swinburne (1986) defends the temporal view of God's eternity, while Leftow (1991) and Helm (1997) defend the timeless conception, and argue that a timeless God could be a person, and could be a creator. Stump and Kretzmann (1981) defend the claim that a timeless God can nevertheless stand in quasi-temporal relations to a temporal world, though at the cost of making simultaneity a non-transitive relation.

15

Omniscience

Introduction

Some writers claim that omniscience generates puzzles at least as perplexing as those raised by omnipotence (see, for example, Stewart 1993: 32). This may be true, but as we will argue, the puzzles which have most troubled theistic writers really depend on their views in other areas of philosophy, and the issues that are really puzzling about divine omniscience have had very little attention.

It is customary to divide human knowledge into three categories: ability knowledge (knowing how to do things); knowledge by acquaintance (knowing objects, persons, places, etc.); and propositional knowledge (knowing truths) (see, for example, Everitt and Fisher 1995: 12). Some writers have insisted that a truly omniscient being ought to be all-knowing in all three categories (see Martin 1990: Chapter 12). Although there is some reason to take knowledge in this inclusive way (e.g. that if one does not, ordinary humans could know things which an omniscient being would not know), in what follows we shall focus exclusively on propositional knowledge.

Divine knowledge

Just as for omnipotence we raised a prior question about the *nature* of God's power, quite apart from its extent, and found that human experience gave some understanding of how it might be conceived, so we will find that a similar strategy works if we ask about the nature of God's knowledge, quite apart from its extent.

There has been a good deal of discussion in recent years about how human propositional knowledge should be analysed, and one distinction which many authors have deployed is that between mediate or indirect knowledge, and immediate or direct knowledge. Some things we know on the basis of other things that we know. From a consideration of the relevant evidence, scientists infer that the theory of evolution is true. The jury infers from the evidence presented in court that the accused is guilty. Here, the knowledge which they arrive at is mediate or indirect because it is inferred from other facts presented as true. By contrast, other things that we know, we know without any process of inference at all – we just know 'straight off' or immediately. Suppose that I am now thinking of the number nine. How do I know that the proposition 'I am now thinking of the number nine' is true? A plausible negative answer would say that I know this immediately; I do not have to infer or deduce from something that that is what I am doing; there isn't a method by the use of which I come to know this. I just know 'straight off'.

Ideally, the theist would like to be able to say that all God's knowledge is *immediate*, just as some human knowledge is immediate. God does not have to work out, or infer or deduce or calculate anything which he knows. He does not *come to know* what he knows, if coming to know suggests any kind of temporal process, at the start of which he does not know some particular truth and at the end of which he does. Rather, he just knows everything which he knows, straight off, without needing to use a method of knowledge acquisition.

The analogy must not be pressed too far. My capacity to know anything will depend on my possession of a brain, and the theist clearly will not want to make a correlative claim about God's knowledge. When I know something immediately, there is doubtless some sort of physiological mechanism at work, even if I have no idea what it is; and the theist does not want to say that divine knowledge is similarly underpinned by any cognitive mechanisms. But the parallel does give us at least a partial understanding of what it is for God to know something. It does not of course give us an understanding of *how* God knows what he knows, but rather of what kind of relationship he stands in to what he knows.

With that as a preliminary let us turn directly to the question of divine omniscience.

Omniscience

How, then, should omniscience be defined? Just as in our discussion of omnipotence, we can start with a simplistic conception:

Definition 1 X is omniscient = For every true proposition, X knows that it is true

Although this might seem immediately acceptable to the non-partisan observer, it faces some problems. We need to notice first one very elegant argument which has been advanced by Grim (Plantinga and Grim: 1993) designed to show that there cannot be a set of all true propositions, and hence that there cannot be an omniscient being who knows all the propositions in this set. Suppose that there were such a set of all truths, call it T. Consider now all the subsets of T. The set of all these subsets is what set theoreticians call the power set of T. To each set in the power set, there will correspond a truth. The truth might, for example, simply specify that there is a subset containing those particular members. So there will be as many truths as there are members of the power set. But it has been proved by Cantor that the power set of any set has more members than the set itself. So, the power set of T will have more members than T itself. So since each member of the power set of T has a truth correlated with it, there will be more truths than are contained in T itself, contrary to our initial assumption that T was the set of all truths. It follows that the very concept of the set of all truths is logically impossible: there cannot be any such set. Consequently there cannot be a being who knows the set of all truths.

This beautiful argument, which illustrates very neatly how debates about theism can be enriched by philosophical ideas coming from wholly unexpected directions, will persuade some at once that there cannot be an omniscient being, by Definition 1 of the term.

This by itself would give theists a motive for wanting an alternative definition of omniscience (though see the response by Plantinga, op. cit.). But in practice they have been moved to this conclusion by other problems (as they see it) with Definition 1. In particular, many theists have thought that there are some grounds for thinking that there are true propositions which God *cannot* know. So, given a prior commitment to the claim that God exists, and is omniscient, the theist would have to reject Definition 1. Of course, an alternative atheist conclusion which could be drawn immediately is that if there are truths which God could not know, then there could not be an omniscient God, and hence since omniscience is one of his defining properties, it will follow at once that God does not exist. But let us assume, at least provisionally that there is some modification of Definition 1 which is both intuitively acceptable (i.e. captures what we might prephilosophically think of as omniscience) and also has the consequence that there could be an omniscient being.

The propositions which are thought to be beyond the reach of even divine omniscience are of two kinds: the first concerns the future free actions of humans, and the second concerns so-called indexicals. Which of these problems the theist regards as serious will depend in part on the view which she takes of God's relations to time and space. Theists agree that eternity and omnipresence are two of God's defining attributes; but as we saw in the previous chapter, each of these attributes can be taken in at least two different ways. God's eternal existence might be either temporal or timeless, his omnipresence might be either spatial or non-spatial.

Very broadly, there is thought to be one problem in combining divine omniscience with the temporal conception of eternity; and a different problem with combining divine omniscience with the timeless conception of eternity (although, as we shall see, this second problem can be extended to cover either conception of eternity). We will deal with the first of these problems in the next section, and the second in the following sections. We will then consider other problems that are raised by the idea of divine omniscience.

Can God foreknow future free actions?

The first problem arises when we combine Definition 1 with the temporal conception of eternity. The problem is this: if God knows on Monday that on Tuesday I will go to London, can my going to London really be free? For if he knows in advance what I am going to do, and he cannot be wrong, then when Tuesday comes, I will *have* to go to London. If I do not go, then God would have been wrong, and that is impossible (omniscient beings do not make mistakes). But if I have to go, then it cannot be true that I go freely. So, in general, if God knows in advance what our actions will be, then none of our actions can be free. Conversely, if some of our actions really are free, then God cannot know in advance what they will be, and hence cannot be omniscient.

This line of thought has proved very seductive to many theists. Some have drawn the conclusion that since God is omniscient by Definition 1, he does know our future actions, and hence that we are not really free after all. Others have said that since we are free, our actions are not knowable in advance, and given that God is omniscient, it follows that Definition 1 of omniscience is faulty: you can be omniscient even if there are things which you do not know. Others again have tried to show that although we are free, God can know in advance what we will do, and hence it is possible to retain Definition 1 after all – at least as far as *this* problem is concerned. We will argue that theists have been unnecessarily concerned about divine foreknowledge of free action: the two concepts are not in any conflict.

We need first to be clearer about what the issue is supposed to be. The problem is not that the initial argument shows that omniscience is a self-contradictory concept. Nor is the problem quite that omniscience is incompatible with the temporal conception of eternity. More nearly, the problem is supposed to be that omniscience *and* the temporal conception of eternity *and* human free will (on a certain understanding of that idea) are incompatible. But even this formulation is not quite right. A better way of putting it is that, as traditionally conceived, the problem is generated by divine *foreknowledge* of free action (whether or not that is accompanied by omniscience) with an existence in time (whether or not that is existence at all times). Putting it this way enables us to see that the problem does not arise for *divine* foreknowledge in particular: if it arises at all, it arises for any foreknowledge of free action. If God's knowledge on Monday of what I will do on Tuesday is a threat to the freedom of my Tuesday action, then Fred's similar knowledge on Monday presents an exactly parallel threat to my freedom. If there is a threat at all, it arises from foreknowledge per se, no matter who has it.

But is there a threat at all? We can present the argument that worries the theist as follows:

Argument A

(1) God knows on Monday that I will go to London on Tuesday (premise).
(2) Necessarily, if God knows on Monday that I will go to London on Tuesday, then I will go to London on Tuesday (premise). So:
(3) Necessarily, I will go to London on Tuesday (from (1) and (2)). So:
(4) If I go to London on Tuesday, I do not go freely (from (3)).

But argument A is a simple logical fallacy. In general, one cannot infer 'Necessarily q' from the two premises 'Necessarily if p, then q' and 'p'. The necessity of the conditional does not imply the necessity of the consequent, even when the antecedent is true. All that follows from 1 and 2 is

(5) I will go to London on Tuesday.

The crucial difference between (3) and (5) is the disappearance from (5) of any necessity about my going to London, and hence the disappearance of any threat to my freedom from action from the fact of God's foreknowledge. It is not as if God's foreknowledge exerts some irresistible causal power that gets a grip of me on Tuesday and forces me to go to London. His foreknowledge exerts *no* freedom-removing pressure at all. I do not go to London in virtue of God's foreknowledge; rather, God foreknows in virtue of what I do. If God foreknows that I will do X, then it follows that I *do* not do not-X. What does not follow is that I *cannot* do not-X. What knowledge of a proposition requires is the truth of the proposition known; it does not require the *necessary* truth of the proposition.

We noted above that the problem does not arise specifically from *divine* foreknowledge. We can now add that it does not even arise from *knowledge*. For consider the following (bad) argument:

Argument B

(6) God remembers on Wednesday that I went to London on Tuesday (premise).
(7) Necessarily, if God remembers on Wednesday that I went to London on Tuesday, then I went to London on Tuesday (premise). So:

(8) Necessarily, I went to London on Tuesday (from (6) and (7)). So:

(9) If I went to London on Tuesday, I did not go freely (from (8)).

All that follows from (6) and (7) is that I went to London on Tuesday, not that it was necessary that I went to London on Tuesday. So the argument is invalid. But if Argument A were valid, then Argument B would be too.

That the problem does not spring from epistemic concepts (knowledge, remembrance, etc.). can be seen when we look at the following argument:

Argument C

(10) It is true on Monday that I will go to London on Tuesday (premise).

(11) Necessarily, if it is true on Monday that I will go to London on Tuesday, then I will go to London on Tuesday (premise). So:

(12) Necessarily, I will go to London on Tuesday (from (10) and (11)). So:

(4) If I go to London on Tuesday, I do not go freely (from (3)).

If Argument C were sound, it would show that it is mere truth, not specifically foreknowledge, nor divine foreknowledge, nor remembrance, which is incompatible with free action. But of course the argument is hopeless. (3) does not follow from (10) and (11), any more than it follows from (1) and (2). All that follows from (10) and (11) is that I will go to London on Tuesday; and that conclusion is compatible with my going freely.

The real source of the pseudo-puzzle about foreknowledge of free action lies in the fact that we can describe events and states of affairs which happen at one time, using descriptions which are true of those events only in virtue of what happens at other times, either earlier or later. Consider the sentence

(S) David Hume's father, Joseph, was born in 1681.

This gives a true description of an event which happened in 1681. However, one of the truth conditions of what it says (namely, that Joseph would later beget David) concerns 1711, the year of David Hume's birth. But this does not mean that when 1711 arrived, Joseph was somehow *compelled* to beget David because of the truth (as we can now express it) that David's father was born in 1681. It is in virtue of Joseph's begetting David in 1711 that (S) is true; it is not in virtue of the truth of (S) that Joseph did the begetting that he did. Events are truth-makers for propositions; propositions are not necessitators of events.

Many theists have tried to show that there is a deeper worry about divine foreknowledge and freedom than this account allows.[1] But it is hard to see that there is a real problem here.

Can God know the truth of indexicals?

The second category of propositions which arguably present a challenge to the possibility of an omniscient being are those which contain indexical expressions. The problem is this: we are familiar with the thought that for some sentences, whether they say something true is independent of who says them, or when and where they are said. For example, if I say 'Water boils at 100° C', you can express the very same fact by using the very same sentence. So too can anyone else, and they can use that sentence at any time, and in any place to express the same fact. Or if you say 'It is better to have loved and lost than never to have loved at all', I can express the very same thought by using the very same sentence – and again, where and when I or anyone else uses that sentence makes no difference to the fact which we thereby state. By contrast, there are other sentences which are such that whether the sentence says something true depends essentially on when or where or by whom it is said. For example, if you say 'I am hot', I cannot state the same fact by using the same sentence. I have to say not 'I am hot' but 'You are hot'. Again, if you say today 'Today it is raining', and I want to express the same thought tomorrow, I cannot use the same sentence you used (another sentence token of the same type): I have to use a different sentence and say 'Yesterday, it was raining' – just as the weather forecaster expressing yesterday the same thought, has to use yet another sentence and say 'Tomorrow it will rain'.

Words that have this feature (what they refer to, and hence the truth of sentences containing them, depends essentially on the user, or the time and place of utterance) are called indexicals, and sentences in which they occur are indexical sentences. It seems that corresponding to indexical sentences (to some at least, and perhaps to all) there is a non-indexical sentence (or perhaps several such sentences) which says *very roughly* the same thing as the indexical. To see what these non-indexicals are like, let us first introduce the idea of a tenseless verb form. Let us use the present tense form to mean not just 'is now . . . ' but 'is, was, or will be'. For example, instead of saying 'I am hot', I could say 'Everitt is (timelessly) hot on 17 March 2003 at 5.23 p.m.' or 'The lecturer speaking in room 3.02 on the 76th day of 2003 is hot' or 'The only person standing in room 3.02 of the Arts Block, UEA at 5.30 p.m. on St Patrick's Day 2003 is (timelessly) hot'. These would be non-indexical sentences which say *very roughly* what the original indexical sentence said; and they are sentences which you or anyone else could use now or at any other time to state *very roughly* the same fact that I was stating when I used the indexical. Let us call such sentences 'the correlates' of the corresponding indexical sentence.

It is an obvious truth that we express much of the knowledge that we have using indexical sentences. And we can divide these indexicals into three main groups: personal indexicals, spatial indexicals, and temporal indexicals, thus:

(1) personal: I, me, mine, you, yours, he/she, his/hers, etc.
(2) spatial: here, there, to the left, to the right, nearer, further, this, that, etc.
(3) temporal: now, in the past, in the future, today, yesterday, tomorrow, soon, and all tensed verbs.

With these preliminaries, we can now raise the question about divine omniscience: on the timeless conception of divine eternity, can God know the truths which we know when we express our knowledge using temporal indexical sentences?

The difficulty is this: Suppose I say 'It is now raining'. I can know that that says something true, in part because I am a being in time who can produce the sentence at one time (when it is raining) and not at an earlier or later time (when it is not raining). But if God is timeless, he cannot do anything *at a time*. In particular, he cannot even have the thought 'It is raining *now*', and hence he cannot think that thought to be true, or know it to be true. We may concede for the moment (although I will later challenge this concession) that he can think, and know to be true, one or more correlates of that indexical sentence. He can think to himself and know to be true the non-indexical sentence 'It is (timelessly) raining on 17 March at 5.15 p.m.'. But he cannot know the very thing that I know when I know 'It is *now* raining'; for he cannot know the truth which I could express by saying 'It is *now* 5.15 p.m. on 17 March'. So there are truths which a timeless being could not know. So, no being can be both timeless and omniscient; so, God does not exist (on the timeless interpretation of his eternity).

A parallel argument applies to sentences with spatial indexicals. We have (at any one time) one and only one spatial position: we are not everywhere, and we are not nowhere. It is in relation to the position of the speaker/thinker (the producer of the token sentence) that terms like 'here', 'there', 'to the left/right', 'over there', 'in front of me', 'behind me', etc. are to be understood. So if I say '*This* building is on fire' or '*Here* is where the fire is', I can say something true, because I can have a spatial relationship to the fire. If I am to know to be true that here is where the fire is, then I must be located in the vicinity of the fire. But a being who was non-spatial could not be located in the vicinity of anything, and hence could not know what I know when I know that the fire is here. Further, a being whose spatial relationship to the fire was exactly the same as his spatial relationship to everything else in the universe (because he was equally present everywhere) could not know any such thing. Again, we can for the moment concede in this context that God can think, and know to be true, one or more correlates of that indexical sentence. He can think to himself and know to be true the non-indexical sentence 'It is raining in Norwich'. But he cannot know the very thing that I know when I in Norwich know 'It is raining here'; for he cannot know the truth which I could express by saying 'Norwich is here'. The problem thus arises from the fact that God's relationship to space (being either everywhere or nowhere) is of the wrong sort to allow him to know to be true sentences which contain spatial indexicals. So there are truths which a non-spatial being could not know. So, no being can be both non-spatial and omniscient; so, God does not exist (on the non-spatial interpretation of his omnipresence).

Let us turn finally to personal indexicals. I can know certain things about myself and express them using personal indexicals – for example, I now have a slight ache in my leg, I am thinking of divine omniscience, I am looking forward to dinner, and so on. As before, we can provisionally allow that God can know the non-indexical correlates of these things I know. He can know, for example, 'Everitt has a slight ache' or 'The lecturer in lecture theatre 3.02 has a slight ache' etc. But since he cannot know that I am Everitt nor that I am the lecturer in room 3.02, it again turns out that there is a range of facts which I can know but God cannot.

As with the problem about spatial indexicals, this problem about personal indexicals arises whatever conception of divine eternity one accepts. So whereas the theist could solve the problem about temporal indexicals by moving to the duration conception of God's eternity; or solve the problem about spatial indexicals by saying that God occupies some regions of space but not others, she is bound to be left with the problem about personal indexicals.

An objection to the argument from indexicals

The argument as I have presented it so far has presupposed that someone who knows the truth of an indexical knows something different from what is known by someone who knows the truth of one or more of its non-indexical correlates. To put it more tersely, we have presupposed that an indexical and its correlates do not say the same thing. That is why above I cautiously said that the correlates say *very roughly* the same as the indexicals, the implication being that they do not in fact say the same thing. Suppose the theist challenges this assumption.

The challenge can go like this: we need to distinguish between what is known on the one hand, and the vehicle of knowledge or how the knowledge is expressed on the other. This is a distinction which is familiar to us from translation between languages. If I say 'Today is Monday' and you say 'Aujourdhui est lundi', then although we have used different sentences or different vehicles of knowledge, what we have said using those different sentences is the same. It would be a mistake to say that *mere* difference of sentence necessarily implied difference of what is said/known. Similarly if I know in 2003 that John F. Kennedy was killed 40 years ago, and what God knows is that Kennedy is (timelessly) killed in 1963, then (according to this line of reply) we know the same thing even though we express our knowledge in different sentences. After all, it might be said, what makes my belief true is the very same historical events, or very same set of historical facts as makes God's belief true. A similar story (the theist might continue) goes for spatial and personal indexicals. If I know that the man facing me has a gun, and God knows something like 'The man facing Everitt has (timelessly) a gun', then there is just one set of people and one set of facts about them that make my belief and God's belief true. So there are no good grounds for saying that my knowledge and God's differ in content, and no reason to say that I know something which God cannot.

Unfortunately for the theist, however, this second line of reply fails. Indexical sentences do not have the same content as non-indexicals, and knowing that an indexical sentence is true is not the same as knowing that its non-indexical pair is true. To establish these claims, we can note in the first place that an indexical and any of its correlates fail to display the most basic requirement which must be met if two sentences are to say the same thing: there is no mutual entailment between them. Take the two sentences:

(A) Kennedy was killed 40 years ago.
(B) Kennedy is (timelessly) killed in 1963.

(B) is true every time it is said. But (A) was not true at any time in the past until 2003, and it will not be true at any time in the future after the end of 2003. Someone who knows that (B) is true cannot thereby deduce that (A) is true; and someone who knows that (A) is true cannot thereby deduce that (B) is true. What makes (A) true is not quite the same as what makes (B) true. For (A) refers to its own time of utterance as well as to what happened in 2003, whereas (B) does not. So there are times when (B) says something true and (A) does not. So someone who knows only (B) is ignorant of something which is known by someone who knows (A); and someone who knows only (A) is ignorant of something which is known by someone who knows (B).

Of course (B) can be deduced from (A), and (A) from (B) if the knower can know

(C) The current year is 2003.

But this is of no comfort to the theist. For (C) is itself an indexical sentence; and how a timeless God could know (C) raises the same problems as how he could know (A).

It is not just in their entailments that (A) and (B) differ. They also differ in their inductive relations. From (A) I could plausibly infer inductively

(D) No one who is now under 38 will remember the Kennedy assassination.

But I cannot infer (D) from (B). And if someone is trying to work out how long ago Kennedy was assassinated, she might reason to herself that (A) is probably true, on the ground that

(E) I am now 46, and Kennedy was killed between my 5th and 8th birthdays.

But (E) by itself would not be good inductive evidence for (B).

Nor is it just in their deductive and inductive relations that indexicals and their correlates differ. They differ also in their explanatory power. Suppose we ask why Lee Harvey Oswald pulled the trigger as and when he did. We get the beginnings of an explanation if we attribute to him a cluster of beliefs, including the following:

(F) *That* man is the President.
(G) If and only if I pull the trigger *now*, will I hit *that* man.

It would not be enough to attribute to Oswald such beliefs as:

(H) The man seated on the left in the back of the third car is (timelessly) the President.
(I) If and only if I fire at 11.32, do I hit (timelessly) the President.

For suppose that Oswald does not also believe that now is 11.32. Then the fact that he believes (I) will not help to explain why he fires at 11.32. Indeed it will make it puzzling that he fires at 11.32, since he must have thought that he was firing at a time when he had no idea whether he would hit the President. Or suppose that he believes (H), but does not believe that *that* man (at whom he is pointing) is seated on the left in the back of the third car. Then (H) would not help to explain why Oswald shot *that* man, for he cannot think that *that* man (at whom he is aiming) is the President.

The moral is that if we are to explain people's actions in part by reference to their beliefs, these beliefs will have to contain some indexicals, otherwise we will not be able to explain why they perform those actions at that time rather than earlier or later, or in that place rather than somewhere else. In short, then, we can say that indexical sentences and their non-indexical correlates differ in three crucial respects: in their deductive relations, in their inductive relations, and in their explanatory power. Because of these differences, an indexical sentence and its non-indexical correlate will play very different roles in a person's overall view of the world, and hence the objection which tries to claim that the sentences are different expressions of a single truth, rather than the expression of different truths, must be rejected.

The upshot of this line of objection to divine omniscience, then, is this: indexicals necessarily have a different content from even their closest correlates. So someone who knows the truth of an indexical sentence knows something different from what is known by someone who knows only the correlates. So someone who knows only the correlates is ignorant of what is known by someone who knows the indexicals. What this shows is that the concept of omniscience (by Definition 1) is self-contradictory: there could not be an omniscient being. He would have to exist at all places, in order to know all truths of the form '*Here* is . . .', and yet also *not* exist in all places, since then no place would be 'here' for him. In relation to time, he would have to exist at every time.

An extension of the argument from indexicals

As a final postscript to this line of criticism of classical theism, I want to raise one much more destructive criticism. The criticism which I have raised so far of divine omniscience has presupposed a distinction between indexical and non-indexical sentences, and allowed that God could know the truth of the non-indexical correlates of indexical sentences. It has denied only that he could know the indexical sentences themselves. The final criticism to consider is whether he could know the truth even of what we have been calling the non-indexical correlates. The reason for thinking that he could not is that what we have been calling the non-indexical correlates themselves are covertly indexical.

Let us see how this is so with temporal sentences first of all. Consider again

(H) Everitt lectures (timelessly) on Monday.

What understanding can a timeless being have of the word 'Monday'? Suppose he knows a number of truths about it –, for example, that it comes between Sunday and Tuesday, that it is for many people the first day of work after a short break, etc. Will that enable him to know which day is being referred to as 'Monday'? It is true that if he knows which day is Sunday or Tuesday, and has a grasp of temporal indexicals such as 'tomorrow' and 'yesterday', he can pin down the reference of 'Monday' on any occasion of its use. But then the same problem could be raised in connection with his grasp of 'Sunday' and 'Tuesday'. It seems that our grasp of each member of this set of weekday terms presupposes a grasp of some indexicals. The same is true of other temporal terms, such as the names of the months and the years.

Do similar considerations apply to our grasp of proper names? That may seem to depend on whether we think of proper names as purely referential or as abbreviated descriptions. If they are purely referential, then there will be a hidden indexical element in them. There will be some 'baptismal' occasion when the speakers of the language agree to call *this* or *that* object 'the Grand Canyon' or 'the Eiffel Tower' or 'the River Thames'. For personal names, the idea of a baptism may be a good deal more literal. 'I name *this* ship *Fairy Mist*' says the celebrity; 'I baptise *this* child John Doe' says the minister. If the referential theory of names is correct, it is in virtue of these indexically imbued occasions that the words have the reference that they subsequently do. Consequently, a being who is unable to know any indexically expressed truths will not be able to know which object is the Grand Canyon, or the Eiffel Tower, the *Fairy Mist*, or John Doe.

However, when we touched on the issue of names in Chapter 1, we opted for the 'abbreviated description' view. So could a timeless God understand the descriptions for which a proper name is an abbreviation? One immediate problem for many proper names is that other proper names appear in the description which the original proper name abbreviates. The Grand Canyon is a canyon in the *USA* through which the *Colorado River* runs; the Eiffel Tower is a metallic structure in *Paris*; John Doe is the son of *James* and *Mary Doe*; and so on. Let us assume, however, that for every proper name, N, we can supply a set of descriptions in purely general terms which do not themselves use any other proper names, and which serve to pin down the meaning of 'N'. The question now to raise is whether a timeless God could ever understand the meaning of any of these general terms. Could he understand the meaning of terms like 'river', 'canyon', 'metal' and 'son'?

We can agree for the sake of argument that the timeless being might know for each general term how it relates semantically to every other general term. Thus he might know that 'river' is semantically connected to 'flowing' and 'water', that 'flowing' is connected to 'movement', and 'water' to 'colourless' and 'liquid', and so on. He might know, as we could put it loosely, the content of a dictionary. But if he knew *nothing* of the form '*That* is a river' or '*That* is some water' or '*That* is a so-and-so', surely he would not know the meaning of the general terms?

For comparison, consider the situation of a standard speaker of English who is a non-speaker of Japanese and who is given a Japanese dictionary which allows her to match each Japanese word (which presents itself to her only as a set of distinctive squiggles) with another set of Japanese words (which she knows only as a further set of distinctive squiggles). Even if she can match every Japanese word with another Japanese word or phrase or sets of phrases which define the original word, it seems clear that this person has not so far learnt Japanese. To count as having learned Japanese, she must have some grasp of how at least some of the squiggles *relate to the world*; and that requires her to have some means of identifying this or that piece of reality. It requires her to know the truth of sentences of the form 'When the world is like *this*, *this* squiggle applies'.

If this line of thought is correct, it shows that a timeless existence would rule out knowledge not just of indexically expressed truths, but of truths in general, because a grasp of indexicals is essential to a grasp of the general terms by means of which non-indexical thoughts are expressed. Far from being omniscient, a timeless being would be hugely ignorant.[2] Even if God exists in time, and so will escape the original objection above to his knowledge of temporal indexical sentences, a parallel argument to the one above will show that he cannot know the truth of spatial or personal indexical sentences. Given the argument that our grasp of a wide range of general terms requires a grasp of indexicals, it will follow that even a God in time will be unable to know a wide range of truths. No matter what other features a being has, he cannot be omniscient. So if omniscience is a defining feature of God, it will follow that God does not exist.

Even if the theist rejects this extension of the argument from indexicals to cover all general terms as well, she will still be left with serious problems over divine omniscience. For even if she can establish that God could know that someone answering your description exists, he could not know that *you* exist. He could not know that you are the person who answers that description. In that sense, he could not have any knowledge of or thoughts about any individuals, as distinct from types of individuals. And if he cannot have any thoughts about individuals, it will follow that he cannot care about any individuals. If he does not even know that you exist, it is not logically possible for him to care about what happens to you.

A revised definition of omniscience

At this point, the theist might wonder whether the problems with her position stem from an over-hasty acceptance of a flawed account of omniscience. Is there some alternative to Definition 1? One possibility that at once suggests itself is:

Definition 2 X is omniscient = For every true proposition p, if it is logically possible for X to know that p (i.e. X's knowing p is consistent with X's defining properties), then X knows that p

If there are some things which it is logically impossible for God to know, in virtue of the fact that by definition he is, for example, non-temporal, or lacks a spatial position, then by Definition 2, the fact that he does not know them would not show that he was not omniscient. Equally, if it is logically impossible for anyone to know in advance what the free choices of a human agent will be, then the fact that God does not know what such choices are would not show that he is not omnipotent.

At first sight, this might seem to be an attractive compromise position for the theist. But it is clear that this definition will be subject to the same undermining line of argument that we applied to a similar definition of omnipotence. Suppose a 'nescient' being is one who by definition knows nothing. It will then be logically impossible for a nescient being to know anything. Yet a nescient being will count as omniscient by Definition 2: if it is logically possible for the nescient being to know that p, then he knows that p – but for every proposition p, it can never be logically possible for the being to know that p. Definition 2 therefore has absurd consequences, and is to be rejected.

Conclusion

It thus becomes clear that the theist faces a number of serious problems in defending the existence of an omniscient God. If God's eternity is construed atemporally, he will be ignorant of a wide range of truths. He will certainly not know any temporally indexical truths. If his omnipresence is either his being non-spatial, or his existing everywhere in space, again he will be unable to know spatially indexical truths. It is also at least arguable that if his eternity and omnipresence are interpreted in these ways, he will not be able to know a very wide range of general truths either. Since he will not be able to have knowledge of us as individuals, neither will he be able to have any concern or care for any of us as individuals. As in the case of the other divine attributes which we have looked at, the theist can respond by seeking to limit the scope of 'omniscient' – in effect to say that someone can be omniscient, even if there are truths of which they are ignorant. But the sceptic is likely to feel that this is a case of moving the goalposts, and that a more honest response would be to say 'God cannot be omniscient after all, and he cannot know nearly as much as we initially thought that he could'.

Further reading

There is a large literature focusing on the relation between divine omni-science and future human free action. Mavrodes in Quinn and Taliaferro (1997) provides a brief but good overview of the problem about future free actions, and the problem about indexicals. In relation to the first, a good starting point is Pike (1965), which argues that given some assumptions, divine foreknowledge of future free actions is impossible. Other important contributions to that debate are Plantinga (1986b), Swinburne (1986) and Hasker (1989). The argument pursued in the text about indexicals was first defended in Perry (1979), but has since been criticised by, among others, Millikan (1990), Abbruzzese (1997) and Jacquette (1999). Abbruzzese also replies to the Grim argument from set theory described in the text, full details of which are at Plantinga and Grim (1993).

16

---◦◯◦---

Conclusion

We have so far looked at a range of arguments in favour of theism, and some objections to those arguments; and a range of arguments against theism, and some objections to those arguments. Our task now is to try to synthesise all this material, and to form a judgement on the truth or probable truth of theism. This is a difficult task that requires judgement rather than the mechanical application of any rules.

Let us leave on one side for the moment the ontological arguments of Chapter 3, and the prudential arguments of Chapter 10. Each of the remaining arguments for theism was found to suffer from more or less serious deficiencies if considered on its own. None of them was strong enough by itself even to make theism more probably true than not, let alone to make it very probably true, or (as some theists think that it is) certainly true. So if the case for theism is considered in relation to any one of the arguments taken singly, that case would be very weak. If we were then to add in all the objections to theism, the case for theism would be annihilated. For this reason, some theists have sensibly urged that the theistic arguments need to be considered collectively. Five independent arguments, each of which is relatively weak, collectively might make theism more probable than not. We need to think here of the analogy of a detective collecting evidence about Bloggs's possible involvement in a crime. To find that Bloggs had a motive does not make it more probable than not that Bloggs was the crook; some eye-witness reports that a person looking like Bloggs was seen near the scene of the crime do not make it more probable than not that Bloggs was the crook; the fact that Bloggs left the country in a great hurry immediately after the crime does not make it more likely than not that Bloggs is the crook. And so on. But facts like these, each of which has only a weak probative force, can collectively build a powerful case for Bloggs's guilt. In a similar way, the theist needs to urge that the theistic arguments should be taken as a collection, and that when so taken they make theism at least more probably true than not.

This move, however, faces a further problem: there is no reason to think that even if each argument has some probative force, it is one and the same

301

being who is referred to in the conclusion of each argument. For all that the arguments show, there might be one being who reveals himself to us in religious experience, another being whose designing intelligence lies behind the apparent design we see in the natural world, a further being who is the First Cause, and so on. Clearly what the theist needs is a second level argument designed to show that each of the first level arguments is referring to the same being. In general, presentations of the case for theism have been negligent in supplying this.[1]

It might seem that an appeal to Occam's Razor will supply what the theist needs. Why say that five arguments establish the existence of five different things, rather than that they are five different ways of establishing the existence of a single thing? But in fact this would be a misuse of the Razor. If my phone rings on Monday, I can infer that someone has phoned me. If a letter arrives for me on Tuesday, I can infer that someone has written to me. If there is a knock at the door on Wednesday, I can infer that someone is calling on me. But Occam's Razor does not give me warrant to say that the hypothesis that it is one person who has phoned, written and knocked, is superior to the hypothesis that three different people are involved. More generally, simply finding some evidence of the existence of a being with property F, and some evidence of the existence of a being with property G, affords no warrant for saying that there is a single being with both F and G. So the Razor by itself will not give the theist what she here needs.

Suppose, however, that this point is waived, and we assume that the appeal to the Razor works. So we allow for the sake of argument that the theist can plausibly say that each of the various arguments does support the existence of a single being. A further problem then arises: that single being is not the God of traditional theism. Suppose for example that some version of the argument from religious experience succeeds. That would at most establish the existence of a supernatural spirit of benign disposition. It would not establish the existence of a being who was omnipotent, or omniscient, or omnipresent, or perfect, or a creator and sustainer, etc. Suppose again that some version of the teleological argument is cogent. That would at most establish the existence of a skilful designer; and let us assume that the appeal to Occam's Razor allows the theist to say that the skilful designer is the very same being as the supernatural spirit who appears to us in religious experience. That still does nothing to establish the existence of a being with *any* of the divine attributes, let alone with all of them. A similar limitation attends the cosmological argument. If either the causal or the modal version succeeds, it shows that there exists a First Cause of the Universe, or that there is a being who exists of necessity – and maybe this being is the same as the benign spirit and the skilful designer. But it does not show that either sort of being is a *personal* being, or one who is omniscient, or caring, or omnipotent, etc.

In short, when we consider the arguments for theism (always remembering that we are here excepting the ontological and prudential arguments), they suffer from three serious weakness. First, they give very poor support to their conclusions. Second, even if each of them gave good support to its own conclusion, there is no reason to think that their conclusions refer to a single being. Third, even if there were reason to think that their conclusions did refer to a single being, there is no reason to think that that being is God. So, even without considering the degree to which the anti-theist arguments undermine the case for theism, theism can put up only a poor defence and one that should not command our rational assent.

However, we have so far been leaving to one side the ontological argument. The reason for doing so is that the strictures applied above do not apply straightforwardly to the ontological argument. In the first place, alone among the theistic arguments, it can claim to be arguing directly for the existence *of God*. In arguing for the existence of a perfect being, or a being than which none greater can be conceived, it is at least arguing for the existence of something which encapsulates a range of divine properties – unsurpassable power, unsurpassable knowledge, unsurpassable goodness, etc. Second, unlike most of the other arguments, the ontological argument presents itself as a proof, in the strong sense of being something whose conclusion follows deductively from premises which are true and can be known to be true. It is, then, a serious contender for the title 'a proof of the existence of God' in a way in which the other 'proofs' are not. It is not surprising then that those who think that it does indeed supply a proof should give it pride of place.[2] The problem with the ontological argument, then, is not that it is not trying to do the right sort of thing: the problem is that it is trying but, for the reasons given in Chapter 3, it is totally failing.

Let us turn now to logical objections to theism. In short, they amount to these: theism has failed to find any definition of omnipotence which is both intuitively plausible in itself, and which leaves possible the existence of an omnipotent being. In connection with eternity, we found that if this is taken to mean atemporal eternity, then an eternal being could not be omniscient, could not be a person, and could not be a creator and sustainer. If eternity means endless duration, an eternal being could not be a creator-sustainer. In connection with omnipresence, if this is taken to be either presence everywhere in space, or nowhere in space, an omnipresent being could not be omniscient. The upshot of these logical points is that the defining attributes of God are either individually self-contradictory (omnipotence) or cannot be coinstantiated (omniscience and omnipotence, omniscience and eternity, eternity and personhood, eternity and creatorship, etc.). It thus follows that not only does God not exist, he *cannot* exist. For ignorant agnostics who unthinkingly proclaim that it is impossible to prove or disprove the existence of God, here is a putative set of disproofs.

When we look beyond the logical objections to the evidence of science, we find two further objections to theism. The first, as we described in Chapter

11, concerns the scale of the universe which modern science reveals, a scale hugely unlike what theism would lead us to expect. The second concerns the fact that if current Big Bang cosmology is correct, past time is finite. If God's eternity is construed as endless duration, this scientific finding entails that God does not exist, since it entails that nothing has had infinite duration.

Finally, there is the very traditional problem of evil: why would there be so much of it, or indeed any of it, in something created by the God of theism? The principal theistic response to this objection is that the evil is a practically unavoidable cost of the valuable gift of free will. Central problems with this reply are first that it relies on an unacceptable (incompatibilist) account of what free will is, and that even if its account of free will were correct, it fails to explain why free will is so valuable – why, for example, it is legitimate to let innocent third parties suffer simply to ensure that guilty persons can enjoy the unfettered exercise of their free will. Also significant in this context is the huge amount of animal suffering which has been going on for tens of millions of years without apparently even being aimed at any good, let alone achieving it.

The conclusion that emerges, then, is that on balance, the empirical evidence tells against theism; and that anyway theism is an ultimately self-contradictory doctrine. But now the theist might object that it is not possible to combine these two kinds of objection to her position: theism cannot be both empirically false and also self-contradictory. If theism is genuinely a self-contradictory doctrine, it might be said, then there cannot be any role for empirical evidence – either for or even against it. Alternatively, if its truth is genuinely an empirical matter, then it must be at least a self-consistent doctrine, and hence not open to the logical objections which have been raised against it in the previous chapters.

This objection however fails through a too narrow conception of the role which empirical evidence can play. That there can be empirical evidence for and against self-contradictory claims is easily demonstrated. A conjunction of the form 'p and q' has two truth conditions: it requires the truth of p and the truth of q, and is false if either conjunct is false. Consider then the limiting case where 'q' is replaced by 'not-p'. The truth of the conjunction 'p and not-p' would require the truth of each conjunct, and would be false if either conjunct is false. If then I discover that p, I have discovered that the second conjunct is false, and hence that the conjunction is false; and there is no reason here why p should not be an empirical proposition. So, I can gain empirical disconfirmation of 'It is raining and it is not raining' by looking out of the window and seeing that it is raining. This disproves the second conjunct and hence disproves the conjunction. What is true is that I do not *need* empirical evidence in order to disprove something self-contradictory – but that is not to say there cannot be any. Hence, even if theism is a self-contradictory doctrine, as the last few chapters have implicitly been arguing, there is no reason why there cannot also be empirical evidence against it.

So combining the arguments for theism, the objections to those arguments, the objections to the truth of theism, and criticisms of those objections, the balance comes down heavily against theism. Overall, there are good reasons for thinking that theism can be *proved* false; and even if those reasons are found not to be compelling, overall there are further good empirical grounds for the falsity of theism.

That leaves us only with the prudential arguments of Chapter 10. It was there allowed that some such argument could give some people a good reason, and even an overriding reason to believe in God – at least to retain a pre-existing belief in God and perhaps even to acquire a belief in God. Since the reason is a consequential and not an epistemic one, and thus has nothing to do with the truth of what is believed, the existence of such a reason, even of an overriding reason, is not in conflict with the conclusion reached above that there are also compelling reasons to think that theism is false. Of course no one person could accept the cogency of both sets of reasons – at least not without being deeply confused almost to the point of total incoherence. But someone who is ignorant of the truth-directed objections to theism, and who is willing to remain that way, could have excellent reasons of a consequential kind for their theism. To adapt a phrase from Marx, it is here that we find at last the very small rational kernel in the mystical shell of theism.

Of course this case against theism does not settle the matter – arguments in philosophy, even putative proofs, virtually never do. In particular, the logical disproofs leave the theist with all sorts of fallback positions. The standard theist strategy, as we have seen in Chapters 13, 14 and 15, is to redefine the allegedly inconsistent divine properties so as to make them internally or mutually compatible. The sceptic's response which I have suggested to that strategy is to argue that the limitations which the theist imposes destroy the substance (as it were) of the divine attributes: no being who is subject to such limitations on his power or knowledge deserves to be called omnipotent or omniscient. The theist will then say that it is up to her, not her opponents, to say what she means when she says that there exists an omnipotent, omniscient, personal creator.

The issue sounds as if it is degenerating into a dispute merely about the meaning of words. But something more is at stake. It is crucial to theism that the God for which it argues will be one who is worthy of worship, and that fact (I suspect) has been a powerful factor in pulling the articulation of theism, and of the divine attributes in particular, towards extreme formulations. Hence, God needs to be not just very powerful, but more powerful than anything else that exists, and indeed more powerful than anything else which does not in fact exist but which might have existed. He needs not just to be very knowledgeable but to know more than anyone else who exists, and indeed be more knowledgeable than anyone else who does not exist but who might have existed. He needs to have existed not just longer than anyone else, but for an infinite past time – or else to have a relationship to time completely unlike that of anyone else. Any falling away from these extreme characterisations opens up the possibility of a being who is more powerful than God, or more knowledgeable, or longer-lasting etc., and hence opens up the question 'But why are you worshipping God, rather than this other being who clearly is greater than God?'. So theism has a constant tendency to adopt extreme characterisations of God – and it is these which provide the opportunity and the motive for the atheist to level his criticisms.

Further reading

S. Davis (1997 Chapter 1) has a good discussion of constraints on proofs in the area of theism, and of what such proofs can achieve. Swinburne (1979 Chapter 12) is a detailed assessment of the cumulative force of the theistic arguments and objections, and one which comes to very different conclusions from those in this chapter.

Notes

1 Reasoning about God

1 Compare Freud's crisp debunking of Tertullian: 'This *Credo* is only of interest as a self-confession. As an authoritative statement, it has no binding force. Am I to be obliged to believe *every* absurdity? And if not, why this one in particular? There is no appeal to a court above that of reason.' (Freud 1973 vol. xxi: 28 'The Future of an Illusion')

2 It should be noted that the quoted words and the text from which they come were not written by Wittgenstein himself. They come from notes taken by students who attended his lectures, and they were never checked personally by Wittgenstein.

3 Strangely enough, Freud combines this thoroughgoing scepticism about the power of reasoning to determine the issue, with the incompatible view that reason comes down fairly heavily against the credibility of religious doctrines. In the same passage he wrote 'Some of them [religious doctrines] are so improbable, so incompatible with everything we have so laboriously discovered about the reality of the world that we may compare them . . . to delusions' (ibid.). If this is not making 'a critical approach' to the doctrines and deciding that they can be refuted, it sounds suspiciously like it.

4 Cosmological arguments

1 I here overlook complications caused by the existence of so called non-denumerable infinite sets. The interested reader is referred to any standard work on set theory, such as Lipschutz 1964.

2 Craig considers and rejects the objection that quantum mechanics disproves the claim that every beginning of existence has a cause. But the form of his reply carries the implication that nothing counts as a beginning of existence unless it starts to exist 'spontaneously out of nothing'. If this is what a 'beginning of existence' is, we have too little experience of them to say whether all such events have causes or not. See Craig and Smith, op. cit. p. 143.

3 We will consider in the next section the problems that arise from supposing that the creator is 'outside' time.

4 For example, his assumption that what exists contingently cannot exist through all time. For a brief but conclusive critique, see Plantinga 1974: 77–80.

5 Rather surprisingly, in the passage above, after referring to 'something which is of absolute or metaphysical necessity', Leibniz continues 'for which itself no reason can be given'. But this must be a slip on his part, for two reasons. In the first place, if he really thought that no reason could be given for the existence of

the necessary being, he would have no reply to an atheist who denied the existence of God while admitting that the existence of the universe was inexplicable. Second, it is clear that Leibniz is committed to saying a reason *can* be given for the existence of the necessary being: its existence follows from its essence.

6 This line of argument will be explored more fully in chapter 15.

7 Swinburne responds to the line of argument presented in the text by arguing that some judgements of probability are wholly a priori. For details, see Swinburne (2001) especially Chapters 3 and 4.

5 Teleological arguments

1 See Flew 1986: 63, where the point is clearly made.

2 Leslie tell us that 'The Anthropic Principle could be stated as follows: *any intelligent beings that there are can find themselves only where intelligent life is possible*'(Leslie 1996: 128); according to Polkinghorne, the Principle says that 'a world containing men is not just any old universe, specified at random so to speak, but it has to have a very particular character in its basic laws and circumstances' (Polkinghorne 1996: 58); Le Poidevin has 'The universe had to be such as to permit the emergence of observers in it at some stage' (Le Poidevin 1996: 59).

3 For those who think Darwin is irrelevant, see Kenny 1969: 188; for those who think he deals a fatal blow, see Dawkins 1986.

4 See, for example, Behe 1996 for the best-known biochemist who has serious reservations about what a Darwinian approach can explain.

5 For a sketch of an empirically possible, and perhaps even plausible account of how life could have originated, see Dawkins 1976: 14ff.

6 Arguments to and from miracles

1 It is worth emphasising this fact since at one point in his discussion, Hume does refer carelessly to 'the absolute impossibility' (op. cit. p. 125) of miracles. But the context makes it clear that this is a slip of the pen. All of his discussion is concerned with the epistemology of miracle reports, not with the reality of miracle occurrences.

7 God and morality

1 If it were possible to benefit currently non-existent people by bringing them into existence, it ought to be equally possible to harm them by failing to bring them into existence. How many countless billions of people would God then have harmed by not bringing them into existence! The clear-headed theist of course is not committed to this lapse in divine benevolence.

2 I here assume that such comforting maxims as that virtue is its own reward, and that the virtuous person cannot be harmed, are false.

3 Davis rather spoils this picture when he continues a few lines further on: 'if God exists, heroic self-sacrifice might be morally justified on the grounds that God will reward it, or on the grounds that God commands it' (ibid.). Why *being rewarded* for doing something, or *obeying a command*, should count as being 'morally warranted', Davis does not explain. If this is Davis's conception of justification, perhaps the non-theist will not after all find it difficult to explain to Davis why morally heroic deeds are justified.

8 Religious experience

1 For a discussion of a fuller range of tests, see Gale 1991: 302ff.
2 By a mystical perception, Alston means what we have been calling religious experience. He rejects the term 'religious experience' as potentially misleading, while recognising that his own use of the term 'mystical' is somewhat unusual (Alston 1991: 34–5).
3 This is a claim which will be investigated more thoroughly in Chapter 9.
4 Though this may be a dangerous way of putting the point. For hallucination implies the possibility of non-hallucination, and the sceptic may want to claim that non-delusory religious experiences are not even possible.

9 Naturalism, evolution and rationality

1 Plantinga produces a variety of closely related arguments in a variety of sources (see Further reading at the end of the chapter for details). This chapter focuses mainly on one version of the argument that he defends in his most recently published account of such arguments, Plantinga 2000.
2 I will assume for the sake of simplicity that natural selection operates on individual organisms, rather than at the genetic level.
3 'Were it not for sin and its effects, God's presence and glory would be as obvious and uncontroversial to us all as the presence of other minds, physical objects and the past' (Plantinga 2000: 214). This comes pretty close to saying that sin is a precondition of atheism, hence that if you are an atheist, you must be a sinner.

10 Prudential arguments

1 For example, sections 2 and 3 of the paper are taken up with discussing the relations between belief and the will.

12 Problems about evil

1 I am thinking here particularly of William Rowe's version, in Rowe 1979.
2 For example, Stump and Murray describe the logical problem of evil as 'largely discredited' (p. 153).
3 Rather surprisingly, Leibniz seems to have thought this worthless justification of evil carries some force. In his *Theodicy*, he argues that God chooses a world which contains evil, and he tries to defend this claim by asserting that 'the best plan is not always that which seeks to avoid evil, since it may happen that the evil is accompanied by a greater good. For example, a general of an army would prefer a great victory with a slight wound to a condition without a wound and without victory'(quoted Pojman 1994: 173). But Leibniz's example here precisely fails to exemplify the point which his argument requires, namely a good which not even an omnipotent being could achieve without the corresponding evil.
4 Adams himself is absolutely clear about this point. He makes it clear that he is addressing only the Leibnizian idea that any world which God creates must be the best possible, and says explicitly that he is not trying to offer a theodicy.
5 I here follow the argument deployed in Everitt 2000.
6 In fairness to Plantinga, we should note that this is merely his preliminary statement of the Free Will Defence. Its detailed elaboration and defence then takes a further 25 pages of closely argued text.
7 Plantinga has placed much weight on the fact that it is not God who performs

the evil deeds but human beings. In his terminology, God cannot *strongly actualise* any state of affairs which consists in a human agent acting freely. So God cannot bring about a world in which every one freely chooses to do what is right. But this is a claim which carries very little argumentative clout. God cannot commit my sins, just as he cannot sneeze my sneezes. But that does nothing to show that he cannot share in the guilt which accrues to me as the sinner. There are more ways of being a guilty party than being the sole perpetrator. Various forms of non-intervention or non-prevention can also incur guilt. In certain cases, the non-intervener is the only guilty party (I watch passively as two toddlers play with an electric socket, one of them eventually pushing the fingers of the other into the socket and giving him a fatal shock).

13 Omnipotence

1 Strictly, of course, just as morality is about more than simply actions, so moral perfection would require more than morally perfect actions. It would require also, for example, morally perfect motives, character traits, etc. But for the sake of simplicity we can proceed here as if morality were concerned only with action.
2 Obviously the doctrine of the Incarnation hovers in the background. Those who think that it makes sense to suppose that Jesus was literally both an individual human being and also identical with God will find no problem with the solution which is rejected in the text.
3 This is substantially the amendment found in, for example, Stewart op. cit. p. 29, though I have omitted an additional moral requirement on omnipotence which he includes. As noted above in the text, this intrusion of moral considerations into a definition of omnipotence is unwarranted.
4 Similar paths to the one followed in the text can be found for example in Plantinga 1967; in Gale 1991; and in Stewart 1993.

14 Eternity and omnipresence

1 For a modern theist who boldly commits herself to the hopeless reading of time-lessness, see Rogers: 'All of space is "here" to God and all of time is "now" . . . All of time is immediately present to God' (Rogers 2000: 79).
2 Swinburne distinguishes God being immutable in that his character does not change, and God being immutable in that *nothing* in him changes at all. He claims that a temporal view of eternity can accommodate the former though not the latter (Swinburne 1986: 212). A similar distinction is found in Helm 1997: 85. We could also distinguish between the claim that God *does* not ever change (although nothing makes this impossible), and the claim that God *cannot* change.
3 I am thinking here of, for example, Wittgenstein's anti-private language argument in Wittgenstein (1963); of Strawson's 'Persons' argument (Strawson 1964); of arguments advanced by Williams and others to the effect that being embodied is a necessary condition of the persistence through time of persons (Williams 1956/57); and of functionalist definitions of mental concepts in terms (partly) of behavioural outputs (e.g. Lewis 1994).
4 Strictly speaking, Swinburne's claim is that this is an 'often expressed' view of what divine omnipresence means. But his later text indicates that he endorses it himself.

15 Omniscience

1 See, for example, Plantinga 1986b. Plantinga argues that the past is 'fixed', that anything 'fixed' to the past must also be 'fixed', and that if future actions are fixed to the past, because they were foreseen in the past, then those future actions must be 'fixed' and hence cannot be free. What is wrong with this is that 'God knew yesterday what I will do tomorrow' is not wholly about the past: one of its truth conditions lies in the future, so even if there is some sense in which the past is 'fixed', it is not a sense which allows the past *per se* to fix the present. See also the reference in Further Reading at the end of the chapter.

2 I say 'hugely' ignorant here, rather than totally ignorant, in case there are some truths (perhaps, for example, within logic or mathematics) which can be known without that knowledge presupposing an empirical application of concepts of the kind presupposed in the text.

16 Conclusion

1 For one honourable exception, see Swinburne 1979: chapter 14.

2 Alvin Plantinga, for example, has argued that there are 'at least a couple of dozen' of 'good arguments' for the existence of God, but the only one to which he has devoted any serious consideration is the ontological argument. See http://www.homestead.com/philofreligion/files/Theisticarguments.html

Bibliography

Abbruzzese, John (1997) 'The Coherence of Omniscience: A Defence', *International Journal for the Philosophy of Religion*: 25–34

Adams, Marilyn McCord and Adams, Robert Merrihew (eds) (1990) *The Problem of Evil*, Oxford: Oxford University Press

Adams, Robert Merrihew (1972) 'Must God Create the Best?', *Philosophical Review* 81, 3: 317–32, reprinted in Morris (ed.) 1987

Alston, William (1991) *Perceiving God*, Ithaca: Cornell University Press

Anselm (1965) *St. Anselm's Proslogion*, translated and introduced by M.J. Charlesworth, Oxford: Clarendon Press

Aquinas, Thomas (1948) *Introduction to Saint Thomas Aquinas*, edited with an introduction by Anton C. Pegis, New York: The Modern Library

Aquinas, Thomas (1963) *Summa Theologiae*, London: Blackfriars and Eyre and Spottiswoode

Aquinas, Thomas (1975) *Summa Contra Gentiles*, trans. Anton C. Pegis, London: University of Notre Dame Press

Atkins, Peter (1994) *Creation Revisited*, Harmondsworth: Penguin Books

Ayer, A.J. (1968) *The Origins of Pragmatism*, London: Macmillan

Bagger, Matthew C. (1999) *Religious Experience, Justification and History*, Cambridge: Cambridge University Press

Barnes, Jonathan (1972) *The Ontological Argument*, London: Macmillan

Beck, Lewis White (1960) *A Commentary on Kant's Critique of Practical Reason*, Chicago, IL: University of Chicago Press

Behe, Michael (1996) *Darwin's Black Box*, New York: Touchstone

Beilby, James K. (ed.) (2002), *Naturalism Defeated?: Essays on Plantinga's Evolutionary Argument against Naturalism*, Ithaca and London: Cornell University Press

Bennett, Jonathan (1974) *Kant's Analytic*, Cambridge: Cambridge University Press

Boethius (1999) *The Consolation of Philosophy*, translated with an introduction by Victor Watts, London: Penguin Books

Cairns-Smith, A.G. (1985) *Seven Clues to the Origin of Life*, Cambridge: Cambridge University Press

Calder, Nigel (1985) *Einstein's Universe*, Harmondsworth: Penguin Books

Chisholm, Roderick (1982) *The Foundations of Knowing*, Brighton: The Harvester Press

Clifford, W.K. (1879) *Lectures and Essays*, vol. 2, London: Macmillan

Copleston, F.C. (1972) *A History of Medieval Philosophy*, London: Methuen

Craig, William Lane (1980) *The Cosmological Argument from Plato to Leibniz*, London: Macmillan

Craig, William Lane (ed.) (2002) *Philosophy of Religion: A Reader and Guide*, Edinburgh: Edinburgh University Press

Craig, William Lane and Smith, Quentin (1993) *Theism, Atheism and Big Bang Cosmology*, Oxford: Clarendon

Cross, Roger (1995) *The Yorkshire Ripper*, London: HarperCollins

Darwin, Charles (1964) *The Origin of Species: A Facsimile of the First Edition*, Cambridge, MA: Harvard University Press

Davies, Brian (1985) *Thinking About God*, London: Geoffrey Chapman

Davies, Brian (1993) *An Introduction to the Philosophy of Religion*, 2nd edition, Oxford: Oxford University Press

Davies, Paul (1992) *The Mind of God*, Harmondsworth: Penguin Books

Davis, Caroline Franks (1989) *The Evidential Force of Religious Experience*, Oxford: Clarendon Press

Davis, Stephen T. (1997) *God, Reason, and Theistic Proofs*, Edinburgh: Edinburgh University Press

Davis, Stephen T. (1999) 'The Cosmological Argument and the Epistemic Status of Belief in God', *Philosophia Christi* 2, 1, 1, 5–15, reprinted in William Lane Craig (ed.) 2002

Dawkins, Richard (1976) *The Selfish Gene*, Oxford: Oxford University Press

Dawkins, Richard (1986) *The Blind Watchmaker*, Harlow, Essex: Longman Scientific and Technical

Dembski, William A. (1998a) *The Design Inference: Eliminating Chance Through Small Probabilities*, Cambridge: Cambridge University Press

Dembski, William A. (1998b), 'Science and Design', *First Things* 86: 21–7 (http://www.firstthings.com/ftissues/ft9810/dembski.html)

Derham, William (1713) *Physico-Theology, or a Demonstration of the Being and Attributes of God from His Works of Creation*, London: Printed for W. Innys

Descartes, Rene (1984) *Philosophical Writings*, vols I and II, trans. John Cottingham, Robert Stoothoff and Dugald Murdoch, Cambridge: Cambridge University Press

Draper, Paul (2002) 'Irreducible Complexity and Darwinian Gradualism: A Reply to Michael J. Behe', *Faith and Philosophy* 19, 3–21

Earman, John (1987) 'The SAP also Rises: A Critical Examination of the Anthropic Principle', *American Philosophical Quarterly* 24, 307–17

Earman, John (2000) *Hume's Abject Failure*, Oxford: Oxford University Press

Everitt, Nicholas (1995) 'Kant's Discussion of the Ontological Argument', *Kant-Studien* 86: 385–405

Everitt, Nicholas (2000) 'Why Only Perfection Is Good Enough', *Philosophical Papers* 29: 155–8

Ferris, Timothy (1997) *The Whole Shebang*, London: Phoenix

Fischer, John Martin (ed.) (1989) *God, Foreknowledge and Freedom*, Stanford, CA: Stanford University Press

Flew, Antony (1961) *Hume's Philosophy of Belief*, London: Routledge and Kegan Paul

Flew, Antony (1966) *God and Philosophy*, London: Hutchinson

Flew, Antony (1976) *The Presumption of Atheism*, London: Elek/Pemberton

Flew, Antony (1986) *David Hume: Philosopher of Moral Science*, Oxford: Blackwell

Flew, Antony and Alasdair MacIntyre (eds) (1963) *New Essays in Philosophical Theology*, London: SCM Press

Frege, Gottlob (1974) *The Foundations of Arithmetic*, trans. J.L. Austin, Oxford: Blackwell

Freud, Sigmund (1973) *The Complete Psychological Works of Sigmund Freud*, London: The Hogarth Press

Gale, Richard (1991) *On the Nature and Existence of God*, Cambridge: Cambridge University Press

Gaskin, J.C.A. (1978) *Hume's Philosophy of Religion*, London: Macmillan

Gaskin, J.C.A. (1984) *The Quest for Eternity*, Harmondsworth: Penguin Books

Geach, Peter (1969) *God and the Soul*, London: Routledge and Kegan Paul

Geach, Peter (1973) 'An Irrelevance of Omnipotence', *Philosophy* 48: 327–33

Gellman, Jerome (1997) *Experience of God and the Rationality of Theistic Belief*, Ithaca: Cornell University Press

Ginet, Carl (1995) 'A Commentary on Plantinga's Two-volume Work on Warrant', *Philosophy and Phenomenological Research* 55.2: 403–8

Gould, Stephen Jay (1996) *Life's Grandeur*, London: Jonathan Cape

Gribbin, John (1993) *In the Beginning*, Harmondsworth: Penguin Books

Gutting, Gary (1982) *Religious Belief and Religious Scepticism*, Notre Dame: University of Notre Dame Press

Hacking, Ian (1972) 'The Logic of Pascal's Wager', *American Philosophical Quarterly* 9: 186–92, reprinted in Craig 2002

Hartshorne, Charles (1973) *The Logic of Perfection*, La Salle, IL: Open Court Publishing Company

Hasker, William (1989) 'The Foundations of Theism: Scoring the Quinn–Plantinga Debate', *Faith and Philosophy*, 15: 1, 52–67

Hasker, William (1998) *God, Time and Foreknowledge*, Ithaca, NY: Cornell University Press

Hawking, Stephen (1994) *Black Holes and Baby Universes*, London: Bantam Books

Helm, Paul (1997) *Eternal God: A Study of God without Time*, Oxford: Clarendon Press

Hick, John (1963) *The Philosophy of Religion*, Englewood Cliffs, NJ: Prentice Hall

Hick, John (1964) *The Existence of God*, New York: Macmillan

Holland, R.F. (1965) 'The Miraculous', *The American Philosophical Quarterly* 2: 43–51

Hollis, Martin (1973) *The Light of Reason*, London: Fontana/Collins

Hughes, Gerard H. (1995) *The Nature of God*, London: Routledge

Hume, David (1935) *Dialogues Concerning Natural Religion*, ed. Norman Kemp Smith, Oxford: Clarendon Press

Hume, David (1957) *Enquiries Concerning the Human Understanding and Concerning the Principles of Morals*, ed. L.A. Selby-Bigge, Oxford: Clarendon Press

Hume, David (1960) *A Treatise Concerning Human Nature*, ed. L.A. Selby-Bigge, Oxford: Clarendon Press

Hume, David (1976) *The Natural History of Religion and Dialogues concerning Natural Religion*, edited by A. Wayne Colver and John Vladimir Price, Oxford: Clarendon Press

Inwagen, Peter van (1995) *God, Knowledge and Mystery: Essays in Philosophical Theology*, Ithaca and London: Cornell University Press

Jacquette, Dale (1999) 'Demonstratives and the Logic of Self', *Philosophical Papers* 28, 1, 1–23

James, William (1918) *Selected Papers on Philosophy*, London: J.M. Dent

James, William (1963) *The Varieties of Religious Experience*, London: Collins Fontana Library

Kant, Immanuel (1949) *Critique of Practical Reason*, trans. and ed. Lewis White Beck, Chicago, IL: University of Chicago Press

Kant, Immanuel (1963) *Critique of Pure Reason*, trans. Norman Kemp Smith, London: Macmillan

Kenny, Anthony (1969) *Five Ways*, London: Routledge and Kegan Paul

Kenny, Anthony (1992) *What Is Faith?*, Oxford: Oxford University Press

Kim, Jaegwon and Sosa, Ernest (eds) (1995) *A Companion to Metaphysics*, Oxford: Blackwell

Kripke, Saul (1980) *Naming and Necessity*, Oxford: Blackwell

Kvanig, Jonathan L. (ed.) (1996) *Warrant in Contemporary Epistemology: Essays in Honor of Plantinga's Theory of Knowledge*, Lanham: Rowman and Littlefield Publishers Inc.

Leftow, Brian (1991) *Time and Eternity*, Ithaca and London: Cornell University Press

Leibniz, G.W.F. (1968) *Philosophical Writings*, trans. Mary Morris and introduced by C.R. Morris, London: Dent Everyman's Library

Leibniz, G.W.F. (1997) *Theodicy*, La Salle, IL: Open Court

Leslie, John (1996) *Universes*, London: Routledge

Lewis, David (1995) 'Lewis, David: Reduction of Mind' in Samuel Guttenplan (ed.) *A Companion to the Philosophy of Mind*, Oxford: Blackwell

Lipschutz, Seymour (1964) *Set Theory and Related Topics*, New York: McGraw-Hill

Locke, John (1955) *A Letter Concerning Toleration*, Indianapolis: Bobbs-Merrill Library of Liberal Arts, 2nd edition

Locke, John (1964) *An Essay Concerning Human Understanding*, 2 vols ed. John Yolton, London: Dent Everyman's Library

Lycan, William G. (1988) *Judgement and Justification*, Cambridge: Cambridge University Press

Mackie, John (1982) *The Miracle of Theism*, Oxford: Oxford University Press

McLellan, David (1987) *Marxism and Religion*, London: Macmillan

Malcolm, Norman (1964) *Knowledge and Certainty*, Englewood Cliffs, NJ: Prentice Hall

Martin C.B. (1959) *Religious Belief*, New York: Cornell University Press

Martin, Michael (1990) *Atheism: A Philosophical Justification*, Philadelphia: Temple University Press

Marx, Karl (1971) *Early Texts*, ed. David McLellan, Oxford: Blackwell

Matson, Wallace I. (1965) *The Existence of God*, Ithaca: Cornell University Press

Mill, John Stuart (1874) *Three Essays on Religion*, London: Longmans, Green, Reader and Dyer

Mill, John Stuart (1967) *A System of Logic*, eighth edition, London: Longman

Millikan, Ruth (1990) 'The Myth of the Essential Indexical', *Nous* 723–34

Moreland, J.P. (1987) *Scaling the Secular City: A Defence of Christianity*, Grand Rapids, MI: Baker

Morris, Thomas (ed.) (1987) *The Concept of God*, Oxford: Oxford University Press

Morris, Thomas (ed.) (1994) *God and the Philosophers*, Oxford: Oxford University Press

Nathan, Nicholas (1997) 'Naturalism and Self-defeat: Plantinga's Version', *Religious Studies* 33: 135–42

Nielsen, Kai (1982) *An Introduction to the Philosophy of Religion*, London: Macmillan

O'Connor, Timothy (1994) 'An Evolutionary Argument Against Naturalism', *Canadian Journal of Philosophy* 24: 527–39

O'Hear, Anthony (1984) *Experience, Explanation and Faith*, London: Routledge

Oppy, Graham (1995) *Ontological Arguments and Belief in God*, Cambridge: Cambridge University Press

Owen, H.P. (1969) *The Christian Knowledge of God*, London: Athlone Press

Paley, William (1826) *The Works of William Paley in One Volume*, Edinburgh: Peter Brown and T.W. Nelson

Parfit, Derek (1992) 'The Puzzle of Reality', *The Times Literary Supplement* 4657, 3 July: 3–5

Parfit, Derek (1998) 'Why Anything? Why This?' *The London Review of Books* 20, 3

Pascal, Blaise (1995) *Pensées and Other Writings*, Harmondsworth: Penguin

Penelhum, Terence (1975) *Hume*, London: Macmillan

Perry, John (1979) 'The Problem of the Essential Indexical', *Nous* 13, 3–21, reprinted in John Perry (1993) *The Problem of the Essential Indexical and Other Essays*, York, 1993

Peterson, Michael L. (1998) *God and Evil: An Introduction to the Issues*, Boulder, CO: Westview Press

Pike, Nelson (1965) 'Divine Omniscience and Voluntary Action', *Philosophical Review* 74: 27–46; reprinted in John Martin Fischer (ed.) (1989) *God, Foreknowledge and Freedom*, 37–73. Stanford, CA: Stanford University Press

Plantinga, Alvin (1967) *God and Other Minds*, Ithaca: Cornell University Press

Plantinga, Alvin (ed.) (1968) *The Ontological Argument*, London: Macmillan

Plantinga, Alvin (1974) *The Nature of Necessity*, Oxford: Clarendon Press

Plantinga, Alvin (1977) *God, Freedom and Evil*, Grand Rapids: Wm. B. Eerdmans Publishing

Plantinga, Alvin (1983b) 'Reason and Belief in God' in Plantinga and Wolterstorff 1983a, reprinted in Sennett (1998)

Plantinga, Alvin (1986a) 'The Foundations of Theism: A Reply', *Faith and Philosophy* 3: 298–313

Plantinga, Alvin (1986b) 'On Ockham's Way Out', *Faith and Philosophy* 235–69, reprinted in Fischer (ed.) 1989, in Sennett (ed.) 1998, in Stump and Murray (eds) 1999, and (partially) in Craig (ed.) 2002

Plantinga, Alvin (1987) 'Justification and Theism' in *Faith and Philosophy* 4: 403–26, reprinted in Sennett (1998)

Plantinga, Alvin (1991) 'An Evolutionary Argument against Naturalism', *Logos* 12: 27–49

Plantinga, Alvin (1993) *Warrant and Proper Function*, Oxford: Oxford University Press

Plantinga, Alvin (1994) http://www.homestead.com/philofreligion/files/alspaper.htm

Plantinga, Alvin (1995) 'Reliabilism, Analyses and Defeaters', *Philosophy and Phenomenological Research* 55.2: 427–64

Plantinga, Alvin (2000) *Warranted Christian Belief*, Oxford: Oxford University Press

Plantinga, Alvin and Grim, Patrick (1993) 'Truth, Omniscience, and Cantorian Arguments: An Exchange', *Philosophical Studies* 71: 267–306

Plantinga, Alvin and Wolterstorff, Nicholas (eds) (1983) *Faith and Philosophy* London: University of Notre Dame Press

Le Poidevin, Robin (1996) *Arguing for Atheism*, London: Routledge

Pojman, Louis P. (1994) *Philosophy of Religion: An Anthology*, Belmont, CA: Wadsworth Publishing

Polkinghorne, John (1996) *One World*, London: Society for the Propagation of Christian Knowledge

Quine, Willard Van Orman (1961) *From a Logical Point of View*, New York: Harper and Row

Quinn, Philip (1978) *Divine Commandments and Moral Requirements*, New York: Doubleday

Quinn, Philip (1985) 'In Search of the Foundations of Theism', *Faith and Philosophy* 2: 4, 469–86

Quinn, Philip (1993) 'The Foundations of Theism Again: A Rejoinder to Plantinga' in Linda Zagzebski (ed.) (1993) *Rational Faith*, Notre Dame: University of Notre Dame Press: 35–47

Quinn, Philip L. and Taliaferro, Charles (1997) *A Companion to Philosophy of Religion*, Oxford: Blackwell

Ray, John (1735) *The Wisdom of God Manifested in the Works of the Creation*, London: printed by William Innys and Richard Manby

Reichenbach, Bruce (1972) *The Cosmological Argument: A Reassessment*, Springfield: Charles C. Thomas

Rogers, Katherin A. (2000) *Perfect Being Theology*, Edinburgh: Edinburgh University Press

Rousseau, Jean-Jacques (1991) *Emile*, trans. A. Bloom, Harmondsworth: Penguin Books

Rowe, William L. (1978) *Philosophy of Religion*, Belmont: Wadsworth Publishing Company

Rowe, William L. (1979) 'The Problem of Evil and Some Varieties of Atheism', *American Philosophical Quarterly* 16: 4, 335–41, reprinted in Stump and Murray 1999: 157–64

Sartre, Jean-Paul (1970) *Existentialism and Humanism*, trans. Philip Mairet, London: Methuen

Schlesinger, George (1994) 'A Central Theistic Argument', in Jeff Jordan (ed.) *Gambling on God: Essays on Pascal's Wager*, Lanham: Rowman and Littlefield, 83–99, reprinted in Craig (ed.) 2002

Schopenhauer, Artur (1974) *On the Fourfold Root of the Principle of Sufficient Reason*, trans. E.F.J. Payne, La Salle, IL: Open Court Publishing Company

Sennett, James F. (ed.) (1998) *The Analytic Theist: An Alvin Plantinga Reader*, Cambridge: William B. Eerdmans Publishing Company

Smart, Ninian (1970) *The Philosophy of Religion*, New York: Random House

Stannard, Russell (1999) *The God Experiment*, London: Faber and Faber

Stewart, Melvill Y. (1993) *The Greater-Good Defence: An Essay on the Rationality of Faith*, London: Macmillan

Strawson, P.F. (1964) *Individuals*, London: Methuen

Strawson, P.F. (1966) *The Bounds of Sense*, London: Methuen

Stump, Eleonore and Kretzmann, Norman (1981) 'Eternity', *The Journal of Philosophy* 78: 8, 429–58, partially reprinted in Stump and Kretzmann 1999: 42–53

Stump, Eleonore and Murray, Michael J. (1999) *Philosophy of Religion: The Big Questions*, Oxford: Blackwell

Sudduth, Czapkay Michael (1995) 'Alstonian Foundationalism and Higher-level Theistic Foundationalism', *The International Journal for Philosophy of Religion* February 1995, 37: 25–44

Swinburne, Richard (1979) *The Existence of God*, Oxford: Clarendon Press

Swinburne, Richard (1986) *The Coherence of Theism*, Oxford: Clarendon Press

Swinburne, Richard (ed.) (1989) *Miracles*, London: Macmillan

Swinburne, Richard (1994) *The Christian God*, Oxford: Clarendon Press

Swinburne, Richard (1996) *Is There a God?*, Oxford: Oxford University Press

Swinburne, Richard (2001) *Epistemic Justification*, Oxford: Clarendon Press

Tomberlin, E. and van Inwagen, Peter (eds) (1985) *Alvin Plantinga: Profiles*, Dordrecht/Boston/Lancaster: D. Reidel

Trethowan, Illtyd (1970) *Absolute Value: A Study in Christian Theism*, London: George Allen and Unwin

Trethowan, Illtyd (1975) *Mysticism and Theology*, London: Geoffrey Chapman

Vernon, M.D. (1966) *Experiments in Visual Perception*, Harmondsworth: Penguin

Ward, Keith (1976) *The Divine Image*, London: Society for the Propagation of Christian Knowledge

Ward, Keith (1982) *Rational Theology and the Creativity of God*, Oxford: Blackwell

Ward, Keith (1996) *God, Chance and Necessity*, Oxford: Oneworld

Williams, Bernard (1956/7) 'Personal Identity and Individuation' in *Proceedings of the Aristotelian Society* 57: 229–52. Reprinted in Bernard Williams (1973) *Problems of the Self*, Cambridge: Cambridge University Press

Wilson, Margaret Dauler (1978) *Descartes*, London: Routledge

Wittgenstein, Ludwig (1963) *Philosophical Investigations*, Oxford: Blackwell

Wittgenstein, Ludwig (1978) *Lectures and Conversations on Aesthetics*, ed. Cyril Barrett, Oxford: Blackwell

Wollaston, William (1726) *The Religion of Nature Delineated*, London: printed by Samuel Palmer

Woodward, Sarah (2000) 'Things To Come', *Cambridge Alumni Magazine* 30: 25

Yandell, Keith (1993) *The Epistemology of Religious Experience*, Cambridge: Cambridge University Press

Yandell, Keith (1999) *Philosophy of Religion*, London: Routledge

Index